EDUCATION FOR LIFE

NATURAL LAW AND
ENLIGHTENMENT CLASSICS

Knud Haakonssen
General Editor

Map of Aberdeen

NATURAL LAW AND
ENLIGHTENMENT CLASSICS

Education for Life
Correspondence and Writings on Religion and Practical Philosophy

George Turnbull

Edited and with an Introduction
by M. A. Stewart and Paul Wood

Latin texts translated
by Michael Silverthorne

*Philosophical Works and Correspondence
of George Turnbull*

LIBERTY FUND

Indianapolis

This book is published by Liberty Fund, Inc., a foundation established to encourage study of the ideal of a society of free and responsible individuals.

𒂼𒄄

The cuneiform inscription that serves as our logo and as the design motif for our endpapers is the earliest-known written appearance of the word "freedom" (*amagi*), or "liberty." It is taken from a clay document written about 2300 B.C. in the Sumerian city-state of Lagash.

Translations, introduction, editorial matter, bibliography, index © 2014 by Liberty Fund, Inc.

Cover art and frontispiece are the Aberdeen detail of the William Roy Map, created from 1747–1755, and are used by permission of the British Library (Shelfmark Maps C.9.b.21 sheet 1/2).

C   14   15   16   17   18   5   4   3   2   1
P   14   15   16   17   18   5   4   3   2   1

Library of Congress Cataloging-in-Publication Data
Turnbull, George, 1698–1748.
[Works. Selections. English. 2014]
Education for life: correspondence and writings on
religion and practical philosophy / George Turnbull;
edited and with an introduction by M. A. Stewart and Paul Wood;
texts translated from the Latin by Michael Silverthorne.
pages   cm.—(Philosophical works and correspondence of George Turnbull)
(Natural law and enlightenment classics)
Includes bibliographical references and index.
ISBN 978-0-86597-621-4 (hardcover: alk. paper)   ISBN 978-0-86597-622-1 (pbk.: alk. paper)
1. Enlightenment—Scotland.
2. Philosophical theology.
3. Turnbull, George, 1698–1748—Correspondence.
I. Stewart, M. A. (Michael Alexander), 1937– editor.
II. Title.
B1302 .E65T87   2014
192—dc23   2014026720

LIBERTY FUND, INC.
8335 Allison Pointe Trail, Suite 300
Indianapolis, Indiana 46250-1684

CONTENTS

INTRODUCTION

Although George Turnbull was a recognized member of the European republic of letters in the second quarter of the eighteenth century, his reputation as an exponent of the moderate Enlightenment was eclipsed soon after his death in 1748. By the turn of the nineteenth century, he had come to be regarded as a figure of little intellectual significance. In 1802, for example, Dugald Stewart indicated that, at most, Turnbull deserved mention as the teacher of Thomas Reid but was otherwise of no interest.[1] Moreover, Stewart's later assertion that the "rise and progress of the Metaphysical Philosophy of Scotland" originated in "the lectures of Dr. Francis Hutcheson, in the University of Glasgow" meant that Turnbull's role in the formation of the Scottish Enlightenment was overlooked by those nineteenth-century writers who championed the merits of the Scottish "school" of philosophy, with the notable exception of James McCosh. McCosh cast Turnbull alongside Hutcheson as a founder of the Scottish "school," yet his positive assessment of Turnbull was largely ignored.[2] Consequently, Turnbull slipped from view until the latter part of the twentieth century, when David Fate Norton stimulated interest in Turnbull's philosophical writings by situating them in the context of Scottish responses to moral and cognitive scepticism. Turnbull's writings on art theory, education, and natural law also began to receive the attention they deserve, as did his teaching at Marischal College Aberdeen.[3] Nevertheless, Turnbull remained a shadowy

1. Dugald Stewart, *Account of the Life and Writings of Thomas Reid, D.D., F.R.S.E. Late Professor of Moral Philosophy in the University of Glasgow,* in Dugald Stewart, *The Collected Works of Dugald Stewart, Esq., F.R.S.S.,* edited by Sir William Hamilton, 11 vols. (Edinburgh, 1854–60), X:326, note B.

2. Dugald Stewart, in Stewart, *Works,* I:427–28; James McCosh, *The Scottish Philosophy, Biographical, Expository, Critical, from Hutcheson to Hamilton* (London, 1875), pp. 95–106.

3. The relevant works by David Fate Norton, Vincent Bevilacqua, Carol Gibson-

figure because a number of basic biographical facts had not been established and important facets of his thought had not been explored.

The Travels and Travails of a Man of Letters

James McCosh was the first scholar to research the details of Turnbull's life and writings. But his biography is flawed because he did not have access to some of the most valuable sources of information regarding Turnbull's life, including the surviving correspondence published below. These sources enable us to construct a richer narrative of his life and the context of his work.

George Turnbull was born on 11 July 1698 in Alloa, near Stirling, the son of the clergyman George Turnbull the elder. The younger Turnbull was probably expected to enter the ministry and was sent to the University of Edinburgh in 1711, where he likely finished his courses in the spring of 1716.[4] He did not graduate formally with his Master of Arts degree after completing his course work and in 1717 entered Edinburgh's divinity school. While studying divinity, he may have been one of the founding members of the Rankenian Club.[5] In the Club, he was close to his fellow divinity student Robert Wallace, the preacher and later minister William Wishart, the surgeon George Young, and the Edinburgh Professor of Universal History Charles Mackie, although each of these friendships later cooled.[6] Apparently disillusioned with a career in the Church of Scotland, Turnbull instead sought employment in the Scottish universities and was elected on 14 April 1721 as a regent at Marischal College Aberdeen.[7]

Wood, M. A. Stewart, K. A. B. Mackinnon, Knud Haakonssen, and Paul Wood are listed in the bibliography.

4. Rev. Robert Paul (ed.), "The Diary of the Rev. George Turnbull, Minister of Alloa and Tyninghame, 1657–1704," in *Miscellany of the Scottish History Society* I (Edinburgh, 1893), pp. 308, 376. Turnbull's name appears in the University of Edinburgh matriculation records in the sessions for 1711–12, 1712–13, and 1714–15. In the first two years he was in the Latin class of Laurence Dundas and in 1714–15 he matriculated in the Logic class of Colin Drummond.

5. M. A. Stewart, "Berkeley and the Rankenian Club," *Hermathena*, 139 (1985): 25–45.

6. Robert Wallace later married Turnbull's younger sister Helen in October 1726.

7. *Fasti Academiae Mariscallanae Aberdoniensis: Selections from the Records of the Marischal College and University MDXCIII–MDCCCLX*, edited by P. J. Anderson, 3 vols. (Aberdeen, 1889–98), II:40; Roger L. Emerson, *Professors, Patronage, and Politics: The*

At Marischal, Turnbull joined a phalanx of young, innovative colleagues, including the distinguished mathematician and leading Newtonian, Colin Maclaurin (1698–1746). Maclaurin was, however, unhappy at Marischal and Turnbull shared his friend's disaffection with academic life at the college. His correspondence shows that in May 1723 he ventured to ask Lord Molesworth to help him find a post as a travelling tutor but without success. In 1724–25 a political battle within the college, which involved both Maclaurin and Turnbull, precipitated their departure. In the spring of 1725 Maclaurin moved to the Edinburgh Chair of Mathematics, while Turnbull took an unofficial leave to become the tutor to Alexander Udny.[8] Turnbull and Udny travelled to Groningen via London in the autumn of 1725, but Turnbull was forced to return to Marischal because he had not been granted a formal leave.[9] In January 1726 he was again lecturing and took his class (which included Udny) to graduation in April. Since he was back in Aberdeen in the autumn of 1726, it would seem that he was neither retained by the Udnys nor able to find another position as a tutor. During the ensuing session he put himself forward as a candidate for the vacant Chair of Ecclesiastical History at St. Andrews and solicited the support of Maclaurin and Charles Mackie in Edinburgh.[10] However, his bid for the Chair failed and he decided to abandon academe, if only temporarily. He resigned from Marischal in the spring of 1727 and was given the first honorary Doctor of Laws degree awarded by the college upon his departure.[11]

Having left Aberdeen, Turnbull became a tutor to Andrew Wauchope of Niddrie. To prepare for travel and study on the continent, Wauchope

---

Aberdeen Professors in the Eighteenth Century (Aberdeen, 1992), p. 38. Prior to Turnbull's appointment at Marischal he obtained a testimonial letter from his father's presbytery in late March and his Edinburgh Master of Arts degree on 5 April 1721; see "Dunbar and Haddington Presbytery Minutes, 1720–34," National Records of Scotland, MS CH2/99/5, p. 36 (29 March 1721) and "First Laureation Album," Edinburgh University Archives, EUA MS IN1/ADS/STA/1/1, where Turnbull's signature appears against the date he was given his degree.

8. M. A. Stewart, "George Turnbull and Educational Reform," in *Aberdeen and the Enlightenment,* edited by Jennifer J. Carter and Joan H. Pittock (Aberdeen, 1987), pp. 97, 100–101; Emerson, *Professors,* pp. 47–48.

9. See below, pp. 15–18.

10. Roger L. Emerson, *Academic Patronage in the Scottish Enlightenment: Glasgow, Edinburgh, and St Andrews Universities* (Edinburgh, 2008), pp. 424–26.

11. Anderson, *Fasti,* II:95.

was enrolled in Mackie's history class at the University of Edinburgh in the autumn of 1727.[12] Three years later we find Turnbull and his pupil in Groningen, where Turnbull attended classes on natural and Roman law.[13] Turnbull may have kept up his legal studies in the hope of securing another academic appointment because he sounded out Mackie about the possibility of negotiating a deal with Mackie's colleague William Scott which would have seen Turnbull succeed Scott as the Edinburgh Professor of Moral Philosophy.[14] But this scheme also proved abortive and he continued in the employ of the Wauchope family. By October 1730, Turnbull and Wauchope had left the United Provinces and were in Paris en route to Italy. In the French capital Turnbull socialized with Dr. (later Sir) John Pringle and apparently visited the Chevalier Ramsay as well as other scholars to whom he was introduced by letters from Colin Maclaurin.[15] A year later, Turnbull was in the south of France and disillusioned with the life of a travelling tutor. Although he was enjoying the company of another tutor, the Cambridge classicist Jeremiah Markland, he reported to Mackie that he would not be going to Italy as initially planned and that he expected to be in England by the spring of 1732. Turnbull was anxious to find another pupil and asked Mackie to put out feelers on his behalf.[16] Mackie did so, only for Turnbull to reject the offer of a position when he arrived back in London in May 1732. Moreover, Turnbull now chose not to return to Scotland, presumably because he believed his prospects were better in England.[17]

Turnbull's last surviving letters to Mackie speak of repeated disappointment and chart the decline of his friendships with Mackie and Maclaurin. By September 1733 Maclaurin was no longer responding to his letters, and there appears to have been no further contact between Mackie and Turnbull after this date.[18] Turnbull was now entirely reliant upon the assistance of

12. Stewart, "Turnbull and Educational Reform," p. 101.

13. See below, p. 20.

14. See below, pp. 21–22.

15. See below, pp. 23–25. For a fragment of a letter of introduction from Maclaurin see *The Collected Letters of Colin Maclaurin*, edited by Stella Mills (Nantwich, 1982), pp. 147–48.

16. See below, p. 26.

17. See below, pp. 28–29.

18. See below, p. 31.

his English patrons and his circle of fellow Scots in the metropolis, which included the poet James Thomson, the physician Alexander Stuart, and his old friend from Edinburgh William Wishart.[19] Although still willing to be a tutor, he decided to take orders in the Anglican Church. To that end, he matriculated at Exeter College Oxford in 1733 and was granted a Bachelor of Civil Law degree.[20] He may have been encouraged in his decision by the Low Churchman and soon to be Bishop of Derry, Thomas Rundle, who had affiliations with Exeter College and was an associate of James Thomson, William Wishart, and one of Turnbull's English patrons Charles Talbot.[21] Turnbull's defense of the credibility of Christ's miracles and his attack on the Deist Matthew Tindal in his early pamphlets on religion would have received a sympathetic reading from Rundle, who likewise defended the reasonableness of Christianity against Deists like Tindal. Moreover, Turnbull's pamphlets would have put him in good stead with Low Churchmen more generally in his search for preferment. Nevertheless, Turnbull failed to find long-term employment in the years 1733 to 1735 and was obliged to accept an offer to become a travelling tutor for the future third earl of Rockingham, Thomas Watson.[22] Unfortunately their Grand Tour is poorly documented. The travel diaries of Alexander Cunyngham (later Sir Alexander Dick) record that he and the artist Allan Ramsay socialized with Watson and Turnbull in Rome in December 1736.[23] Otherwise we know little about their itinerary or the duration of their trip.

19. On Thomson see James Sambrook, *James Thomson 1700–1748: A Life* (Oxford, 1991), p. 155. Turnbull probably first met Thomson in Paris in the winter of 1730, when Thomson was there as a travelling companion to Charles Richard Talbot, the son of the then solicitor-general.

20. Turnbull had also received a Doctor of Laws degree from Edinburgh on 13 June 1732; David Laing, *A Catalogue of the Graduates in the Faculties of Arts, Divinity, and Law, of the University of Edinburgh, since its Foundation* (Edinburgh, 1858), p. 256. See also Joseph Foster, *Alumni Oxonienses: The Members of the University of Oxford, 1715–1886: The Parentage, Birthplace, and Year of Birth, with a Record of Their Degrees,* 4 vols. (Oxford and London, 1888), IV:1448.

21. On Rundle and Talbot, see the *Oxford Dictionary of National Biography* (*ODNB*).

22. George E. Cokayne, *The Complete Peerage of England, Scotland, Ireland, Great Britain, and the United Kingdom,* edited by Vicary Gibbs, revised edition, 12 vols. (London, 1910–59), XI:59.

23. *Curiosities of a Scots Charta Chest, 1600–1800. With the Travels and Memoranda of Sir Alexander Dick, Baronet of Prestonfield, Midlothian Written by Himself,* edited by the Honourable Mrs. Atholl Forbes (Edinburgh, 1897), p. 114.

Prior to leaving London, Turnbull subscribed to the fledgling Society for the Encouragement of Learning, which eventually began formal meetings in May 1736. Initially the Society's membership was largely made up of antiquarians and Scots living in London, leavened with a few Jacobites, physicians, and men of science.[24] Turnbull's involvement in the Society marks a turning point in his career, for he now began to move in the circles of virtuosi and antiquarians in the metropolis centered on Dr. Richard Mead. It is unclear when Turnbull first met Mead, but by the late 1730s Turnbull had access to Mead's spectacular library and collections. Turnbull cultivated Mead's patronage, not least in dedicating his *Three Dissertations* (1740) to Mead.[25] Mead, however, rebuffed Turnbull's overtures. Consequently, Turnbull remained on the periphery of the metropolitan antiquarian community.[26] By contrast, in 1737 Turnbull succeeded in befriending Mead's close associate, the Rev. Thomas Birch. Turnbull probably first encountered Birch in the Society for the Encouragement of Learning and, in 1739, Turnbull turned to Birch for help with his ordination as an Anglican priest.[27] Even though Turnbull did not understand the mechanics of the process, he managed to be ordained by one of the leading Low Churchmen of the day, the Bishop of Winchester, Benjamin Hoadly, to whom he had apparently been introduced by the Bishop's protege and Birch's friend, Arthur Ashley Sykes.[28]

Faced with an uncertain future, Turnbull turned to his pen to improve

---

24. Clayton Atto, "The Society for the Encouragement of Learning," *The Library*, 4th series, 19 (1938): 263–88. Turnbull had signed on as a subscriber by 1 August 1735 and he began attending the Society's meetings on 7 April 1737; see British Library, Additional Manuscripts 6184, fol. 2v, and "Memoirs of the Society for the Incouragement of Learning taken from the Register of Their Meetings, and Minute Books of the Committee," BL Add. Mss 6185, p. 34.

25. See below, pp. 281–86.

26. His marginality is reflected in the fact that he failed in his bid to replace the Scottish antiquary Alexander Gordon as Secretary of the Society for the Encouragement of Learning in 1739; see below, pp. 34–35.

27. See below, pp. 35–36.

28. See below, p. 38. For a helpful discussion of the steps involved in ordination, see W. M. Jacob, *The Clerical Profession in the Long Eighteenth Century, 1680–1840* (Oxford, 2007), pp. 31–37. Birch had been ordained by Hoadly; A. E. Gunther, *An Introduction to the Life of the Rev. Thomas Birch D.D., F.R.S., 1705–1766* (Halesworth, 1984), p. 8.

his finances. In 1739 he published a greatly expanded third edition of his popular pamphlet, *A Philosophical Enquiry concerning the Connexion betwixt the Doctrines and Miracles of Jesus Christ*, as well as his *Treatise on Ancient Painting*. The year 1740 saw the appearance of *The Principles of Moral and Christian Philosophy*, his *Three Dissertations*, and *An Impartial Enquiry into the Moral Character of Jesus Christ*. A spate of books followed in 1741, including his heavily annotated translation of Johann Gottlieb Heineccius's *A Methodical System of Universal Law*, his repackaging of the plates from the *Treatise of Ancient Painting* under the title *A Curious Collection of Ancient Paintings*, and his student edition of Marcus Junianus Justinus's history. Then, in 1742, he produced his last major publications, his *Observations upon Liberal Education, in all its Branches* and his abortive translation of Blainville's *Travels*. Most of these works reveal that Turnbull was desperately, and largely unsuccessfully, searching for patronage. He dedicated his books to a number of prominent public figures, notably his old acquaintance the Bishop of Derry, Thomas Rundle, and the Duke of Cumberland. The Duke did not accept Turnbull as a client, but his brother and rival, Frederick Lewis, the Prince of Wales, appointed Turnbull as his chaplain in 1741. Turnbull moved to Kew, where the Prince had his primary residence outside of London, and set himself up as a schoolmaster.[29] Rundle rewarded Turnbull in 1742 by making him rector of the remote rural parish of Drumachose, County Derry, to which he apparently travelled since he was in Dublin, probably in 1742 or 1743.[30]

None of Turnbull's correspondence survives from this point onward, and hence the details of his life become increasingly obscure. We know that he made a further trip on the Grand Tour with Horatio Walpole, the eldest son of the politician Horatio or Horace Walpole.[31] Turnbull and Walpole

29. See below, p. 40, and Stephen Duck, *Hints to a School-Master. Address'd to the Revd. Dr. Turnbull* (London, 1741).

30. An undated letter from the Dublin physician James Arbuckle (1700–1746) to the Rev. Thomas Drennan (1696–1768) in Belfast bears the added inscription "to the Care of the Revd Dr Turnbull." The letter thus suggests that Turnbull visited Dublin (where he was likely inducted as rector of his parish by Rundle) and Belfast while en route to Drumachose. See James Arbuckle to Thomas Drennan, undated, Public Record Office of Northern Ireland, MS D531/2A/3.

31. The elder Walpole was the brother and political ally of Sir Robert Walpole.

set out in October 1744 and visited Milan and Turin before residing in Florence from June 1745 until April 1746. For much of the time Turnbull suffered from a debilitating attack of what he described as "rheumatism," a condition that had already afflicted him in 1739.[32] His illness became so severe that in January 1746 the British resident in Florence, Sir Horatio Mann, confided to the young Walpole's cousin, Horace Walpole, that Turnbull was "in a bad way, and I don't believe will recover."[33] But despite being incapacitated, Turnbull went to Rome with Walpole because he had been engaged by Horatio Walpole senior and the Duke of Newcastle to gather intelligence about the Jacobite uprising launched in Britain in the summer of 1745. After a period in the Eternal City, Turnbull and Walpole went on to Naples before returning to England in the spring of 1747.[34] Turnbull then drops entirely from view until his death from unspecified causes in the Hague on 31 January 1748. What took him to the United Provinces is unknown, but it is said that he was again spying on exiled Jacobites for the British government.[35]

Turnbull's Place in the Enlightenment

Turnbull's intellectual identity was defined by his formative experiences as a student at Edinburgh and his understanding of the relations between the different branches of human learning. At the turn of the eighteenth century, proponents of what we now identify as Enlightenment in Europe were consolidating their hold over the cultural institutions of Edinburgh.[36] Thanks to the Gregory family, the University became a bastion of Newtonianism in the 1690s, while other parts of the curriculum were gradually updated, especially following the adoption of the professorial system of teaching in 1708. When Turnbull arrived in 1711, he would have encoun-

32. See below, p. 40.

33. Mann to Walpole, 4 January 1746, in *The Yale Edition of Horace Walpole's Correspondence,* edited by W. S. Lewis, 48 vols. (New Haven, 1937–83), XIX:192.

34. *Walpole Correspondence,* XIX:184, note 12; John Ingamells, *A Dictionary of British and Irish Travellers in Italy, 1701–1800* (New Haven and London, 1997), p. 976.

35. *The London Magazine: Or, Gentleman's Monthly Intelligencer,* 17 (1748): 236.

36. Roger L. Emerson, "Sir Robert Sibbald, Kt, the Royal Society of Scotland, and the Origins of the Scottish Enlightenment," *Annals of Science* 45 (1988): 41–72.

tered a residue of scholasticism mixed with newer currents of thought, including the natural law theories of Grotius and Pufendorf. He would also have been given a good grounding in Greek and Latin; significantly, his Latin professor, Laurence Dundas, apparently used Justin's epitome of Pompeius Trogus's *Philippic Histories,* which Turnbull subsequently edited.[37] Turnbull then studied divinity under the Principal, the Rev. William Wishart, and the Professor of Divinity, the Rev. William Hamilton. Wishart was an orthodox Calvinist who had been sympathetic to the Covenanters in his early years, whereas Hamilton was said to have instilled in his pupils "moderation and a liberal manner of thinking upon all subjects."[38] Outside of the classroom, Hamilton's moderate form of Presbyterianism seems to have inspired the discussion of religious topics in the Rankenian Club.

We know little about the proceedings of the Club. Comments made by Robert Wodrow in the mid-1720s show that the Rankenians were known to be critical of orthodox Calvinism.[39] A manuscript dating from before 1720 by Wallace challenging the use of "Creeds or Confessions of faith" and Turnbull's contemporaneous manuscript on civil religion published below, indicate that they debated whether the state or a national church can legitimately regulate religious belief.[40] These manuscripts show that the Rankenians registered not only the case for religious toleration advanced by John Locke, but also the arguments involved in the Bangorian Controversy sparked by Benjamin Hoadly and the disputes over subscription to formulas such as the Westminster Confession of Faith that had recently flared up in Ireland, England, and Scotland.[41] Moreover, Turnbull's letter

37. For a detailed discussion of the Edinburgh curriculum in Turnbull's day see M. A. Stewart, "Hume's Intellectual Development, 1711–1752," in *Impressions of Hume,* edited by M. Frasca-Spada and P. J. E. Kail (Oxford, 2005), pp. 11–25.

38. [James Oswald], *Letters concerning the Present State of the Church of Scotland, and the Consequent Danger to Religion and Learning, from the Arbitrary and Unconstitutional Exercise of the Law of Patronage* (Edinburgh, 1767), p. 23.

39. Robert Wodrow, *Analecta: Or, Materials for a History of Remarkable Providences; Mostly Relating to Scotch Ministers and Christians,* 4 vols. (Glasgow, 1842–43), III:175.

40. Robert Wallace, "A Little Treatise against Imposing Creeds or Confessions of Faith on Ministers or Private Christians as a Necessary Term of Laick or Ministeriall Communion," Edinburgh University Library, MS La II 620/18.

41. Colin Kidd, "Scotland's Invisible Enlightenment: Subscription and Heterodoxy

to John Toland written in 1718 (below, pp. 3–4) suggests that the club members were exploring the writings of Toland and other English Deists and flirting with radical Enlightenment ideas. The place of religion in society and the credibility of Christianity continued to preoccupy Turnbull over the next two decades. His letters to Molesworth show that in private he echoed the Deists in railing against priestcraft and the imposition of creeds, and that he had read Anthony Collins.[42] But Turnbull was also a theist who maintained that the design and order of the moral and natural realms evinced in the work of Newton refuted "atheism," in both its ancient and modern forms.[43] Moreover, in the early 1720s he was already familiar with the debate over miracles sparked by Spinoza's *Theological-Political Treatise* (1670), which rumbled across Europe for a century.

Turnbull entered this debate in *A Philosophical Enquiry concerning the Connexion betwixt the Doctrines and Miracles of Jesus Christ*, which appeared anonymously in 1731 while he was on the continent. The *Enquiry* was ostensibly a letter written "to a Friend" dated 10 April 1726 (that is, while he was still teaching at Marischal College) and signed "Philanthropos" (lover of humanity). In the "Advertisement" to the first two impressions of the pamphlet he explained that he had delayed publication because he had

> expect[ed] to see a Discourse upon Miracles, promised by the Author of the *Grounds and Reasons of the Christian Religion,* [but] does not know whether that Discourse is at last published or not, [or] whether a late Book entitled, *Christianity as old as the Creation,* takes any notice of miracles; and is, in one word, an utter stranger to what has been publish'd in *England* for two years past.[44]

The "Author" referred to here was Anthony Collins, and Turnbull's puzzlement was genuine because Collins mentions his "Discourse upon Mir-

---

in the Eighteenth Century Kirk," *Records of the Scottish Church History Society,* 30 (2000): 28–59; M. A. Stewart, "Rational Dissent in Early Eighteenth-Century Ireland," in *Enlightenment and Religion: Rational Dissent in Eighteenth-Century Britain,* edited by Knud Haakonssen (Cambridge, 1996), pp. 42–63; M. R. Watts, *The Dissenters,* 2 vols. (Oxford, 1978–95), I:371–82.

42. See below, pp. 10, 13–14.

43. See especially Turnbull's graduation theses, below pp. 43–74.

44. [George Turnbull], *A Philosophical Enquiry concerning the Connexion betwixt the Doctrines and Miracles of Jesus Christ. In a Letter to a Friend* (London, 1731), p. [iii].

acles" in *The Scheme of Literal Prophecy Considered* (1726), but the "Discourse" remained unpublished at Collins's death in December 1729.[45] The *Enquiry* was thus most likely initially conceived as a response to Collins's argument that miracles were no proof of the truth of Christianity, which he likewise advanced in *A Discourse of the Grounds and Reasons of the Christian Religion* (1724) and the *Scheme*. Turnbull may also have been prompted to publish because of the furor over Thomas Woolston's six discourses on Christ's miracles published in the years 1727 to 1729. Woolston's pamphlets, his imprisonment for blasphemy in 1729, and the deluge of attacks on him ensured any contribution to the dispute over miracles a wide readership, which the *Enquiry* evidently enjoyed. And although Turnbull did not fundamentally alter the miracles debate the way Hume later did, his ingenious argument that Christ's miracles provided "experimental" or empirical proof of the truth of His teachings was a striking attempt to show that belief in the miraculous foundations of Christianity was as rational as a belief in the truth of Newtonian natural philosophy.[46]

Turnbull and his bookseller likewise took advantage of the controversy aroused by Matthew Tindal's *Christianity as Old as the Creation* (1730) by publishing *Christianity Neither False nor Useless, Tho' Not as Old as the Creation* as a pendant to the *Enquiry*. Turnbull here insists that in humanity's fallen state, unaided reason can discover the basic principles of morality, but not establish the truth of the doctrines of the resurrection, a future state, the forgiveness of sins, and divine rewards and punishments. These doctrines, he argues, are necessary to "enforce sufficiently upon [humankind] obedience" to the law of nature; hence we need revelation to assist us in the pursuit of virtue. Against Tindal, he maintained that the moral teachings of Christianity amount to more than simply the dictates of natural law, and that miracles are not only credible but also provide us with the necessary evidence of the truth of revelation.[47] *Christianity Neither False nor Useless* was thus not merely a cynical attempt to promote the *Enquiry*

45. [Anthony Collins], *The Scheme of Literal Prophecy Considered; in a View of the Controversy, Occasioned by a Late Book, Intitled, A Discourse of the Grounds and Reasons of the Christian Religion*, 2 vols. ([The Hague], 1726), II:420.
46. See below, pp. 91–170.
47. See below, pp. 177, 182–83, 191–93.

among readers of Tindal.[48] Rather, Turnbull's pamphlet is intellectually significant because it underlines his debt to Samuel Clarke's blend of rational Christianity and moderate Enlightenment.

Turnbull's indebtedness to Clarke resurfaced in his last pamphlet, *An Impartial Enquiry into the Moral Character of Jesus Christ* (1740). Turnbull elaborated on Clarke's assertion that Christ's spotless character showed that he was "neither an *Imposter* nor an *Enthusiast,*" and that Jesus' moral integrity "add[s] great Weight and Authority to his Doctrine, and make[s] his own Testimony concerning himself exceedingly credible."[49] Using the epistolary form, Turnbull addresses himself to a Deist and endeavors to persuade this imaginary friend that Christ was an even greater teacher of morality than Socrates and that Christ's exemplary behavior and good works attested to his divine mission. Turnbull was implicitly arguing that Christ's unimpeachable character and his miracles constitute "extrinsic" evidence for the truth of Christianity which complements the "intrinsic" evidence derived from the excellence of his teachings. Together, this evidence suffices to persuade the candid unbeliever of the reasonableness of Christian belief.[50] With the *Impartial Enquiry* (and *The Principles of Moral and Christian Philosophy*), therefore, Turnbull's protracted dialogue with Deism and his public defense of the reasonableness of Christianity (and hence of the moderate Enlightenment) came to an unresolved end.

Turnbull's apologetic agenda in his writings on religion was set while he was a student in Edinburgh. His Aberdeen graduation theses, which doc-

48. See also on p. 187 the puff for his friend and brother-in-law Robert Wallace's *The Regard due to Divine Revelation, and to Pretences to It, Considered* (London, 1731).

49. Samuel Clarke, *A Discourse concerning the Being and Attributes of God, the Obligations of Natural Religion, and the Truth and Certainty of the Christian Religion,* seventh edition (London, 1728), pp. 370–71.

50. In making this distinction Turnbull drew on the Port-Royal Logic, first published in 1662; Antoine Arnauld and Pierre Nicole, *Logic or the Art of Thinking: Containing, Besides Common Rules, Several New Observations Appropriate for Forming Judgment,* translated and edited by Jill Vance Buroker (Cambridge, 1996), p. 264. The distinction subsequently became a standard one in the apologetic literature in Scotland; see, for example, Alexander Gerard, *Dissertations on Subjects Relating to the Genius and Evidences of Christianity* (Edinburgh, 1766), pp. ix–x, and James Beattie, *Evidences of the Christian Religion; Briefly and Plainly Stated,* 2 vols. (Edinburgh, 1786), I:12.

ument the transformation of the curriculum at Marischal College in the
1720s, likewise show that his teaching reflected his studies at the University
of Edinburgh and his conversations in the Rankenian Club.[51] The theses
demonstrate that much like his colleagues he was conversant with a wide
range of ancient and modern writers and that he incorporated the ideas of
Bacon, Descartes, Locke, and Newton into his lectures. But the theses also
indicate that his courses differed significantly from those of the other regents. First, his topics for student disputations contain little on metaphysics
and logic, which suggests that he limited the time spent on these subjects.
It seems, therefore, that he went further than some of his colleagues in
removing scholastic remnants from the curriculum. Second, as noted, the
theses reveal his preoccupation with countering the threat of irreligion.
Such apologetics was by no means novel, for the primary aim of a university
education was to inculcate sound moral and religious principles. The formulation of his argument was, however, original because he relied exclu-
sively on the argument from design to refute atheism and he blended
Newton's theocentric vision of the physical universe with Shaftesbury's
conception of a benevolent natural and moral order to illustrate the design
in nature.[52] Third, the disputation topics set in 1726 imply that his teaching
of ethics and politics was framed in terms of the natural law tradition.
Regents in the two Aberdeen colleges had drawn on the writings of Grotius
and Pufendorf from the latter part of the seventeenth century onward, but
it was Turnbull (along with his fellow regent at Marischal David Verner)
who did most to recast the study of moral philosophy in the mold of natural
law.[53] Last, Turnbull was the first Scottish regent or professor to state ex-
plicitly that moral philosophy ought to be studied using the same method
as that employed by Newton in natural philosophy. Much had been made

51. Paul Wood, *The Aberdeen Enlightenment: The Arts Curriculum in the Eighteenth
Century* (Aberdeen, 1993), pp. 35–49.

52. See below, pp. 43–74.

53. See below, pp. xxxi, 73–74; Wood, *Aberdeen Enlightenment,* pp. 6, 39–40, 46, 60.
It is telling that Turnbull later said that he lectured on pneumatology at Marischal "by
way of preparative to a course of lectures, *on the rights and duties of mankind.*" That is,
he taught natural law and saw it as being founded on the science of human nature. See
George Turnbull, *The Principles of Moral and Christian Philosophy,* edited by Alexander
Broadie, 2 vols. (Indianapolis, 2005), I:17.

in the natural law tradition of the methodological unity of the two main branches of philosophy, and there is little doubt about Turnbull's debt to Grotius, Pufendorf, and Richard Cumberland in this regard. Nevertheless, his 1723 thesis struck a new note when he appealed to Query 31 of Newton's *Opticks* to justify his claim that the moral realm ought to be investigated empirically using the methods of analysis and synthesis.[54] Turnbull was thus an early promoter of the Newtonian form of scientism adopted by successive generations of moralists not only in Aberdeen but throughout the European Enlightenment more generally.[55]

Like the Edinburgh virtuosi who shaped the early Scottish Enlightenment, Turnbull believed that all branches of human learning formed a coherent and unified system which he likened to a tree of knowledge.[56] This view underwrote his belief in the methodological unity of the natural and moral sciences, and it also enabled him to delineate the cognitive relations between his historical and antiquarian interests and his broader philosophical concerns. His fascination with history and Roman antiquities was something that he probably originally shared with his fellow Rankenian Charles Mackie. At Edinburgh (and elsewhere) history was taught as an adjunct to law, so that for Turnbull and Mackie the study of these subjects was closely intertwined.[57] Once Turnbull became a travelling tutor his taste for "the Study of the Antients" deepened, while his contacts with antiquarians and historians in London turned his researches in new directions.[58] His work on antiquities and history was also deeply influenced by French models, as seen in his *Three Dissertations* and his edition of Justin.[59] These late works register his indebtedness to the critical scholarship championed

54. See below, p. 50; compare Turnbull, *Principles,* I:7–8, 47–66.

55. Paul Wood, "Science and the Pursuit of Virtue in the Aberdeen Enlightenment," in *Studies in the Philosophy of the Scottish Enlightenment,* edited by M. A. Stewart (Oxford, 1990), pp. 126–49; McCosh, *Scottish Philosophy,* p. 99.

56. Paul Wood, "Thomas Reid and the Tree of the Sciences," *Journal of Scottish Philosophy* 2 (2004): 119–36, especially pp. 123–25.

57. Turnbull, *Observations,* pp. 333–37. On Mackie see L. W. Sharp, "Charles Mackie, the First Professor of History at Edinburgh University," *Scottish Historical Review* 41 (1962): 23–45.

58. See below, p. 6.

59. See also Turnbull's *Curious Collection.*

by the Parisian Académie des Inscriptions et Belles-Lettres and to the rationale for the study of history articulated by the noted historian and pedagogue Charles Rollin. The *Three Dissertations* pays tribute to Richard Mead's collection: one of the engravings Turnbull included illustrates the celebrated ancient painting owned by Mead that was taken to portray Augustus, Agrippa, Maecenas, and Horace, while the other depicts a bas relief of actors and a musician that had recently been uncovered in Rome, which Turnbull believed was worthy of Mead's ownership.[60] Two of the three essays which he translated from the *Histoire et mémoires de l'Académie des inscriptions et belles lettres* discussed antiquarian topics related to these engravings. The third described the notable collection of paintings and statues amassed in ancient Rome by the infamous Gaius Verres. Turnbull used this essay as a vehicle to state what he believed were the proper ends of collecting the remains of the past. According to Turnbull, true collectors like Mead sought to benefit the public by opening up their cabinets to foster "the ambition to excel in the Arts of Design" and to promote "the Study of polite Literature" among their fellow citizens. But in Britain their efforts to arouse the "natural Genius" of the nation were sadly hampered by the lack of institutions comparable to the state and provincial academies in France. Turnbull here echoed a common complaint among men of letters that the British government did far too little to foster the advancement of learning.[61]

Turnbull's discussion of the value of historical knowledge in the preface to his edition of Justin's *History* complements his extended treatment of the topic in his *Observations upon Liberal Education*.[62] As in the *Observations*, he paid tribute to Rollin's achievements as a historian and apologist for the study of history and, following Rollin and the humanist tradition, emphasized that historical knowledge is valuable insofar as it can be used to teach moral and political lessons.[63] This view of the primarily didactic

---

60. See below, pp. 280, 283; Craig Ashley Hanson, *The English Virtuoso: Art, Medicine, and Antiquarianism in the Age of Empiricism* (Chicago and London, 2009), p. 173.

61. See below, pp. 283–86, 287–91.

62. Turnbull, *Observations,* pp. 331–45, 355–65, 372.

63. See below, pp. 308–9, 323–24; compare Turnbull, *Observations,* pp. 331, 339, and 340, where he cites Bishop Bossuet as a model.

function of history—what has come to be known as "exemplar history"—
is encapsulated in Lord Bolingbroke's dictum "that history is philosophy
teaching by examples how to conduct ourselves in all the situations of private and public life."[64] For Turnbull civil history was thus the grounding
for ethics and politics just as natural history was for natural philosophy.
Moreover, he insisted that the facts of both branches of history illustrate
broader moral and religious principles, and it was the recognition that the
facts serve such higher ends that for him distinguished the true historian
and antiquary from those who were guilty of mere "cockle-shellship," that
is, the random stockpiling of objects and information with no eye for their
meaning.[65]

Turnbull's *Treatise on Ancient Painting* explored another facet of his tree
of knowledge, namely the connection between philosophy and oratory, poetry, and painting. His discussion hinged on his claim that painting is a
language that can be employed to express the truths discovered in the moral
and natural sciences. Painting can thus play a role in a liberal education
akin to that of history, for paintings can illustrate the workings of natural
laws and moral principles and hence serve as "Samples or Experiments" of
those laws and principles.[66] In the selections reprinted below, however, we
see that his main aim in the *Treatise* was not simply to justify the study of
classical art. Rather, his reflections on the uses of the fine arts in education
were the starting point for a general exposition of his pedagogical ideals,
which he claimed mirrored those of the leading moralists of ancient Greece
and Rome. This claim masked the extent to which his views on education
reflected his own experiences as a pedagogue as well as his reading of more

64. George H. Nadel, "Philosophy of History before Historicism," *History and Theory* 3 (1964): 291–315; Lord Bolingbroke, *Historical Writings,* edited by Isaac Kramnick
(Chicago and London, 1972), p. 25. It is probable that Turnbull met Bolingbroke because
they were both members of the Prince of Wales's circle.

65. See below, pp. 320–24; compare below, pp. 13–14, and Turnbull, *Observations,*
pp. 331–32, 339–40, 355–56. In the *Three Dissertations,* Turnbull was likewise critical of
empty erudition; see below, pp. 292–95.

66. See below, pp. 341, 412–27, and George Turnbull, *A Treatise on Ancient Painting*
(London, 1740), pp. 145, 179.

recent educational tracts.[67] His belief that education ought to foster the cultivation of both private and public moral and political virtue could be traced back to the ancients, but it had also been forcefully enunciated by Shaftesbury and Molesworth in their calls for educational reform.[68] Furthermore, Turnbull's remarks on the educational rationale for foreign travel owed more to Molesworth's preface to *An Account of Denmark* than to the writings of Greek or Roman authors.[69] And although he credited the ancients with the map of learning that justified his scheme for a liberal education, his conception of a unified system of the arts and sciences was in fact the creation of modern thinkers and was something that he shared with fellow exponents of Enlightenment.[70] In effect, the *Treatise* provided the ancient precedents for a thoroughly modern plan for a liberal education, and Turnbull's deployment of erudition in the service of pedagogical reform illustrates how classical antiquity was used to underwrite Enlightenment in eighteenth-century Europe.

Who, then, was George Turnbull? His life fits the pattern of the "Scotsman on the make" seeking a career in London and exploiting the opportunities opened up by the Union of 1707.[71] His ideas and values were those of the virtuosi who fostered the European Enlightenment. In Edinburgh, Turnbull and the Rankenians built on the cultural and institutional foundations laid by Sir Robert Sibbald and the generation who brought Enlightenment to Scotland. Their diverse inquiries in medicine, mathematics, natural and moral philosophy, history, chorography, and antiquarianism

67. On Turnbull's educational views see the editorial introduction to Turnbull, *Observations,* pp. ix–xviii.

68. See below, pp. 393, 405–6; [Lord Shaftesbury], *Several Letters Written by a Noble Lord to a Young Man at the University* (London, 1716); Robert Molesworth, *An Account of Denmark. With Francogallia and Some Considerations for the Promoting of Agriculture and Employing the Poor,* edited by Justin Champion (Indianapolis, 2011), pp. 14–17, 20–23.

69. See below, pp. 351–60, and Turnbull, *Observations,* pp. 290–91, 418–21; Molesworth, *Account,* pp. 7–14.

70. See below, pp. 339–45, 370–84; Richard Yeo, *Encyclopaedic Visions: Scientific Dictionaries and Enlightenment Culture* (Cambridge, 2001).

71. *Scots in London in the Eighteenth Century,* edited by Stana Nenadic (Lewisburg, 2010). The phrase is J. M. Barrie's.

were shaped by their Baconian belief in the unity of all branches of human knowledge. Turnbull refashioned their view into his own tree of the arts and sciences. He immersed himself in the early Enlightenment debates over religion and politics, but he became increasingly fascinated by the textual and material remains of ancient Greece and Rome. Turnbull can thus be seen as an exemplar of the enlightened virtuoso.

EDITORIAL PRINCIPLES

In editing printed material we have retained, as far as possible, the spelling, punctuation, and capitalization practices of the original compositors. We have silently corrected obvious typographical errors. Original pagination is indicated using angle brackets thus, <1>. Different works from different dates and different publishers show some variation in the conventions used to mark footnotes. We have not standardized the footnote markings themselves, although we have modernized the placement of Turnbull's footnote markings. Where necessary we have also modernized the use of quotation marks. Editorial amplification interpolated in Turnbull's footnotes is indicated by square brackets. The editors' own annotations on the texts are supplied in a numerical sequence below the original author's notes. Unless otherwise noted we have used the standard Loeb editions of Greek and Latin works, although in some instances M. A. Stewart and Michael Silverthorne have provided revised translations.

Turnbull's biblical references cannot always be corroborated in known editions of the Bible. In our editorial annotations we have used the King James version as published in 1998 in the Oxford World's Classics series. We have supplied references to the King James Bible for all of the biblical passages Turnbull quotes or alludes to, except where Turnbull's own references correspond to the relevant passage in the King James version. Where there are multiple citations in Turnbull's notes, our references follow the sequence of Turnbull's citations. There are also instances where Turnbull's biblical references make no sense and we have indicated such instances in our notes.

Where possible we have tried to refer the reader to Turnbull's sources in reliable modern editions, but it has sometimes been necessary to draw attention to features of the editions that Turnbull himself cites. Many of the

editions of the seventeenth- and eighteenth-century works to which Turnbull refers are readily available in either microfilm or digital form. Further
information on a number of the British subjects identified in the editorial
annotations can be found in the *Oxford Dictionary of National Biography.*

In editing manuscript material, we have again followed as far as possible
the spelling, punctuation, and capitalization of the originals. Even though
Turnbull retains archaic spellings that have long gone out of use (for example, "wiew" for "view"), we have made no attempt to modernize or stan-
dardize his spellings. Turnbull's use of punctuation may seem erratic to a
modern reader, but it is no more so than was common in his day. However,
where his lack of punctuation creates significant ambiguity, we have clari-
fied his sense by inserting the necessary punctuation enclosed in angle
brackets thus, < >. Occasionally syllables and words have been duplicated
and in these cases the duplication has been silently deleted. Where it has
seemed essential to adjust erroneous or missing lettering to convey the intended sense the editorial revision is inclosed in angle brackets thus, < >.
We have also indicated the pagination of Turnbull's "The Religion of the
State" using angle brackets thus, <3>. Contractions have been silently expanded. Characters in superscript have been printed on the line. In order
to provide easily readable texts, we have not recorded authorial insertions
or deletions. Instances of such revisions in the manuscript and letters tran-
scribed below are relatively infrequent and of no consequence for the meaning or interpretation of Turnbull's writings. Editorial notes to the manuscript and to the letters are provided in a numerical series of footnotes.

Our presentation of Turnbull's letters is modelled on that of the published correspondences of Adam Smith and Thomas Reid. At the head of
each letter we have provided information about the address (when given)
and the source used for the text. We have stated the place of origin and
date of writing in that sequence at the top right of each letter thus, "Edinburgh, 13 November 1718." We have not standardized the places of origin
given, but we have standardized the form of the date on which the letter
was written. Where information relating to addressee, provenance, or date
of a letter is conjectural, this is supplied in square brackets.

LIST OF ABBREVIATIONS

AUL   Aberdeen University Library

BL   British Library

EUL   Edinburgh University Library

HMCR   *Historical Manuscripts Commission: Report on Manuscripts in Various Collections. The Manuscripts of the Hon. Frederick Lindley Wood; M. L. S. Clements, Esq.; S. Philip Unwin, Esq.* Volume 8 (London, 1913).

NLI   National Library of Ireland

ODNB   *Oxford Dictionary of National Biography: From the Earliest Times to the Year 2000,* edited by H. C. G. Matthew and Brian Harrison, 61 vols. (Oxford, 2004). Also available online.

Shaftesbury, *Characteristicks*
      Anthony Ashley Cooper, Earl of Shaftesbury, *Characteristicks of Men, Manners, Opinions, Times,* edited by Douglas Den Uyl, 3 vols. (Indianapolis, 2001).

ACKNOWLEDGMENTS

The editors would like to thank Michael Silverthorne for his translations of George Turnbull's two Latin graduation theses and the Latin and Greek passages found in the selections from Turnbull's *A Treatise on Ancient Painting*. We would also like to thank Alexander Broadie, John Cairns, Claire Carlin, Roger Emerson, Stephen Snobelen, Jeffrey Suderman, and, especially, Knud Haakonssen for their help during the lengthy gestation of this book. In addition, Paul Wood would like to thank John Sterk, QC, for his work as a research assistant and the Social Sciences and Humanities Research Council of Canada for research funding.

For permission to reproduce manuscript material and letters we are grateful to the Special Collections Centre, University of Aberdeen; the Department of Manuscripts and the Board of the British Library; and Edinburgh University Library, Special Collections Department. Turnbull's three letters to Lord Molesworth were first published, in edited form, in the Historical Manuscripts Commission's combined account of the papers of the Molesworth and Clements families, who were related by marriage; see HMC, *Report on Manuscripts in Various Collections, Vol. VIII: The Manuscripts of the Hon. Frederick Lindley Wood; M. L. S. Clements, Esq.; S. Philip Unwin, Esq.* (1913). The whole collection was microfilmed at some point in the twentieth century and a master copy placed in the National Library of Ireland, before the manuscript originals were sold at Sotheby's, London, in 1977. The purchaser, Mr. Martin Townsend of Letchworth, Hertfordshire, kindly gave permission for M. A. Stewart to publish eight letters from several authors in this collection, and he generously supplied photocopies of as many as he could find, including two of the Turnbull letters, with permission for transcriptions to be published from the microfilm for the remainder.

Translations from the following titles are reprinted by permission of the publishers and the Trustees of the Loeb Classical Library. Loeb Classical Library® is a registered trademark of the President and Fellows of Harvard College.

Cicero, *De finibus bonorum et malorum,* Loeb Classical Library, vol. 40, translated by H. Rackham, pp. 133 35, 199–205, 201, 205–7, 293, 339–41, 417 (Cambridge, Mass.: Harvard University Press, 1914).

Cicero, *De natura deorum and Academica,* Loeb Classical Library, vol. 268, translated by H. Rackham, pp. 139–43, 151, 155–57, 159, 205–9, 257–59, 263–65, 283, 365 (Cambridge, Mass.: Harvard University Press, 1933).

Cicero, *De officiis,* Loeb Classical Library, vol. 31, translated by Walter Mitter, pp. 13–19, 65 (Cambridge, Mass.: Harvard University Press, 1913).

Cicero, *De oratore, De fato, Paradoxa Stoicorum, and De partitione oratoria;* Loeb Classical Library, vols. 348–49, translated by E. W. Sutton and H. Rackham (2 vols.), pp. 17–19, 141–45, 225 (Cambridge, Mass.: Harvard University Press, 1942).

Plato, *Euthyphro, Apology, Crito, Phaedo, and Phaedrus;* Loeb Classical Library, vol. 36, translated by Harold North Fowler, pp. 113, 335–39 (Cambridge, Mass.: Harvard University Press, 1914).

Correspondence, 1718–1741

෩ ෩ ෩

1. *To* JOHN TOLAND[1]

Address: To Mr John Toland To the care of Mr Roberts[2] in
Warwick lane London[3]
MS: BL Add. MS 4465, fols. 17–18; unpubl.

Edinburgh, 13 November 1718

Sir

I have read some of your performances, & I have all the reason in the
world to think, that I may tell my Sentiments to you freely, & that if you
differ from me, you will, for the sake of truth, give your self the trouble to
shew me why you do so: and therefore I have fairly ventured to begin a
coresspondence with you, and I would perswade my self, that when we have
exchanged some few letters, you will not incline to drop it.

Sir I am a Freethinker, and I glory in the character. Some people are
pleased to say that I am no good Christian; and in good faith if these two
characters are in the least incompatible, I shal very frankly yeild it to them
that I am not. But if to prove all things & to hold fast that only which is
good, be true Christianity; I am as orthodox as any man can pretend to be.
I neither regard custom, nor fashion, authority nor power; truth & reason
are the only things that determine me. And I can never believe that to be
a fool, is the way to get into the favour of infinite wisdom; or that one must
be stript of his reason, to be made meet for the society of pure & perfect
spirits. Sir I don't know how it comes about, that it hath always been cast
in the Atheist's teeth, that he hates the restraints of virtue, & would gladly
take up with any hypotheses, to get rid of the fears of another world. Per-

---

1. John Toland (1670–1722), Irish Deist, Whig political pamphleteer, and author of
Christianity Not Mysterious (1696) as well as many other works.

2. James Roberts (ca. 1669–1754), printer and bookseller, who sold books authored
by John Toland.

3. The address is not in Turnbull's hand.

haps it may be so with some. For my part, I have no prejudice against the being of a God; nor do I think, the practice of virtue, can be any hardship upon those, that have a true taste of life; but the only difficulty, that I can see, about the immortality of the soul, arises from the principles of the Theists themselves. An eternal Series may go on to eternity; but if you stop at the one end, you must stop at the other too. To suppose a God at the top of an Infinite scheme, that sees all his designs at once, is in reality to suppose a thing finite & infinite at the same time. For that which is seen must be finite; so that if God sees all his works, his works must have an end. Infinite knowledge, or an Infinite scheme perceived, is the most glaring contradiction imaginable. A succession of things may be vastly long, but end it must if it be perceived.

And in truth, Sir, the notion of God seeing all his works at one wiew, affords us no very extraordinary Idea of the divine blessedness. To be always fixed to the same Ideas, is a happiness, that I don't envy even the Godhead it self. Let the wiews of the Deity be as large & wide as you will: I like much better to skip merrily from one thing to another at my pleasure. To have always just & true notions, is very desirable, but to be eternally humming over the same story, or to have always the same objects before one's eyes, is the dullest entertainment under the heavens.

I have a great deal more to say to you, Good Sir, about the principles of religion, if you incline to keep up the corespondence, but this is enough at once. I long very much to know what you mean by your immortal government.[4]

I am Sir

with the greatest respect
and sincerest friendship
your most humble servant
Philocles[5]

PS. Please to direct for me. To Mr Ebednezar Shovel at Edinburgh[6]

---

4. A reference to John Toland, *Nazarenus: Or, Jewish, Gentile, and Mahometan Christianity* (London, 1718).

5. Turnbull uses a pseudonym drawn from the name of one of the interlocutors in the dialogue "The Moralists, a Philosophical Rhapsody," in Shaftesbury's *Characteristicks*.

6. This letter is endorsed in the hand of Thomas Birch, "Mr. G. Turnbull Nov. 13. 1718." Birch's endorsement confirms that Turnbull was the author of this letter.

2. *To* [VISCOUNT MOLESWORTH][7]

MS: NLI, Microfilm n. 4082, p. 3753[8]

Tinninghame East Lothian, 3 August 1722

My Lord

I have long admired your steady & firm adherence to Liberty & the interests of your country, & in my heart blessed you and all your Generous Designs. But when the E. of Shaftsbury's Letters to you, that have been lately published,[9] came to my hands, Pardon me, My Lord, if it was then my Esteem rose highest, and my breast began to glow with the Warmest affection towards your merit. Good and Honest surely must he be who was the Friend and Trustee of the truly Good and Upright Shaftsbury.[10] And worthy indeed hath your Lordship's conduct always been of so noble a Friendship.

I have, My Lord, studied with great care the works of that Excellent man, & must own I never received so much real benefit from any Uninspired writings; so incomparably perfect is the composure of all his peices, & so divine the Energy with which these form the genuine principles of Virtue & goodness, and a true relish of beauty & Truth of every sort in the mind of a well disposed Reader. And I have now conceived so just a veneration for his memory, that there is nothing can give me more pleasure than to hear of him & his Friends, and particularly of his worthy Lady and promising Son.[11] I have often, My Lord, regretted that none of his Friends have

---

7. Robert, 1st Viscount Molesworth (1656–1725), Irish politician and leading "Old" or "true" Whig. Politically he was an ally of the third Earl of Shaftesbury, and he was also a patron of John Toland.

8. Excerpts from this letter are published in HMCR, VIII, 343–44.

9. *Letters from the Right Honourable the late Earl of Shaftesbury, to Robert Molesworth, Esq., now the Lord Viscount of that Name. With Two Letters written by the Late Sir John Cropley. To which is Prefix'd a Large Introduction by the Editor,* edited by John Toland (London, 1721).

10. Anthony Ashley Cooper, 3rd Earl of Shaftesbury (1671–1713), English moralist and author of *Characteristicks of Men, Manners, Opinions, Times,* 3 vols. ([London], 1711), as well as other miscellaneous writings.

11. Shaftesbury married Jane Ewer (1689?–1751) in 1709. In 1711 they had a son, Anthony Ashley Cooper, who later became the 4th Earl of Shaftesbury.

given the world an account of his Life. Sure I am it would not be an Idle tale; but a profitable history. The progress of his studies & improvements, and the Steps by which his Lordship, inter scabiem tantam et contagia Lucri,[12] arrived to such a surprising height of Virtue & so polite a taste in all usefull science, must undoubtedly be very curious & worthy of observation, and the account of 'em very Entertaining & instructive.

May I presume, My Lord, to Enquire of your Lordship how a copy of the Letter he wrote to an English Lord with his peice upon the judgement of Hercules which I am informed was only printed with thirty copies of his works, may be procured?[13] Or if there is any thing else of his that I can have access to see. I have no news to write from this place that can be so agreable to your Lordship as that even in this narrow bigotted country there are severall of my acquaintance who are sincere Lovers of Truth & Liberty. I am heartily Sorry, My Lord, that there should be any dispute about your election & am heartily concerned with several others here about the final event.[14] My Lord I am setled a Professor of Philosophy in the new College of Aberdeen;[15] & hope now to have Leisure to apply my self to the Study of the Antients, the Study to which my humor & Genius leads me; And in my publick Profession shal always make it my business to promote the interests of Liberty & Vertue & to reform the taste of the Young Generation. But oh! My Lord, Education in this country is upon a miserable footing; And why should I say in this country, for is it not almost Every

12. Horace, *Epistles*, I.xii.14: "in the very midst of the contagious itch of gain."

13. *A Letter concerning the Art or Science of Design, written from Italy (on the occasion of Some Designs in Painting), to my Lord ****,* which appeared in a limited number of copies of the first edition of Shaftesbury's *Characteristicks; A Notion of the Historical Draught or Tablature of the Judgment of Hercules, according to Prodicus, Lib. II. Xen. de Mem. Soc.* (London, 1713). The *Notion* also appeared in a few copies of the first edition of the *Characteristicks*. See Robert Voitle, *The Third Earl of Shaftesbury, 1671–1713* (Baton Rouge and London, 1984), p. 418.

14. Turnbull refers here to Molesworth's abortive campaign in the 1722 General Election. Molesworth had served as MP for Westminster from 1715 until 1722. He again stood as a candidate in the 1722 General Election but then withdrew.

15. Turnbull was elected as a Regent at Marischal College on 14 April 1721.

where? And must it not be so while Philosophy is a Traffick, and Science is retailed for a peice of bread?

If your Lordship should do me the honour of a Letter I must put you to the trouble of enclosing it under a cover to Mr George Young Chirurgeon at Doctor Pitcairn's head Edinburgh;[16] for I shal for some time be very litle in one place; and he is a very honest worthy Friend of mine, to whom I committ my affairs at Edinburgh in my absence.

I am with the sincerest respect

My Lord

your Lordships

most humble and

devoted servant

Geo: Turnbull

P.S. When I was just going to put up this Epistle a Friend of mine came upon me, who would needs have me to present his humble respects to your Lordship & most hearty wishes for your prosperity & the success of all your noble designs.[17] He is a Gentleman of a very fine taste a truly Worthy Honest Fellow. 'Tis to him I in a great measure owe my acquaintance with the E. of Shaftsbury's works; and there is none perhaps who has studied these Excellent writings more, or understands them better. He was Educated by his Presbyterian Friends for the Sacred Function & 'Een commenced Preacher before he came to his present free State of mind & just notion of Religion & Vertue. But is now a very sincere promoter of Liberty & true Vertue by his sermons & otherwise. And indeed he is very well fitted to do service here in the honest cause being wise as well.

---

16. George Young (1692–1757) was a fellow member of the Rankenian Club.

17. William Wishart (ca. 1692–1753), another member of the Rankenian Club and later Principal of Edinburgh University. Wishart graduated from Edinburgh with his Master of Arts degree in 1709 and then studied divinity there until he was licensed by the Presbytery of Edinburgh in 1717. After a brief spell in the United Provinces he returned to Edinburgh in 1719 and was made a preacher at Skinner's Close, where he remained until 1724. Wishart also corresponded with Molesworth.

3. *To* VISCOUNT MOLESWORTH

Address: To The Right Honourable my Lord Molesworth. To the care of
Mr Valentine[18] Bookseller at the Queen's head in Fleet Street London
MS: NLI, Microfilm n. 4082, p. 3753[19]

Settled now at Aberdeen, 5 November 1722

My Lord

Upon the reading your most good & condescending Letter (which I
received much sooner than I was flattering my self as earnestly as I longed
for it) methought I felt all that was Good & Honest in me redoubled. Every
line is so full of the true Philosopher the worthy Honest man. The applause
of the truly Good & Upright is indeed a strong & powerfull incentive to
those who are but just Entred upon the paths of virtue: And it was truly
generous in your Lordship weel knowing the charm to Encourage so Liberaly my honest inclinations. You my Lord who have always been acting
the noblest part any Mortal can be Engaged in upon this earthly Stage,
when you are wrestling for liberty & your country, does not the presence
& applause of your friends & weel-wishers to your cause add something
to your Zeal & Courage? Or is that divine pitch of honest boldnes & that
overpowring force of Publick affection which you discover in your publick
actings no more than what you can easily command at any time or in any
cool & solitary hour. This indeed were more great & Godlike. But the most
Elevated Virtue among mankind, I think, reaches not so high. For my own
part (My Lord) I act in a much Lower orbit, and my Strugles are not to be
compared with these your Lordship hath undergone in pursuing your far
greater & nobler undertaking. But I should never be able to maintain my
Virtue in the warmth & Vigour that is necessary to bear one up under the
Difficulties that Lie Even in my way; Did I not frequently Endeavour by
Strength of Fancy to supply the want of a real presence & applause. And
thus (My Lord) have I at Last presumed to address my self to your Lordship,
with whose imagined presence, I have long been very familiar, that by (A

18. We have been unable to identify this bookseller.
19. Brief excerpts from this letter are published in HMCR, VIII, p. 352.

Macte Virtute)[20] A real approbation & good wish from one so far advanced in the ways of honour & Merit, (a condescension I weel knew your uncommon Generosity would readily comply withall as soon as the weightier matters you are Ever employed about should permit you) I might obtain the most Effectual motive I could in my imagination devise to animate & Enliven my faint & Languid Vertue and to give new life & vigour to all my honest purposes & resolutions.

That your Lordship after the toil of many years Employed in fighting with vice & Tyranny, now when your constitution is become crazy & inhabile & your days are fast hastening to the natural period instead of Ease & retirement can yet think with pleasure of Strugling for the Public weal & the same Glorious cause of Liberty, is indeed a proof of the Strongest & most Indefatigable Virtue & the Sincerest affection to your country. But oh my Lord how it moves me to the heart! And how afflicting should it indeed be to all the Friends of Liberty, that means have been found by mercenary avaricious men, Enemies surely to the common interest & all that is Good & Honest to debar such an old Experienced approven Patriot from all access to serve his country in a legal way; Spirit worn out in his country's service & yet willing to Sacrifice the remnants of old age & a crazy body to her interests, the Cato of our time & nation.[21] Indeed in these degenerate times the truly honest Patriot who resolves to act faithfully, & to continue to his country's interest is likely to have a very hard fighting task: But tho' Vertue hath seldom been triumphant, the Strugle is glorious & a few honest Champions against Slavery & arbitrary power have always been of great use at least to moderate matters & keep the measures of Wicked men a little more tolerable than otherwise they might have been.

20. "Be increased in your virtue" or "go on and prosper."

21. Marcus Porcius Cato (95–46 B.C.E.), also known as Cato of Utica or Cato the Younger, a Roman politician who committed suicide rather than compromise his political principles. In early eighteenth-century Britain Cato was widely regarded as someone who had defended liberty in the disinterested service of the Roman republic and was thus seen as an exemplar of republican *virtù* and Stoical virtue. Cato was much admired by Molesworth and the Old Whigs, as well as by less radical figures like Joseph Addison (1672–1719), whose *Cato: A Tragedy* (1713) served to popularize the image of Cato as a patriotic opponent of the tyrannical designs of Julius Caesar.

But if our few faithfull honest men are shut out from all capacity of Exerting themselves in a legal way what shal become of us.

But I must contain myself.

The learned youth of the University of Glascow (with some of whom I have the honour to be acquainted) have indeed given proofs of a free & generous spirit which deserve to be commended. And I am sure they have a very gratefull sense of the Encouragment you have been pleased to give them.[22] Would to heaven (My Lord) I could say our college were as yet in any respect upon a better footing than her sisters. Sure I am I should reckon my Self a happy man if I can contribute any thing in my capacity to promote the interests of liberty truth & the love of mankind. 'Tis indeed on the Education of the youth that the Foundation stones of Publick Liberty must be layed. But oh (my Lord) when shal a Formal dogmatical spirit which hath brought true Philosophy & usefull Scholarship into such contempt be seperated from the gown; And our Academies become realy good & Wholesome Nurseries to the Publicke. O when shall all that Idle Pedantick Stuff which is now alass the most innocent cargoe our youth can carry with them from our Universities be banished; And that Philosophy which once governed States & Societies & produced Heroes & Patriots take place in its room. And for this effect when shal the Sprightly arts & Sciences, which are so Essential in the formation of a gentiel & liberal Caracter be again reunited with Philosophy from which by a fatal Error they have been so long severed! But what do I talk of? All this surely is meer Romance & Enthusiasm. For how can it be so while our Colleges are under the Inspection of proud domineering pedantic Priests whose interest it is to train up the youth in a profound veneration to their Senseless metaphysical Creeds & Catechisms, which for this purpose they are daily inured to defend against all Doubters & Enquirers with the greatest bitte<r>ness & contempt, in a stiff formal bewildering manner admirably fitted indeed to Enslave young understandings betimes and to beget an early antipathy against all Free thought. My lord I have read with great pleasure several late

22. Molesworth was a political figurehead for the group of students opposed to the University administration that included the Irishmen John Smith (d. 1771) and James Arbuckle (d. 1742). Turnbull was in contact with members of this group, who all shared his political and religious views. On Arbuckle, see also below, note 26 on p. 13.

performances of a truly noble & generous Spirit, particularly the Independent Whig & the letters subscribed Cato, & with my soul wish weel to the worthy undertakers.[23] No doubt they are known to your Lordship & they are certainly men of a fine turn, throughly good & honest Lovers of mankind. I admire that noble warmth of honest Enthusiasm which give such uncommon life & vivacity to these Excellent papers: And yet more that comprehensive knowledge of mankind by which it is influenced & supported. For indeed it is in the histories of mankind that the value of liberty is best learned, as weel as the ways by which it has been lost & preserved: And this brings it to my mind to ask your Lordship if there is any translation in any of the more known languages of the Laws of Denmark, for I have a great inclination to see these laws which are so weel spoken of in that most judicious account of Denmark published in 1692.[24] How weel pleased should I be that there were such accounts of all the other States in Europe that by that means I might supply the want of travel with the hopes of which I fear I must not flatter myself.

My Lord I cannot read what you say of your age & constitution without the most passionate Emotions. May heaven be so kind to mankind as to prolong your days. But to your self I must believe your age is noway uneasy. For Cato like you have the vertuous labours of a weel spent life & Philosophy the never failing refuge of a learned Honest man, to solace you in these days which appear only Evil to a youthfull taste. And that Philosophy which hath made you so compleatly good & Vertuous must undoubtedly have Enabled you long agoe to Despise Death that Head Gobling & all its terrors. Your body (my Lord) may be frail & decaying apace But your virtue is still lively & vigorous & this methinks presages it shal never die, but when

---

23. Thomas Gordon (d. 1750) and John Trenchard (1668/69–1723). Gordon authored the pamphlet *The Character of an Independent Whig* (London, 1719), and then collaborated with Trenchard and the Deist Anthony Collins (1676–1729) in publishing the paper *The Independent Whig,* which appeared in 1720. The individual weekly numbers were collected as *The Independent Whig* (London, 1721). In 1720, Gordon and Trenchard also began to contribute letters to Trenchard's paper, the *London Journal,* using the pseudonym Cato; the letters were eventually brought together to form *Cato's Letters,* 4 vols. (London, 1723–24).

24. Robert Molesworth, *An Account of Denmark, as it was in the Year 1692* (London, 1694).

its present crazy habitation fails Exchange it for another more suited to its perfection & Excellence. The Great motive, your lordship knows, which perswaded the wisest antients to the belief of a future state unrevealed to them was purely the love of virtue in the persons of these great men the Founders and Preservers of Society. And indeed even amidst all the Light the Christian revelation affords concerning futurity there is something in this argument peculiarly satisfying to good & virtous minds. For surely if Wisdom & Goodness be chief & predominant in nature whatever difficulties & hardships may be necessary to form as weel as prove a true & genuine virtue; yet after Virtue has strugled thro' much opposition & by suffering arrived to perfection, it cannot continue any longer to be suppressed & born down; But must at last triumph over all opposition and be placed in such circumstances as it may Exert all its benignity & goodness & act like it self. But it is now high time to beg pardon for detaining your Lordship so long and giving too loose reins to an Impulse for which I have nothing to say but that it is truly honest. And indeed it had got vent much sooner had I not been obliged to a continual wandering since I received yours. I am my Lord with the sinc<e>rest respect your most obliged humble servant.

Gco: Turnbull.

4. *To* VISCOUNT MOLESWORTH

Address: To The Right Honourable The Lord Molesworth at Breckdenston near Dublin
MS: NLI, Microfilm n. 4082, p. 3753 [25]

Edinburgh, 14 May 1723

My Lord
    I am unwilling to trouble your Lordship too often; But now I Long exceedingly to know how you are & in what state of health.
    I thank your Lordship mos<t> heartily for your most acceptable & obliging complement & there is nothing indeed of that kind I would be prouder

---

25. Excerpts from this letter are published in HMCR, VIII, pp. 360–61.

of than to have your works in my Library Ex dono the worthy Author. If you please therefore to transmit the peices you mention to Glascow directed to the care of Mr James Arbuckle Student of Divinity he will forward them to me.[26]

I have seen Mr Collins' treatise on Free-thinking some years agoe & another peice of the same Author's (as it is commonly said) upon liberty & necessity; & I should be glad to know if he is still alive & what is become of him.[27] Toland who was said to have been of his Club I know is gone.[28] I beg Leave to tell your lordship that I wrote a small treatise about four years agoe upon the Religion of the State which had it not been for the timidity of Printers had seen the light long since.[29] The design of it was to shew that a fair & impartial excercise of reason was the best & worthiest part an understanding creature could act in matters of thought or faith & that no rational society could have any common interest in matters of that sort but the common defence of this common & noblest priviledge of rational be-ings. I Endeavour to shew that the interest of true religion only requires that the Publick Magistrates & Guardians should protect all the members of the societies under their care & tutorship equally in the easy & quiet use of the thinking & reasoning Liberty: And that all other publick medling in religion must be prejudicial to religion trade learning politeness & in fine to all the common right & interests of mankind whether Civil or Spirituall. But now My Lord tho I be as sincere & hearty a lover of free-thinking as ever, I begin to doubt a litle whether upon an impartiall balance of all the

26. Arbuckle took his Master of Arts degree at Glasgow University in July 1720. He then became a divinity student and remained in Glasgow until 1724. Arbuckle was one of the leaders of the campaign to revive the rectorial elections at the University, and his involvement in student politics brought him into contact with Viscount Molesworth, who later became his patron in Dublin.

27. Anthony Collins, the leading English Deist; [Anthony Collins], *A Discourse of Free-Thinking, Occasion'd by the Rise and Growth of a Sect call'd Free-Thinkers* (London, 1713); [Anthony Collins], *A Philosophical Inquiry concerning Human Liberty* (London, 1717).

28. Toland had died on 11 March 1722. In using the term "Club" Turnbull probably means no more than that Collins and Toland were fellow Deists and friends of long standing.

29. See below, pp. 79–89.

interests & advantages of Society some Established worship & mode of
religion & publick order of Priests or Teachers would not be found absolutely necessary if not for the upholding of society, at least for the right
management of it.[30] The decision of this question depends upon a thorough knowledge of mankind & a judicious observation of the ways by
which they have been governed in different ages & circumstances. And I
should be glad to have your Lordship's sentiments upon that head weel
knowing your own deep insight into human affairs & that your notions of
government & politicks are founded upon solid history & observation. In
the mean time I can't but think it very plain from history that some orders
of Priesthood have been very pernicious to Society & that most that ever
were might have been under regulations much more advantageous to true
religion & Virtue & all the learned & polite arts.

What you tell me my lord of the breaking up of my last surprised me
not a litle; But it was a sincere esteem of your Lordship's uncommon love
to truth liberty & virtue that alone induced me to hasten so forwardly in
to your friendship & this I am proud to own in the face of all the flatterers
of Arbitrary power that I have more real pleasure in the virt<u>ous correspondence in which you are pleased to allow me than in all the gawdry
pomp & honours of their most caressed minions I am my Lord with the
sincerest respect your

Lordships most obliged
humble servant
Geo: Turnbull

PS. I do not know my lord if I should venture upon so short & distant an acquaintance with your lordship to desire of you to recommend me, if it fall in
your way, to go abroad governour to a young gentleman, for that to be sure is
what one of your wisdom & honesty will not do rashly; But so impatient is my
desire of an opportunity of that sort for my own improvement; & so satisfied
am I at the same time that my natural turn fits me for a trust of that kind more
than any other that I shal presume to tell your lordship that it would be the
greatest favour you could do me & that I am far from proposing your lordship
should do any thing of that kind without using any methods you think proper
for knowing more of my sufficiency for that business.

30. Compare below, pp. 103–5.

5. *To* CHARLES MACKIE[31]

Address: To Mr Charles Macky Professor of History in the university
of Edinburgh
MS: EUL, La. II. 91; unpubl.

London, 3 September 1725

Dear Sir

We are just going to Leave this place; & having as yet received no account
of Mr Duncan's[32] inclinations I cannot write any formal commission of
Substitution & Factorship[33] But shal do it as soon as I know the person
you agree with. And I do by this give you full & ample power to transact
& bargain with him or any other person in my name to be my Substitute
and Factor at Aberdeen to teach my class for me & uplift all the Emolu-
ments & Salaries due to me at the term of Martimass next & thereafter till
the bargain & transaction you shal make in my name be duly revoked and
do by this missive to you oblidge my self to hold firm & stable any bargain
or transaction you shal make with any person in my name and for the above
mentioned effect as if done my self personaly; as also to give a formal commission of Factory and substitution to the person you shal agree with upon
stampt paper as law requires as soon as you notify the particulars of the said
bargain & transaction to me. And for you<r> trouble in this & many other
favours shal always be Dear Sir your most oblidged

humble servant
George Turnbull

PS. I am realy anxious to have the affair of the Substitution fairly setled. I shal
write to you as soon as we setle at Groninghen. mean time if there is occasion

31. Charles Mackie (1688–1770), Edinburgh Professor of Universal History (1719–
65). Turnbull probably first met Mackie in Edinburgh in 1719, while Turnbull was a
divinity student. They were fellow members of the Rankenian Club prior to Turnbull's
departure for Aberdeen in 1721.

32. Robert Duncan, a Scot who had studied at Groningen. Duncan corresponded
with both Mackie and the Rev. Robert Wodrow (1679–1734) of Eastwood.

33. Even though Turnbull had not obtained a leave of absence from Marischal College
Aberdeen, he had clearly approached Duncan to act as his substitute and teach for him
during the forthcoming academic year. When his colleagues at Marischal learned that
he intended to absent himself from the college, they demanded that he return before the
start of the session in order to teach his class.

to write let letters be directed to the care of John Gordon Factor in Roterdam[34] Tell Mr Maclauran[35] that it has been impossible for me to get out to the country to wait on Jeriswood.[36]

6. *To* CHARLES MACKIE

Address: To Mr Charles Macky Professor of History and Antiquities in the University of Edinburgh North Britain
MS: EUL, La. II. 91; unpubl.

Groninghen, 20 October 1725

Dear Sir

Your friend Rossal[37] is very kind & oblidging; and I hope in a litle time I shal be acquainted with him. Mr Udney[38] & I wait upon his history colledge; which he has but jus<t> begun. Monsieur Cramant[39] is still here &

---

34. Unidentified.

35. Colin Maclaurin (1698–1746), Professor of Mathematics at Marischal College Aberdeen (1717–25) and then at the University of Edinburgh (1725–46). When this letter was written, Maclaurin was about to take up his post in Edinburgh and was presumably already residing there.

36. George Baillie of Jerviswood (1664–1738), a prominent Scottish Squadrone politician who occupied a number of important public offices during his political career. He was removed from the Board of Trade in 1725 but continued to serve as an MP until 1734. Baillie's wife, Lady Grisell (1665–1746), was the sister of Alexander Hume Campbell, 2nd Earl of Marchmont (1675–1740), whose son Maclaurin had tutored from 1722 to the son's death in 1724.

37. Michael Rossal (d. 1744), Professor of Greek at Groningen (1717–44), where he had held an adjunct position since 1706. From 1724, he held his chair jointly with that of Logic. He published on the Stoic philosophy of Epictetus (Groningen, 1708) and other classical and religious subjects. Mackie had studied under Rossal in 1707–8, and the two of them continued thereafter to correspond.

38. Alexander Udny of Udny, who graduated in Turnbull's class at Marischal College Aberdeen in April 1726. Udny became an advocate in Edinburgh in 1728 and a Commissioner of Excise.

39. Unidentified.

was Exceedingly weel pleased to hear of your weelfare & desired to have his compliments returned to you. I believe I shal pass this winter pretty pleasantly But by what I can see yet I should not care to be here another. I wrote to Mr Duncan lately my mind about my affair at Aberdeen I should be much oblidged to him if he could think of it; & I leave the terms Entirely to you. But what are our folks inclinations at Aberdeen I know not. I am afraid the folks I thought would be easiest may be most uneasy. For I have wrote twice or thrice both to Dr Mackail[40] and Mr Varner[41] & have had no answer If they will make me uneasy I cannot help it: But this winter I neither will nor can come home.[42] Let them do what they please. And indeed I wish heartily I may be so lucky as to have no more to do with that place. But I know I need not put you in mind how much I want to be delivered from Aberdeen; & how much I wish something better would cast up. I should be glad to know if you have made any steps in the Glascow project[43] & what you think of it But I must either finish this letter now without saying any more or lose this post for I am called to the other Room to attend Mr Barbeyrac[44] who is come to honour us with a visit. I suppose Mr Duncan has given you an account of his colledges.[45] I realy like his

40. Matthew Mackail (1691/92–1733), Professor of Medicine at Marischal College Aberdeen and a friend of Turnbull's.

41. David Verner or Warner (ca. 1688–1752), Regent at Marischal College Aberdeen and a friend of Turnbull's.

42. Turnbull subsequently changed his mind and was back in Aberdeen by January 1726.

43. It may be that Turnbull was hoping to replace the ailing Professor of Humanity at Glasgow, Andrew Ross (ca. 1682–1751). The University had to find substitutes to teach for him in the period 1726–29.

44. Jean Barbeyrac (1674–1744), French Huguenot refugee, who studied and for a time taught law at Lausanne, before becoming Professor of the Law of Nature and Nations at Groningen (1717–44). Best known for his translations into French and commentaries on the natural-law theories of Grotius and Pufendorf, and for his contributions to the learned journals of the day, he also translated the English natural-law theorist Richard Cumberland. His views of biblical criticism and the early Church were too liberal for many in the Reformed tradition.

45. Unlike Turnbull, Duncan had a low view of Barbeyrac's teaching. See his letter to Mackie of 29 February 1724 quoted in James Moore, "Natural Law and the Pyrrhonian Controversy," in *Philosophy and Science in the Scottish Enlightenment,* edited by Peter Jones (Edinburgh, 1988), p. 22.

colledge on the Institutes[46] but he has given it over because he had not above five to wait on it. I am Dearest Sir

Your most obliged
humble servant
George Turnbull.

7. *To* CHARLES MACKIE

Address: To Mr Charles Macky Professor of History in the university of Edinburgh
MS: EUL MS La. II. 91; unpubl.

Aberdeen, 23 January 1727

Dearest Sir

Tis indeed a dismal and affecting story that gives occasion to my troubling you at this time. Poor James Hadden's melancholy death.[47] Now Dear Sir may I adventure to speak of my self to you for that profession & entreat your friendly asistance. I know by many proofs the sincerity of your kindness & friendship towards me. If it was possible to get me into that business I would be very happy: And I can't think considering how litle there is to do in such a profession but I might turn my studies so as in time to be able to do tolerably in it. I never thought such a profession should be a sine cure; nor was I in such a one would I incline to make it so: But on the contrary apply my self to it with all vigour and application. Dear Sir I need not tell you more particularly what I would have you do for me<.> I write to Mr Maclauran at the same time: I cannot say but I am somewhat uneasy Mr Duff's presentation is not yet come down.[48] But I am very sure that if in that or any thing that casts up it be proper to medle for me neither Mr

46. The Institutes of the Roman emperor and jurist Justinian (527–65).

47. James Haldane (ca. 1686–1727), Professor of Ecclesiastical History at St. Mary's College in St. Andrews, who died in a fire at St. Salvator's College on 17 January 1727.

48. William Duff, who replaced Turnbull as a Regent at Marischal College Aberdeen. Duff was formally appointed on 25 July 1727.

Maclauran nor you will forget me. I had once some thoughts of writing to the Sollicitor[49] or my Lord Provost of Edinburgh.[50] But considering how litle I have the honour to be of their acquaintance I thought it better to refer all to you and Mr Maclauran. I am Dearest Sir

with the sincerest respect

your most

humble servant

George Turnbull

8. *To* CHARLES MACKIE

MS: EUL, La. II. 91; unpubl.

[Utrecht], 10 January 1730

Dear Sir,

I heartily wish you many happy returns of years. I was indeed Longing most impatiently to hear from you; But your friendship I could never suspect; nor would I fear the indolence you complain off did any opportunity offer of doing me or any friend a real service. Your letters will ever be most agreable to me when they bring me good accounts of your self & your's; But this last indeed brought me news which gave me a very sensible uneasiness. Poor Trotter[51] is he indeed taken from us! And must Mr Scot[52] also die! How vain and uncertain is human life sed ita visum Superis![53] I am glad however to hear my other friends are so weel; & that Mr Warrender[54]

---

49. Charles Erskine (1680–1763), who was appointed Solicitor General on 29 May 1725.

50. George Drummond (1687–1766), whose first term as Lord Provost of Edinburgh was from 1725 to 1727.

51. Unidentified.

52. William Scott the younger, who succeeded his father as the Edinburgh Professor of Greek in 1729. Scott the younger died in December 1729.

53. "But so it pleased the Gods!"

54. Hugh Warrender (ca. 1714–54), Professor of Hebrew at St. Mary's College in St. Andrews. He had taken his Master of Arts degree in Edinburgh in 1728.

is to come abroad with that young Lord: sure I am his Lordship is very lucky: And how earnestly must I wish who know & like Warrender so weel that he would come to this place & that it might be our mutual happiness to travel together. And indeed this is an exceeding good place for study. Mr Wauchope[55] who gives his kind service to you & with whom I am very happy gives great application & with Excellent success. But I need not trouble you with an account of the colleges he attends. Lord George Hay[56] who is just come here within these few days, I would gladly hope, will follow his good Example. He is recommended to my care in the most obliging manner by the Marquis;[57] & lodges in the same house with us. Allow me to give some account of my self<.> I attend the college of Mr Otto upon the Pandects & believe me it is an Excellent one.[58] I have likewise a privatissimum upon Grotius in conjunction with Mitchel,[59] who you may be sure remembers you most kindly, & My Lord Cornberry[60] with whom I have the honour to be very weel acquainted & who is indeed the most virtous wise young gentleman I ever knew & at the same time has a vast deal of Life & wit. No doubt you know Mr Otto's Thesaurus juris is now finished & the price mounts every day.[61] It is certainly a curious collection. Mr Cunninghame[62] to whom Otto has been vastly obliged in making that

55. Turnbull's pupil, Andrew Wauchope of Niddrie (1711–84).

56. George Hay (d. 1787), fourth and youngest son of Charles Hay (1667–1715), 3rd Marquess of Tweeddale. Lord Hay eventually became the 6th Marquess of Tweeddale in 1770.

57. John Hay, 4th Marquess of Tweeddale (ca. 1695–1762), an opposition politician.

58. Turnbull attended the public lectures of the Professor of Civil and Public Law at Utrecht, Everhard or Eberhard Otto (1685–1756), German jurist, formerly at Duisberg. Otto was later also the Professor of Feudal Law. Otto gave public classes on Justinian's *Pandects* or *Digest*.

59. Turnbull's fellow student in the private class was Andrew Mitchell (1708–71), who initially studied law at the University of Edinburgh and continued his legal studies in Holland. Mitchell went on to enjoy a successful political and diplomatic career.

60. Henry Hyde, Viscount Cornbury (1710–53); see below, note 87 on p. 28.

61. Only the first volume of Everhard Otto's *Thesaurus juris Romani, continens rariora meliorum interpretum opuscula, in quibus jus Romanum emendatur, explicatur, illustratur,* 5 vols. (Leiden and Utrecht, 1725–35) was published at this time. The *Thesaurus* was devoted to an edition of and commentary on the *Pandects* or *Digest* of Justinian.

62. Alexander Cunningham of Block (1650/60–1730), the Scottish legal and classical scholar and bibliophile, who had also served as a traveling tutor to various sons of the

collection says it has much dimi<ni>shed the value of a Law library he had
gathered from all parts of the world with great care. And By the bye Cunninghame has been here severall days; he is a worthy good man but the
most entetaea about his readings of Horace & Phaedrus.[63] I have been often
with him & he with me; & I am sure I could divert you a litle if I durst;
But all I dare say is that you will soon see another learned work of his in
which he is to defend as warmly as ever he attacked a certain Learned Doctor
at the Expence of a very Reverend prelate.[64] Mr Duker[65] whose Thucidides
we will now have in three months gives Mr Wauchope a privatissimum
upon Sueton.[66] He is realy as Good as he is learned & the last he has given
unquestioned proofs of. He is likewise busy just now in giving the finishing
stroke to some notes upon Livy upon his collegue Mr Drakenburg's[67] account a book the world will likewise very soon see. You see then Dear
Charles how I employ my time here. And tho I am Exceeding happy in Mr

---

Scottish nobility. He suffered a stroke shortly after this letter was written and died later
in the year in The Hague.

63. "Entêté" in French means stubborn or obstinate. Cunningham continued to work
on his annotations to Horace until the end of his life. Provoked by Dr. Richard Bentley's
(1662–1742) 1726 edition of the fables of Phaedrus (ca. 15 B.C.E.–ca. A.D. 50), Cunningham prepared a rival edition, which was eventually published posthumously as
Phaedri Augusti liberti Fabularum Aesopiarum libri quinque (Edinburgh, 1757).

64. Cunningham had earlier attacked Bentley's edition of Horace in *Q. Horatii Flacci
poemata, ex antiquis codd. & certis observationibus emendavit variasque scriptorum & impressorum lectiones adjecit Alexander Cuningamius* (The Hague, 1721) and *Alexandri
Cuningamii animadversiones, in Richardi Bentleii notas et emendationes ad Q. Horatium
Flaccium* (The Hague, 1721).

65. Karl Andreas Duker (1660–1752), a native of Westphalia, formerly vice-rector of
a school at The Hague, was a Professor of History and Rhetoric at Utrecht (1716–34).
He published works on both Greek and Latin grammar and classical jurisprudence. His
bilingual (Greek and Latin) edition of Thucydides' *History of the Peloponnesian War* was
published at Amsterdam in 1731. It was a revised edition of an earlier scholar, Joseph
Wasse, to which Duker added further commentary and extensive indexes. The Foulis
brothers republished Duker's texts alone, without commentary, in Glasgow in 1759.

66. Gaius Suetonius Tranquillus or Suetonius (b. ca. A.D. 70), Roman author of *The
Lives of the Caesars* and *The Lives of Illustrious Men*, a collection of biographies of noted
Roman men of letters.

67. Arnold Drakenborch (1684–1748), a native and law graduate of Utrecht, was a
Professor of History and Rhetoric there (1716–48). By this date he had published an
edition of the Roman historical poet Silius Italicus (Utrecht, 1717), but he is better known
to posterity for a seven-volume edition of Livy (Amsterdam, 1738–46).

Wauchope & will never part with him upon any consideration while he has
any use for me; yet you know sufficiently my inclinations do not give me
to be a Wanderer: if therefore Will Scot happens to die (which I sincerely
pray heaven may forbid) Could it possibly be brought about, the profession
of the law of nature is much to my taste and I would willingly make a
bargain with Mr Scot about it: The Greek Class is the most profitable &
perhaps if other folks could be brought to consent to it he would not be
averse to return to it upon certain terms.[68] And I have now three hundred
pounds good. No doubt you sufficiently understand me & I would have
you to talk with my good friend Mr Maclauran about it. To no other but
you two will I ever write or speak of the matter. I can't think but considering
how long I have chiefly applied my self to that study & the opportunities
I just now have of farder improving my self; it might be said I might be
trusted with that profession. And in short what upon that melancholy event
which it seems there is reason to dread I would have proposed to Mr Scot
is that I should be made professor of the Law of nations & that he should
return to the Greek but supply both till it please God to send me safe back
with Mr Wauchope & *have both salaries;* & that upon my return I should
enter upon the profession & the salary & pay him a reasonable consideration. If this appears to you Romantick & unpracticable it is only told to
a friend with whom I can trust any thing & who I know would very gladly
serve me. My kind respects to my good friend Mr Maclauran<.> I thank
him for all his favours & particularly his goodness to my brothers. pray
remember me to Mrs Macky[69] & to John Stevenson[70] & all our friends in
the castle<.> pray let me hear from me now & then. I wish you would write

68. Turnbull had evidently not heard of Scott's death and was confused as to which
chair Scott occupied. The Edinburgh Chair of Public Law and the Law of Nature and
Nations was then treated as a sinecure appointment by the incumbent, Charles Erskine;
on Erskine, see above note 49, p. 19.

69. Ann Hamilton (d. 1770), who had married Charles Mackie on 3 February 1726.

70. John Stevenson (1695–1775), who became the Edinburgh Professor of Logic and
Rhetoric in 1730. Stevenson was a close friend of Mackie's and a member of the Rankenian Club.

to Doctor Mitchel[71] who is now at Paris & send the letter to me that I may write along with it<.> I want to corespond with him for he can be of great use to me<.>

your's
G. Turnbull

9. *To* CHARLES MACKIE

Address: A Monsieur Charles Macky Professeur en Histoire a Edinburgh par Londre
MS: EUL, La. II. 91; unpubl.

Paris, 23 October 1730

Dear Sir

I long now to hear from you & hope you'l give me that pleasure soon. We had a very agreable journey allong the Rhine; & were so agreably disapointed at the German courts we saw that we design to see more of them; in going to Italy we will pay a visit to the Court of Lorrain & so see Strasburg Munich perhaps Vienna & go thro the Tirroll. The Court at Brussels is vastly stupid; But Brussels is a delightfull place. To Enjoy the company at Spa & Aix la chappelle we deserted the Rhine came thro Treves a wretched country saw luxembourg a town I don't know whether it may not at present be the strongest in the world: its mines are prodigious. At Spa we had very good company & at Aix no less so; for the prince of Orange was there: who Every body agrees, was his body as good as his spirit, would be a very Extraordinary young prince.[72] We chose after that to go into Brabant & Flanders & from thence to come to Paris that we might see a litle of its mag-

---

71. Dr. John Mitchell (d. 1751), who took his M.D. at Rheims in April 1713 and later studied at Padua (1717) and Leyden (1721). He became secretary to Sir Richard Ellys (see below, note 93 on p. 30) and was elected a member of the Spalding Gentleman's Society.

72. William IV (1711–51). When he came of age in 1729, he became the Stadtholder of Friesland, Groningen, Drenthe, and Gelderland in the United Provinces.

nificence before we take up our winter quarters which I suppose will be at
Angiers if there are not too many English there. There are vast numbers
here But I can give no account of any of em for we never go to the English
coffeehouse but shun our country men as much as is possible. I only see
Doctor Pringle[73] sometimes; a valuable acquaintance I assure you. Pray
write to me & send me a copy of a letter in latin you have describing
Winesene house;[74] you had it from Mr Anderson[75] But I have almost quite
forgot where it is only I remember you read it to me & I must see the place
& have the description. pray send it to me. & if in any thing I can serve I
am sure you know you have nothing to do but to command. Forget not
my compliments to your Lady Nor to any of my Friends: I need not name
em. I never was in better health; & I am very easy every way: yet this travelling life with all the pleasures that attend it has its allay. Mitchel[76] is returned to Holland to study Law at the Corpus another winter But joins us
in the beginning of summer some where or other. This is a place one would
not soon weary of did not they spend so much time at cards & game so
high: But on that account I believe it is impossible to get much into the
grande monde here: And perhaps the loss is not great. There are fine things
to be seen; & very good company of another taste to be found. I want much
to hear from Mr Maclauran<.> I hope he will be so kind as to introduce
me to some of his acquaintances.[77] I think to see the Chevalier Ramsay[78]

73. Dr. (later Sir) John Pringle (1707–82), took his M.D. at Leiden in 1730. He subsequently became the Professor of Moral Philosophy at the University of Edinburgh
(1734–44) and had a distinguished medical career in the British army and in London.
He also served as the President of the Royal Society (1772–78).

74. The Château de Vincennes, east of Paris.

75. William Anderson (ca. 1690–1752), Professor of Ecclesiastical History at the University of Glasgow.

76. See above, note 59 on p. 20.

77. Maclaurin provided Turnbull with letters of introduction; see *The Collected Letters of Colin Maclaurin,* edited by Stella Mills (Nantwich, U.K., 1982), pp. 147–48.

78. Andrew Michael Ramsay (1686–1743), philosopher and Jacobite, best known as
the author of *The Voyages of Cyrus,* first published in French and then in English translation in 1727. After Ramsay left Scotland in 1708, he maintained close connections with
Scottish men of letters.

this afternoon; But what I'll think of him I don't know; his caracter is a meer proteus. But I want to be with all sorts of folks if I can. Prithee let me know if there are any changes among our friends since I heard from you last. None of my brothers ever write. I give my self here entirely to reading french authors. Sometimes however I steal a look of a Roman & sometimes of a Greek author I like to see the difference: speaking french with the volubility of a french man I'll never attain; But I understand & am understood: and perhaps that is enough. I begun Italian last winter & that I am sure I'll find an easier task to master even as to speaking. When I begin to write to you or any of my friends I find a pleasure I imagine my self with you & become tedious without saying any thing. it is time to take leave I am

Sir
Yours most sincerely
& affectionately
George Turnbull

10. *To* CHARLES MACKIE

Address: To Mr Charles Macky Professor of History at Edinburgh par Londre
MS: EUL, La. II. 91; unpubl.

Marseilles, 23 September 1731

My Dear Sir

It is now long since I had the pleasure of hearing from you: your colleges are now over & I may venture to trouble you. We are to go for Lions in a few days; & after some litle stay there to Geneve. We are four in company & have had hitherto a very pleasant journey. But to say the truth there is not much worth the while in this voyage: I did flatter my self with spending some time in Italy before seeing you But when friends press coming home & young Gentlemen have no very great taste for Antiquities the Governours would be in the wrong to press an Italian voyage & that is my case

& that too of my brother Governour in company; one of the Best men & Best scholars I know Mr Markland of Cambridge who published the Epistola Critica to Dr Hare & after that Statius.[79] Will you forgive me my Dearest friend if I open my mind a litle to you & tell you that as the time of coming home draws near my cares increase. I can't bear the thoughts of being out of business: travelling again or the care of some body at home is all I can project: and I wish I could be sure of some such good opportunity. I will be at home in time enough to go abroad again the next season for setting out. And I sometimes am thinking with my self who there is in our country that is worth the while: sometimes the Marquis of Clidsdale[80] comes in my head tho' he be too young to travel: and the Marquis of Tweddale[81] honoured me frequently while I was at Utrecht with very kind letters. Sometimes my Lord Eglinton[82] comes into my head. Can you forgive all this *foiblesse:*[83] Or is there any in giving sin<c>ere vent to a sincere friend? If there is any occasion casts up may not I be mentioned tho' I am not home since I am to be so soon. And if any thing does may I not Expect better terms than I have at present for in truth there is nothing to be gained by a hundred pound abroad if one does as must be done to be acceptable to company in france. But enough of this you understand me; & I am sure have me at heart. I fancy we may be in England next spring early. There are troubles & cares innumerable in the charge of a young Gentleman abroad was he ever so good & wise and I am lucky enough: But there are cares & troubles in Every Station of Life; & if nothing else offers a good

79. Jeremiah Markland (1693–1776), classical scholar and Fellow of St. Peter's College Cambridge (1718–28). The works Turnbull refers to are: *Epistola critica: ad . . . Franciscum Hare . . . in qua Horatii loca aliquot et aliorum veterum emendantur* (Cambridge, 1723) and *P. Papirii Statii Silvarum libri quinque* (London, 1728). Markland was tutor to William Strode, with whom he traveled on the Grand Tour from 1728 until 1733.

80. James Hamilton (1724–58), Marquess of Clydedale (1724–43) and then 6th Duke of Hamilton.

81. See above, note 56 on p. 20.

82. Alexander Montgomerie (1723–69), who became the 10th Earl of Eglinton on 18 February 1729 on the death of his father. He was educated at the grammar school in Irvine.

83. The eighteenth-century spelling of *faiblesse,* meaning weakness or feebleness.

opportunity of travelling again would give me joy because it would give me something to do. My humble service to your lady, to Mr Maclauran & all friends. pray tell Mr Maclauran that his treatise upon motion is much longed for abroad; & much wanted.[84] It is long since I said to several who are impatient to see it that it would be soon published: But I have forgot whether he designed it in English or in Latin: if in English I wish he would get it translated into french. I never write to any body a journal of my travels; all I have seen has been described again <and> again. The affair of the Jesuite & the Girl of which you have certainly heard is still in dependence before the Parliament of Aix; & is the only subject of conversation in these parts of the world. The Jesuites Exert all their force to get him innocented. But the populace are warm & zealous against them evrywhere.[85] I don't know if ever you was in the south of France: for antiquities there is nothing remaining tolerably entire Except at Nismes.[86] The new part of this town is very beautifull. And Aix is the finest town I ever saw. But what is all this to the purpose Fareweel my Dear Sir and believe me with the sincerest respect & affection

your most humble servant

George Turnbull.

84. In 1728 Maclaurin wrote a treatise dealing with the controversy over the correct measure of the force of moving bodies which elaborated on ideas contained in his essay on the percussion of bodies that won a prize from the Académie des Sciences in Paris in 1724. He circulated the treatise in manuscript but it remained unpublished. Maclaurin later incorporated materials from these works into the twelfth chapter of *A Treatise of Fluxions,* 2 vols. (Edinburgh, 1742), where he refers to his treatise (2:437).

85. See the report on this scandal in *The Gentleman's Magazine* 1 (1731): 453–54. The Jesuit, Father Jean-Baptiste Girard (1680–1733), was accused of the seduction of Marie-Catherine Cadière. The case became a flash point in the struggle between the Jesuits and the Jansenists, and when it was brought before the Parlement in Aix-en-Province in 1731, twelve judges found Girard guilty and twelve found him innocent. The split decision meant that he went free. The verdict aroused considerable popular outrage and Girard was forced to return to his birthplace of Dole in the Jura. A number of books and pamphlets related to the affair were published in English translation in the period 1730–32, including *The Case of Mrs. Mary Catherine Cadiere, against the Jesuit Father John Baptist Girard. In a Memorial presented to the Parliament of Aix,* 10th ed. corrected (Edinburgh, 1730).

86. Extensive Roman remains survive at Nîmes, notably the aqueduct known as the Pont du Garde, the ruins of a Roman tower and baths, an amphitheater, and two temples.

11. *To* CHARLES MACKIE

Address: To Mr Charles Macky Professor of history at Edinburgh
MS: EUL, La. II. 91; unpubl.

London, 13 May 1732

Dear Sir

I had your's of the 23 of March Last night. I arrived here thursday evening <and> thought indeed to have been here two months agoe; but it is
not easy to leave Paris. Your Long Long silence made me not a litle uneasy;
But I could never call the sincerity of your friendship in question. Your
concern in looking about for me in my absence is a new proof of it I will
never forget; and no doubt you must wonder I have not wrote to you sooner
about that proposal. But this is first post after my receiving your's & after
giving you a great many thanks for your kindly concern about me allow
me to ask the favour of you to make my most humble compliments to that
young Gentleman's curators & to thank them for the honour they do me
in offering me that charge which I can't accept off being engaged already.

That is all that it is necessary to say to them but I must trouble you with
more of my story; nor do I believe you will think it any trouble to know
any thing that concerns me. I have had the good Luck to be very agreable
to several English I met with abroad. My Lord Cornbury[87] whom I believe
I have named in former letters to you is much my friend: has often assured
me that there is no man he would sooner choose to oblidge than me (These
are his own words) has begged me again and again to let him know if he
could serve me. I have at last named something to him and I am sure of
his readiness to do for me to the outmost He knows very weel my situation
& that I don't incline to travel with any charge if I could do better &
diswades me from it. But if nothing casts up for me soon I design to accept

87. After Cornbury met Turnbull in Groningen in the winter of 1729–30, he became
closely involved in the Jacobite cause and paid a secret visit to the Old Pretender, James
Stuart, in Rome in January 1731. Following Cornbury's return to England, he was elected
as the MP for the University of Oxford on 26 February 1732.

of a very generous offer made me by one whom I like with all my heart to make the tour of Italy with him not as a governour for he is of age but as a comrade: He has no great fortune so I can Expect nothing by him but the pleasure of making that tour with him with litle or no Expence to my self. a twelvemoneth hence I am engaged If I can possibly to make the same tour with another English Gentleman of a very great fortune whose bounty & generosity & regard for me I have already had several proofs of & who proposed the thing to me in the most handsome manner & is able to reward me very Liberaly. Thus I am sure in a manner of passing two or three years more very agreably; and am not without hopes that before that time what I have in eye as my grand restor<a>nce for Life may suceed by my Good Lord Cornbury's means. As for travelling with a young man & being answerable for his conduct the <trifle> of what I had from Mr Wauchope would not engage me to do it unless I was under an absolute necessity of doing it. I have been very happy with Mr Wauchope I have told him & do acquaint his friends this post that I cannot have the pleasure of going to Scotland with him. I told Colonel Stclair[88] of it today & I hope they will go to Scotland together. Mr Wauchope has behaved very weel abroad & I am glad to see that those who knew him formerly think I have done my duty to him not without sucess tho' *entre nous* to have made the improvement as I could have wished, he ought to have been at least a year longer abroad and never to have seen the Gentleman who from a generous principle he brings home with him. This *entre nous* it was a delicate point to me to medle with. My kind service to Mr Maclauran if he yet remembers me. I am sure I will always love & esteem him. my humble service to your Lady & all friends & pray henceforth give me not the pain of fearing I have forfeited your friendship<.> I thank you for naming me to Dr Mitchel.[89] I will endeavour soon to have the pleasure of waiting upon him.

I am Dear Sir
with the sincerest respect
your most obliged humble
servant George Turnbull.

88. James St. Clair or Sinclair (1687/88–1762), a colonel in the 22nd Foot regiment and MP for the Dysart burghs. David Hume later served as his secretary.
89. See above, note 71 on p. 23.

12. *To* CHARLES MACKIE

Address: To Mr Charles Macky Professor of History in the university of Edinburgh
MS: EUL, La. II. 91; unpubl.

London, 27 May 1732

My Dear Sir

Excuse this trouble for last time I wrote to you nay a few post<s> agoe when I wrote to Mr Maclauran I did not know that what I now desire would be of any use to me. Mr Hamilton[90] to whom I refer you will tell you what I propose. My service to all my Friends & acquaintances in your society.[91] I make no doubt of their giving me a very favourable testimonial<.>[92] you'l please to speak to them all in my name & assure them of my most humble respects from a sence of many obligations I lie under to almost all of them<.> And believe me my Dear Sir

Your's affectionately
George Turnbull

I am to dine with Sir Richard Ellis[93] some day next week when I will have the pleasure to see your Friend.

90. Unidentified.
91. The University of Edinburgh.
92. An allusion to the honorary Doctor of Laws degree given to Turnbull by the University of Edinburgh on 13 June 1732.
93. Sir Richard Ellys (1682–1742), bibliophile, biblical scholar, and English Presbyterian.

13. *To* CHARLES MACKIE

Address: To Mr Charles Macky Professor of History Edinburgh
MS: EUL, La. II. 91; unpubl.

London, 15 September 1733

Dear Sir

I Long prodigiously to hear from you and beg that favour soon: I know I had the last from you: But you'l Excuse me I have been in a very great hurry for some time. For Mr Maclauran I have wrote to him several times & asked very sensible favour's such as I thought I might ask from so old an acquaintance But it seems I have offended him I know not how I heartily wish him weel but must it seems reckon no longer upon his assistance in any project, not so much as a favourable recommendation.

Dear Charles I trust in your friendship thoroughly and hope you will not forsake me.

You know my scheme; But tho' I have friends it is difficult very difficult to succeed. And yet it was by Every bodie's advice whom I could trust here I took the resolution: And indeed, that way of life would be very agreable to me. I would fain have a pupil in the mean time who was to be in England for some time & have been looking about: two have been proposed but nothing is yet done tho' I would not be nice about the terms

This moment I was interrupted by a visit from Doctor Stewart[94] who came to make me proposals from the Marquis of Annandale's[95] friends but that is to go abroad<.> they offer good terms And it gives me courage afresh to think I am sought after. If I go abroad I am resolved to go into orders first. And I am to go to Oxford soon to have the degree in Law ad eundem.[96]

94. Alexander Stuart (1673–1742), a Scot from Aberdeen who was physician to Westminster Hospital and later St. George's Hospital in London.

95. George Johnstone (1720–92), 3rd Marquess of Annandale.

96. A degree "ad eundem" was granted on the basis of an equivalent degree awarded at another university. In Turnbull's case, he had been given a Doctor of Laws degree by both Marischal College Aberdeen and the University of Edinburgh. Turnbull matriculated at Exeter College Oxford on 10 October 1733 and was given his Bachelor of Civil Law on 16 November 1733.

This is by Mr Talbot's advice who has wrote to Oxford about it long agoe.[97] This they think necessary in England. Some of my Lord Eglinton's[98] friends here have spoke to me about him but they had no commission: they say he is to be Educated in England & that they would give good terms. I would rather stay in England as I have already said. Dear Sir I have wrote you a long letter about my self but it is a pleasure to give vent to a sincere friend. Was I with you I have a great deal to say But will write no more

My kind Compliments to Mrs Macky<.> As for what I have wrote in the beginning of my letter about Mr Maclauran I know you'l soften it: it would give me pleasure to know I had yet any share in his friendship. I heartily wish him joy & all of you a good session. I am my Dear Sir

Your's most affectionately

George Turnbull.

I am just come to town have been in the country for six weeks.

14. *To* [ALEXANDER GORDON][99]

MS: BL, Add. MS 6190, fols. 56–57; unpubl.

London, 10 March 1737/38

Dear Sir

I had the honour of your kind Letter by which you acquaint me of the resolution of the committee of the Society of Learning with regard to my work.[100]

---

97. Charles Talbot (1685–1737), Solicitor-General (1726–33), Lord Chancellor (1733–37), and 1st Baron Talbot of Hensol (1733), was a Fellow of All Souls College Oxford.

98. See above, note 82 on p. 26.

99. Alexander Gordon (ca. 1692–1754), Scottish opera singer and antiquarian who served as the first secretary of the Society for the Encouragement of Learning (1735–49).

100. At a meeting held on 24 February 1737/38 the managing committee of the Society for the Encouragement of Learning instructed Gordon to write to Turnbull to

I reckon my self under the greatest obligations to the Honourable & worthy members of the committee for their very generous resolution to encourage my undertaking, in a private capacity. I should never have thought of carrying on my design by subscription, had I not been perswaded that the Society not having a fund for undertaking it, it was impossible to accomplish in any other way what had already cost me a very considerable Expence. I will take it as a very great favour to be allowed to wait on the committee from time to time in order to have their opinion of my work as it advances, Having nothing more at heart than to have it Ex<e>cuted to the satisfaction of such good judges & generous Encouragers of all the ingenious arts & Sciences.

At the next meeting of the Committee I will have the honour to wait on them & shew them several Specimens of the Engraving with which I flatter my self they will be very well pleased.[101]

I am very sensible from the obliging manner in which the Committee received my proposals and hath all along treated me, that the Encouragement of Learning for which the Society was formed, is entrusted with persons disposed to promote that noble design with the greatest zeal agreably to the Excellent rules of the Society. I beg leave to return my most sincere & hearty thanks to the Committee in general & to Every member of it in particular for all their favours and for their Last very generous resolution which you did me the favour to communicate to me. I am fully perswaded that very great advantages must redound to Learning from their Excellent management. Please to communicate this to the Committee and you will highly oblige Dear Sir

Your most obedient

humble servant
George Turnbull.

---

inform him that the Society was unwilling to sponsor the publication of his *Treatise on Ancient Painting*.

101. Turnbull was apparently allowed to show the managing committee some of the engravings for the *Treatise* at their meeting of 3 March 1737/38.

15. *To* THOMAS BIRCH[102]

Address: To The Reverend Mr. Thomas Birch Over Against
Mr. Bettenham's[103] in St Johns Lane near St John's Gate[104]
MS: BL, Add. MS 4319, fols. 279–80; unpubl.

26 February 1738/39

Reverend Sir

Allow me to ask your friendly assistance in an affair that was proposed
to me yesterday. Many candidates appearing for the Secretary-ship to the
Society &c if Mr Gordon goes some of my friends chid me for not thinking
of my self & got my consent to use their interest for me.[105] I can't help
thinking that a member has a better title to ask it than one who is not. You
have a very universal acquaintance with the members; and are very justly
esteemed by all who know you; and you are therefore able to do me very
great service in this affair, and to Lay a very great obligation on

Reverend Sir
your very humble
and obedient Servant
George Turnbull.

Dear Sir[106]

I would have waited on you with the above letter of my freind Mr Trumbulls:
which I just received, but was affraid of your being abroad & therefor have sent

102. Thomas Birch (1705–66) was a clergyman and man of letters who was a Fellow
of both the Royal Society of London and the Society of Antiquaries. He is best known
as the editor of *The Works of the Honourable Robert Boyle* (1744) and the author of *The
History of the Royal Society of London* (1756–57). Birch was also closely involved in the
affairs of the Society for the Encouragement of Learning. He served as treasurer (1736–
38) and was a member of the Society's Committee of Managers.

103. James Bettenham (ca. 1683–1774), printer.

104. The address is in the hand of Andrew Millar (1705–68), prominent London
bookseller and a close associate of his fellow Scot, the poet James Thomson (1700–1748),
author of *The Seasons.* Millar sold books on behalf of the Society for the Encouragement
of Learning and published works by Thomas Birch.

105. Alexander Gordon did not in fact resign as the secretary of the Society for the
Encouragement of Learning until May 1741.

106. This postscript is added in the hand of Andrew Millar.

it you knowing you'l have as great a regard to the desire of that Gentleman as if I had delivered it. I Asshure you it will be doing me a wery great favour if you can serve him in this point, & I am sensible it will be serving the Society & oblidging a worthy man. I am

Dear Sir
Your very humble Servant
And: Millar

Monday Afternoon
4 O'Clock

16. *To* THOMAS BIRCH

Address: To The Reverend Mr Thomas Birch
MS: BL, Add. MS 4319, fols. 281–85; unpubl.

7 April 1739

Reverend Sir

I know very well that you have a great deal to do; and I am very unwilling to take you off one moment from the useful way in which you are always employed; the more so that I am fully convinced of your extreme readiness to do good offices for any one you think has any degree of merit & your disposition to think favourably of Every one. But Kind Sir I must beg you to accomplish what you have begun. I have already found by the kind reception I have met with from Dr Sykes[107] that your recommendation hath the weight with him I was perswaded it must have with all who know you. I should be glad on several accounts to have the affair over;[108] I am a<n>xious to have it done; & my Friends daily press me more & more not to delay it. Yesterday the Doctor asked me if I continued in my resolution to which I answered I had always devoted my self to that Study & only repented my having delayed so long going into orders; and therefore I en-

---

107. Arthur Ashley Sykes (ca. 1684–1756), a noted clergyman and one of the leading Low Churchmen of the day.

108. Turnbull's ordination in the Church of England. The ordination process varied to some extent depending on the officiating bishop. Typically, a bishop required

treated him to speak to the Bishop[109] that it might be done as soon as possible; which he most obligingly undertook. But the Doctor leaves town after Easter & in that case I may happen to fall into an unknown Chaplain's hands; whereas now after the conversations I have had with the Doctor & the obliging things he has been pleased to say I look upon my Examination as almost pass'd.[110] I have no manner of title to ask the Bishop to appoint a day for me alone; yet I would gladly have private ordination & should be very proud to be known to the Bishop. I might I am sure press the Doctor himself. But tho' I have seen a good deal of the world I believe I shal always continue timid in my own affairs. It is proper my name should be given in form to the Bishop; and I should be glad to know from you what testimonials are necessary.[111] I am very well known to Dr Freind & his son[112] who I think is one of the Bishop's chaplains; But I am afraid they are not in town. I know very few other <C>lergymen beside your self Except some at Oxford & three or four in town<.> I have been confined to the house ever since I had the pleasure of seeing you by a severe Cough a disease quite new to me other wise I would have waited upon you instead of writing.

It is proper I should know in time whether a title is absolutely necessary or not that is whether the Bishop demands there should be one because in

---

candidates to provide their names and addresses two weeks before their ordination so that the bishop could verify their personal details and qualifications. Candidates were then examined, and they were also required to subscribe to the thirty-nine articles of the Anglican Church and to take the oaths of allegiance and supremacy before being formally ordained. Turnbull's comments in this letter indicate that he had little idea of what was normally involved in the ordination process.

109. The Bishop of Winchester, Benjamin Hoadly (1676–1761), who was a patron of Arthur Ashley Sykes. Both Hoadly and Sykes were friends of Thomas Birch.

110. Candidates for ordination were usually asked if they felt called to the priesthood and they were also examined on their knowledge of the scriptures, the basic doctrines of Christianity and the thirty-nine articles of the Anglican Church, and their facility in Latin and Greek.

111. Turnbull was required to provide at least three or four "testimonials" or letters of reference from clergymen attesting to his suitability for holy orders. The clergymen were expected to have known the candidate for ordination for two or more years, depending on the standard imposed by the officiating bishop.

112. Dr. Robert Freind (1666/67–1751), Canon at Christ Church Oxford, and his son, the clergyman William Freind (1715–66).

that case it is time to look about me in order to get one.[113] I can't help
wishing you had more idle time on your hands for I am now about revising
a work which has long lain by me called the Moral philosopher that I should
be very glad to have your opinion about.[114] The shortest wiew I can give
you of the Design is this: "The phenomena in the material world are justly
reckoned to be well Explained physicaly & moraly when they are reduced
to good general laws: The phenomena therefore in the moral world that
are reduced to good general laws are likewise well Explained physicaly &
moraly. & I attempt to point out several good general laws to which many
phenomena in the moral world are reducible" But in order to prepare my
way I begin with showing how natural philosophy proceeds; and next that
General laws in the moral world are so far from being inconsistent with
liberty that the activity, power or dominion of created agents necessarily
supposes the prevalence of general laws as far as it extends. I have set apart
this summer for revising this work & reading what hath been published,
that I have not yet seen, upon the subject. I must not forget to tell you that
I think I have set a future state that is the arguments for it in a light somewhat uncommon. And I conclude with shewing that the doctrine of the
gospel concerning God's government of the world is Exactly agreable to
reason & yet receives a new, a different Evidence from testimony. And by
gathering together into proper Classes all the texts relative to a future state
I have endeavoured to take off an objection made against Christianity as
not giving us any satisfactory account of a future State tho it pretends to
have brought *life & immortality to light.* I would fain hope that some time
this summer you may find time to breath Harrow on the Hill air.[115] I shal
have a bed for a friend; and I should be overjoyed to have an opportunity

113. A "title" stated where the candidate was going to be employed and what his salary
was going to be. Bishops would refuse to ordain candidates who did not present legitimate titles.

114. An allusion to the work published as *The Principles of Moral and Christian Philosophy* in 1740. See George Turnbull, *The Principles of Moral and Christian Philosophy*,
edited by Alexander Broadie, 2 vols. (Indianapolis, 2005).

115. Harrow on the Hill is northwest of the center of London and the location of the
noted public school founded by Royal Charter in 1572. Turnbull may therefore have been
working as a private tutor when this letter was written.

of laying all this train of reasoning before you of which no one is a better judge. I am

Reverend Sir
with the sincerest respect
your most obedient
humble servant
George Turnbull.

17. *To* THOMAS BIRCH

Address: To The Reverend Mr Thomas Birch at
Rathmall's Coffee-house[116]
MS: BL, Add. MS 4319, fols. 286–87; unpubl.

28 April 1739

Reverend Sir

I am just going out of town to take the air I shall be back on tuesday. It would be very convenient for me on many considerations if the Bishop[117] could be prevailed upon to give me orders tomorrow se'night and priests orders the sunday after. If you could prevail upon Dr Sykes[118] to urge it I will reckon it a very great obligation. Dr Hoadley[119] has promised sunday next to take an opportunity of speaking of me to his Father.

I beg pardon for giving you all this trouble about me; But if <I> am troublesom blame your self you have engaged me to take all this freedom by your friendly obliging manner and I am with the sincerest respect your most obedient

humble servant
George Turnbull.

116. Rawthmell's Coffee House, located at No. 25 Henrietta Street, Covent Garden.
117. Bishop Hoadly; see above, note 109 on p. 36.
118. Arthur Ashley Sykes; see above, note 107 on p. 35.
119. Dr. Benjamin Hoadly (1706–57), the eldest surviving son of Bishop Hoadly and physician to St. George's Hospital and the Westminster Hospital in London.

18. *To* THOMAS BIRCH

Address: To The Reverend Mr Thomas Birch
MS: BL, Add. MS 4319, fol. 288; unpubl.

Friday Evening 18 May 1739

Dear Sir

Tho' I have not had it in my power to go further than Rathmell's coffee-house[120] to Enquire after you yet I am afraid you may be indisposed since you have not been there for some time. I want much to see you some time tomorrow where you please. I have a testimonial in my pocket[121] which I would gladly have your name to<.> pray let me know where you will be tomorrow <at what> hour: if you chance not to be at home when this comes to your house I beg to see you tomorrow Evening at Rathmell's.

I am Reverend Sir
your most obedient
humble servant
George Turnbull

19. *To* [THOMAS BIRCH]

MS: BL, Add. MS 4319, fol. 289; unpubl.

4 February 1739/40

Dear Sir

I know how busy you are and therefore that I can't hope to have the pleasure of seeing you till I am able to wait on you. I hope that may be soon.

Mean time knowing your friendship I take the Liberty to send you some proposals. I hate to be idle, can not afford to live so; and would gladly be useful in some way. perhaps you may not know that it is but returning to

---

120. See above, note 116 on p. 38.
121. The testimonial was needed for Turnbull's ordination.

my first business for five years in the university of Aberdeen. and since that time I became again a student in the same way at Groninghen and Utrecht. It is not amiss my friends who are so kind as to mention this scheme should tell it is not a new business to me.[122] I persuade my self of your readiness to serve me on Every occasion. I have had proofs of it and wish I could be of any use to you.

I am Dear Sir
your most obedient
humble servant
George Turnbull

I thank you for introducing me at the coffee-house.[123] I Expected great pleasure by being often there; but almost ever since I have been very ill. I begin now to recover if <a> change of weather do not demolish me.

Pray Excuse the want of better paper.

20. *To* THOMAS BIRCH

Address: To The Reverend Mr Birch
MS: BL, Add. MS 4319, fols. 293–95; unpubl.

Kew,[124] 24 April 1741

Reverend Sir

I beg you would add to the many former instances of your friendship your interest to get Encouragement to this design. It hath been the Study

---

122. Turnbull was thus beginning work on his translation (published in 1741) of Johann Gottlieb Heineccius, *Elementa iuris naturae et gentium, commoda auditoribus methodo adornata* (Halle, 1738). See Johann Gottlieb Heineccius, *A Methodical System of Universal Law: Or, the Laws of Nature and Nations, with Supplements and a Discourse by George Turnbull,* edited by Thomas Ahnert and Peter Schröder (Indianapolis, 2008).

123. Possibly Tom's Coffee House in Devereux Court, near Temple Bar, a favorite of Birch's.

124. Turnbull probably moved to Kew when he joined the entourage of the Prince of Wales in 1741. While living in Kew he opened a school.

of many years, & I think such a work is much wanted. may I hope to see you at Kew. It would be a great favour to one who tho' I have but few pupils can't come to town to Enjoy my friends. I am

Reverend Sir

your most obedient

humble Servant

George Turnbull

I send you 12 receipts from 157 to 168[125]

---

125. A printed subscription form (numbered 157) is enclosed with this letter. The form reads: "I promise to pay to George Turnbull, LL.D. or Order, on the Delivery of _____ Book _____, entitled, A System of the Laws of Nature and Nations, &c. conformably to the Proposal, _____ Guinea _____."

Graduation Theses

ဟော ဟော ဟော

Philosophical Theses

On the Association of Natural Science
with Moral Philosophy

Which, with the Annexes, under the assistance of the Great and Good
GOD, will be publicly defended, in the New College of the Caroline University of Aberdeen[1] at the customary hour and place on the 11th April, by
GEORGE TURNBULL, President,

and the following Candidates who are to be Honoured with the Degree of
Master

Alexander Howie	George Turner	*John Craig*
Alexander McBean	William Catto	*John Farquharson*
Alexander Maitland	*William Forbes*	John Hardie
Alexander McQueen	*William Middleton*	John Harrow
ALEXANDER REID	William Thomson	*John Milne*
Alexander Skeen	James Lumsden	*John Mowat*
Charles Gordon	James Milne	Patrick Milne
Daniel McLean	*James Robertson*	Robert Maulde
George Forbes	James Sime	
George Gordon	*James Strachan*	

Published at Aberdeen by James Nicol, Printer to the City and University,
in the Year of our Lord 1723. <2>

---

1. In 1641 the two Aberdeen colleges (King's and Marischal) were united into one university called "King Charles University" by an Act of the Scottish Parliament. Although the Act was rescinded in 1661, the term "Caroline University" continued to be used and appears on the title pages of graduation theses from Marischal College published in the 1720s. Marischal was known as the "New College" because it was a younger foundation (1593) than King's (1495).

To The Great and Most Illustrious

THOMAS
Earl of Hadinton &c.

Knight of the Most Ancient and Noble order
of St. Andrew.[2]

Also
To his Noble Son, Distinguished Scion
of his most Honourable Family,

Charles,
Master of Binning,[3] &c.

These Philosophical Theses are dedicated,[4] as a token of
his great Devotion and everlasting respect

by GEORGE TURNBULL President <3>

---

2. Thomas Hamilton, 6th Earl of Haddington (1680–1735), a prominent Squadrone politician and a representative peer of Scotland in the House of Lords.

3. Charles Hamilton, Lord Binning (1697–1732), Haddington's son.

4. Reading the abbreviation "D.D.C.Q." as "dono dedit commendavitque," that is, "has given and entrusted as a gift to."

Philosophical Theses

Since the real usefulness of any Science in human life is to be measured by its relation to Moral Philosophy (which has rightly been called by Wise Men the Guide and Parent of life),[5] we must now briefly investigate the connection that Natural Science has with it.

There is no need of a full discussion here about natural Philosophy and its recent development and advances. But anyone who has tasted this Science even with the tip of his tongue, can see that, in its present state, it rests on a very firm foundation, since it is sustained not by fanciful hypotheses or unfounded conjectures, but entirely by either Mathematical reasoning or clear and certain experiments[6] and Analogy. That this is the only method by which a real knowledge of nature could be advanced and developed, was prescribed long ago by the most Perceptive *Verulam*.[7] And it is by this method that it has indeed come about that this Science has reached such a peak of perfection in our time, especially through the wonderful insight and industry of the most illustrious Newton.[8] In explicating the nature and the Phenomena of light (to make the matter clear by one or two examples) that Great Man first investigated and proved by Analysis the innate differences between rays of light as regards refrangibility, reflexibility and colour, and their alternating phases of readier reflection and transmission, as well

5. Compare Cicero, *Tusculan Disputations,* V.ii.5.

6. The Latin term *experimentis* could also mean "experience." This ambiguity was typical of seventeenth- and early eighteenth-century usage.

7. Sir Francis Bacon, Baron Verulam, (1561–1626), English politician and man of letters. Bacon's most detailed exposition of his view of the scientific method is found in the *Novum organum* or *New Organon* (1620).

8. Sir Isaac Newton (1642–1727), English natural philosopher and author of *Philosophiae naturalis principia mathematica* or *Mathematical Principles of Natural Philosophy* (1687) and the *Opticks* (1704) as well as other works.

as the properties of the bodies, both opaque and transparent, on which the reflections and colours of the rays depend. Once he had discovered these things, he assumed them as principles, in order to explain by Synthesis the Phenomena that flow from them. In the same way, after he had derived from celestial Phenomena, by Mathematically demonstrated propositions, the forces by which bodies tend towards the Sun and each of the Planets, he derived from those forces, by propositions equally Mathematical, the motions of the Planets, of Comets and of the Moon. And thus he elaborated an Astronomy which was complete in every respect. Every explanation of Corporeal Effects admitted by modern Physicists rests on exactly the same kind of reasoning. And Newton himself observed some time ago that "if natural Philosophy by pursuing this method eventually becomes a <4> perfect Science complete in all its parts, it will undoubtedly result in a similar extension of the boundaries of Moral Philosophy."[9]

II

From the most excellent order, harmony and Beauty of the corporeal world is derived a thoroughly lucid argument, by which one may demonstrate, against all Supporters of Atheism, Demonism and Polytheism, that all parts of the world were fashioned in the beginning and are at all times governed by One GOD of supreme intelligence in accordance with the very best design. It is certain that no truth has greater significance than this for the advancement and development of moral Philosophy. *For such a great, harmonious, accordant, uniform complex of things could certainly not come about, if all things were not maintained by One Divine and Uniform Spirit.*[10] There are very many arguments derived from the abstract and Metaphysical consideration of cause and Effect, of Necessary and dependent existence, fash-

9. "And if natural Philosophy in all its Parts, by pursuing this Method [of analysis and synthesis], shall at length be perfected, the Bounds of Moral Philosophy will be also enlarged"; Sir Isaac Newton, *Opticks: Or, a Treatise of the Reflections, Refractions, Inflections, and Colours of Light,* 3rd ed. (London, 1721), p. 381. The passage appears in Query 31 of Newton's *Opticks,* which was added to the first Latin edition of the work published in 1706; see Isaac Newton, *Optice: Sive de reflexionibus, refractionibus, inflexionibus & coloribus lucis libri tres* (London, 1706), p. 348.

10. A partial paraphrase of Cicero, *De natura deorum,* II.vii.19.

ioned[11] and refined by Metaphysicians with consummate skill, which invincibly demonstrate that GOD exists and rules all things by his Most Wise Providence, even if they are inaccessible to most people, because they are constructed purely of reasoning.[12] Hence we certainly do not give our support to those who repudiate and reject every exemplary and Metaphysical Proof for establishing the Divine Existence and Providence. But at the same time we do not hesitate to maintain that the argument drawn from the most perfect ordering of the corporeal world in confirmation of these things, not only rests upon a very firm foundation but is suited beyond all others to command the assent of a candid mind, free of evil disturbances.[13] For just as no kind of reasoning expands and extends its usefulness more widely in human lives than that which is derived from experiments and evidence and is founded on analogy, so there is none which affects the Understanding more pleasantly or in which the human mind more securely acquiesces; so perfectly are our minds adjusted to the condition of human life. And this itself is no small sign of a supremely good Providence, which presides over the whole of nature and by its own initiative promotes the welfare of all things but especially the welfare of human beings.

III

It is well-known to the learned that Anaximander, Democritus, Leucippus,[14] and all the ancient Atheists, however much they disagreed with each other, always agreed in this, that they recognized nothing but bodies. It is also well known that some recent writers have used all their ingenuity to

11. Reading *excussa* for *excusa*.

12. Probably an allusion to Samuel Clarke (1675–1729), *A Demonstration of the Being and Attributes of God: More Particularly in Answer to Mr. Hobbs, Spinoza, and their Followers* (London, 1705).

13. On the greater intelligibility and broad appeal of the argument from design see, for example, Ralph Cudworth, *The True Intellectual System of the Universe: The First Part; Wherein, All the Reason and Philosophy of Atheism is Confuted; and Its Impossibility Demonstrated* (London, 1678), p. 683.

14. Anaximander (d. ca. 547 B.C.E.), Democritus (b. 460–57 B.C.E.), and Leucippus (fl. 5th century B.C.E.) were all ancient Greek atomists whose ideas were later popularized by Epicurus (341–270 B.C.E.) and Lucretius (fl. 1st century B.C.E.).

support this opinion. The most prominent are Spinoza, Hobbes, and To-land.[15] But now the true Science of nature has clearly proved that the whole mass of matter is by itself inert, that it is bound and ruled by necessary laws <5> chosen and determined in utter freedom by the infinitely Wise cause, and thus that no mechanical motion could have either begun or sur-vived for the smallest moment of time apart from a uniform intelligent Cause, which is utterly different in its nature from matter.[16] Nearly all Phys-icists agree that gravity, fermentation, and cohesion, which seem to be the three effective principles from which all the properties and actions of cor-poreal things follow, are to be directly resolved into the Divine Virtue.[17] But even if they did not stop here, and were to discover some very subtle cause of these principles (as some believe they will one day), it would not therefore be legitimate to infer that mechanical motions do not depend on some Supreme intelligent Cause. For it is abundantly confirmed by all ex-periments and in fact by the whole science of matter and motion, that physical causes are simply natural laws and forces, fashioned and preserved with consummate skill by the Most Wise Creator of nature. And in fact, if matter could understand and will and order and direct itself, the possi-bility of reaching any certain conclusion about the powers and laws of mat-ter would be so remote that nothing more Chimerical could be attempted than a mechanical explanation of nature. But we can best see how much light and advancement this science of matter has brought to moral Phi-losophy from the fact that this science has made it clear that the supreme Author of nature is Spirit or immaterial substance. And to the extent that

15. Benedict de Spinoza (1632–77), whose reputation for heterodoxy rested primarily on his *Ethics* (1677) and *Theological-Political Treatise* (1670); Thomas Hobbes (1588–1679), notorious for his *Leviathan, or the Matter, Forme, and Power of a Common-wealth Ecclesiasticall and Civill* (1651) among other works; and John Toland (1670–1722), whose materialism was advanced in his *Letters to Serena* (1704).

16. For this argument see Richard Bentley, *The Folly and Unreasonableness of Atheism Demonstrated from the Advantage and Pleasure of a Religious Life, the Faculties of Human Souls, the Structure of Animate Bodies, & the Origin and Frame of the World: In Eight Sermons Preached at the Lecture Founded by the Honourable Robert Boyle, Esquire; in the First Year MDCXCII* (London, 1693) and the "General Scholium" added to the second edition of Newton's *Principia* in 1713.

17. Newton highlights the importance of the "active principles" responsible for grav-itation, fermentation, and cohesion in *Opticks,* pp. 376–77.

we can understand from natural Philosophy what the first cause of things is, to that extent we shall know more clearly by the light of nature our duty towards him and the worship which is acceptable to him.[18] This too is how we learn that that in us which thinks, though attached to the body, is very different from it in its nature. From this it is reasonable to infer that the human mind does not necessarily perish with the body, but can exist when liberated from all admixture of body. And if this is the case, nothing seems to come closer to the truth than the immortality of our souls. Nothing certainly is more joyful than the hope of eternal life or fills the honest mind with more pleasing delight. In the midst of sorrows, it brings us relief and consolation. It gives strength and courage to those who fight for GOD, for their Country and for Virtue.

IV

Many disasters proceed from the organization of our earth, to wit, plagues, earthquakes, storms, shipwrecks, and many, many other natural events, very much to the detriment of human life. But anyone who is the least conversant with these matters knows that the very wise laws which govern the world offer a beautiful explanation of these <6> calamities. Here too we may briefly see how much natural Science has contributed towards explaining the administration of the moral world. The system of our world is one, and fully finished from its first formation, and uniform without any mutations, except those which happen in accordance with the very laws by which it is governed by the most perfect Author of nature. And hence it happens that Philosophers have at last succeeded in giving an excellent explanation of almost all its Phenomena, forces and laws, by uniting Geometry with observations, by means of Analysis and Synthesis. The moral world on the other hand is so extensive and complex, that we have been able[19] to understand only a very small part of it. And what is more important, it seems continually to develop, not to be completed in this present state of things, so far as it is known to us by the light of nature. And if this

18. Newton, *Opticks,* pp. 381–82.
19. Reading *potuerit* for *poterit.*

is so, it is inevitable that many of its Phenomena should be inexplicable to us. Yet even at first sight we see that very many things in it are governed by a design which is wise and analogous to the organization of the natural world. And a whole number of things which are completely obscure at first and inexplicable become clear and very easy to explain when they have developed a little. Therefore if we combine our knowledge of the moral world and of the natural world, we may surely conclude with the very best of reasons, if it is ever legitimate to reach a universal conclusion on the basis of evidence and examples, that the whole world is subject to one most wise dominion; and that there is one Providence which guides all things most beautifully; and constantly handles the reins of the moral world as well as of the natural with a benevolent and prudent hand. And if we could attain to a full knowledge of the natural world and an equal knowledge of intelligent beings and of their various powers, faculties, dispositions and orders, *we would see that all act in concert and are bound by one force and one agreement of nature*—as Cicero tells us that certain ancients also thought[20]— and finally that through the universal bond of nature there is a most beautiful subordination and harmony of all things. But whatever difficulty may be experienced in clarifying the administration of the moral world by the light of nature, one has to admit that the order of the corporeal world is most elegant and exceedingly neat. And it certainly offers us a very fine pattern of life and morals. For we find that as all its parts move in harmony, all are united and as it were banded together in a communion which is very well suited to preserve it and keep it safe; and from this it is certainly reasonable to argue that it is most pleasing to the supreme Creator <7> and Ruler of nature, the Great and Good GOD, that all whom he has made to share in reason and a social sense[21] should pursue the common good of all intelligent beings. The human mind has been so made by nature that the same passions contribute to private and to public use. And it is through

20. Cicero, *De oratore*, III.v.20: "And in my own view the great men of the past, having a wider mental grasp, had also a far deeper insight than our mind's eye can achieve, when they asserted that all this universe above us and below is one single whole, and is held together by a single force and harmony of nature." This passage from Cicero also figures in a work that Turnbull was deeply indebted to, namely "The Moralists, a Philosophical Rhapsody" in Shaftesbury, *Characticks*, II:161.

21. *Sensus communis.*

that just and regular moderation of the passions by which we constantly cooperate for the common good of intelligent beings that the most beautiful harmony of life and morals is preserved, which is in accord with the regularity of the world, and is acceptable to the infinitely holy GOD, and finally wins the approval of all who are familiar with the measures and rhythms of true life. But nothing is more repulsive or more out of accord with the Harmonious fabric of the world than the evil man, who is governed by no sure mode of life and reason, but is agitated by contradictory passions and is at odds with himself in his whole manner of life.[22] And for this reason, men were said by the Ancients to be born to contemplate the world and to imitate it in the moderation and consistency of their lives.

V

The Association by which natural Science and moral Philosophy are connected with each other, is clearly seen in the following. Just as Reason could not fully enjoy the corporeal world without investigating and admiring its order and construction, so no study conducted by reason alone is more closely united with virtue by its own nature or produces more humane passions in our mind. *The knowledge of nature fashions us to modesty and magnanimity. For (as Cicero says)*[23] *the observation and contemplation of nature is like a kind of natural food for our minds and intellects. We are lifted up, we seem to take a broader view, and in thinking on Higher and Heavenly things, we despise our own affairs as small and petty.* Further the love and admiration of any kind of order and harmony, does much to induce a humane and sociable frame of mind by itself, and enlarges and supports virtue, which is nothing other than a desire for the order that expresses itself in life and morals. And nothing is more beautiful than the most graceful frame of the world, nothing more delightfully and powerfully attracts our souls by its

22. Turnbull's Latin echoes Horace, *Epistles*, I.i.99: "aestuat et vitae disconvenit ordine toto." In translation the relevant passage reads: "What, when my judgement is at strife with itself, scorns what it craved, asks again for what it lately cast aside; when it shifts like a tide, and in the whole system of life is out of joint, pulling down, building up, and changing square to round?"

23. Cicero, *Academica,* II.xli.127.

magnificence, constancy and dignity. And certainly the frequent and attentive contemplation of it goes a long way towards expelling evil passions and instilling good order into the mind by a kind of natural efficacy and Sympathy. And finally it is very clear that a true knowledge of nature is well fitted to banish Superstition in Physical matters. By Superstition in Physical matters we mean the conviction that attributes all sorts of wonderful effects <8> to natural causes, even if neither reason nor experience can discern any connection between the cause and the effect. "A not infrequent evil and (as the Learned Werenfelsius S.S.T.P. Bas. well shows in his dissertation on this question) most inimical to a good mind, and if a man once imbibes it, nothing is too ridiculous to find credence with him."[24]

VI

Although there are many other things which clearly confirm a beautiful association and Analogy of Physiology with Ethics, it seemed sufficient for our present purpose to select just a few of the more general points. But before we end this dissertation, it is worth noticing how much power a true explanation of nature has had to refute all the subtleties by which Spinoza and his Acolytes so earnestly pretend that they have undermined the miracles which were performed to confirm the Divine Religion.[25] For the true Physiology clearly proves that the links and sequences of natural things are not so rigid and unbreakable that the Supreme Lord of the world is not at liberty to perform miracles when it seems good to him to do so. The infinitely powerful and Wise GOD has made and ordained the laws of nature in complete freedom, and he can without doubt fashion and refashion them, and change and alter them at his own discretion. Consequently,

24. Samuel Werenfels, *De Superstitione in rebus physicis,* in *Opuscula theologica, philosophica, et philologica* (Basel, 1718), pp. 633–44. Werenfels (1657–1740) was Professor of Sacred Theology at the University of Basel.

25. See especially Benedict de Spinoza, *Theological-Political Treatise,* edited by Jonathan Israel and translated by Michael Silverthorne and Jonathan Israel (Cambridge, 2007), chap. 6, "On Miracles." One of Spinoza's earliest "Acolytes" in England was Charles Blount (1654–93), whose *Miracles, No Violations of the Laws of the Nature* (London, 1693) incorporated material Blount translated from chapter 6 of the *Theological-Political Treatise.*

whenever it seems good to him, he has the power to perform any miracles he pleases that seem to him to be appropriate to confirm any doctrine that he wishes to be revealed and confirmed to men. And it would be easy to prove against Spinoza that the miracles performed to confirm the Christian doctrine were in their nature the best and most suitable evidences and examples of that most excellent doctrine. But we may not spend time on this.[26]

ANNEXES

1. *Logic which trains the mind for the Analytic and Synthetic method of investigating and confirming truths by quite simple examples best prepares the way to the other Sciences. 2. All our Ideas arise from either sensation or reflection. 3. The root of possibility is not to be derived from the Divine will. 4. Animals are not automata. 5. The will by its nature is free. 6. The state of nature is not a State of absolute licence. 7. Moral rightness is founded in nature, but derives its obligation properly so-called from the Divine Authority to forbid and to command.*

26. Turnbull develops this argument in his *A Philosophical Enquiry concerning the Connexion between the Miracles and Doctrines of Jesus Christ,* below pp. 125–29.

Academical Theses

*On the Most Beautiful Structure
of the Material and the Rational World*

Which, if GOD Wills, are to be defended, under the presidency of
GEORGE TURNBULL, Professor of Philosophy, in the Public Auditorium
of the New University of *Aberdeen* at the customary hour on the 14th day
of *April* by the following young gentlemen, who are honourably contending for the degree of Master.

Alexander Blackwell	*George Black*	*James George*
Alexander Charles	George Blackwell	James Lesly
Alexander Gairden	George Rose	James McWilliam
Alexander Schanks	George Thomson	James Robertson
Alexander Udny	William Carnagie	*John Douglas*
Alexander Walker	William Erskine	*John Milne*
Andrew Webster	William Keith	John Rae
Archibald Chalmers	William Lessel	John Stuart
Arthur Forbes	William Moir	John Walker
Charles Forbes	James Barclay	*Robert Paterson*
David Mitchel	James Brodie	Thomas Forbes
David Reid	James Darling	Thomas Gordon
David Young	*James Dugquid*	Thomas Reid.

Published at Aberdeen by James Nicol, Printer to the City and the University, *in the Year of our Lord* 1726. <2>

To the Distinguished and Honourable

Patrick Duff, Esquire
of *Premnay*,[1]

noble Rector of this gracious University,

universally regarded for his singular humanity,

devoted friend of all good arts

these Academic Theses are gladly dedicated,
in witness of homage due,
by GEORGE TURNBULL, President. <3>

1. Patrick Duff of Premnay (1692–1763), advocate, was elected Rector of Marischal College Aberdeen in 1726 and continued to serve as Rector until 1729. He subsequently became a J.P. and a Commissioner for Supply for Aberdeenshire. He defended the political interests of the Argathelians led by the 2nd Duke of Argyll, John Campbell (1680–1743), and his brother Archibald, the Earl of Ilay and later 3rd Duke (1682–1761).

Academical Theses

Those who insist that the World is not governed by mind are obliged to attribute design and reason to a Nature which neither perceives nor thinks. It is no less absurd to imagine that there are several deities, unless a belief is the more credible, the further it is from simplicity. But nothing is simpler than truth. There is therefore one mind which by its own force and reason moves and governs the whole of Nature. That this mind, to which all things are subject and obedient, is not jealous and malevolent, seems to us to have been proved by the sounder Ancients in the following argument. *Where there is no clash of opposed interests, there is no malice. Without an adversary there is no conflict. The first and universal cause is not beholden or subordinate to any nature, and nothing can resist it. It is therefore utterly remote from all malignity of heart.*[2] And if there is one Father and Governor of all things, it is certain that his own advantage cannot be opposed to the safety and preservation of all things. He cannot intend anything with his mind but the most perfect provision for nature, nor can he go beyond that; and on the other hand there is nothing that can provoke him. An infinite Deity of an intractable and malignant character is in truth nothing but a ridiculous mingling in the same thing of perfect and imperfect, of powers and deficiencies that mutually destroy each other. It is therefore an infinitely good and perfect mind that moves and governs the whole mass of nature, and it manages all things most beautifully. That is powerfully confirmed by this Argument, which is also very easy to understand. On the assumption that there is a God—as assuredly there is—and all things are governed with the most excellent skill and design, it is nevertheless inevitable that many things will appear imperfect to us which are in fact most perfect and possessed of

2. Turnbull draws on Cicero, *De fato,* xiii.30 and *De natura deorum,* II.xxx.77.

no fault.[3] For a mind that has no grasp of the whole succession and Relationship of things, where all things are connected and adapted to each other, does not have <4> a full view of anything. But if there is no GOD—which it is wicked even to suppose—there can be no order, no consistency, and in short no good at all. For what can one expect from a blind impulse but randomness and inconstancy; or what from omnipotent evil but perpetual misery and disasters all around?

II

The supreme Craftsman himself alone has power to embrace the whole fabric of the World in his mind and thought. But the more closely we can see into the powers and motions of things, and the more extensive the portion of nature we can grasp with our minds, the more clearly we see that all things are ruled by the same divine reason, and on more careful examination many things which at first glance seem to be far otherwise, are discovered to give evidence of the most provident and cunning art. All things pretty well appear to be one, controlled by a single force and a single harmony of nature. From this it is reasonable to conclude that nothing misses its Mark, and that we should in all modesty acknowledge the feebleness of our minds, if anything seems to us to be inconsistent with this art. Before we can say of anything that it is well or ill designed, we must first of all inquire what is the function of the properties with which it is endowed, and what power they have in themselves; which parts are neatly fitted and combined with each other and which are less consistent with its purpose; or whether indeed it is subject to a nature outside of itself and what the effect of that is. For generally speaking it is most true that no finite thing can be said to be beautiful or perfect absolutely, but only in the relation which is has with another thing. And anything that is moved and governed by rules, and would either completely perish or be forced into a worse condition if the rules were changed, has been rightly and properly fashioned,

3. Turnbull's Latin echoes a famous phrase of Lucretius: "nequaquam nobis divinitus esse creatam / naturam mundi: tanta stat praedita culpa," that is, "the nature of the universe has by no means been made for us through divine power: so great are the faults it stands endowed with"; Lucretius, *De rerum natura*, 2.180–81 and 5.198–99.

and deserves a place among the varied productions of infinite art. Nor is the Artificer to be charged with error for anything that happens of necessity because of the very nature of the thing, or as a result of the laws by virtue of which all members beautifully conspire together for the security and perfection of the whole. Anyone therefore who wishes to make a fair judgement of the system of the world, must obtain a thorough knowledge of the sizes, positions, and powers of each of the Planets, as well as of the properties of the orbits in which they turn. It is only by collating and comparing them with each other that we can distinguish the order in that structure from the aberrations. It is by the same process that we must judge of the earth, our home, and of all things, animate and inanimate, <5> with which it is filled. So too if the question is raised about man as to what the perfection of human nature consists in and in what ways it fails of perfection. And certainly nothing is so important for us as to make a most careful inquiry into this subject. Since man consists of body and mind and is equipped both with organs of sense and with intellect and will, the question can only be investigated on the basis of the force, the use and the mutual relations of these faculties.

III

The true Physiology clearly proves that the solar system was constructed in the beginning with the best design and is so governed at all times.[4] Gravity, by whose universal force this structure holds together in its proper state and which is the cause of almost everything that happens in it, is not natural and necessary to it.[5] If that law were changed, the whole wonderful union of things would come crashing down as well as the cementing force of nature, so to speak, which favours the preservation of the world. All the planets below and above our world, so far as their structure is known to us,

4. The "true Physiology" being the Newtonian system.

5. Sir Isaac Newton insisted that the force of gravity was not inherent in, or essential to, matter. Rather, he argued that the cause of gravity was unknown. See Newton's "General Scholium" in Isaac Newton, *The Principia: Mathematical Principles of Natural Philosophy*, translated by I. Bernard Cohen, Anne Whitman, and Julia Budenz (Berkeley, Los Angeles, and London, 1999), p. 943.

have been admirably constructed and located for essential purposes. We think too much of ourselves if we imagine that we deserve such great things to be set in motion for us. It looks as if the fabric of the world could have been organized far more economically if it had only been necessary to create things that served human purposes. But although a greater purpose than the preservation of mortal things is intended for the Sun, the Moon and the other heavenly phenomena, and although there is a greater benefit from their activities than this, even so a design for our benefit was also laid down from the beginning of things, and it appears from the order imposed upon the world that concern for us was not the least consideration.[6]

IV

As for the earth itself, its figure, firstly, seems to have been selected with excellent sense. Situated in the most favourable position in the world, it is seen to be solid and spherical and drawn in upon itself all around by its own inclinations.[7] We also see that it is clothed and adorned with an infinite variety of things, for all of which nature has made excellent provision, and at the same time everything is organized for the maximum utility and benefit of the human race. No one who has had even a taste of Physics fails to see that all the arguments drawn from the unequal distribution of heat, eclipses of Moon and Sun, earthquakes and the sterility of waste lands, with which Ancient Atheists laboured to crush the belief about divine providence that is so deeply implanted by nature <6> in human minds, are trifling and ridiculous.[8] It is also clear from many considerations that the seas too are essential to the composition of this earth, and that a smaller amount of water would not be adequate for essential purposes. But in truth how great is the beauty of the Sea! How pleasant are her shores and coasts! Nor will anyone still find fault with[9] towering mountains and their terrifying

6. Turnbull here challenges Lucretius, *De rerum natura,* 5.156–94.

7. Turnbull's Latin in this passage echoes that found in Cicero, *De natura deorum,* II.xxxix. The argument of this section of the thesis is also derived from Cicero.

8. Compare Lucretius, *De rerum natura,* 5.195–234.

9. Reading *accusabit* for *acusabit.*

ruggedness, once he has followed in his rambles, under the guidance of Physics, the cold and ever-flowing springs and the clear waters of the streams, and knows also how to appreciate the hidden veins of gold and silver and the infinite amount of usable rock. Who can enumerate all the useful properties of air? At one time, extended and thinned, it rises; at another time it thickens and gathers into clouds, and collecting moisture it fertilizes the earth with showers; and at another time again it spills out in all directions and gives rise to winds. It is also responsible for the annual alternations of cold and warmth; it sustains the flight of birds; and drawn in as Breath it nourishes and sustains living creatures. It is reasonable to put up with the disadvantages of a thing from which so many advantages come.

V

The lower animals belong to the class of natural things since they lack reason and all of their actions are done by instinct.[10]

If we look at them more closely (for it would be an endless task to speak of every thing on earth individually) how great is the variety of animals! And what a drive in each of them to persist in its kind; and the incredible multitude of them all is marked by inexhaustible variety. For all of them nature has provided, largely and plentifully, the food that is suitable for each. All those whose pleasure it is to make curious investigations into these things, as well as professional Anatomists, know well what a cunning and subtle division of parts there is in the bodies of each of them for capturing and consuming this food, and how cunning and subtle it is, and how admirable is the structure of their limbs. They are all formed and placed in such a way that none is redundant, none not essential for the maintenance of life. The pains that torment their lives arise either from Elements which it is normal for them to be subject to by nature, or from a natural concatenation of elements, the absence of which would empty the world of a great part of its riches and <7> beauty.

10. The argument of this section is derived from Cicero, *De natura deorum,* II.xlvii–lii.

VI

But no intelligence can devise laws that are to be perpetual and universal and yet do not involve some disadvantages. Therefore if anyone should prefer that nature operate haphazardly and that the world not be governed by a consistent and unchangeable order, let him be aware of what he wishes for. For without the consistency and perpetuity of laws there could assuredly be no charm in nature, no beauty.

What then remains for us but to conclude that the government of the world has nothing in it that can be faulted? For from the natures that were to be created, the best situation that could be brought into being has been brought into being. If anyone thinks otherwise, let him show that it could have been better. But no one ever will. And if anyone tries to amend anything, he will either make it worse or will long vainly for what could not be.[11]

"You see therefore the material (*says Maximus of Tyre*)[12] with which the Supreme Artificer has to deal. If it receives any improvement, that must be wholly attributed to his art. But if certain things on earth that are not as well ordered as they should be betray anything unworthy of his art, beware of laying the blame on his artistry (for never does the design of an Artificer fail in point of skill any more than the design of a legislator fails in point of Justice), not to mention that the divine mind attains its end much more surely than human art. And in the mechanical arts the art itself produces certain effects directly as it seeks its own end, and certain effects unworthy of the art are unavoidable consequences of the work, and they necessarily arise from the work process but are not produced directly by the Craftsman himself. In the same manner in the case of those earthly ills which we say occur occasionally in human affairs, the art is to be acquitted of all blame, since they are no more than certain unavoidable states that are an integral part of the overall structure of the whole. For what we call evils and corruptions, which we lament, these the Craftsman calls the perfection of the

11. This paragraph is derived from Cicero, *De natura deorum,* II.xxxiv.86–87.

12. Oration 41.4. See Maximus of Tyre, *The Philosophical Orations,* translated and edited by M. B. Trapp (Oxford, 1997), pp. 327–28.

whole. For he has regard to the whole, for the sake of which it is sometimes necessary that parts be corrupted."

VII

If anyone says: *Concern for those who use reason is the most important evidence for establishing the Providence of the Great and Good GOD,*[13] *and we would therefore be no more justified in inferring from the beauty of material things viewed in itself, that the mind which is responsible for them <8> is of a beneficent character and furnished with all the virtues, than if we should conclude that any particular man is upright and good, and looks after his family properly, from the fact that his house and gardens have been most exquisitely laid out to please. From the choice and elegant composition of any Work of Art we are justified in inferring nothing but skill and practice in that art, and just as a consummate Painter or Architect is not always a good Father to his family, so perhaps he who constructed and equipped the fabric of the world with such wonderful skill and such a sense of order is not good and perfect in every respect. At any rate, it does not seem to follow necessarily from this single factor, or to be completely evident to us, unless care for intelligent beings accords and goes along with it?* There are indeed some people who thus boldly spout this kind of nonsense. But we do not have to look far to find a reply to them. For the Wisdom which is in the Author of nature, necessarily implies full and completely perfect virtue. If we ourselves fall away from the true pattern of life and morals, it is a result either of ignorance or a lack of self-control, or because we are led astray by an opposed appearance of advantage or pleasure. No other cause can be suggested which induces anyone partaking of reason to violate and disturb good order. But such things cannot affect that Mind which the very material structure of the world obviously shows to be infinitely Wise and Powerful. He who in the most immeasurable expanse of material things has so disposed and positioned the individual parts that nothing can be conceived either better or more beautiful, is certainly endowed with an infinite understanding; and he cannot fail to

13. *DEUS Optimus Maximus.*

know what is best in every circumstance. But it is absurd to say that infinite Mind, which never fails to see what perfect reason requires in every circumstance, should have been motivated in the government of the world by so great a desire for order and beauty together with free choice, and yet not always and everywhere have hit upon that which is most excellent; particularly in the governance of rational creatures, since a superior Species of beauty more properly attaches to this class of things.

VIII

But our argument does not stop even here. For we see not only that the whole structure of matter is so laid out that nothing could be more elegant in appearance, but we also find that all things above and below, as far as we can <9> see into them, are designed for essential uses and benefits with the most cunning skill and foresight. Our earth, in comparison with the other Planets which look towards the same centre, is the best made and the best situated, as also are all of them in their relation to it. And the individual parts of the Earth are so very well mutually adjusted to each other, that it is a habitat fit to nourish and sustain an almost innumerable multitude of animals and especially to make the life of men who far excel the rest by nature, sufficiently convenient and prosperous. Nor is it reasonable to hold a different opinion about the other planets if we consider them and undertake reasoning by analogy. And if we examine the powers and faculties of men and the material available to each individual, as well as the laws by which they can and should be directed, we shall quickly recognize that the human race is no less a regular system than the wonderful assemblage of the Planets. Nor are the falsehoods and fictitious hypotheses of philosophers any more required for exhibiting its beautiful regularity than Cycles and Epicycles are needed to explain the pattern of that assemblage.[14] In truth all the factors deployed to disprove the divine care for men either have no force or prove that man ought to be nothing other than an accumulation in one of all the gifts and powers of nature; or rather that nothing should

14. Turnbull alludes to the use of epicycles and other mathematical devices in the geocentric system of astronomy derived from Ptolemy's *Almagest*.

exist except that one thing which is most perfect among the innumerable kinds of living creatures which divine power is able to create: than which nothing is more absurd.

IX

Many things can be cited from which it is possible to see how many things GOD has given to men and how extraordinary they are. For men are of the earth not as inhabitants and dwellers, but as spectators of superior and heavenly things, the viewing of which is available to no other species of living creature.[15] With the intelligence with which man is endowed, he not only develops many skills, some of which are needed for the purposes of life and some for pleasure, but his special quality is the ability to learn the natures and causes of things. From these he receives his knowledge of GOD, and this is the origin of Piety; united with Piety is justice and the other moral virtues; and these are the source of a happy life for a living being capable of reason. Also man has complete dominion over the good things of the earth. And nature <10> supplies material to the senses with unstinting hand. And nothing could have been made which was more subtle or more adaptable to a great variety of purposes than the whole structure of the senses; with this caveat however that we always get the greatest pleasure from them when reason commands them and allots their tasks so to speak. This in itself proves with sufficient clarity that the divine mind oversees human things with particular care. And although man is mortal, that which the vulgar call death is nothing but the beginning of immortality and the birth day of the life to come. As for the distresses with which human life is beset, they proceed either from its conjunction in our present state with the corporeal world and by the bond by which the mind is united with the body, or from licentiousness of heart and a wicked abuse of the gifts of nature. But these things cannot be blamed unless we want to alter the whole structure of the corporeal world. For these reasons it is fair to blame only ourselves. For the divine care for the human race is only to be judged

15. Compare Cicero, *De natura deorum,* II.liii.133, and Robert Boyle, *Some Considerations Touching the Usefullness of Experimental Natural Philosophy,* in *The Works of the Honourable Robert Boyle,* edited by Thomas Birch, 5 vols. (London, 1744), I:423–43.

by the purpose and powers of the faculties which nature has kindly bestowed upon us; and by the laws which Reason as the interpreter of the
Divine Mind lays upon us, which all conduce by their own force and nature
to preserve the most beautiful order among men. The things that wickedness of heart like a mother conceives and brings to fruition are to be retorted
squarely upon ourselves. We alone are at fault; and the Great and Good
GOD could not have given us a more excellent or noble gift than that liberty
which alone renders us capable of law and right. Man is born and as it were
charged with the preservation of society; and for this reason it was fitting
that men should be vested with diverse powers and natures and established
in very different conditions and roles in human life. So too man has been
so designed by nature that he does not achieve wisdom without hard work
and education. Nor does the innate freedom of our will permit us in the
conduct of human affairs to be directed by impetuous instincts beyond the
normal order of nature. But nature has intended that our mind should be
always its own guide; it moves itself by its own force in accordance with
the judgments which it can form for itself by the association and comprehension of events with their consequences. Moreover the needs of human
life absolutely require that men should excel in swiftness of memory and
acquire for themselves by study and habit a ready ability to perform any
tasks whatsoever; and therefore it is essential that repeated associations of
thought and inbred moral habits <11> should have great force and be difficult to break. And from these powers and laws of our nature reason may
be rendered sufficiently well-adjusted, as it seems to us, to the whole condition of mortal men and to almost all the ills and troubles by which men's
lives are most vexed, particularly if we also add that the Sanctions which
fortify the laws to which GOD has willed that men should adapt their conduct, have a special relation to the future life. This is fully proved by many
arguments, but it is also quite clear from this, that it exhibits to us a concept
of a moral World which is consonant with nature in the most complete
way and is consistent with itself in every way. And when the true doctrine
of revelation about the origin of men and the future state are brought to
its assistance, the whole thing becomes far clearer and richer. This is a great
argument for the authority which it claims for itself, and an argument more
convincing than any other to persuade a true Philosopher to embrace it.

Corollary

From what has been said it is quite clear, as it seems to us, that the Physiology which lays out the true order and constitution of the Natural world must underpin moral Philosophy. For such a Physics is nothing other than acquaintance with the mind which most perfectly rules all things; and anything certain found in natural Theology that is not known to us from Physical Principles can be quickly completed. *Socrates* is said to have been the first to bring Philosophy down from the stars to the earth and the life of men.[16] But nothing certainly could have been more acceptable to him than a Physiology which does not simply explicate the Mechanism of the world, but above and beyond that, makes a particular point of showing how it is that nature does nothing in vain and whence the splendour and beauty of the whole world has arisen. He himself shows us in *Plato's Phaedo* why he disdained the Physics that flourished in his time. This true Philosopher desiderated a Physics that should point out the causes of things, that should first say whether the earth is flat <12> or round, and when it had pronounced on this, should add the reason and the necessity, and should deal with other natural things in exactly the same way, affirming that which is better and that it is better that it should be so.[17] This is the genuine Physiology which we owe above all to the quite wonderful penetration of the Great NEWTON.

ANNEXES

I. The will of the great and good GOD about what is to be done and what not to be done, is known to us by nature uniquely from the fact that certain things are wicked and disgraceful by nature, others beautiful and good; and therefore we infer the divine moral will from the natural turpitude or goodness of actions, and we do not, as some prefer to think, deduce the natural turpitude or goodness of actions from the divine will.

16. Diogenes Laertius, *Lives of Eminent Philosophers,* II.20–21.

17. Plato, *Phaedo,* 97b–99d; Turnbull gives a paraphrase and, in part, a straight translation of 97d5–e3.

2. If there is any certain mark by which the true may be discriminated from the false, by the same mark the right is discriminated from the wrong.

3. What nature itself teaches us is bad or good, right or wrong, receive their obligatory force, properly so called, from the divine will.

4. Unless man was obligated to discern the moral laws, he could not have been obligated to follow them.

5. Neither Understanding nor will can be compelled.

6. That alone which harms the state is liable to a civil penalty.

7. The right to do or not to do at our discretion is to be regarded as derived from GOD no less than the obligation to do or not to do; there are therefore laws which are purely permissive.

8. All dominion over things and persons derives from GOD.

9. All rights belonging to men by nature are inalienable by contract.

10. One who is in severe need has a right to other people's property, exactly as if it had not been occupied by another.

11. Without divine inspiration no man becomes truly good, pious or brave.

The Religion of the State

ৼ ৼ ৼ

NOTE ON THE TEXT

The manuscript of Turnbull's "The Religion of the State" is incomplete. It consists of two four-leaf quires, the first lacking the first leaf. We have therefore supplied the title, which is taken from Turnbull's letter to Lord Molesworth, 14 May 1723, above, p. 13. In the manuscript, pages 3–16 are paginated, whereas the "Postscript" is unpaginated. We have included continuous pagination in our transcription. Although there is no explicit indication of authorship in the manuscript and the handwriting differs from that found in Turnbull's letters, there are good reasons to think that the manuscript is a version of the "Small Treatise" Turnbull mentions to Molesworth. First, the manuscript is part of a collection of papers (AUL MS 3107/1–9) discovered at the University of Aberdeen in 1982 that illustrates various phases of the Aberdeen Enlightenment. The provenance of the manuscript thus points to an author who, like Turnbull, worked in Aberdeen during the course of the eighteenth century. Secondly, internal evidence points to the likelihood that Turnbull wrote the manuscript, notably the stylistic mannerisms that Turnbull derived from the writings of Shaftesbury and the use of quotation marks to enclose loose paraphrases of material cited from other writings. Moreover, the author's emphasis on the use of reason in religion and the stress placed on practical morality are consistent with the view of religion expounded in Turnbull's writings and reflect the religious preoccupations found in his roughly contemporaneous letters to Toland and Molesworth. Furthermore, the references to "the principles & offices of honesty & vertue" and to "sociality" (pp. 82, 84) speak to Turnbull's interest in Cicero and the natural law tradition. Last, the attack on the blending of scholastic metaphysics with theology and the view of pedagogy advanced in the manuscript also resonate with Turnbull's vision of a liberal education. We therefore believe that the manuscript can be identified as a copy of Turnbull's "Small Treatise."

MS: AUL, MS 3107/6/14.

The Religion of the State

. . . if I cannot see reason to rely upon it, but reject it, what ever the consequences may be. To beleive is either no act of a reasonable mind at all, or it is an act of the judgment & understanding faculty. And therfore to beleive without seeing reason to bel<e>ive is to see without seeing, or understand without understanding. So that when I beleive a doctrine to be true, I see reason to rely upon the certainty of what it contains: & when I beleive it to be false, I must perceive good reason to reject & despise it. And in order to a reasonable reception or contempt of any proposition offered to my consideration all that is in my power to do is to rub up my intellect carefully & set it a canvassing the matter with all the strictness & attention I am capable of. And whatever be the effect of that it is as necessary and inevitable, as it is for mee to see green or yellow when such colours are realy presented to my sight. In one word faith must be either reasonable or unreasonable & when it is built upon no reasons it is most certainly sensless and unreasonable & there is no way to make it reasonable but by giving reason full power over it to let it out & keep it in warm it & cool it at his pleasure. Any other guide but reason & understanding must be something different from reason & understanding & consequently something that neither reasons nor understands & that of course can produce nothing that is either wise or reasonable.

This, my Freind, is the summ of the whole affair that concerns the nature of faith & the plain consequence of it is that in order to beleive with reason & judgment I must be convinced & that there is no possible way to promote any reasonable faith but by giving free reins to fair reasoning and argument <4>

So that for the magistrate to pretend to propagate any reasonable faith by cajolling its pretended admirers & affronting & persecuting those who neglect & despise it: Or to think that they can realy do any benefit to the reasons & judgements of men by these methods is just as wise as if they should take it in their heads to teach men merchandize & the affairs of trade by whipping & scourging them instead of excercising them to accompts & real trafeck: Or to make men see in the dark & while their eyes are shoot give right judgments of the objects around them. Men must be reasoned into opinions & whatever is not the effect of reason & judgment is not rational faith or intellectual persuasion.

And when we take a weiw of the faith or religion of the commons in any country, what is in it that deserves the name of rational? Is there any understanding or judgment connected with <it>? Are they the wiser or the more knowing for it? Or can their understandings indeed be said to be better furnished by all the Cathe<c>heticks which they have learned by rott? They are indeed early taught to hear & repeat certain awfull mysterious sounds with the profoundest reverence, and to look on others as the language of Devils & most incensing to heaven. But do they understand what they say or have they ever examined the meaning & intent of the sounds which they blindly worship? Men whose intrest lies at the stake may talk as bigly as they please of the diffusive light & knowledge which in these most illuminated times prevails even among the lowest herd of mankind by the happy dispensation <5> in which they are cheif. But there is no man that ever conversed with the Catechumans or innitiated pupills of any sect or exaimined any of the various systems of modern Theology so widely different among them selves but will clearly see that it is impossible for any of the commoner sort of mankind, who have not been tutored in metaphysical universities to understand one single article of all that from their earlyest times they have been inured to revere as most holy & divine. For my own part I have made the experiment in many instances & still it held. And it can not indeed be otherwise unless there may be knowledge & distinct perception without clear ideas; or clear ideas without the necessary means of attaining them.

The circumstances of mankind do not make slavery and misery necessary to any sort of men but the circumstances of mankind make it necessary that there be different degrees & conditions of men. And as it would be impossible to make distinct clearheaded scholars of several of these degrees of men especialy the lowest & labouring sort: so neither does their happiness require, but rather forbid it. And therefore I have ever thought schemes of doctrine to propagate principles of deep & abstruse divinity through all sorts of people, to say no worse of them, owing to a very unaccountable ignorance of the humane nature & the circumstances of mankind. It is true indeed the motives upon which these constitutions are framed pretend to look beyond this life & to take their rise from higher & nobler ends than any of the temporal intrests <6> of humane society. And indeed the souls of men & their eternal salvation are by far of greater moment than all the litle concerns of this brittle state: and to mind this life only would be a policy too narrow & confined considering the immortal nature of our better part. But can it be to fit us for heaven & eternal felicity, that such pains are taken to learn us our metaphysical cathechism by heart? Is it to prepare us for the society of angels & spirits of the most refined natures that we are sermonised so often with such venerable awfull overbearing mysteriousness about things tho we could understand them would neither make us wiser nor better; And that we must learn to repeat like parrots so many hard bewildring distinctions & divisions of persons properties subsistences essentialities coessentialities & the Lord knows what? If it is so we are most exceedingly beholden for this extraordinary & dissenterested charity for our souls. But we wou'd be much more so if our reverend tutors could let us see, if it be not among the things inuterable & that cannot yet be understood, how such a discipline can make us more ready for heaven & a state of happyness & perfection: Whither at our first entrance upon that hereafter life we are to be catechised by rott & to get our eternal assig<n>ments according to the strength of our memories & the darkness of our understandings; or if we are to have our chance as we have lucked upon the scheme of favourite or odious terms. Or what indeed is the rule by which we are to be tried & what connection there is between this parrot tutorage & the favour of a wise being; or happiness in a thinking or rational state. If they would but condescend thus far to <7> instruct us in the reasonableness of their soul:policy; we might all perhaps rest satisfied with their authority and become most humble & submissive pupills. But

as for those whose misfortune it has been once to have begun to think a
litle for themselves they must till these knotty questions are solved remain
in a very indifferent opinion either of their design or of the heaven & Diety
they have in wiew. For how any sort of constitution that never makes men
the more wiser or the more knowing should be of use to recomend us to
the favour & approbation of the best & wisest beings hereafter: Or why in
any good and reasonable goverment persons shou'd be preferred honoured
or rewarded according to any other rule than their temper disposition or
ability to serve & to do good are things those will never be able to digest
who have ever exercised their reasons so far as to have formed just notions
of goodness & wisdom just & unjust.

Thus, my Freind, it is pretty evident that the attempting to instruct the
lower herd of mankind which ever will be the greater part in dark & in-
tricate systems of atributes, predestinations, imputations, & satisfactions
is of no use either with regard to this present or any future life. And for this
reason the bussiness of goverment is not to provide for that sort of cate-
chetick and instruction: but to encourage learning & true philosophy by
all proper methods & constitutions that so there may be the best means of
adwancing all the fine arts & sciences, & of educating such a convenient
number in all the useful parts of knowledge as may be fit to serve the publick
in these spheres <8> of life which require such a preparatory institution.

It is indeed necessary to the publick happiness to have a sort of publick
instructers: but then their business must be not to explain upon any particular system of speculations; but to instruct in the principles & offices of
honesty & vertue. That lectures of this moral sort may be adjusted to all
capacities is plain from experience which afoords many instances of a much
better understanding in morals among the illiterate part of mankind than
those who of late years have been tutored in universities & instructed in
school philosophy as it is called. And that these lectures would be of publick
use is very evident; good morals being the only necessary basis of society
& the publick happiness. but as for schemes of divinity or philosophy different creeds and persuasions the nature of society does not require that the
publick instructers should have any further medling with them than to recomend peace & love to all sectories, as the cheif & only thing necessary;
as that which is agreeable above all things to the supreme being & that alone

can entitle to his favour either here or hereafter. And if this was the publick religion to enculcate universal love and charity it would be the Protectrix of Philosophy liberty politeness & honest morals. Nor would any freedom that cou'd in the least promote the happiness of society or the entrests of vertue and reason be in the least restrained by it. <9>

'Tis true the beleif of a God cou'd not according to this scheme be publickly impugned & so far some may think the Philosophical licence wou'd be cramped. But what harm this confinement wou'd do I cannot see as much a lover of the reasoning liberty as I am. For if there were no other publick fetters upon philosophy than this there wou'd be sufficient place for free disquisitions of that sort in private closets. And in the mean time the belief of a principle the most reasonable as well as confortable in it self wou'd be applyed not as a meer political tool to base and mean ends; but to purposes truly worthy of it the encouragment of vertue & philosophick liberty & the repressing of a malign unsocial persecuting spirit. And thus the best of principles would be made the Patroness of the best of constitutions; & produce the most happy & beneficial fruits. But while other religious tests are framed, particular creeds pick'd out, and all nonconforming schemes marked with odium, & given over by publick authority to holy violence & fury it is impossible that ever <10> true piety or real religion can be promoted. But on the contrary a false superstitious zeal must do more mischeif to mankind than can possibly arise from any other cause.

It is needless to insist upon the horrible ravage & havock that false religion has in all ages produced. For it is plain from the nature of things<.> suppose we had no histories to look into that while the belief of Deity is not applyed to the encouragment of mercy justice gratitude love & all that is good & social; but on the contrary to inflame men's mind<s> with a false mischevous fancy of a divine regard for whims & sounds about which men while they are men will ever differ<.> it were much better for society that there were no knowledge of Diety at all in it; but men were left to the simple workings of these natural affections with which wise providence has very aptly fur<n>ished us. Sure I am if we can have any just notions of goodness or true majesty the Diety would much rather that they never thought of him than that they should by false & corrupt conce<i>ts concerning <11> his glory or honour be made to imagine that they can please & gratify him

in contending with violence & rage over the bowels of all that is benign or
social in his nature for any speculations whatsoever. What can it be to a
good & wise diety if a man cultivates the social & generous affections which
make him a natural & useful member of his kind; whither he prefers the
blue or the green colour; or whither he likes a flute or an organ best. And
what, Prythee My Freind, are the notions miscalled religious about which
sectaries have hated & persecuted one another in all ages; but meer speculations that have as litle connection with vertue & sociality. Wou'd any man
that merits the caracter of wise and good put the happiness of humane
society in competition with empty insignificant trifles or even with his own
favourite taste and fancy?

> Heus age responde, minimum est, quod scire laboro:
> De Jove quid sentis? Estne ut praeponere cures
> Hunc cuiquam? Cuinam? Vis Staio? An scilicet haeres?
> Quis potior Judex, pueris quis aptior orbis?
>
> Per: sat 2d[1] <12>

A just conception of the Deity is certainly the most strong incitement to
great & good actions: & <a> never failing source of rational comfort to an
honest generous mind conscious of its own worth and integrity. And therefore it is a great pity that due care shou'd not be taken to make this motive
as universal as possible in its influence. It is plain from the history of mankind that they will alwise be influenced by some religious beleif. And it is
as true that this cheifly depends upon the publick leading. And for this
reason the principle art in the modelling of society is to make this beleif
of the best & most beneficial sort. And how ever difficult it may be to root
out any religion when it is become old and has been long established &
revered: And indeed I beleive nothing is more so: Yet I cannot see why in
the original forming of things a good beleif might not be as easily planted
& made as universal in its influence by the publick authority as a bad one.
And my enquiry with you, My Freind, is about the religion of the state.

---

1. Persius, *Satires*, 2.17–20, in *Juvenal and Persius:* "Hey then, tell me (it's a tiny thing
I strive to know), what is your view of God? Would you care to rank him above—who?—
'Who?' How about Staius? or would you hesitate at that? Who is a better judge, who a
more suitable guardian for orphan boys?"

Or what shou'd be the religious part of the constitution in a <13> weel constructed policy. A great deal of mecanical zeal there must be in every society and that just of the complexion of the publick faith whatever it be. And if the publick faith were good this mecanical zeal wou'd do as much good as now for the most part it does harm. If the beleif of the state were "That there is a God of infinite goodness who loves mankind vertue sociality and free:examination & whose favour is only to be gained by loving mankind justice and liberty" and this was duly inculcated upon us by dignities that wou'd indeed be venerable if this was their office & that with all the solemnities which now gain reverence & promote zeal for things of a very different nature. Then wou'd the publick beleif concenter with the very design of society; & all the zeal or warmth it coud produce wou'd be zeal & warmth for society & its happiness. Then wou'd the publick religion be the guardian of all the common entrests of mankind and our publick instructers faithful defenders of mankind's best & most valuable priviledges. And this, My Freind, is the established religion I am pleading for. The only <14> useful publick leading either to religion or mankind.

But to discuss this question about the state religion a litle more formally allow me to enquire whither it be practicable to alter a constetution so far as to introduce this happy nay only happy publick religion. And then for a further illustration of our argument to glan<c>e a litle more particularly at the bad effects that flow from other establis<h>ed creeds.

"Machiavel that admirable Politician observes that even when one wou'd change the constitution of a state to bring the alteration into a likeing & the better with every ones satisfaction to maintain it he must keep the form or shaddow of the ancient customs. For thus the people who are not able to look further than the outward appearances of things seing the same officers, the same courts of justice, and other external formalities, are insensible of any innovation, and beleive themselves in possession of their old goverment tho indeed it be quite changed. The Romans knowing this necessity when first they lived free, having in place of one King created two consuls wou'd not suffer them to have more then twelve Lectors, because this was the number that attended the King. And when <15> the yearly sacrifice was made in Rome which cou'd not be done without the presence of the King that the people by the absence of a King might not find any deficiency in the old ceremonies; they created a head of that sacrifice whom they called the King Preist, who yet was in <a> lower degree than the high Preist. And thus the people was satisfied with that sacrifice and had no occasion by any default to miss their Kings; or wish them restored. And this rule says he they ought all to observe that wou'd cancell the old manner of living in a city and reduce it to a new & free course. All novalties some what move mens minds & therefore all reformers shou'd Endeavour to work their designed alterations as much as may be into the old mould & shape. Thus if the magistrates both in number durance & authority differ from the ancient at least they shou'd retain the same name."[2]

And certainly this policy is good whither the changes be designed in the civil or the sacred constitutions of a state. And when I have reflected upon this political observation; I have frequently been tempted to think that it wou'd not be altogether impossible to make considerable changes in a publick religion, as difficult as innovations of this sort are commonly accounted, if the thing was but managed with suitable wisdom & policy. Thus let us have reverent garbs, holy places, orders, times, and all the other external forms of a Mother Church; & I cou'd almost beleive, her doctrines instead of metaphysical unintelligible cant, or pernicious inflammatory po<i>son <16> might be most agreeably metamorphosed into good plain wholesome food & the greater bulk of her zealous votaries not perceive the change. And sure I am if the disguise of the vehicle took, & it got leave to ly in the Stomach till it was weel concocted & had but once mixed with the blood, it wou'd quickly make such a sweet alteration on the temper & constitution as wou'd sufficiently recomend it afterwards; & discard for ever all the former sour corrupting stuff which they wou'd then find to have been of the most noxious & disturbing quality; and to have produced the most distructive plagues and convulsions with which their body politick has ever been tormented.

But oh! My Freind, in order to carry on this happy change how many things are necessary what a spirit of liberty & true philosophy what love

2. Turnbull paraphrases Book I, chapter 25, of Niccolò Machiavelli's *Discourses on the First Decade of Titus Livius.*

of God & mankind what disenterestedness & publick affection must first possess & actuate the souls of those who move in the higher orbits of life! The secondary sort of mortals are but attendants to the first & higher orders and are intirely guided & influenced by their movements. Or at least they might easily be deceived by proper policy as children are by flattery & sweet meats to go to school or do any other thing their Parents and tutors think good for them. But who shall give generosity and honest boldness to those who must begin & carry on this blessed change. All I fear is reavery, My Freind. <17>

Postscript

The worthy & ingenious Mr Harrington in the second chapter of his third book of the art of law giving where he proposes prac<ti>cably the religious part of his model of goverment reasons thus for the necessity of a national religion.

"There is nothing (says he) more certain or demonstra<ble> to common sense than that the far greater part of mankind in matters of religion give themselves up to the publick leading. Now a national religion rightly established or not coercive is not any publick driveing b<ut> only the publick leading. If the publick in this case not lead such as desire to be led by a party whe<re> would be the liberty of conscience as to the state? W<hich> certainly in a well ordered common weal<t>h being the p<ublic> reason must be the publick conscience. Nay where <would> be the liberty of conscience in respect of any party wh<ich> should so proceed as to shew that without taking their libe<rty> of conscience from others they cannot have it themse<lves?> If the publick refusing liberty of conscience to a party wou'd be the cause of tumult how much more a par<ty> refusing it to the publick? And how in case of such a tumult shou'd a party defend their liberty of conscience or indeed their throats from the whole or far greater par<ty> without keeping down or tyrranizing over the whole or greater party by force of arms? These things being now understood it is no wonder that men living like men have not been found without a government or that any government has not been found without a national religion. That

is some orderly or known way or publick leading <18> in divine things &
the worship of God.<">[3] And having thus proved a national religion to be
necessary he proposes. "That the national religion be excercised according
to a directory in that case to be made & published by act of parliament.
That the national minestry be permitted to have no other publick preferment or office in the common wealth. And that no religion being contrary
to or destructive of Christianity be protected by or tolerated in the state
but that all other religions be tolerated & protected by the council of religion. And that all professors of any such religion be equaly capable of all
elections magistracys preferments & offices in the common wealth according to the orders of the same."[4]

Mr Harrington very justly observes that in every state the greater part
will always follow the publick leading in religion. And for this very reason
nothing concerns the happiness of a government more than a right publick
leading in religion. A publick leading there must be but then it ought to be
of such a nature as is werth the following and by being followed wou'd be
realy useful to the publick. And the question in politicks is to find out the
publick leading in religion that would be the most advantageous and beneficial to the publick. Whatever establishments the majority are for the
lesser party must needs submit

But the question about the religion of the state is, what should be the
publick concience or reason. Or what publick leading in religion is wisest
& fitest. Whither upon ballance of all consequences conveniencies &
unconveniencies considering the nature of religion liberty truth error
<tra?>de science & every thing that ought to be the care of <the> publick
governours it be not the best part the state <19> can act to make liberty of
examination & honest morals the only publick leading. If the goverment
should endeavour after a publick following in any particular articles of faith
or if it be not rather their business to promote charity and universal benevolence and for this effect to ma<i>ntain a national ministry whose work
it shall be to enstruct in wholesome morals leaving it to such as have opportunity & capacity to examine into matters of faith & speculation & to

3. James Harrington, *The Art of Lawgiving in Three Books,* in *The Political Works of
James Harrington,* edited by J. G. A. Pocock (Cambridge, 1977), pp. 678–79.
4. Harrington, *The Art of Lawgiving,* p. 681.

think for themselves & borrow all the helps from others they can in their enquiries. Genuine <and> uncorrupted Christianity is indeed the best of all religions & good Christians will ever be the best & worthiest members of society. But neither the nature of the Christian institution nor the design of society allows <that> it be reduced to a parliamentary standart & made an engine or tool of state. In short the only usefull publick leading in religion <is the> care of liberty & of free examination and any other medling e<ver is> & ever must be pernicious to every thing that is valuable <to> mankind or that should be protected by society as the common rig<ht> & priveledge of reasonable creatures. The way to determine the question is to bring matters by fair count & reckoning to a just ballance of loss & gain & whoever wou'd shew that this or the other scheme of beleif should have a publick leading in any state must go to political arithmetick with it and take all things into the account which it is the design of any weel model'd society to cherish & promote. What I have attempted in this short essay is to shew that it is the entrest of society to make the publick leading the Protectrix of liberty & all honest good subjects whatever their schemes of Philosophy or faith may be and tho perhaps I have not been full enough in stating all the particulars which shou'd be brought into this account yet I have said enough to shew you, my Freind, what are my real sentiments of that affair and how I think the question ought to be managed.

A Philosophical Enquiry concerning the Connexion between the Miracles and Doctrines of Jesus Christ

ാ ാ ാ

NOTE ON THE TEXT

The first edition of the *Philosophical Enquiry* exists in two versions. The first printing was published by the London bookseller R. Willock in 1731 and cost six pence. The pamphlet was then reset and a second printing was published by Willock on 7 May 1731, which sold for one shilling.[1] The second version incorporates minor changes in punctuation, spelling, and capitalization, as well as different textual ornaments and minor variations in accidentals. In both versions Turnbull used the pseudonym "Philanthropos" to sign the preface and was not named as the author on the title page or in the text.

The second edition of the *Philosophical Enquiry* was published by Willock in 1732 and sold for one shilling and six pence. Turnbull's name appeared on the title page, and the fact that he was styled "A.M." suggests that the pamphlet was published before he was given his honorary Doctor of Laws degree from the University of Edinburgh on 13 June 1732. The text of the second edition is reset. It is also thoroughly revised and substantially enlarged. In the preliminary matter, the preface is no longer signed "Philanthropos" and the advertisement has been reworded. In the main body of the pamphlet, Turnbull made numerous minor changes of punctuation and wording, expanded the text of some footnotes, inserted new footnotes, deleted some footnotes, and added sentences and paragraphs, as well as a new section in Part II, two new sections in Part III, and a set of six "Queries" at the end of the work.

The third edition of the *Philosophical Enquiry,* again published by Willock, bears a new title page. Turnbull has reworded and expanded the

---

1. The pamphlet is listed among the "Books published in May, 1731" in *The Gentleman's Magazine* 1 (1731): 228.

subtitle of the work and is now styled "LL.D." The order of the preliminary
matter has been altered, with the advertisement from the second edition
now preceding the preface. Both have been reset with new ornaments and
incorporate minor textual revisions. The "Advertisement to this Edition"
has been added after the preface. Turnbull has not revised pages 1–86
(pp. 103–62) and they appear not to have been reset. The original page 87
(pp. 162–63) has been replaced with one and a half freshly set gatherings
(pages 87–98; below pp. 162–70). Queries IV to VI have been reset, and
Queries V and VI incorporate minor revisions. Turnbull has added Queries
VII and VIII and reworded the concluding paragraph on page 89 (p. 163).
The appendix (pages 89–98; below pp. 164–70) has also been added, as
indicated on the title page.

A

Philosophical Enquiry

CONCERNING THE

CONNEXION

BETWEEN THE

Miracles and Doctrines

OF

JESUS CHRIST.

IN WHICH

MIRACLES are considered in a new Light; and it is proved that the Works Jesus Christ performed to evince the Truth of his Doctrines, are a natural, proper, and full Proof of them, in the strictest and most philosophical Sense of Proof or Evidence.

By *GEORGE TURNBULL, LL.D.*
The Third Edition.
To which is added, An APPENDIX.

LONDON:
Printed for R. Willock, at *Sir Isaac Newton's-Head*
in *Cornhill.* MDCCXXXIX.

[Price One Shilling and Six-pence.]

ADVERTISEMENT

Upon reviewing the first Edition of this ENQUIRY, I thought it proper to make some few changes and additions in order to render it a full and compleat demonstration of the Connexion between the *Doctrines* and *Works* of JESUS CHRIST: And I have now no more to say upon that subject. As for the other part promised, I only want some short time to put in order for the press, what I have long had by me upon that argument, so the Publick may expect to have it very soon.[1] <iii>

---

1. See below p. 118, note †. The projected second part was not published.

THE PREFACE

If a Preface or Apology be necessary in any case, it is certainly when a Letter to a Friend assumes a more publick character; and instead of a private missive, becomes an epistle to the world.

By way of apology may it therefore suffice, That tho' the Author was advised, nay pressed, to send this private letter to the press; yet what only prevailed with him to do it, was, that he seriously thought it might chance to convince some one doubter or other, of the truth of Christianity: *And if it does, he is sure of thanks for publishing it from such; if it does not, some body will probably take the trouble to point out the lameness of the reasoning; and so may perhaps give him new light, shew him his mistake, or help him to a better argument; and in that case too he will have his reward; for truth is his search and delight.* <iv>

ADVERTISEMENT TO THIS EDITION

This ENQUIRY, with the APPENDIX, is offered by the Author to the consideration of some late writers against Christianity, to the *Moral Philosopher* in particular; for he thinks it contains a satisfying answer to all that Author has said about miracles, after many others.[2] He begs leave only to ask them one question, and it is, Whether they think it probable that virtue would be more prevalent and universal in a state where the genuine doctrines of Christianity concerning our duties to GOD, ourselves and our neighbours, and a future life, are believed; or in a state where a future life is not believed, and moral duties are not inculcated or inforced from that belief? If this should be said to be a Query that does not belong to the question about the truth or falshood of the Christian Religion, yet sure it cannot be said to be a Query that does not relate to the happiness of mankind and human society. As for the truth of Christianity, it must come to the plain simple question stated and answered in the following Essay, Whether the doctrine of JESUS CHRIST concerning a future state, which is obviously a strong motive to virtue, be not proved true by the Miracles which CHRIST wrought to prove it, in a way that is strictly philosophical and unexcep-

---

2. As Turnbull indicates on p. 164 below, he had read or at least seen the first two volumes of Thomas Morgan's *The Moral Philosopher;* a third was subsequently published in 1740. For Morgan's view of miracles see [Thomas Morgan], *The Moral Philosopher. In a Dialogue between Philalethes a Christian Deist, and Theophanes a Christian Jew* (London, 1737), pp. 98–100, and especially [Morgan], *The Moral Philosopher. Vol. II. Being a farther Vindication of Moral Truth and Reason; Occasioned by Two Books lately published: One Intitled, The Divine Authority of the Old and New Testaments asserted . . . by the Reverend Mr Leland. The other Intitled Eusebius: Or, the True Christian's Defence, &c. By the Rev. Mr Chapman* (London, 1739), pp. 26–40, 48–52, 65–68, 70–71, 196–97, 235–36, and "A Letter to Eusebius," in *The Moral Philosopher. Vol. II*, pp. 7–18, 23–25, 29–32, 55–57, 67–74.

tionable, at the same time that it is obvious to the meanest capacity; and that it is, must be admitted by all who allow experimental proof to be a good proof, or, in other words, samples to be samples of what they are samples; for the works of CHRIST are proper and adequate samples of his doctrine. The way in which Miracles are considered in this Essay is quite new, tho' very simple and obvious, and indeed demonstrative; I have not met with it in any defence of Christianity; and I am sure it hath never been adverted to by any writer against Christianity.

I think myself obliged to take notice, that the abridger of this Essay, in the *Bibliotheque Raisonneè,* has no where mistaken my meaning but in one place, *p. 22. But says a noble author,* &c.[3] I don't say that Lord *Shaftsbury* intended to make an objection against Christianity; I only give his words, and thence I take occasion to expatiate at greater length upon the evidence which CHRIST gave of the truth of his doctrines, and to prove that as power can only be proved by samples, so honesty can only be proved by samples, and therefore that CHRIST gave full proof of his doctrine by giving proper samples of his honest and good intention, as well as of all the power and knowledge he claimed. <1>

---

3. *Bibliothèque raisonée des ouvrages des savans de l'Europe* 7 (1731): 340–41.

An Enquiry, &c.

Introduction

Christianity, my Friend, has been attacked with so much zeal of late; that a meer stranger would certainly imagine, the happiness of mankind depended upon being delivered from it. That it was a belief of the most fatal, pernicious influence; a dismal enslaving doctrine, which rendered its disciples incapable of living agreeably. For who could think that any one, who had the least regard to his own private interest, or that of society in general, would take pains to ruin the credit of a prevailing faith, which evidently tends to encourage virtue and to curb every vitious affection? Yet these who have so keenly disputed the evidence of the Christian Religion, never dared to find fault with the morals <2> it teaches. And hardly will any one adventure to say, "That the perswasion of a future state, is not a most powerful motive to the practice of virtue and a good life: or that mankind would be more virtuous without such an incitement."

To correct the false doctrines and tenets of certain professing Christians, is indeed a good office. And the corruptions and abuses that prevail in Churches, most undeservedly called Christian, ought to be exposed in their proper colours. Or, in one word, if any Christian teachers represent the doctrines of CHRIST in a false light; and put the stress of Religion and our salvation upon any thing, besides the sincere love and practice of every moral virtue, their error ought to be discovered and refuted. And our SAVIOUR himself has shewn us the way, by his manner of reasoning with the Jewish Doctors.[4] But this is the sum of Christianity: "That there is a future

---

4. See, for example, Matthew 15.1–20 and 22.23–40; Mark 7.1–23 and 12.18–34.

state of happiness for the good: and of punishments, for the vitious. The sincere and steady practice of virtue is every where inculcated by our Sav-iour and his Apostles, as what only can recommend with any advantage to the Divine favour and approbation here, or hereafter." And consequently to attack the true and genuine doctrine of Jesus Christ, is indeed to fight against a belief the most comfortable and beneficial.

'Tis certainly meer enthusiasm, to think that society can subsist without a publick leading in religion.* And if the Christian religion <3> is the best publick one that can be devised, is it friendly to undermine and destroy it? why diminish the obligations to virtue, which at least are the most easily conceived by the vulgar, and are the fittest to work upon those who cannot enquire, or philosophize: but are powerfully struck and over aw'd by the belief of miracles and inspiration.

I have often had it in my head to publish, for the use of modern un-believers, a dissertation upon the religion of *Cicero,* that I have had by me some time; it is certainly fit to put them in mind, how that Academic ex-amines the various opinions concerning Deity and providence; his way of treating the publick established superstitions in his time; and his senti-ments† of those philosophers who endeavour'd to destroy the belief of

---

* *See Lord* Shaftsbury's *Essay upon* Enthusiasm. [Shaftesbury, *Essay,* in *Characteris-ticks,* I:11–14. See also Turnbull's "The Religion of the State," pp. 79–89, above.]

† Quod si in hoc erro, quod animos hominum immortaleis esse credam, lubenter erro: nec mihi hunc errorem, quo delector, dum vivo, extorqueri volo: sin mortuus (ut minuti philosophi censent) non vereor ne hunc errorem meum mortui philosophi irrideant. *Cic. de Senect.* [Cicero, *De senectute,* xxiii.85: "And if I err in my belief that the souls of men are immortal, I gladly err, nor do I wish this error which gives me pleasure to be wrested from me while I live. But if when dead I am going to be without sensation (as some petty philosophers think), then I have no fear that these seers, when they are dead, will have the laugh on me!"]

Polybius, *who was certainly one of the best judges of mankind and matters of government, observes, that the belief of a future state is one of the greatest restraints from villany; and therefore speaking politically makes this remark, (I choose to give it in the words of* Casau-bon's *translation)* "Idcirco mihi videntur veteres nec temere, nec sine gravi causa istas de Diis opiniones, & de poenis apud inferos, in vulgus induxisse. Contra autem qui nunc vivunt temere ac sine rationeillas rejicere. εἰκῇ καὶ ἀλόγως ἐκβάλλειν αὐτά." *Lib.* 6. [Polybius, *The Histories,* VI.56.12: "For this reason I think, not that the ancients acted rashly and at haphazard in introducing among the people notions concerning the gods

immortality and future rewards and punishments, tho' it was no article of the publick religion. *Socrates,* and abundance of other examples, might very seasonably be set before them. For my part, was I an unbeliever, I would look upon myself as obliged to confute such false notions and representations of the Chri-<4>stian doctrine, as tend to the hurt and ruin of true morals, and consequently of society and mankind; but at the same time to support genuine Christianity to the utmost of my power, for society's sake.

But I believe, and am to give you at present the reason of my belief, for you are curious, it seems, to know at full length, what I meant th'other day when I said, "That the works of CHRIST were natural proper samples of his doctrines; and that I was not a little surprised, none of the Apologists for Christianity had considered his miracles in that view; the connection is so simple, and obvious."

To proceed regularly in this enquiry, one ought to consider, what doctrines may be proved by works; and what doctrines cannot; or stand in no need of such a confirmation.

SECTION I

Beautiful and natural fables, parables, or allegories, are so in themselves independently of any works the teacher may perform. And no works can prove an allegory, parable, or fable, to be natural and elegant, if it is not indeed so: if its beauty and fitness does not discover itself to every discerning hearer or reader. For would it not be reckoned very odd and ridiculous for a Poet, who happened at the same time to be an able Physician, to appeal to the wonderful cures he performed, to prove his poetry elegant; or a Painter to prove his painting true and judicious. <5>

'Tis therefore evident, that works of the most extraordinary kind, can be of no other use, with regard to fables, allegories, and parables; except to excite the attention of the hearers; to gain authority to the teacher; get him a hearing; and make every body attend with due care; the vulgar especially

---

and beliefs in the terrors of hell, but that the moderns are most rash and foolish in banishing such beliefs." Turnbull cites the edition of Polybius's *Histories* published in 1609 by the noted philologist and scholar Isaac Casaubon (1559–1614).]

who stand much in need of instruction in that familiar insinuating way, and yet are not to be moved without an extraordinary awakening.

The parables of our SAVIOUR justify themselves abundantly; nor did he work miracles to prove their propriety and beauty.

SECTION II

Common sense is certainly sufficient to teach those who think of the matter with tolerable seriousness and attention, all the duties and offices of human life; all our obligations to GOD; and our fellow-creatures, all that is morally fit and binding. And there is no need of works, to prove that to be morally fit and obligatory, which common sense and reason clearly shews to be so. Nor can any work on the other hand, prove that to be morally fit, and becoming, which common sense and reason proves to be the reverse. The moral fitness or unfitness of actions can only be deduced from the nature of the actions and agents; their constitution, situation, and relations. And therefore works of the most extraordinary nature can be of no further use, with regard to precepts and lessons of morality, except to beget attention, and to make the spe-<6>ctators and hearers reflect seriously upon that moral fitness, which common sense clearly points out to every thinking person.

But if at any time common sense is quite asleep or buried; or if by the cunning of corrupt designing teachers, false notions of religion and virtue are become universal; and the vulgar especially, who are easily misled by crafty deceivers, can hardly be brought to attend to the wholesome instructions of undebauched pure sense and reason; extraordinary works are certainly fit in such a case; nay almost necessary to give sufficient weight and Authority to a reformer; and to rouse mankind to that attention which is necessary, in order to their being undeceived and soundly instructed. Their eyes must be opened, their sleeping understandings awakened, their prejudices and false notions must be quite rooted out, before truth can enter into their minds with any success, or produce any desired change. And hardly can a talk so difficult, be performed by a teacher with no more than ordinary skill or authority.

Such was the condition of mankind in general, of the Jews particularly, when our divine Reformer appeared in the world. And even his extraordinary, marvellous, works, scarcely were sufficient to create attention to the moral doctrines and precepts he taught; which however are evidently in themselves of the most excellent kind: in every respect wholsome, true, just, perfect. He did not work his miracles to prove the moral fitness; the reasonableness and excellency of these; these prove themselves sufficiently: whoever will but attend to them must <7> necessarily discover their natural, immutable, eternal truth, and fitness.

SECTION III

Doctrines that can be demonstrated to be worthy of GOD and the divine perfections; and their opposites, or contraries, inconsistent with our natural and just conceptions of GOD and his moral qualities, are necessarily true. Thus, for instance, could it be proved that the immortality of human souls is worthy of GOD; and their mortality inconsistent with the true idea of GOD and the divine perfections; it would follow necessarily, that our souls are immortal; and no works, of whatever kind, could prove that they are mortal. Nor would there be upon that supposition, any need of works to shew that they are immortal. All that any works could do in that case would be, to excite attention to the necessary connexion of that doctrine, with the true notion of GOD and his moral attributes.

The argument holds equally good with regard to the reunion of our souls with bodies, or any other doctrine; supposing that the doctrine could be proved, by necessary consequences, to be worthy of GOD, and its contrary utterly repugnant to the divine nature and perfections. But however probable and likely these doctrines, of immortality and the reunion of our souls with bodies, may be in themselves, upon several considerations; yet hardly will any one say, that their truth is demonstrable. How these therefore may be proved to be true by works, is to be enquired. <8>

SECTION IV

But it must also be observed, before we go further; that no works of whatever kind, however surprising or extraordinary, can prove reasonings to be just and conclusive which are evidently false; and solid, accurate reasonings stand firmly upon their own bottom; there is no need of any works to prove that they are so. There are indeed certain reasonings from facts or works; as from experiments, for instance, in physical philosophy. But in that case the facts, works, or experiments are the principles; the premisses, as the schools speak, from which the conclusions are inferred. And therefore with regard to such reasonings, the works may be said to prove the conclusion. But any other kind of reasoning which is offered as compleat in itself, distinctly from the works that are produced by the teacher, or in which the conclusion is deduced, not from the works but other principles, must not be judged by the works, but by comparing the conclusion with the principles from which it is drawn, examining first the truth of the principles, and next the connexion betwixt these and the conclusion inferred from them. In short, it is only when the works are the principles, the foundation, upon which the doctrine is built, that works can be taken into the consideration, when the question is about the justness of a reasoning or conclusion. <9>

Thus when our SAVIOUR reasons with the Jewish doctors concerning the Resurrection, for instance, from this argument that GOD calls himself the *God of Abraham, Isaac, and Jacob;* and that GOD is not the *God of the dead but of the living:** here is a conclusion drawn from a certain topic, which his works can neither prove to follow, nor not to follow. This and such like reasonings must be judged of by themselves without any regard to his works.†

And now, my friend, you will understand, why t'other day, when I had not leisure to explain my self fully, I said, that in proving the truth of the Christian Religion, "it was necessary to distinguish betwixt the reasonings of our SAVIOUR and his apostles; and their pure simple, positive, doctrines,

---

* Matth. xii. [Matthew 22.32; see also Luke 20.37–38.]

† *See Bishop* Tillotson's *excellent sermon upon that text, in which that reasoning is set in a clear light.* [John Tillotson, "A Sermon Preached at the Funeral of the Reverend Mr. Thomas Gouge, the 4th of November, 1681. At St. Anne's Black-fryars; with a Brief Account of his Life," in *The Works of the Most Reverend Dr. John Tillotson, Late Lord Archbishop of Canterbury: Containing Fifty four Sermons and Discourses, on Several Occasions. Together with the Rule of Faith. Being all that were Published by his Grace Himself,* 2nd ed. (London, 1699), pp. 251–70. The text for Tillotson's sermon is Luke 20.37–38.]

for the proof of which miracles were wrought."* Nothing can be more out
of the way, than to say in the general, all the reasonings of our SAVIOUR
and his apostles must be good, and all his fables and allegories must be
perfectly just and well chosen, because he wrought such and such miracles.
The reasonings and the parables sufficiently justify and prove themselves.†
And the miracles only can be compared with these simple positive assertions, or doctrines, to prove the truth of which they were wrought; and
which can be inferred from the <10> works, as any other conclusion from
its principles.

What should we think of a Mathematician, who pretended to give demonstrations of his propositions; and after all argued thus; That his demonstrations must be just, because he could perform certain extraordinary
feats in chymistry or medicine: Or of a moral philosopher, that appealed
to such like marvellous productions to prove his moral scheme firmly built,
every conclusion just, and the whole system well connected. Whatever was
thought of the works to be sure, we would judge of the pretended reasonings and demonstrations by themselves, without regard to the works.

"One general use however, of the works of our SAVIOUR, with regard
to the whole of his lessons and instructions, is obvious from what has been
said. They serve to shew he was a teacher that deserved to be noticed; they
were fit to rouse and excite his hearers to give due attention to what he
taught." <11>

---

* Inter Apostolum & Doctorem, *to speak with the learned.* ["Between the apostles and
the doctors." Turnbull's focus on the New Testament and, in particular, the Gospels in
defining the fundamentals of Christianity is, in general terms, reminiscent of the ap-
proach to the Bible taken in, for example, John Locke's *The Reasonableness of Christianity,*
edited by John C. Higgins-Biddle (Oxford, 1999), esp. p. 166.]

† *One may truly say upon this head; Wisdom will ever be justified of her children.* [A
paraphrase of Matthew 12.19, "But wisdom is justified of her children," and Luke 7.35,
"But wisdom is justified of all her children."]

Part II

section i

But now it is time to enter into the main question; the connexion betwixt the Works and the Doctrines of Jesus Christ.

And in order to conceive distinctly; how, or in what case, works can prove a doctrine to be true; let us attend a little more particularly to the nature of those reasonings just now mentioned, which are deduced from facts, or experiments.

It is by experiment, that the natural philosopher shews the properties of the air, for example, or of any other body. That is, the philosopher shews certain effects which infer certain qualities: or in other words, he shews certain proper samples of the qualities he pretends the air, or any other body that he is reasoning about, hath. Thus is it we know bodies gravitate, attract, that the air is ponderous and elastic. Thus it is, in one word, we come to the knowledge of the properties of any body, and of the general laws of matter and motion. The same way, if a philosopher, a physician, an architect, a painter, or any artist, pretends to a certain <12> degree of skill or power; he must prove his claim by giving proper samples of that very degree of skill or power he professes. 'Tis by proper samples or experiments only of power and knowledge, that we can be assured, one actually possesses a certain power or knowledge.

Just so it is only by samples or experiments, that we can judge of one's honesty, benevolence, or good intention. We conclude a man honest and worthy of trust and credit, because he has given proof and evidence of his integrity and merit. It is from the works of the Supreme Being, that we infer his infinite wisdom, power, and goodness; as from so many samples and experiments, by which we may safely judge of the whole. 'Tis thus we are satisfied about our own faculties and abilities natural or acquired. 'Tis thus we reason in a thousand instances every day about ourselves and others.

It is in one word, from one's works only that we can infer his ability, skill, or power, of any kind or degree, as from proper samples or experiments of that power or quality; in the same way that it is from effects, that we conclude in natural philosophy, that the air, or any body, possesses a certain quality; as from so many proper and analogous samples or experiments of that quality. And it is the same what the power claimed be, of what kind, sort or degree; provided the power claimed be exemplified by proper analogous proportional samples or experiments.

If therefore certain doctrines of Jesus Christ evidently are, or can be, reduced to assertions of his having a certain degree of power or <13> knowledge: his works may be a proper proof of these Doctrines; because they may be proper samples or experiments of the power, or knowledge claimed by these assertions. For with regard to such doctrines or assertions, all that can be required by way of proof is, samples analogous in kind, and proportioned in quantity or moment, to the power or knowledge claimed: just as in natural philosophy, or the common reasonings in life every day about the properties and qualities of things, or agents.

SECTION II

It remains therefore to be considered, what doctrines of our Saviour can be taken in this light; or compared in this manner with his works.

And there are three doctrines of Christianity that are evidently of this kind.

"The doctrine of future rewards and punishments."

"The doctrine of the resurrection of the dead."

"The doctrine of the forgiveness of sins."

But before we advance farther it is proper to take notice, that it is evident from what was said before, of the proper proof of any claim to a certain degree of power or knowledge, that <14> it must be the same, whether these three doctrines are reduced to a claim of knowledge or a claim of power. The works will have the same relation to these doctrines, whether they are considered in the one way or the other. For a pretension to knowledge of a certain kind must be proved by samples of that kind; and a pretension to power of a certain kind must be proved by samples of that kind. The same samples therefore will prove the one, that prove the other, if the power and knowledge are of the same kind.

Either these three doctrines must be considered as a claim to knowledge in this way;

"I know certainly that the dead shall be raised."

"I know certainly that there is a future immortal State of rewards and punishments."

"I know certainly that sins will be forgiven upon a certain condition."

Or these doctrines must be considered as a claim to power in this way:

"I have power to raise the dead."

"I have power to forgive sins."

"I have power to make happy or miserable in the life to come."

And which ever way they are taken, the question about the works must come to the same <15> thing. For in the one case it will be, whether they are samples of the knowledge pretended to; and in the other, whether they are samples of the power pretended to. But the power and knowledge being evidently of the same kind; their objects the same; the works that are of kind with the one, must be of kind with the other.

In which way then are these doctrines to be considered? As a claim to power certainly. For thus our SAVIOUR himself is represented in his history as always declaring these doctrines. "I will raise the dead; that all men may know I have power to forgive sins," &c.

But these three doctrines must be examined severally, and compared with their samples.

SECTION III

Let us first consider the "Doctrine of the resurrection of the dead."

If our SAVIOUR had said: "I certainly know that the dead shall be raised": What would have been the proper proof of his having that knowledge? He behoved certainly to have given instances of the possibility of a resurrection from the dead; and of his having that knowledge, by actually raising from the dead. But observe how the doctrine runs; it is not an assertion of knowledge but of power: He does not say; "I know certainly the dead shall be raised." But he asserts his power to <16> raise the dead: and always teaches that doctrine in these terms; "I will raise the dead; I will give eternal life."

And what is the proper evidence when the claim runs in this strain? The same as in the other case. It was necessary to give samples, or experiments, of this power he claimed. And accordingly he raised from the dead;[a] and gave power to his Apostles to raise from the dead.[b] And to put his pretensions beyond all doubt, he himself submitted to death, that he might give an incontestible proof of his being actually possessed of that power, by rising himself from the dead the third day,[c] according to his own prediction.[d]

To ask then whether JESUS CHRIST gave a sufficient or proper proof of his having power to raise the dead; is to ask, whether raising the dead is a sample of power to raise the dead.

All the Objections of certain Sceptics against the doctrine of a resurrection from the dead, have been examined and sufficiently answered by Dr *Samuel Clarke,*[e] Mr *Locke,*[f] and others; to whom I refer you. To say the

a. Matth. xii. 25. Luke vii. 9, &c. John xi. 14, &c. Matth. iii. 24. [Matthew 9.25; Mark 5.35–42; Luke 7.12–15; John 11.1–44.]

b. Matth. xxviii. Matth. x. 18, &c. Mark xvi. [Matthew 10.8.]

c. Mark iii. 15. Luke x. 8, &c. Luke xxiv. [Matthew 28; Mark 16; Luke 24; John 20.]

d. Luke vii. 9, &c. Luke xii. 12, &c. John xx. [Matthew 20.19; Mark 10.34; Luke 9.22 and 18.33.]

e. *See the Doctor upon the* Being *and* Attributes. [Samuel Clarke, *A Discourse concerning the Being and Attributes of God, the Obligations of Natural Religion, and the Truth and Certainty of the Christian Revelation,* 7th ed. (London, 1728), pp. 356–59.]

f. Locke's *Commentary on the* Epistles; *and Dispute with Bishop* Stillingfleet. [John Locke, *A Paraphrase and Notes on the Epistles of St. Paul to the Galatians, I and II Corinthians, Romans, [and] Ephesians; to which is Prefix'd, An Essay for the Understanding of St. Paul's Epistles, by Consulting St. Paul Himself,* in John Locke, *The Works of John Locke Esq.,* 3rd ed., 3 vols. (London, 1727), III:168, 202–9, 227, 254, 288–89, 303–5, 321, 350, 375; Locke, *Mr. Locke's Reply to the Right Reverend the Lord Bishop of Worcester's Answer to his Second Letter: Wherein, besides other incident Matters, what his Lordship has said concerning Certainty by Reason, Certainty by Ideas, and Certainty by Faith; the Resurrection*

truth, the difficulties moved against a resurrection from the dead, do not touch that doctrine as it is de-<17>livered by our SAVIOUR and his Apostles; but the chimerical additions to it of some Divines; who imagine the same particles of matter, which were united with the soul when it acted the bad or the good part, must likewise be sharers in the rewards or the punishments; forgetting their own principle, the immateriality of our thinking part, and that matter is utterly insensible; nay incapable of being made, even by the Deity himself, to think, feel, or perceive.[5]

SECTION IV

But our SAVIOUR not only asserted his power to raise from the dead:* but to give us immortal, incorruptible[†] bodies and to make perfectly happy, or compleatly miserable in the life to come.

And who are to be happy, and who are to be miserable, according to his doctrine? The virtuous and regular are to be rewarded; the vitious and immoral are to be punished. Every one is to be judged by his works, by his conduct, and approved or condemned accordingly.

Instinct, Reason, and the universal consent of all nations and ages of the world, conjoin to render this doctrine probable, which our SAVIOUR has set beyond all doubt, by the samples he gave of his power to bestow blessings, or inflict miseries of every sort. Consider but his works in this light; and were they not all so many experiments or instances of this power? he made the <18> ignorant and simple wise in a moment: changed the tempers and dispositions of men almost instantaneously: cured the most malign, inveterate, diseases by a word of his mouth: delivered in the same instantaneous, wonderful, manner, from infirmities of every kind: and bestowed upon whom he pleased, the most marvellous and surprizing gifts

---

of the same Body; the Immateriality of the Soul; the Inconsistency of Mr. Locke's Notions with the Articles of the Christian Faith, and their Tendency to Scepticism; is examin'd, in Locke, *Works,* I:483–98, 565–67.]

   * John v. 20, &c. [John 5.21.]

   † 1 Cor. xv. [1 Corinthians 15.42–54.]

   5. Turnbull thus rejects Locke's suggestion that God could "superadd" the power of thought to matter; John Locke, *An Essay concerning Human Understanding,* edited by Peter Nidditch (Oxford: Clarendon Press, 1975), IV.iii.6.

and talents.* His transfiguration was a plain specimen and example of the glory and lustre he could give to our bodies after the resurrection. And all his works, in one word, were one continued series of proper and analogous experiments, to prove his power to curse or bless; banish diseases and infirmities; bestow blessings of every kind, moral or corporeal: make happy; compleatly happy, or compleatly wretched.

SECTION V

Our SAVIOUR also taught the forgiveness of sins.† And how did he prove his pretension to this power? By these very experiments and samples that he gave of his power to deliver from miseries, and render happy. For what is it to forgive sins? is it not to deliver from those miseries sin justly merits; or to which it renders the sinner obnoxious?

And accordingly he asserted his power to forgive sins: but that all men might know he had <19> indeed that power; he ordered the lame, whose sins he pronounced remitted and forgiven, to arise take up the couch and walk. The dumb spoke; the deaf heard; the lame walked strait and firmly: he cured all diseases; and bestowed health, strength, and all sorts of blessings: at his command also the dead arose; to prove that he could forgive sins, or deliver the penitent from all the pains and miseries his sinful life had righteously deserved.‡

Let us take notice however, how cautious he was of giving any encouragement to the wicked, by his doctrine of the forgiveness of sins.§ It was only to those who seriously repented and reformed, that he gave the agreeable hopes of finding pardon. It was not to such as continued in their sins, in spight of frequent Remorses and professions of repentance: but to such

---

* Matth. xiv. 25, &c. Mark iv. 40, &c. Matth. ix. 35, &c. Matth. xiv. 14, &c. Matth. xii. 25, &c. Matth. xv. 21, &c. Matth. xx. 35, &c. Matth. xxi. 14, &c. Luke xii. 32, &c. Luke x. 8, &c. Mark iii. 15. [Mark 4.39; Matthew 12.22, 15.28, and 20.34; Luke 10.19.]

† Matth. xxviii. Mark xvi. Luke xxiv. John xx. [Turnbull's references make little sense. See, for example, Matthew 6.14; Mark 3.28, 4.12, and 11.25; Luke 6.37, 7.48, and 11.4.]

‡ Matth. ix. 5, &c. Mark ii. 10. Luke v. 20, &c. Mark xiii. II, &c. [Matthew 9.2–8; Mark 2.3–12; Luke 5.18–26.]

§ Matth. xiii. 58, &c. [Turnbull's reference makes little sense. He may have in mind Matthew 18.21–35.]

as really turned to the love and practice of virtue; and sincerely forsook their wicked ways, in the habitual course of their lives and practice.

And therefore we find that where there was no Faith, he refused to work cures. Where there was no Faith: that is, where he found not that sincere, unprejudiced; that pliable, docile temper, that is necessary in order to reformation, or receiving wholesome instruction: but on the contrary, obstinacy, stubbornness, malignity of disposition, and every bad quality. That this is the meaning is plain, because he upbraids them for their malice and blind obstinacy; the hardness of their hearts; and calls them children of <20> the Devil sometimes; a phrase that sounds harsh in our tongue; but is well known by those who are skill'd in the original languages, to mean no more, but that they hated the light and loved darkness, because their works were evil, as he himself speaks at other times.

Thus in the whole of his conduct, he carefully shunned, by a promiscuous bestowal of his favours and blessings, to give any handle to the most terrible, pernicious abuse of his doctrine concerning the forgiveness of sins; as if in consequence of it, *men might sin that grace might the more abound.** And at the same time gave full assurance of his power to deliver sincere reformers, from the just demerits of their former evil practices; if an infinity of instances of power to deliver from all sorts of pains and miseries, and to confer all kinds of blessings, are proper and adequate samples of a power to curse and bless, make happy or miserable.

SECTION VI

Add to these three, the promise of assistance to all those who being convinced of the truth of our SAVIOUR's doctrine and pretension; seriously set themselves to reform every evil habit; and to improve daily in virtue and goodness.

It was necessary that the Apostles, who were, after our SAVIOUR's ascension, to preach and promulgate his doctrine, should have an extra-<21>ordinary assistance;† the gift of tongues; the power of healing diseases;

---

* Luke vii. 9, &c. Luke x. 9, &c. John xi. 14, &c. Matth. x. 19, &c. Matth. viii. 42, &c. [Matthew 10.8 and 8.26–33.]

† *See the texts already cited. And the whole history of the Acts of the Apostles is full of samples and proofs to this purpose.*

and of raising from the dead. And accordingly we have already seen that all necessary power and assistance was actually given to them. So that the effusion of gifts upon them at *Pentecoste;* their bold and undaunted perseverance in spight of all opposition; their heroic sufferings; and all the extraordinary works they performed; were an infringible proof and confirmation of our SAVIOUR's ability to bestow every virtue, every quality, every degree of power: and at the same time of his veracity and faithfulness, that he would not fail to fulfil all that he had promised. And consequently were an indisputable argument of the truth of all his doctrines; of his whole claim. A proper proof in particular of his being able to give the assistance he hath promised to Christians.

He proffers his spirit to them who ask it.* He hath said that if Christians are not remiss and slothful, but give all due pains on their part; that their endeavours shall be successful; that they should feel their irregular appetites and passions weaken apace; and the good ones gain new life and vigour every day. And more especially that they should find proper aid in time of trial; an extraordinary assistance to counterbalance the extraordinary attacks their virtue might suffer in certain circumstances from the side of pleasure and its enchantments; or distress and its terrors. And seeing he accom-<22>plished to the full, what he promised to his Apostles; why should we doubt of his ability, or good-will to do all he undertook? He who did the greater, can he not, will he not, do the less? In short, all the courage, wisdom, sincerity, and steadiness of the Apostles; all their gifts, talents, and works, are, in the nature of things, the fittest *Specimens* that can possibly be imagined, of our SAVIOUR's capacity to make good all he promised. And that no distance of time or place could make any difference, or alteration, with regard to his will or power. Samples of power to bestow a certain quality, or blessing, are certainly a proof of power to bestow it.

SECTION VII

I have not time to give you an exact history or detail of the works of our SAVIOUR recorded in the gospels; nor is it necessary: after these hints it

---

* *He hath promised in innumerable places to* Give his Spirit to those who ask it.

will be easy, in reading over the gospels, to refer the works narrated there, to these doctrines.

But, says a noble author,* "Signs of power may prove power, but cannot prove honesty, or create trust."

And to say the Truth, it was this way of speaking about miracles, that first gave me the hint of considering the miracles of our SAVIOUR as samples of his pretended power. But in answer <23> to this, let us consider how honesty and good intention can only be ascertained. To be sure it must shew itself by an uniform untainted conduct and behaviour; by a continued course of honest and benevolent deeds; by a series uninterrupted of samples of goodness and sincerity. And was not the whole of our SAVIOUR's conduct the fittest that can be imagined to gain him credit in this way? what ground did he ever give to suspect his fidelity, or call his truth and honesty in question? Were not these very works,† that proved his power at the same time, so many irrefragable evidences of his goodness, sincerity, and benevolent honest intention? It was necessary to give some examples of his power to curse as well as to bless. For such is the nature of the common herd of mankind, that one instance of suffering makes more impression upon their weak and fearful minds, than a thousand examples of happiness. But he chose to shew his power to inflict pains and miseries to blast and curse by such examples as might serve the purpose sufficiently, and yet do very little mischief: as in cursing the fig-tree,‡ and sending the Devils into the swine.§ He delighted not in cursing, but in blessing; he rejoiced in works of mercy and benevolence; and went about continually doing good. But there is the less reason to insist upon this article, that even those who have called him an impostor never adventured to <24> charge him with malice, or any bad mischievous design: but on the contrary, have been obliged to acknowledge,

---

* *The Earl of* Shaftsbury *somewhere in his* Moral Rhapsody. [A paraphrase of Shaftesbury, *The Moralists,* in Shaftesbury, *Characteristicks,* II:188.]

† *I need not put you in mind upon this head, that by Devils are to be understood violent terrible maladies; for that has often been made plain, and is now, I believe, generally agreed on. And I shall be obliged to treat of that affair at more length in the second part of this* Enquiry; *when I come to consider the facts, and their evidence.* [The projected second part of the *Philosophical Enquiry* was never published.]

‡ Matth. iv. 19. Mark xi. 14, &c. [Matthew 21.19–20.]

§ Mark v. 13, &c.

that he gave all the possible marks of a good, generous, and well-disposed Teacher of the soundest morals.[6]

In judging however of our SAVIOUR's pretension; his conduct, and the evidences that he gave of his honesty, and sincere good disposition, must certainly be taken into the account. He himself tells his disciples, that they were not to trust to miracles only; because not only might false teachers *work miracles,* but there should actually come after him *false Christs,** false prophets, working miracles; but that, together with the miracles they were to consider the doctrine and the conduct of pretended extraordinary Teachers: to judge of the *tree by its fruit.*[†]

SECTION VIII

But having considered the samples JESUS CHRIST gave of the power he claimed by his doctrines: it must be observed next, that he pretended to a divine commission to teach these doctrines: and by them to encourage and excite to the practice of virtue, and to discourage sin and vice.

And with regard to his pretended mission: it is evident, that if the particular doctrines, that is, the particular assertions of power, are sufficiently justified and proved by proper samples; the truth of the mission follows in course. <25> For what reason can there possibly be to doubt of the mission, when the particular power the missionary claims, as missionary, is sufficiently ascertained by proper samples?

But besides, the whole series of the miracles of JESUS CHRIST may be

---

* Math. xxiv. 24. Mark xiii. 22.

† Matth. xii. 33.

6. Turnbull may be alluding to Charles Blount's *The Two First Books, of Philostratus, concerning the Life of Apollonius Tyaneus* (London, 1680). Apollonius of Tyana (fl. first century A.D.) was a Neo-Pythagorean said to have performed miracles. His teachings formed the basis of a cult after his death and he was likened by some pagans to Christ. Blount noted the parallels between the lives of Apollonius and Christ that had been drawn in classical antiquity and even though he denied the legitimacy of the comparison his denial seems disingenuous. It is also possible that during Turnbull's travels on the continent he had read *Le Traité des trois imposteurs,* either as a clandestine manuscript or in the form published in *La Vie et L'Esprit de Spinosa* ([The Hague], 1719). In the *Traité* Moses, Christ, and Muhammad are depicted as men who exploited fear and ignorance in order to dupe their followers.

justly considered as one continued proof of the general pretension to a mission: as one continued proof that, as he asserted, all power was given unto him of GOD who sent him.* For by his works he shewed, that he had an universal command of nature: a power that nothing could controul.† The seas, the winds, all the elements, every thing above or below obeyed his all-commanding voice. His works therefore in this case are still proper adequate samples.

In fine, a divine mission can be nothing else, but a certain degree of power or knowledge given of GOD; or ordered by GOD to be exerted for a certain end: such as the "ascertaining the truth of certain doctrines." And therefore samples or experiments of power and knowledge analogous to the doctrines preached: or to the power and knowledge claimed; and proportioned likewise in quantity or number; are a proper proof of a divine mission; if power or knowledge can in any case be evidenced by samples, or experiments. And sure, as has been said, there can be no other way of shewing power, or knowledge, but by giving certain specimens of it.

But to leave no room for doubt or scepticism, let us enquire yet more particularly what is necessary to prove a mission. <26>

And when one pretends to a mission, there are three things requisite to compleat his credentials. "The doctrines he teaches must be of importance; such as it concerns mankind much to be assured of; and have an evident connexion with our peace and happiness, and tendency to promote virtue and piety."

And such certainly are the doctrines which JESUS CHRIST taught: they are such as the wise in all ages have earnestly wished to be assured of by a proper evidence. They are, in one word, the only doctrines that have any connexion with virtue and piety;‡ or the happiness of mankind, which natural reason is in the dark about, and cannot ascertain beyond all doubt.

"Next the missionary must behave himself in such a manner, as that we may have sufficient reason, from his conduct, to trust and put full confidence in him."

---

* Mark iv. 39, &c. [Turnbull's reference makes little sense.]
† Ibid. vi. 11. [Matthew 8.26; Mark 4.39; Luke 8.24.]
‡ *Well might our Saviour say,* That such who know the will of GOD, and do it; must own and acknowledge his doctrines to be of GOD. [John 7.16–17.]

And such certainly was the whole of our SAVIOUR's conduct and behaviour; that either we may safely rely upon his word, and believe in his
honesty; or no marks, no samples of goodness, sincerity, and faithfulness,
are sufficient to create trust.

"Last of all, the pretended missionary must give a proper and full evidence, that he really is possessed of any degree of power he claims; and of
the knowledge that is necessa-<27>ry to render him capable of ascertaining
these doctrines to us which he asserts and teaches."

And have we not already found that he gave proper and adequate samples
of the power he claimed by his doctrines? and do not all his works shew
that universal knowledge of nature, and the government of the world;
which is sufficient to put his capacity to teach us the doctrines he taught
beyond all controversy? Who is sufficient to instruct us, if he who gave
samples of such extraordinary knowledge was not? What greater degree of
knowledge can we require in an instructor; or what other samples of the
knowledge requisite to instruct us? consider him as pretending to come
from GOD, to tell us that he had power given unto him of GOD *to raise
the dead, to forgive sins,** and to make the virtuous happy, and the wicked
miserable, in the life to come. And as this was indeed his pretension; so we
have already seen that his works were proper and proportioned samples of
his right to claim such power. Consider him as pretending to come from
GOD, to teach mankind that there will be a future state, and a resurrection
of the dead; and that those who repent and reform their lives, will be forgiven and made happy in a future life; but that the impenitent, and such
as continue to lead vitious and disorderly lives, will be punished in that
after-life. And still his works are proper and adequate experiments, that he
had the knowledge requisite to give us this information. For he shewed that
the dead could be raised; that he knew how to raise the dead; and could
<28> actually raise them; that he could make happy or miserable in any
degree; that he could forgive sins; or give full and compleat evidence when
sins were forgiven; because he could deliver those whose sins he pronounced
forgiven, from any sorts of pains or miseries, to which sin renders obnoxious. In like manner he proffers assistance to the virtuous; and at the same

* John v. 19, &c. Matth. xi. 27. [John 5.21; Matthew 9.6.]

time shewed his ability to confer every good quality when at a distance, as well as when present.

To conclude, if we abstract from the history of our SAVIOUR, and inquire with our selves what would be a full and compleat evidence of a mission from GOD to teach; it is not difficult to find out what the evidence must be. For we know what doctrines of importance, with regard to GOD and ourselves, natural reason is not able to satisfy us fully about.

We have so much knowledge of GOD, as to be able to determine what doctrines he would instruct us in, by an extraordinary missionary; if he should ever condescend to teach us in that manner. These very doctrines to be sure, which have a connexion with virtue and piety, that natural reason is not able to deduce certainly from any principles; and such are the doctrines which JESUS CHRIST taught. And as for what regards testimony, we all know the evidence that is requisite to render it credible and worthy of our reception. All, to be sure, that can be demanded is, that there be good ground to trust our informer as to his honesty; and next, that he give sufficient samples of the kind of knowledge he pretends to, or that is necessary in order to his giving us such and such information: <29> samples analogous in kind, and proportioned to the degree of knowledge he claims, by pretending to inform us of certain truths. We must reason concerning the proper credentials, or evidence of testimony, in every case the same way: in this just as in any other.

Having therefore shewed that our SAVIOUR gave samples of his sincerity and honest design; and at the same time adequate samples of the power and knowledge he pretended to; it follows necessarily, that there is all the reason in the world to believe in him, and give him full credit.

SECTION IX

And is this then, perhaps you'll say, the whole of Christianity? Yes it is; and a noble and perfect system indeed it is, containing all the encouragements that can be thought of, or desired, to virtue, piety, and goodness, the love of GOD and our fellow-creatures; which common reason sufficiently tells us, if we would but hearken to its dictates, is the whole duty of man.

These doctrines above explained are clearly insisted upon by our SAV-

IOUR and his Apostles.* These doctrines are ever and ever insisted upon by
them, as the chief; as the only doctrines of consequence they had to instruct
us in.[†] These doctrines <30> are ever inculcated by them, as motives to the
practice of virtue. These are the doctrines the best of the ancient philosophers, would have rejoiced to have found sufficient evidence to believe.
And these doctrines being ascertained, we are fully instructed in every thing
that relates to virtue, or this life, or the life to come, that it concerns us to
know. Had I not then good reason to say in the beginning of this letter,
my friend, "That the doctrine of a future state is the sum of Christianity."
For the doctrines abovementioned are easily reducible to this one proposition, "That the vitious are to be punished in the life to come; and the
virtuous to be assisted in their serious endeavours here; and made perfect
in virtue and happiness hereafter." With this single additional circumstance, "That after our souls have been for some time separated from their
bodies, they are to be again embodied." There is nothing in the christian
doctrine that has not a relation to a future state, as its main end and scope.[‡]
And consequently to fight against Christianity, is to fight against a belief
the most chearing and comfortable; the most strong and powerful persuasive to a virtuous and good conversation.

There are several obscure places, especially in the epistles of the Apostles,
about the interpretation of which the learned Criticks and Divines have
been much divided in all the after-ages of Christianity. But that is argument
enough, <31> that Christians are not obliged to know their meaning. That
can never be said to be revealed, which is not made plain; or which remains
liable to various and uncertain interpretation. Our salvation cannot possibly depend upon that which it is difficult, not to say impossible, even for
much learning to determine. Not to mention that common sense and reason tells plainly and indisputably, that it is only virtue and goodness that
can recommend, or make acceptable to GOD, who is all virtue, all reason,

---

* John v. 2. —vi. 38, 44. —xiii. 44. —xiv. 33. Acts ii. 29. —iii. 26. —iv. 10. —x. 42.
—xviii. 30. 1 Cor. xv. [John 5.21; 6.26–59; 13.3, 19–20, 31–35; 14.1–31. Acts 2.29–36; 3.15,
20–26; 4.8–12; 10.34–43; 17.31. 1 Corinthians 15.1–58.]

  [†] *See the texts cited in the foregoing pages.*

  [‡] *The Apostles in all their discourses, and the Fathers in all their apologies, insist upon the
resurrection as the principal doctrine of Christianity: the great end and purpose of christian
preaching.*

all goodness. And indeed to imagine otherwise, is to suppose that the most useful quality is not the most valuable: or that GOD, who is infinite wisdom, doth not delight most in that which is of all other qualities the most excellent and deserving.*

We are called by JESUS CHRIST to believe in him: that is, to believe he really had a mission to inculcate virtue by these doctrines he taught; and really had the power he claimed by these doctrines: that thus believing in him we might fall in love with virtue, and seek earnestly for glory, honour, and immortality, by a sincere and firm adherence to virtue, in spite of all temptations and seducements. To believe in him is nothing else than to believe the authority he had to excite to virtue and piety by his doctrines; his power to forgive sins and raise the dead; and to assist and prosper our earnest aims in the pursuit and study of virtue. And this faith can be of no value or merit, unless it <32> produces good fruits; unless the end of his teaching is gained, which is to perswade to live a natural, manly, and virtuous life; in every circumstance to behave as becometh a thinking, reasonable being; to love GOD; and, like him, to delight in doing good. Without such works faith is dead.†

A great many questions are asked and disputed, about the state of those who have not heard of CHRIST. But the answer to them all is obvious. Those who have not heard of CHRIST, cannot believe: but those have yet a law within themselves, teaching them their duty; the duty CHRIST taught; the whole duty of man.‡

That the doctrine of CHRIST however is not more generally known throughout the world, is the fault of Christians, who take not the right method to propagate it; but have, the greater part, ever done their utmost, either foolishly or wickedly, to marr its progress. The Christian Religion can only be propagated in the rational way of argument and persuasion; and it is the integrity and purity of the lives of professing christians; and their moderation and humanity towards unbelievers, that ever will have the

---

* *If there is a* GOD; *and that there is, all nature cries aloud, he must delight in virtue. Virtue is the perfection of the human nature.*

† James iii. 20. [James 2.17.]

‡ *This is the Apostle* Paul's *account of the matter,* Rom. ii. [See especially Romans 2.13–15.]

greatest influence to recommend Christianity, and promote the belief and love of it. The temper and spirit which true and genuine Christianity inspires, is a spirit of meekness and gentleness, charity and compassion; *slow to wrath; ready to forgive; prompt to good works.** And <33> where this temper is not found, there is not the same spirit that was in CHRIST and his Apostles; nor the disposition that only can render agreeable to GOD who sent him into the world to teach humility, and benevolence, and to reprove every vitious affection; to exemplify all the moral virtues in his life and conduct; as well as to give the strongest inducements to the practice of them by his doctrines.

SECTION X

But by this time, my friend, I am afraid you begin to dread a sermon. And therefore to return to the argument:

If it is allowed, as it must certainly be, that the doctrines so often repeated are the chief doctrines of Christianity; Christianity carries the same evidence along with it, that any doctrine does, which is confirmed by the plainest, the most proper, or analogous experiments.

"The works of JESUS CHRIST considered as samples of the power he claimed, are not *Disperates,* with regard to his doctrines, as *Spinosa* alledges miracles must be with regard to doctrines."[7]

It is true, miracles, when considered in a general abstract view, do not appear to have any relation to doctrines: nothing at first sight can seem more distinct or remote the one from the other. And therefore it is commonly objected against the proof offered from miracles: what can miracles have to do in the case; miracles <34> may prove power; but what is that to the truth of doctrines? But take the doctrines and the works of CHRIST, and compare them together; and the relation and connexion is obvious. Samples of power to raise the dead, prove the power to raise the dead: and samples

---

* James iv. 1 Cor. xiii. [James 3.]

7. Benedict de Spinoza, *Theological-Political Treatise,* edited by Jonathan Israel, translated by Michael Silverthorne and Jonathan Israel (Cambridge, 2007), chap. 6, "On Miracles." Turnbull restates his criticism of Spinoza in *The Principles of Moral and Christian Philosophy,* edited by Alexander Broadie, 2 vols. (Indianapolis, 2005), II:903–4.

of power to make happy, prove the power to make happy: in the same way that samples of gravity prove gravity; or samples of elasticity prove elasticity; or that samples of skill in any sort, prove skill of that sort. There is the same relation, in one word, betwixt the doctrines of JESUS CHRIST and his works, that there is betwixt any experiment, and the conclusion that naturally follows from it.

"Nor are the works of JESUS CHRIST arguments *ad ignorantiam,* (as the same author says) miracles must ever be."[8] For the works of JESUS CHRIST, however much above our comprehension, bear a plain relation to his doctrines; and it is only the truth of the facts or samples, and their relation to the doctrine, that we are concerned to understand. That can never be said to be a proof *ad ignorantiam,* the connexion of which with the thing proved, or the conclusion inferred, is clearly perceived.

The works of JESUS CHRIST are not arguments of power, we know not what: they are arguments of the very power he pretended to; because samples of that very power. Arguments of his power to raise the dead; forgive sins; make happy or miserable. Arguments of an universal knowledge of nature; and unlimited authority over all things; arguments, in short, <35> of the whole of his pretension; because samples of all he pretended to.

Tho' we understand not the nature of that power which raises the dead; tho' the raising the dead be a work above our ability and comprehension; yet a sample of power to raise the dead, proves that power; and the connexion betwixt the sample and the power pretended to is not above our comprehension, but is easily understood. Attraction, say all the philosophers, is above our comprehension: they cannot explain how bodies attract: but experience or samples certainly prove that there is attraction. And proper experiments or samples, must equally prove the power of raising the dead, tho' we do not understand, or cannot explain, that power.

But because there is so much controversy about that common distinction betwixt things above our reason, and things contrary to our reason, it may not be amiss, on this occasion to say something about it.[9]

8. Spinoza, *Theological-Political Treatise,* esp. pp. 81–82, 84.
9. A distinction made popular by, but not original with, [Robert Boyle], *Some Con-*

And an example taken from natural philosophy will soon clear the matter: Attraction can only be known by experience, and samples abundantly prove it. But it is above our reason or comprehension? What is the meaning of that? why it is only to say, that a thousand questions may be ask'd about it, to which no answer can be given; because we know not enough about it, to answer them. We know that it is; and some of the laws according to which it produces its effects: And that is all we know of it. And our not being able to give satisfying answers to <36> other questions, that may be asked about it, only proves that there is a great deal relating to it, we do not know.

In the same manner a thousand questions may be ask'd about raising the dead, which we can't answer. A sample however proves the possibility: and many samples as certainly prove the power to raise the dead; as samples of attraction prove attraction. Nor indeed can the power of raising the dead, be said to be above our comprehension in any sense, that attraction, and twenty other properties of bodies, may not be said to be above our comprehension. What we clearly see to be absurd, we clearly see to be so; but there is a great difference betwixt seeing a thing to be absurd, and not knowing every thing that belongs to it; or not being able to answer every question that may be asked concerning it. Some seem however to confound insolvable questions about a truth, with insolvable or invincible objections against a truth. And because there may be difficult, nay unanswerable, questions relating to a known truth; maintain there may be insolvable objections against a known truth. But an insolvable objection against a truth, is an argument *ad absurdum* against a truth, or a proof that a known truth cannot possibly be true.* Those who delight in sophistry and grubbing, may

---

siderations about the Reconcileableness of Reason and Religion (London, 1675); [Robert Boyle], *A Discourse of Things above Reason. Inquiring whether a Philosopher should admit there are any such* (London, 1681); [Robert Boyle], *The Christian Virtuoso: Shewing, that by being addicted to Experimental Philosophy, a Man is rather Assisted, than Indisposed, to be a Good Christian. To which are Subjoyn'd, I. A Discourse about the Distinction, that represents some Things as Above Reason, but not Contrary to Reason. II. The first Chapters of a Discourse, Entituled, Greatness of Mind promoted by Christianity* ([London], 1690); Locke, *Essay,* IV.xvii.23 and IV.xviii.7–11.

* *It is worth while to read a discourse of Mr* Leibnitz, de Fide & Ratione, *in which this*

perplex the ignorant or incautious: and no science has escaped this puzzling, perplexing art. But by a fatal calamity, none has suffer'd more than Divinity. Yet when the artful terms of the schools, intro-<37>duced on purpose to darken and embroil the clearest truths, and to be an everlasting source of controversy and wrangling; when all artful, captious, equivocal terms are thrown aside; and truths are expressed in common, simple, plain language, the sophistry is easily seen thro', and its mists evanish.*

This way of considering the works of JESUS CHRIST, as samples of his doctrines, makes the connexion betwixt his works and his doctrines obvious to every capacity. Because we all reason in this way every day, about a thousand different things: thus the meanest labourer of the ground, or poorest mechanick, must argue frequently: we judge of friends and enemies by samples; by samples and experiments, in short, almost all our affairs in life are regulated. And therefore in this way of handling the question concerning the connexion betwixt the works and the doctrines of our SAVIOUR, I can't be blamed for having talked so much of miracles hitherto, without giving a definition of them. Because taking the miracles of JESUS CHRIST in this view, nothing more is necessary than to consider them as certain works that shewed such and such power.

It does not belong in the least, to the question, whether these works are above, or contrary to, the established laws of nature; whether superior to human power, as they plainly are; or whether above the power of all created <38> agents. But only what they were; and what power they were samples or experiments of. And of this any body may judge; the relation and connexion is so conspicuous and glaring.

The only thing I fear, my friend, is, that you think I have been too te-

---

question is handled. [Turnbull refers to G. W. Leibniz's "Preliminary Dissertation on the Conformity of Faith with Reason" in *Theodicy: Essays on the Goodness of God, the Freedom of Man, and the Origin of Evil,* edited by Austin Farrer, translated by E. M. Huggard (La Salle, Ill., 1988), pp. 73–122. The *Theodicy* was first published as *Essais de Theodicée sur la bonté de Dieu, la liberté de l'homme, et l'origine du mal* (Amsterdam, 1710). Turnbull refers to a subsequent Latin translation: *Godefridi Guilielmi Leibnitii tentamina Theodicaeae de bonitate Dei libertate hominis et origine mali* (Frankfurt, 1719).]

* *Pray look into an incomparable Dissertation by* Werinfelsius, *Professor of Theology at* Basil, de Logomachiis Eruditorum. [Samuel Werenfels, *Dissertationiis de logomachiis eruditorum,* in *Opuscula theologica, philosophica, et philologica* (Basil, 1718), pp. 449–576.]

dious; and have taken too much pains to make a connexion evident, that is obvious at first sight. For what can be more clear than what I have been so long insisting upon? "That he who shews by experiments and samples, that he has a certain degree of power; really shews that he has that power. And that he who shews by a long train of honesty and goodness, that he is good, and honest, and worthy of trust; really shews that he is good, and honest, and worthy of trust."

Nor would I have dwelt so long upon this argument; had ever the works of our Saviour been considered in this light, by any writer upon the subject that I have seen. <39>

Part III

I would not however be understood, my friend, as if there was no other way of reasoning from the works of Jesus Christ, to prove the truth of the religion he taught. On the contrary, there is another argument which to me seems beyond all exception. It runs thus:

"A great number of works that shew a power superior to human power, and to the established laws of nature which limit human power; when produced by a preacher of good doctrines, as signs of the divine approbation; upon a solemn appeal to God for these signs of his approbation: are the most natural signs of the divine approbation we can conceive.

"And it is inconsistent with the idea of the divine wisdom, and with the order that must obtain in the moral, as well as the natural world; in consequence of a divine providence; to suppose that such works could be produced by an impostor. For in that case the most likely and natural tokens of divine approbation, we can form any notion of, <40> would accompany a presumptive, deceiving pretender; and thus a cheat would be attended with the natural and probable marks of truth."

This argument, I think, must hold good; because it is not so difficult a matter to determine what works shew a power superior to human power, and the laws of nature. Experience teaches clearly certain established uniform laws of nature which we cannot controul, alter, or suspend. "To raise the dead; and cure diseases by a word of our mouth, are, for example, evidently works of that *kind.*"

And tho' we know not the spheres of activity of other beings; the laws which limit their faculties: nor, in one word, what degrees of power created beings, superior to mankind may possess; and consequently know not what works God alone can produce: yet knowing what works are superior to human power; and that these works are wrought by a preacher of good doctrines, as signs of the divine approbation, upon a solemn appeal to the divine approbation; we must conclude, that such a preacher really has the divine mission he pretends to. Or we must say, that such works produced in such a manner, are not proper signs of the divine approbation. And at the same time it is certainly impossible to conceive more likely signs of the divine approbation; or how indeed the divine approbation can possibly shew itself, but by such signs upon an appeal to GOD by the preacher for his approbation.

It is justly added to this reasoning, by way of a corroborative adjunct, that a being of a malig-<41>nant disposition, would never exert its power to preach and excite to virtue and piety; nor one of a good disposition to deceive, and thus our SAVIOUR himself argues concerning his doctrine and mission.*

But this argument has been so fully and elegantly displayed in all its force, by several authors, (Dr *Samuel Clarke*† particularly, and the Bishop of *Salisbury*)‡ that there is no occasion for dwelling longer upon it. Only because I fancy the considering the works of JESUS CHRIST as samples, adds no inconsiderable force to it; it may not be improper, to take a short view of it in all its strength, when this additional consideration is taken into the reckoning. That thus we may have a full view how far the considering the works of CHRIST as samples reaches.

SECTION II

It consists then of two propositions to be examined separately.

"The moral world would be irregular and disorderly; if things were not so ordered, that the most natural and likely signs or marks of the divine mission and approbation, should never accompany an impostor."

---

* Mark iii. 25, &c. [Mark 3.22–30.]

† *Demonstration of the Being,* &c. Part II. [Clarke, *Discourse,* pp. 369–86.]

‡ *See* Hoadley's *Tracts. See* Grotius de Veritate, *&c.* [Benjamin Hoadly, "A Letter to the Reverend Mr. Fleetwood. Occasion'd by his Essay on Miracles," in *Several Tracts formerly Published: Now collected into One Volume* (London, 1715), pp. 1–31; Hugo Grotius, *The Truth of the Christian Religion. With Jean Le Clerc's Notes and Additions,* translated by John Clarke and edited with an introduction by Maria Rosa Antognazza (Indianapolis, 2012), pp. 100–102.]

"But signs of power superior to human power, which are proper and adequate sam-<42>ples, of the power claimed as a divine messenger, when produced in great numbers and unfailingly, by a preacher of doctrines in themselves good and probable; as signs of the divine mission and approbation, are the most natural and likely signs we can conceive of the divine mission and approbation."

If these two propositions are true it must follow, because such were the works of CHRIST, that he is not an impostor, but really sent of GOD.

SECTION III

The idea of order, wisdom, and providence, necessarily infers the truth of the first: "That the proper marks of the divine approbation cannot accompany an impostor." For what could produce greater confusion or disorder in the moral world, than the contrary permission. And on the other hand, the restraint upon the powers and faculties of beings superior to man, which such oeconomy in the government of intelligent agents supposes, cannot possibly have any bad effect. And, in one word, we must either conclude, that there is such a restraint, and such a law in the government of the moral world: or we must suppose it impossible for GOD, in consequence of his own administration, to instruct mankind by a mission. 'Tis to no purpose to say, that we can't reason about what may, or may not be permitted, because sins and errors of the grossest kinds are permitted. For there is a manifest difference betwixt permitting free agents to mis-<43>use their liberty, and commit sins, which they themselves, and all other intelligent beings, know to be sins; or permitting errors to prevail, which all rational beings may clearly see to be such; who will but open their eyes, to consider and examine them: And permitting the criterions and marks of truth to be confounded with those of falsehood; the most likely and natural signs and tokens of the divine mission, and approbation to accompany and attest an impostor. In the one case, free agents are not restrained by an overpowering preternatural force, from exerting their natural powers and faculties in a free choice or election. But sin and vice remain essentially and immutably distinguishable. In the other, truth and error are confounded; imposture and presumptuous falsehood carries away with it the proper marks of the divine authority and approbation. And can we suppose GOD to look on inactive, and see his authority trifled with, nay trampled upon, and prostituted.

In fine observe the laws in the natural world, and the order and harmony that results from the steady, uniform observance of them; and judge whether it is not likely, that equal order and regularity must prevail in the moral. But how can it be so, if it is not an established law in the moral world, that whatever the powers of any beings are, the evidences of truth should never accompany an impostor! Balance the inconveniencies that must follow, if there was no such rule; with the consequences of such a rule; and it will be no difficult matter to see on which side the probability lies. <44>

But that there is such a law, is a plain consequence from the divine veracity. "And that GOD is truth, all nature cries aloud."

'Tis the full and perfect knowledge of truth, order, and beauty; together with the unchangeable love of it; and power incontroulable to execute his design, that render a being all perfect. And because the whole of things, as far as we can trace it, is an uniform, consistent system, in which truth, harmony, and proportion, are exactly observed; and in which all works towards the general good; justly may we conclude, that the author of it is a GOD of truth and order; infinitely wise and good; as well as almighty. And that the further we are able to pry into his government, by all our searching, the more we shall be charmed with its beauty, goodness, and perfection. And to suppose GOD acting inconsistently, or departing from truth and order: infinite truth and wisdom having recourse to chicanery and fraud; and acting the impostor; is a contradiction in terms. And what can possibly be called acting contrary to truth; or using fraudulent, deceitful measures; if giving all the marks of approbation, favour, and protection, to a *lying deceiver,* that can be given to a *Divine Mission,* is not really so? <45>

SECTION IV

"That works which shew a power superiour to that of mankind; and to the established laws of nature; and are samples of the very power claimed; when produced by a preacher of good and wholesome doctrines to prove his mission; are proper signs of a divine mission, is likewise certain."

Mankind in all ages hath had that notion; that if GOD did ever reveal himself; or shew his approbation of any extraordinary teacher, it would be by such signs of power as above described. *That is, by miracles.** And therefore if an argument can be fetch'd in any case, from the universal consent and opinion of mankind, it may in this.

Besides, if a being preaches good doctrines, and gives all evidences of piety and sincerity, there can be no ground to suspect such a being of claiming a mission, that he is not really invested with. Is it probable, that any being of an order superior to mankind, would run the risque of being baffled in his pretension to a divine mission? And every such being must necessarily be supposed to know, as well as we, that GOD hath power supreme, infinitely above <46> all created power: And that he can easily oppose and ruin such a claim: which if it is not true, such a being must likewise very well know to be most presumptive and impious. Is it not then more likely that any being who can be supposed to teach good doctrines; and produce extraordinary works to confirm them; if he had no mission, would pretend to none; but meerly seek his own honour and glory, by the works he wrought and the doctrines he taught? And thus, if I am not mistaken, our SAVIOUR himself reasons to prove his mission. "I came not, *saith he,* to seek mine own honour; but the glory of him who sent me." [10]

And therefore so far am I from thinking, that the divine mission and approbation is not proved, if claimed, when all the circumstances already described concur: that is, when the doctrines are good in their tendency; the preacher gives indisputable evidence of sincerity and good intention; the signs shew power superior to human power, and to the laws of nature; and are samples of the power claimed and the doctrines asserted; that on the contrary, I should rather imagine, that the only small ground of sus-

---

* *This is evident from the conduct of antient politicians, who to give the more authority to their laws and institutions, pretended to inspiration; or an extraordinary intercourse with some revered Deity, or heavenly being,* &c. [Turnbull echoes the argument of Book I, Chapter 11 of Niccolò Machiavelli's *Discourses on the First Decade of Titus Livius;* see also above, pp. 85–86.]

10. A paraphrase of, for example, John 8.50 and 8.54.

picion, in case of such teaching, would be, if a divine mission was not claimed; and if the preacher ascribed all to his own generosity and benevolence towards mankind, without pretending to any divine order or mission. And yet even in that case there would be no sufficient reason to reject such instruction. Because samples of power necessarily prove that power of which they are samples: and marks of sincerity must needs be deemed marks of sincerity. And if a teacher has all the power and knowledge that is <47> requisite, in order to the giving us certain information: and at the same time gives sufficient evidence of his honesty and candor; there can be no ground to mistrust him.

But further, if the doctrines preached are not consistent with our natural notions of GOD and virtue; or if the conduct of the preacher is not suitable to the claim of a divine mission; whatever the works are, we have good reason to conclude, that there is no mission. In that case the cheat is manifest. Common sense may easily see through the mask, and discern the imposture.

And if there is no criterion, no certain mark neither in the doctrines themselves, nor the works, nor the behaviour of the preacher, by which the falshood of the claim can be known: GOD being superior to all created agents, can easily refute and baffle the daring, impudent pretender.

And therefore when the conduct of the preacher, and the doctrines themselves are in every respect consistent with our justest notions of GOD and virtue; signs of power superior to the laws of nature, which are samples of the power claimed, and of the doctrines taught; must be held as signs of the divine approbation, to prove which they are produced without any controul. Such works are justly assignable, if not to the immediate hand and operation of GOD himself, at least to his order and mission. Nor can any shadow of reason be alleged why they are not: no circumstance being wanting in them that could render any works more so. At least <48> it must be said, that in such a case GOD refuses not his approbation, because he does not check or contradict the pretender. And in such circumstances we may safely argue, "That approbation not refused is given": for it is only the refusal by thwarting or opposing the pretender, that can evidence its not being granted. Nay, when these very signs of supernatural power, which GOD is called upon by the preacher to produce, or allow to be produced, to vouch his authority and mission, are actually produced; GOD, by these signs, if they are likewise samples of the very power claimed, declares, speaks aloud, as it were, his consent and approbation. He gives the properest samples and tokens of it, that we are able to form any notion of.

Because it is by certain supernatural appearances or signs, that the divine mission must be declared and sealed. And to us who know not the boundaries of created power, "Any supernatural effects which have all the characteristicks again and again defined, are as fit and proper signs of the divine mission, as any supernatural signs whatever can be." They have all the marks and characters of such signs that can be required, or indeed conceived.

Such appearances, or works, demonstrate the approbation of some being superior to man, and to the laws of nature. They are marks of such an approbation, because they are marks and samples of such a power. The question therefore is only, whether they are marks of the divine approbation. And they are marks and samples of it, because GOD is appealed to; his mission and approbation is claimed; and the <49> works are samples of all the power claimed as GOD's messenger, and of all the doctrines taught.

And a divine mission can only be ascertained by supernatural effects produced upon such an appeal; which are adequate samples of all the power claimed. For in reality, the only thing that can make any difference as to the fitness or unfitness of supernatural effects, produced without any controul or opposition, to vouch the divine approbation, is the relation or affinity, more or less, which they have to the doctrines preached, and the particular kind of power or knowledge claimed by the pretended mission. And therefore this was what always seemed to me of chief account, with regard to the signs of power, when a divine mission is claimed: the only quality indeed that is requisite to render supernatural effects proper proofs and signs of the divine approbation and mission; viz. "That the signs produced to prove a mission, have a plain connexion with the doctrines taught; and be samples of the very power and knowledge claimed as a missionary from GOD." And I am indeed surprized, that this consideration hath never been called into the reckoning; in making up the proper evidence of a divine mission to teach and confirm certain doctrines.

If the works were not of that kind and nature; one might justly call the claim in question; and ask; "But why no samples of the very power and knowledge claimed? Why signs of all supernatural power, except that particular kind of it, which the very mission <50> itself specially announces?" Such a defect in the signs offered would indeed be no slight ground of doubt and suspicion: it being easy to GOD to enable his messenger to give proper analogous samples of the power and knowledge he pretends to particularly, as sent by him to teach and confirm certain doctrines: and natural and reasonable to think, that it was the power and knowledge specified by the doctrines, that ought to be particularly exemplified by proper signs and experiments. Thus, for example, if a preacher of the resurrection from the dead, should give ever so many proofs of extraordinary supernatural power; but did not raise the dead; would there not be good reason to ask, But why no samples of this power to raise the dead? would it not be natural and reasonable to expect, that this would be the power he would principally choose, to exemplify by samples and experiments. The reasoning will hold equally good, with regard to any other doctrines that may be taught by a pretended messenger from GOD, and the works he produces to testify the truth of his mission and doctrines.

But when the extraordinary works shew all the power and knowledge that is claimed by the mission; all is proved by experiment that is claimed: when the works are samples or experiments of the doctrines themselves, all is confirmed by experiments and samples that is asserted. And consequently the whole claim is sufficiently vouched and exemplified, Or samples of power and knowledge are not a proper evidence of power and knowledge. That is, samples of a certain quality, are not samples of that quality. <51>

In one word, let any one try with himself, if he can possibly devise any other tokens, or signs, by which GOD can declare his mission and approbation of a preacher, besides supernatural effects produced to testify such a mission upon an appeal to GOD, for these very signs of his mission and approbation, which are signs and samples of all the power and knowledge claimed as a missionary, and of all the doctrines taught as such, and he will soon be convinced, "That such signs are indeed the only language by which GOD can converse, or have any communication with us mortals. The only marks or tokens by which he can manifest his will and authority. That such works are indeed, in the nature of things, proper samples or experiments

of the divine approbation; or, that they have all the properties and characters, that can render supernatural effects such experiments or samples.
And consequently that, according to the natural order, contexture, and language of things, and our common, natural, and necessary way of reasoning
from samples and experiments in every other case, they must be referred to
that end, and held as such." Any thing that is taught us in this manner,
concerning the order and connexion of things, is taught us in the very way
that we learn every thing we know concerning the order and connexion of
things in nature; that is, by specimen or experiment. <52>

SECTION V

When the several branches of this argument are laid together, it shortly
amounts to this:

If a preacher of doctrines in themselves probable; or at least not inconsistent with our justest ideas of GOD and virtue, to prove his divine mission,
not only in the general works samples of extraordinary supernatural power;
but also gives particular samples of every doctrine he teaches, and of every
particular kind of power or knowledge he claims, as a teacher sent of GOD;
and all this upon an appeal to GOD that he was indeed sent of him; and
had power from him to work such signs to shew the divine approbation;
the mission is certainly proved beyond all controversy. Or a mission may
be pretended to; and the most likely signs of it, we can form any notion
of, may accompany an impostor without any opposition or controul: That
is to say, a divine mission cannot be proved at all; whatever signs of extraordinary power are given to establish and confirm the pretension to it;
in so great uncertainty are we about the *Regularity* or *Irregularity* of the
divine conduct. Or in other words it is to say; That it is impossible for GOD
to instruct mankind by a mission; because such are the powers he hath given
to created agents; or rather such is his administration, that no certain marks
can be given of it. He hath not reserved to himself any sure unquestionable
signs and tokens, by <53> which he can make his will and pleasure known.
He allows the proper, natural marks and credentials of his mission to be so
abused and prostituted, that in reality we can never be certain, when there
is a divine mission, or not; even tho' all the conceivable signs, samples, or

experiments of it are given that can possibly, in the nature of things, be given. And that is indeed to suppose GOD strangely limited; nay embarrassed in consequence of his own government of the world: to suppose a government which we can hardly reconcile with our ideas of wisdom, order, and regularity; or with what we know of the divine providence in the natural or moral world.

Or to take the argument in another view, it is to say, That when all the power and knowledge that is claimed by the pretended mission, is proved by experiments analogous in kind, and proportioned in quantity and moment; all is not proved that is claimed. That when all the doctrines preached, are shewn to be true by proper and adequate samples and experiments of their truth; all that is taught is not proved. And that therefore there is something more necessary to prove a conclusion, than experiments of that conclusion.

But to set this reasoning yet, if possible, in a stronger light; let us suppose it possible that GOD may connive at a false pretension to a mission, and suffer it to be vouched by the most proper marks and tokens of a mission, for reasons incomprehensible to us; consistently however with his truth and goodness in the government of the whole. And this may be, is <54> all that ever was, or indeed can be said in opposition to the former reasoning from the divine veracity. Supposing therefore this possibility, let us see how the argument will stand upon that footing. All that can be meant by such a *Possibility*, is that for what we know it may not be *inconsistent* with the good of the whole, to allow such and such credentials to accompany an impostor. And in whatever case it can only be said, for what we know a thing may not be inconsistent; it may be said on the other hand with equal reason; for what we know it may not be consistent. Such a possibility amounts to no more than the not being able to determine repugnance or non-repugnance. But in the nature of the thing, there must be one or other. And therefore when neither the repugnance nor the consistency is capable of proof; the one *may be,* balances the other *may be:* and no regard is to be had to either, in judging of what really happens. Thus then in the present case, supposing neither the consistency nor the inconsistency determinable; the argument from real appearances must run thus: "The doctrines are not inconsistent with our justest notions of GOD and virtue, but on the contrary in themselves probable. The conduct of the preacher is in every respect suitable to the pretension of a divine mission. And the works are such in every respect as can possibly be required to vouch a mission; such in every article and circumstance as GOD would produce, or order to be produced, to shew his approbation, in case of a divine mission; according to all the ideas we are able to frame of proper and fit credentials to testify a mission. The works are al-<55>so proper and analogous samples of all the power and knowledge claimed by the pretended mission; or necessary to prove the truth of the doctrines taught by the missionary." And therefore according to all appearances there is indeed a mission; there is all the proof of the mission and of the doctrines that the nature of the thing admits: and more could not possibly be done to vouch and ascertain a mission, or to establish and confirm the doctrines of the missionary. And not to judge according to appearances; or according to the natural tendency and connexion of things; upon the account of a meer *may be* counterpoised by a contrary *may be;* would certainly be absurd, and contrary to our way of reasoning in every other case.

But perhaps, the comparing this argument with another reasoning somewhat of a kind, may help not a little to clear the matter.

That in nature GOD does not multiply causes; but works always in the same uniform way; producing similar effects by similar causes, is a maxim in natural philosophy justly thought to be evident of itself; and to stand in no need of demonstration.[11] Simplicity and uniformity are so inseparable from wisdom according to all our ideas of wisdom and perfect working. And that GOD, to serve any other purpose whatsoever; will not allow the signs and tokens of his approbation to be produced if he does not approve, seems to me as clear; and to stand as little in need of demonstration. For darkness is not more contrary to light, than encouraging and confirming error and falshood <56> is repugnant to truth and wisdom; if there is any certainty at all in our clearest moral ideas. And what can be called encouraging error and imposture, if giving all the marks and signs of favour, coun-

---

11. Turnbull alludes to the first of Isaac Newton's "Rules for the Study of Natural Philosophy"; see Isaac Newton, *The Principia: Mathematical Principles of Natural Philosophy,* edited by I. Bernard Cohen and translated by I. Bernard Cohen, Anne Whitman, and Julia Budenz (Berkeley, Los Angeles, and London, 1999), p. 794.

tenance, and protection, to a false pretence, that can be given to a real mission, is not so?

But supposing it quite indeterminable, whether GOD may consistently with his wisdom in the government of the whole, multiply causes and produce like effects by very different causes; yet who would doubt, upon the account of that *may be;* that indeterminableness of consistency or inconsistency; to refer all like effects to the same known familiar cause, which is found to be universal as far as our examination can reach? 'Tis but judging according to appearances; and according to the nature of things, to refer all like appearances to the same known cause. And to conclude otherwise would be to judge contrary to all we see and know; contrary to what nature itself points out to us; and calls upon us, as it were, to conclude.

In like manner in the other case, supposing the indeterminableness of the consistency, or inconsistency with divine wisdom and truth, of error's having all the marks of truth; or an impostor's being honoured with all the marks and credentials of a divine mission: yet it is but judging according to the nature of things, to conclude a divine mission, when all the marks of a divine mission that can be conceiv'd, or desired, concur: and to conclude doctrines true, of the truth of which all the proper and requisite experiments are given, that the nature of <57> the thing is capable of. And to conclude otherwise would be to judge contrary to all appearances; contrary to the plain language of the facts and experiments; contrary to what the very nature and context of the affair calls, as it were, upon us to conclude.

I find the old objection against taking the nature of the doctrines into the consideration, revived by a late author, and great stress laid upon it: *viz.* "That it involves in a circle."

"Suppose, *says that author,** one should ask me why I regard a doctrine to day as true, which formerly I considered as indifferent; I would answer,

---

* *I have only seen the treatise in* French, *and his words are:* "Supposez que l'on me demandât, pour quoi regardez vous aujourdhui comme vraye une doctrine qui vous paroissoit auparavant indifferente? Je répondrai parce qu'elle est confirmée par des miracles. Si l'on continue a me demander, pour quoi regardez vouz ces miracles comme divins? (car il faut qu'ils soient tels afin de pouvoir fournir une preuve) il me semble que ma réponse sera tout à fait liée avec les principes de Mr *Clarke,* si je dis, je les regarde comme

because it is confirmed by miracles? If it is asked, why I take the miracles to be divine, (for such they must be in order to furnish a proof) I think my answer would be suitable to Mr *Clarke*'s principles, if I should say, because the doctrine is possible, or at least indifferent."

But let any one read what Dr *Clarke* hath said, and he must be surprized how any one of so distinct, clear an apprehension as that author ap-<58>pears to be, could possibly mistake Dr *Clarke*'s reasoning so widely; considering how clearly that excellent author always writes. For what the Doctor says, is to this purpose: That if the doctrine is bad, we may be sure the miracles are not of GOD. But if the doctrine is not bad, but rather good, such however as cannot be proved from principles of reason to be true; then miracles may prove its truth. But how do miracles prove the truth of such a doctrine according to the Doctor? Not because the doctrine is indifferent; which would indeed be reasoning in a circle; but because the doctrine being of itself indifferent; if any one should pretend to a mission to prove its truth; and work miracles to attest his mission; was there indeed no mission such a claim would be controuled; such miracles would be overcome and baffled as the Magicians were by *Moses*. Miracles then prove an indifferent doctrine to be true, because there is reason to conclude, from the divine veracity, "That if the doctrines are in themselves indifferent, miracles without controul would not attend a false pretension to a mission from GOD for teaching these doctrines." [12]

That is the hinge upon which the Doctor's argument turns. And is it a circle to say, that a thing is in itself absurd and consequently incapable of being proved by testimony? Or on the other hand to say, a thing is not absurd, and therefore may be proved by testimony? Don't we reason in that manner every day, about pretended facts or events? we are only at pains to examine the qualities of the testimony offered to prove a thing; when it is in itself possible or not absurd. And is not the reasoning about <59> doctrines precisely parallel? when it is said, "Such and such doctrines are absurd,

---

de bonnes preuves parce que la doctrine est possible ou du moins indifferente." *Traité sur les miracles par Jacq. Seris, p.* 14. [Jacques Serces, *Traité sur les miracles* (Amsterdam, 1729).]

12. Clarke, *Discourse,* pp. 379–82.

their falshood is palpable and evident; and therefore they cannot be proved to be true by any testimony?" Or when it is said, on the other hand, That such and such doctrines are not absurd in themselves, and therefore may be proved to be true by testimony of a certain sort; or attended with such and such qualities; and miracles, or certain works are necessary to render the testimony such as may be relied upon? And why then is one of two reasonings, precisely parallel, condemned as a sophistical circle; and the other constantly admitted without any scruple?

In one word; doctrines which are in themselves consistent, that is, not absurd; tho' they cannot be demonstrated from internal principles, or from the nature of things; may however be proved to be true by proper testimony; by a sort of extrinsick evidence: and what renders a certain extrinsick evidence credible, when a mission from GOD is claimed, is the absurdity of supposing an extrinsick evidence, so and so qualified, to attend an imposture or falshood.[13] And there cannot possibly be any circle in such reasoning, unless in the general it is a circle to say, "There is no reason to call the possibility of the thing in question; and the testimony is unexceptionable; therefore the thing must be true." A way of reasoning the most common, the most useful; nay, necessary in all our affairs of the greatest concernment in life.

And as there is no ground to accuse the argument, from miracles, of a circle, when it is <60> taken upon this footing; so there is none to be sure to charge it with that failure, when the miracles are found to be samples of all the power and knowledge claimed, as a messenger from Heaven to instruct us; or samples and experiments of all the doctrines taught, and of all the authority pretended to as a Divine Teacher. And such I think I have already proved the works of JESUS CHRIST to be, with regard to his doctrine and his pretension.

13. Compare Antoine Arnauld and Pierre Nicole, *Logic or the Art of Thinking: Containing besides the Common Rules, Several New Observations Appropriate for Forming Judgment,* translated and edited by Jill Vance Buroker (Cambridge, 1996), p. 264. Religious apologists made a distinction between the internal and external evidences for the truth of Christianity. The internal evidence was provided by the "excellence" or intrinsic merits of Christian teachings, while the external evidences were drawn from prophecy, miracles, and historical testimony.

SECTION VI

It is said that "The great pretension of JESUS CHRIST was; That he was the Messias prophesied of to the Jews: And that miracles cannot prove prophecies to be fulfilled which were not fulfilled: and that it is only from the fulfillment of these predictions in JESUS CHRIST, that his pretension can be proved."

This is the topic of late much insisted upon. But to say the truth, this objection never mov'd me much; nor appeared to me of very great weight.

Because it is obvious, That prophecies cannot be plain and determinate, without producing great confusion and mischief in the world: But must ever run in a poetical, mystic, figurative, obscure stile; liable to various and uncertain interpretation before the event, and even after the event: unless some other circumstances concur to evince the fulfillment. <61>

And this is the case with regard to the antient predictions of the Jewish Messias. They are, as prophecies must necessarily be, in an obscure, figurative, mystic stile. But when we compare the character of JESUS CHRIST, and the circumstances that attended his appearance in the world, with these obscure prophecies, we see these prophecies can be applied to him: and something else renders the fulfillment of them in him indisputable; the mighty works he wrought;* together with his moral character. For he applies them to himself, claims the character of the Messias prophesied of; and at the same time shewed by his works, and the whole of his conduct, that we had sufficent reason to trust him.

If the prophecies could not be applied to him in any tolerable consistent sense; that would indeed be a considerable difficulty, with regard to his pretension. But if they can be applied to him, as clearly as the nature of prophecy admits, and can be applied to nothing else, all circumstances taken in, so consistently, and fully: his applying them to himself is enough, considering what he did to confirm this application. In fine, the only question about this pretension to the predicted Messiaship is, whether from the doctrine, the life, the works of our SAVIOUR, there is not reason to trust

---

* *Observe only the answer our* SAVIOUR *gives to St* John'*s message from prison,* Matth. xi. 2, &c. [Matthew 11.5; Luke 7.22.]

his application of certain obsure prophecies to himself? When all the al-
ledged prophecies of the Messias are laid together; they amount to no more
than predictions of an extraordinary teacher, and deli-<62>verer, and
worker of miracles to appear to the Jews, teaching repentance, the forgiveness of sins, and the resurrection from the dead. And was not our SAVIOUR
such a teacher, such a deliverer; and did he not appear in, and about the
time prophesied of, if the meaning of these antient prophecies can at all
be guessed at, or ascertained with any tolerable degree of probability?

But whatever be said of these antient prophecies; I must believe, that he
who raised the dead, had power to raise the dead; that he who could make
happy and miserable; cure all diseases; and banish all infirmities; had power
to make happy and miserable.

Say therefore that there never were such prophecies of a Messias; say the
arguments fetched from them, were only arguments *ad hominem;* taking
advantage of a prevailing notion and expectation, neither of which there
is any reason to suspect: say, in short, whatever you please upon this head
of prophecies; it will still remain certain and indisputable, "That the doctrines JESUS CHRIST taught were excellent doctrines; that he gave by the
whole of his conduct, all the possible evidences of sincerity and honesty;
and that his works were exact and perfect samples of the power he claimed:
the power of raising the dead; forgiving sins; and making the good and
virtuous happy, and the vitious and unworthy miserable, in the life that is
to come: samples of all the power and knowledge he pretended to as our
Divine Instructor; and consequently the fittest proofs and experiments,
<63> in the nature of things, of his being sent of GOD, with all the power
and authority he claimed, to instruct us in the knowledge of these doctrines
which he taught: and that is all I have undertaken at present to prove."

It would be impertinent to insist longer upon this article, when I have
nothing new, or that has not been fifty times repeated of late, to offer.*

---

* *Allow me to recommend to you, upon this question,* Limborchii amica collatio cum
Judaeo. *No doubt you have seen several excellent treatises upon this subject, occasioned by the*
Enquiry concerning the Grounds and Reasons, *&c. those particularly of the learned and*
worthy Bishop of Lichfield *and* Coventry. [Philip Limborch, *De veritate religionis Chris-*
tianae amica collatio cum erudito Judaeo (Gouda, 1687); Anthony Collins, *A Discourse of*
the Grounds and Reasons of the Christian Religion (London, 1724); Richard Smalbroke,

SECTION VII

Having thus, my friend, answered my principal design; allow me just to add a few remarks upon the Christian doctrine, and the reasons why Christianity hath been so much disputed, and controverted.

And the first and chief reason is certainly because natural religion is not sufficiently understood; nor its principles fully comprehended. If those who represent the Christian doctrine in certain lights; understood the principles of natural religion; they could not possibly entertain such notions of Revealed Religion. And if Christianity was not sadly misrepresented; those who understood and believed natural religion, could not possibly find fault with Christianity; <64> or at least oppose themselves to it, so obstinately and vehemently.

Was I even in doubt about the being of a GOD; and an over-ruling providence, I behoved to reason thus with my self. Tho' there was no GOD; no providence; virtue would still be the interest of mankind in general, and of every individual in particular: and if there is a GOD (and that there is all nature cries aloud throughout all her works) the way, the only way, and the infallible way to please him, and recommend our selves to his favour, is by the love and practice of virtue. Virtue therefore is in any case my duty, my interest; if it is my duty and my interest to make myself as happy as I can; or if it is my duty and my interest to promote the interest of society and my kind to the utmost of my power; and these two are inseparably joined and connected together, in the nature of things. Virtue and social affection work at once towards the publick good of mankind, and the private happiness of every particular person. Vice and unsocial affection, on the contrary, work unavoidably towards private as well as publick misery.

Whether therefore there is, or is not a GOD, my duty and my interest remains the same.

Further, was I in doubt about the Being of a GOD and a providence; the authority of one who shewed by his works an extraordinary superiority in nature, an extraordinary power and knowledge, would be sufficient to

---

A Vindication of the Miracles of our Blessed Saviour; in which Mr. Woolston's Discourses on them are particularly Examin'd, his pretended Authorities of the Fathers against the Truth of their literal Sense are set in a just Light, and his Objections in point of Reason are Answer'd, 2 vols. (London, 1729–31).]

remove my doubts, and assure me that there is a GOD and a providence; for I could have no reason to <65> suspect such a teacher, if he shewed in all his conduct the greatest benevolence and compassion towards mankind, and taught a doctrine so consistent; so plausible; so likely of itself (to say no more of it). And so contrary in its tendency, to any end a deceiver can possibly be supposed to have in view. "That there is a GOD and a future state, and that the only way to recommend to the divine favour and approbation, either here or hereafter, was by the practice of virtue, by leading a social rational life." If such testimony or information was offered, all that could be required to render it credible, is an evidence of such knowledge of nature, and the government of the world, as shews the teacher of an order superior to man; and in such a situation that he may certainly know that truth without any absurdity. And therefore in this sense it may be said, that even the principles of natural religion, the being of a GOD and a providence, may be proved by revelation, or taught by a divine mission.

But no divine mission can possibly teach another religion than that which nature and reason sufficiently establisheth, if we would but hearken to its dictates. "That the way, the sure way, the only way to please GOD, or gain his approbation, is by the love and practice of virtue, by imitating his goodness and benevolence, in our sphere, to the utmost of our abilities."* As soon as we form an idea <66> of GOD; we must needs draw this conclusion concerning the way to obtain his favour; "That the way to please GOD is not by sacrifices; but by works of justice, charity, and mercy." To speak in the stile of the sacred writings, or in the words of a pagan poet:

> *Compositum jus fasque animo, sanctosque recessus*
> *Mentis, & incoctum generoso pectus honesto.*
> *Haec cedo ut admoveam templis & farre litabo.*
>   PERS. Sat. ii.[14]

Nature does indeed leave us a little in the dark, not as to the being of a GOD and a providence; that there is no need of an extraordinary teacher

---

* Matth. xii. 30, &c. Luke vi. John xv. 12. James ii. 28. Matth. v. vi. vii. Tit. ii. 11, &c. iii. 6, &c. John iv. [Matthew 12.31–37; James 2.8; Titus 2.11–14 and 3.7–9.]

14. Persius, *Satires,* II.73–75: "a heart rightly attuned towards God and man; a mind pure in its inner depths, and a soul steeped in nobleness and honour. Give me these to offer in the temples, and a handful of grits shall win my prayer for me!"

to ascertain; but as to a future state. And therefore it is reasonable to think, that it must be the main end of a divine mission, if ever GOD instruct mankind in that way; to satisfy them fully, as to the truth and reality of a future existence: and when this is done, it must infallibly be in this way, so often already repeated. "That the practice of virtue is the only way to happiness in the future state; and vice that only which can render miserable in it." And because it is by JESUS CHRIST that immortality is fully ascertained; and the terms of acceptance with GOD, and of eternal happiness, made clear and sure; well may it be said; "That life and immortality are brought to light by his gospel."

This is evidently the account given of a future state in the gospel of CHRIST; and no other could be received as true, by those who have just notions of GOD and natural religion: and <67> therefore if certain christian teachers attended to this lesson of natural religion, they would not place religion, the christian religion, in what they do; or adventure to point out any other road to future and immortal happiness, but this one: which natural reason tells us must be the only way to future happiness, if there is a future state of rewards and punishments: and christianity shews us to be indeed the way to eternal happiness in that future state, which it alone has set beyond all doubt.

And seeing this really is the doctrine of the gospel of JESUS CHRIST; who can find in his heart to oppose Christianity; who would not wish Christianity was true; who would not naturally be prejudiced in its favour? every virtuous man certainly would; for it is natural to every virtuous spirit to wish for honour, glory, and immortality.

Even those who, unluckily for them, had not the inward satisfaction of believing, would wish well to Christianity for the sake of society and mankind, and like to see so noble, so comfortable, so beneficial a belief prevail universally, and universally produce the good works which it is the end and tendency of the Christian doctrine to promote among mankind.

Let then Christianity have fair play; let us look for the genuine doctrines of Christianity in the gospel of our SAVIOUR; and let us distinguish betwixt them and the vain additions and commandments of men, by which indeed the doctrines and commandments of GOD are rendered of little or no effect; and what is con-<68>trary to virtue and to piety, and consequently to Christianity, let us set our selves together with all our might to destroy it. But let none who wish well to mankind and society ever think of diminishing the obligations to virtue, the great bond of society and human happiness.

Let us never think of extirpating the most agreeable, the most cheering belief of a future state; the belief that tends so much to promote virtue and goodness, and without which there is too much ground to fear very little virtue would remain in the world. Let us consider before we declare against Christianity, even tho' at a time we should happen to doubt, whether men would be better fathers, or better husbands; better sons, or better subjects; in one word, better members of society, without the belief which true Christianity is designed to propagate in the world; for wilfully to endeavour to make men worse than they are, is certainly the worst, the most malicious office.

Christianity hath not added any thing to our duty, either towards GOD or our fellow creatures, that natural reason doth not teach and demonstrate to be our duty; it only sets the duties of natural religion, or which our natural light teacheth in a clear light; and sheweth their full and perfect extent, in opposition to false and corrupting misrepresentations, and urgeth to them by motives and considerations the most forcible and engaging, which natural reason is not able to ascertain. Certain motives and inducements to sanctity of life and manners; and means of improving in piety and virtue; together with such gratitude to our SAVIOUR him-<69>self, as such an extraordinary benefactor, well deserves at our hands; are, properly speaking, all that is *Revealed.* All the duties to GOD, our neighbours, or our selves, CHRIST enjoins, are naturally and essentially obligatory; and demonstrable from our natural relation to GOD and our fellow-creatures. For to love GOD and our neighbour is, according to the doctrine of our SAVIOUR, the whole duty of man: The sum of the commandment: The sum of the Law and the Prophets. That is, the great end and purpose of Revelation, in all its different periods and appearances; and particularly of his Gospel, who, so to speak, came to give the finishing stroke to Revelation, and in that sense to fulfil and perfect the divine law.

And this puts me in mind to observe, that I never met with any objection against the morality of the Christian Religion, except one; "That friendship was not recommended."* And this not a little surprized me; because we have a remarkable example of friendship betwixt our SAVIOUR and his disciple *John.* And at the same time that general benevolence is strongly inculcated by Christianity, without which there can be no truly virtuous friendship; and which naturally must produce friendship, when proper occasion offers of contracting that intimate union of souls, emphatically so call'd, which can't subsist but betwixt honest hearts; and is better understood by feeling than it can be by any de-<70>finition;† nor need I describe it to you, who duly experience its sincere delights.

SECTION VIII

But that we may have a just idea of the whole of the Christian Religion; let us take a short view of the means recommended to Christians for their improvement in virtue and goodness.

In order to become good, and to make progress in virtue, a certain discipline of the mind must be carefully maintained: our life and conduct must be often reviewed and impartially examined. The fancies, the opinions, must be catechized, and often called to a strict account. The excellency of virtue, and the folly and unreasonableness of vice; the shortness and uncertainty of human life; the immortality of our souls, and the certainty of future rewards and punishments; the Divine Providence and perfections; and, in one word, all the great Principles of religion and morality must be often brought to remembrance, duly weighed, and forciby impressed: We must often think seriously upon what is right and becoming in this or t'other circumstance; and what otherwise; and whence the difference proceeds. 'Tis thus on-<71>ly that the mastership of the passions can be obtained; or the habit of acting rationally and deliberately can be acquired; and that one can arrive at such a force and strength of reason as to have

---

* *See* Characteristicks, Vol. III. [Shaftesbury, *Characteristicks,* I:62–63.]

† *To see how naturally true virtuous friendship springs from the universal benevolence Christianity teaches, one needs only read what Lord Shaftsbury says upon that subject in his incomparable treatise upon virtue and merit; where one will see the difference betwixt generous true friendship, and partial friendship elegantly described.* [Shaftesbury, *Characteristicks,* II:63–66.]

ever at command the sense of duty; a clear and just apprehension of fit and unfit; and to be habitually in a capacity to act in every situation, with ready discerning, the same worthy and reasonable part.

This self examination so often inculcated by ancient moralists, as absolutely necessary to the right government of the mind and passions; and living according to the laws of nature and reason, is enjoined upon christians* in the strongest manner: Private prayer, or private serious address to GOD, in consequence of meditation upon his infinite excellency and perfect administration, is another exercise recommended to christians, in order to their advancement in virtue. And it has indeed been acknowledged by the wise philosophers† to be naturally a proper mean for conquering every unreasonable appetite, and for strengthening and nourishing the rational virtuous disposition.‡ <72> We christians in our devotions, according to the model set before us in the Lord's Prayer (as it is commonly called) and the other directions given us, are to acknowledge with thankful hearts the divine bounty and goodness; and to resign with contentment and approbation, to the divine care, all our outward affairs; and to breath earnestly after all these virtuous qualities which only can render happy and acceptable to our Great Creator, and which it is in our own power to obtain, if we are in good earnest about it; to confess our faults and resolve upon more diligence, caution and circumspection in our future conduct; to adore the divine perfections, his benignity and mercy particularly; implore the divine

---

* *Thus we are often called to think upon our ways; to examine our selves; to know what manner of spirit we are of.*

† *I shall only observe upon this head, that* Juvenal *in his tenth satire, the argument of which is known to be taken from the second* Alcibiades *of* Plato, *and the doctrine of* Socrates *concerning prayer, seems indeed to be laughing at prayer altogether; even prayer for the moral qualities he so beautifully describes; as plainly appears from his saying,* monstro quod tibi ipsi possis dare; *compared with what he says before,* ut tamen & poscas aliquid: *Yet according to the doctrine of* Plato *and* Socrates, *praying for, or seeking, the moral qualities was one of the best natural means of acquiring them.* [Juvenal, *Satires*, X.363: "What I commend to you, you can give to yourself"; Juvenal, *Satires*, X.354: "that you may have something to pray for"; Plato, *Alcibiades*, II, esp. the argument presented by Socrates at 148B–150B.]

‡ *See the 12th chapter of the gospel of St* Luke, *and compare it with several other parallel places in the other gospels.* [Luke 11.1–13; compare Matthew 6.1–21 and Mark 11.24–26.]

guidance and assistance; and indulge our selves in generous and benevolent wishes towards all our fellow-creatures; even those who may have on any account merited our displeasure.*

And surely it is not possible but the mind must be better'd and improved by this exercise, if frequently and duly performed. Nothing can contribute more to humanize and sweeten the temper; to correct and subdue all unruly and inordinate passions; and to confirm and invigorate every good and generous affection.

But besides these two which Philosophy hath ever recommended in some sort; and Christianity only sets in a better and clearer light; there are other means peculiar to Christianity, which are no less proper and fit, in the nature of <73> things, to ripen and improve the virtuous habits: such as the assembling our selves together the first day of the week, in commemoration of our SAVIOUR's resurrection from the dead; the great foundation-stone of our Christian belief; to hear our common faith and common duties explained; profess publickly the sense we have of our obligations to love GOD and all mankind; to do justice, and to delight in charity and mercy; to forgive injuries, and to walk humbly with GOD; that is, to maintain a full resignation of mind to infinitely wise Providence, with regard to all that we can neither foresee nor prevent, by our care and anxiety; and a sincere steady inclination to do what depends upon ourselves wisely and becomingly; to act a reasonable part in every circumstance of life whether prosperous or adverse. In one word, to profess our common faith; and to have the impression of our duties refreshed and enlivened by publick prayer, praise, and instruction. This is the end of christian assemblies: and when the publick worship and teaching are suitable to this design, or according to this rule, the effect must be good. And therefore an excellent author very justly observes, "That it would have rejoiced the heart of a *Socrates,* or any of the antient moralists, to have seen a publick institution for the instruction of all men in their common duties, and in doctrines that have so strict a connexion with virtue and human happiness." [15] An insti-

---

* *We are particularly enjoined in our addresses to* GOD, *to declare our sincere forgivance of all offences done to us.*

15. "How would the heart of a *Socrates* or *Tully* have rejoiced, had they lived in a nation, where the law had made provision for Philosophers, to read lectures of morality and theology every seventh day, in several thousands of schools erected at the publick

tution in every respect perfectly well calculated to civilize men, and render them wiser and better: not to mention other lesser advantages, such as, the rest it gives to the labouring part of the creation, to the lower sort of mankind, as well as to the brute animals. <74>

Baptism is another christian institution, very proper for gaining the same virtuous end. It is a very proper rite for preserving the memory of the facts upon which the Christian Faith is founded; and pointing out emblematically that purity and sanctity which is the chief end of Christianity: and is besides, a chain or link by which Christians are particularly knit together; without any design however to confine human love within more narrow bounds, than nature itself hath marked out to us.

And the Eucharist, or Lord's-Supper, is another christian institution, very wisely adapted to the same purposes; with this additional advantage, that whereas Baptism is administred regularly to the infants of christian parents, while they are not capable of reflexion; the act of communicating in the supper, is an act of reason and judgment: an act of our own free choice, in which he who believes the generous condescension of our SAV-IOUR, to suffer death for the good of mankind; while he meditates upon so noble an example of benevolence and goodness, must needs feel all the generous and noble affections work within his breast, in the most improving as well as delightful manner; and form sentiments and resolves that can't fail to have a happy and lasting influence upon his temper and disposition.

In all these exercises however, it is recommended, and indeed is absolutely necessary that reason preside; and that the mind preserve a certain calmness and sedateness; otherwise contemplation, admiration, and the warm affections which these naturally produce, may run into ex-<75>cess; and at last destroy the balance in which soundness of mind consists. The caution the excellent philosopher *Aristotle** gives to young contemplators

---

charge throughout the whole country, at which lectures all ranks sexes without distinction were obliged to be present for their general improvement?"; Joseph Addison, *The Evidences of the Christian Religion* (London, 1730), p. 208.

* *Nor was this prohibition (as a noble Author observes) "of the wondering or admiring habit, in early students, peculiar to one kind of philosophy alone. It was common to many; however, the reason and account of it might differ in one sect from the other. All Moralists, worthy of any name, forbid the forward use of admiration, rapture, or extacy, even in subjects they esteemed the highest and most divine, to all tyro's in philosophy; being well appriz'd, that in religious concerns particularly, the habit of admiration and contemplative delight, would,*

in Philosophy, is equally necessary in Theology. Too great a warmth of affection is dangerous, and ought to be guarded against. And therefore reason must take care to keep the reins, that it may be able to check and controul, examine and regulate, every action and commotion of the mind.

But not only are these means naturally fit and proper exercises, under the guidance of a cool and clear judgment, for the cultivating and improving virtue; but besides, it is promised to Christians, that in the diligent use of them, they shall receive the spirit of CHRIST, the spirit of Grace; an extraordinary assistance.*

The excellent bishop *Tillotson* hath shewn in several of his sermons, that we are to understand by this assistance; by the spirit of GOD, and the seal of the spirit: not any extraordinary revelation from the spirit of GOD to the minds of good men, telling them in particular, that <76> they are the children of GOD; but strength and firmness of mind, generous principles, sentiments, resolutions and desires influencing the mind and all our conduct.[16] And it is well known, that several of the antient philosophers† thought a divine *afflatus,* or assistance, necessary, in order to one's arriving to an uncommon pitch of virtue; of fortitude, and publick spirit particu-

---

by over-indulgence, too easily mount into high Fanaticism, or degenerate into abject Superstition." Characteristicks, Vol. III. p. 37, 202, 203. [Shaftesbury, *Characteristicks,* III:24, p. 124 note.]

   * *See St* Luke xiii. 24. *St* Matth. vii. 7, *&c. and several other texts might be quoted.* [Turnbull's references make little sense. Of the many relevant passages that could be cited see, for example, Romans 8.1–27, Galatians 3.14, and Ephesians 1.13–14, 4.20–25, and 5:9.]

   † *Several passages might be brought from the antient philosophers to prove this; was that needful to one who is so well acquainted with them.* Absque divino afflatu (*says* Cicero) nunquam vir bonus aut fortis. ["Without a divine breath there has never been a man who was (either) good or strong." Turnbull's Latin is a variant of Cicero's *De natura deorum* II.lxvi.167: "Nemo igitur vir magnus sine aliquo adflatu divino umquam fuit./ No one, then, has ever been a great man without some breath of the divine." For Samuel Clarke's use of this passage from Cicero see below, p. 203.]

   16. John Tillotson, "The Danger of Zeal, without Knowledge," "Honesty the Best Preservative against Dangerous Mistakes in Religion," "Of the Ordinary Influence of the Holy Ghost, on the Minds of Christians," and "The Fruits of the Spirit, the same with Moral Virtues," in *The Works of the Most Reverend Dr. John Tillotson, Late Lord Archbishop of Canterbury: Containing Two Hundred Sermons and Discourses, on Several Occasions,* edited by Ralph Barker, 2nd ed., 2 vols. (London, 1717), I:200–206, 235–53, II:298–310, 311–18.

larly. Nor can this doctrine of assistance to the virtuous, be charged with any absurdity, meerly because we cannot point out the way how it is conveyed; unless every thing is held for absurd that we cannot fully explain. It is certainly very easy to comprehend what it is for noble, generous sentiments and principles to work within our minds, in a strong active, vigorous manner, in consequence of meditation, and other spiritual exercises; so much may be understood, or rather felt by experience; and as for the extrinsic conveyance, or assistance in this case, we cannot be more in the dark about it, than we are about the original conveyance or impression of our ideas of sense: for all philosophers are agreed, that they are conveyed into, or impressed upon, our minds by GOD himself, or at least by some extrinsic cause independent of us: but how, they pretend not to explain.[17]

Certain ways of speaking among Christians, about the spirit of GOD and its operations, have been confounded with the genuine doctrine of Christianity about assistance to the virtuous; <77> and by this means the true doctrine hath suffer'd not a little. But take it by itself as it really stands; as a promise of growth in knowledge, grace, and virtue; a promise of firmness and steadiness in times of trial and assault; to be acquired in the use of means which are naturally fit to replenish the mind with noble sentiments; and to confirm and strengthen the good affections. Take the Christian doctrine in this view, and no objection can possibly be made against it; whatever may be said of certain false notions concerning the divine spirit and its workings; whether the produce of melancholy, or of hypocrisy and spiritual pride. There is nothing in the thing promised, in the fact itself unintelligible: and the assurance of such assistance must needs be, to all

17. Turnbull most likely alludes to Nicolas Malebranche and George Berkeley as the philosophers who maintain that God conveys our ideas into our minds. See Nicolas Malebranche, *The Search after Truth,* translated and edited by Thomas M. Lennon and Paul J. Olscamp (Cambridge, 1997), pp. 217–35; George Berkeley, *A Treatise concerning the Principles of Human Knowledge,* in *The Works of George Berkeley Bishop of Cloyne,* edited by A. A. Luce and T. E. Jessop, 9 vols. (London, 1948–57), §§ 26, 33, 146. As representatives of the second group of philosophers Turnbull probably alludes to René Descartes and John Locke, although both Descartes and Locke did explain how our sensory perceptions are caused. See, for example, the fourth Discourse of Descartes' *Optics,* "Of the Senses in General," in René Descartes, *Discourse on Method, Optics, Geometry, and Meteorology,* translated by Paul J. Olscamp (Indianapolis, 1965), pp. 86–90; Locke, *Essay,* II.viii.11–13.

who believe it, a strong inducement to the serious pursuit of virtue. It is in the power of all men to be good, if they will but be in earnest about it: the chief difficulties to be overcome arise from evil customs, from contracted vitious habits. But it is not only in our power to conquer these by due diligence and labour; but it is in the power of Christians to do more than others, if they are not remiss in their endeavours; because of the assistance promised to them. And if the virtues of heathens reproach Christians, and cast them at a distance; it is because they are wanting to themselves; and do not give due pains to do honour to their master and his religion. If they did; they should indeed shine as lights in the world; and others seeing their glorious example, would give glory to GOD; and fall in love with a religion which produced such useful members of society; such noble patterns of every good and praise-worthy action. And indeed the lives of heathens ought <78> to render christians ashamed; and to excite a noble emulation to excel them: and for that reason, What do we more than others? is a question Christians cannot too frequently put to themselves.

I have not entered upon the enquiry, What is precisely meant by the spirit of GOD; the spirit of CHRIST; the HOLY GHOST the comforter; and such like phrases. An assistance is plainly promised to Christians, and that is the main point. And it is enough to our present purpose, to have shewn, that the works of CHRIST are proper samples of his power to impart this promised assistance: and that the proofs he gave of his sincerity and his ability, are more than sufficient to satisfy us, that we may depend upon his word and promise.

I likewise forbear enquiring into the meaning of certain ways of speaking, concerning the personal dignity and rank of our SAVIOUR: not that there seems to me any considerable difficulty in the matter; notwithstanding of all the disputes upon that head, when scripture language is attended to, and all foreign scholastic terms are laid aside. But because upon this subject, I could not possibly do more than transcribe from pens I am not able to imitate. His mission and relation to Christians, as our instructor and SAVIOUR, is clearly told. And how his works, together with the indisputable evidences he gave of sincerity, and good generous intention, prove that point; (which must be acknowledged to be of main consequence) we have already seen. One thing however may be added: "That tho' we know not the various <79> degrees of created agents, and communicated power;

and cannot determine what works GOD only can do: yet greater works than those of JESUS CHRIST, the raising the dead particularly we cannot conceive, unless it is creating: and therefore the works he wrought are as proper samples as could possibly be given of his claim to any order or rank in being whatever it be: and consequently we have sufficient proof of that claim; especially when the evidences of his truth and sincerity are taken into the account; and it is likewise remembred what ground we have shewn there is to believe, *That* GOD *would have controuled and opposed him, if his claim had been false or blasphemous.* 'Tis power and knowledge in different degrees, that makes the difference amongst beings; GOD, for example, is supreme, because his power and knowledge is underived and infinite: And power or knowledge of any degree, can only be proved or made known by samples of power and knowledge in that kind and degree."

Thus we see that the rules Christianity gives for the conduct of life are excellent. Whatsoever is noble, generous, or praise-worthy; it is that, we are commanded by JESUS CHRIST to seek after. To give all diligence, to add virtue to virtue, that we may obtain glory, honour, and immortality, is the whole of our christian calling. And how then can we ever induce ourselves to think, a teacher an impostor, who taught so pure and perfect a system of religion and morals, without any allay of folly or superstition; and who had no other end in view, but to make men wiser and better. And <80> after all, if he is supposed an impostor, our obligation to live according to the very same precepts and rules he gave must be acknowledged; if a rational creature is obliged to act rationally; or if there is any difference between wisdom and folly, reasonable and unreasonable. For virtue is certainly the interest of every particular person, as well as of mankind in general, even when this world only is taken into the account; and much more must it be owned to be so, if any regard ought to be had to another life; to which every thinking person will reckon himself obliged to have regard, if the notion cannot be clearly demonstrated to be a dream without any foundation. And that was never yet pretended.

SECTION IX

But because there are some obscure passages even in the gospels; tho' that is easily accounted for; another remark that I would make, is; That there cannot possibly be any article of faith about what is obscure and disputable as to its meaning in the christian revelation, but this one; "That it is obscure and disputable; and GOD can never require of us to understand that which is not made plain." To throw away or despise what is clear, and evidently useful in any work, because there are other things we can't make any certain sense of, is certainly most unreasonable. And for those who are agreed together in the belief of what is plainly told, to fall out, and treat one another rudely, because of different opinions about what is obscure, is no less so. And yet would but <81> christians remember this, the controversies that divide them so much, would soon be at an end; or at least all disputes among christians would be carried on and managed in a most amicable, agreeable manner. Whatever obscurity there may be elsewhere, there is none at all in the precepts, which are of indisputable obligation. Charity, benevolence, moderation and humanity, are clearly enjoined: and to the practice of these virtues it is, that eternal life and happiness is as clearly promised. Is it not therefore very odd and surprizing that christians who consent in this; that the practice of these duties is the chief thing; and that the doctrine of a future state and a resurrection from the dead, is the main doctrine of Christianity, the doctrine of chief importance; should not reason with one another about the meaning of certain places in the sacred writings, which they both own to be of difficult interpretation, with all calmness, good nature, and modesty?

In the mean time nothing can be more certain than that what is not plainly and distinctly revealed to us, and of easy certain interpretation, can only be designed for an exercise of charity and friendly conference or dispute.

To believe that what is obscure is of vast importance, and that our salvation depends upon the hitting the meaning rightly; is a notion contrary to all our natural ideas of GOD and his divine perfections; it is supposing a divine revelation a snare, or sphinx. If therefore there is any thing obscure and difficult in the sacred writings; let those who have time and leisure endeavour to explain it. And if men of learning <82> differ in their sentiments; let them not however tear and devour one another on that account as wild beasts: but remember that love is the end of the commandment: and that tho' one should have the gift of interpretation; nay the gift of working miracles and of prophecying; yet if he hath not charity *all is vain and of no value.* GOD *is love and he that is of* GOD *is love.* If it is said; that after all there cannot be much virtue or merit in the faith of the common-people, because they cannot possibly philosophize about miracles, and their connexion with doctrines: I answer, that I am far from thinking that it is belief, however rational and well founded, that can recommend to GOD; it is only a good life and conversation. And if the faith of the common-people produce this effect, they will be accepted of GOD, because of their virtue, piety and goodness, without regard to the grounds upon which their belief is founded. But the great advantage of Christianity is; that it is able to give rational satisfaction to the philosopher, about points of the greatest importance; and at the same time to excite the inferior herd of mankind to the practice of virtue, in the way that they are most capable of being moved and influenced. And yet however difficult it may be to make the common-people understand the bulls of popes, the creeds of councils, a metaphysical catechism; it is not so hard a task to make the meanest mechanic comprehend the genuine doctrines of *Christianity,* and their connexion with the works of CHRIST. Nor is the historical evidence, when represented in a simple familiar light, as it may easily be, above the vulgar reach. Every body reasons about things of the same kind every day. <83>

If you ask me, my friend, how an unbeliever, living among christians, ought to be treated by christians? I answer; with all tenderness, compassion, and good will, for so humanity requires, so Christianity teaches; and that is the only way to bring in those that are without.

If you ask me, what may be his fate hereafter? I answer, "Every man will be judged by his works." And one who is conscious to himself of no prejudice against Christianity, that he has examined it fairly, and yet can't help doubting; if at the same time he leads a virtuous and regular life; has nothing to fear; so Christianity as well as reason teaches me. Virtue is the main thing, the end of believing; and the best and worthiest part that one can act in matters of opinion and belief, is to examine impartially. This is an eternal immutable truth: "That he who feareth GOD, loveth mercy, and worketh righteousness, will be accepted of GOD; who hath no respect of persons, but will judge every one according to his works."* But no

---

* *And this is what* GOD *hath taught us by* JESUS CHRIST, Acts x. 34, *&c.* [Acts 10.34–35.]

unbeliever, who loves mankind and society, will take it amiss to be put in mind; that whatever his opinion may be of the evidences and grounds of the Christian Religion; it is doing a real mischief to mankind and society, to endeavour to destroy or diminish the faith and persuasion of a future state of rewards and punishments. Οὐχ ὁρᾷς, ὅτι τὰ πολυχρονιώτατα καὶ σοφώτατα τῶν ἀνθρωπίνων, πό-<84>λεις καὶ ἔθνη, θεοσεβέστατά ἐστι καὶ αἱ φρονιμώταται ἡλικίαι θεῶν ἐπιμελέσταται.

ΞΕΝΟΦΩΝΤΟΣ
ΑΠΟΜΝΗΜΟΝΕΥΜΑΤΩΝ
Κεφ.δ΄. ις΄.[18]

In my next I will give you my sentiments concerning the historical evidence of the works of JESUS CHRIST; and at the same time my opinion of the antient Magic, so much talked of. In the mean time it is obvious, "That those who were eye-witnesses to the works of our SAVIOUR, had the same evidence for the truth of his pretension, That those have of the skill of a painter, who see him draw a fine picture; or of the truth of a conclusion who see the experiments performed, from which it naturally and necessarily follows."

I am, &c. <85>

---

18. "Do you not see that the wisest and most enduring of human institutions, cities and nations, are most god-fearing, and that the most thoughtful period of life is the most religious?"; Xenophon, *Memorabilia,* I.iv.16–17.

Queries[19]

QUERY I

Whether samples of a certain power, do not prove that power: Or if any thing else is necessary to prove a certain power, besides samples of that power: samples analogous in kind, and approportioned in quantity or moment?

And in consequence of this, whether samples of a power to raise the dead, do not prove a power to raise the dead; and whether samples of a power to deliver from all kind of diseases and infirmities, do not prove a power to deliver from all kind of diseases and infirmities; and whether samples of power to confer certain qualities and blessings, do not prove power to confer these qualities and blessings? <86>

QUERY II

Whether the principal, if not all the doctrines of CHRIST are not assertions of his having power to raise the dead, and deliver from miseries; and confer blessings; to deliver from such kind of miseries, and confer such kind of blessings as his works were proper and natural samples or experiments of? And what sample or samples are wanting, to make the evidence of his having any power he claimed by his doctrines, full and compleat?

QUERY III

Whether it is more natural and reasonable to think, that GOD would controul the power of any Being who pretended a mission from him which he

---

19. Turnbull's eight Queries were reproduced with minor variations in accidentals and wording in Caleb Fleming, *Animadversions upon Mr. Tho. Chubb's Discourse on Miracles, Considered as Evidences to Prove the Divine Original of a Revelation* (London, 1741), pp. 63–66.

had not; and not suffer him to produce all the extraordinary works he appealed to, as signs of the divine mission and approbation? Or that GOD would let one appeal to him for his approbation; and give all the evidences and signs of it, to which he appeals as proofs, without any check or controul; full samples of all the power and knowledge he pretended to as a divine missionary? which of these two conclusions is most consonant to our notions of order and wise administration; our natural conceptions of GOD; and to what we know of the divine government of the natural or moral world? <87>

QUERY IV

Whether an uninterrupted course of honesty, goodness, faithfulness, and benevolence, be not sufficient to create trust? And whether there was any thing in the conduct of JESUS CHRIST, that could beget diffidence and mistrust; or any thing wanting to put his honesty, sincerity, and good intention beyond all doubt?

QUERY V

Which of the doctrines of our SAVIOUR has not a direct tendency, and powerful influence, to excite and encourage to the practice of piety and virtue; and what is wanting to render the doctrine of our SAVIOUR, a compleat system of religion and morality, in point of precepts, motives or means: what in point of duty, that reason does not demonstrate to be duty; what in point of motive, that is not in itself probable tho' not certain; or what in respect of means that is not fit and proper in the nature of things, to improve and promote virtue and goodness to the highest degree of perfection human nature is capable of?

QUERY VI

Whether therefore abstracting from the truth of Christianity, a better publick doctrine can be devised; whether mankind would live more comfortably and virtuously without the belief of a future state of rewards and punishments, and the other motives Christianity furnisheth to the practice of benevolence and righteousness; and consequently whether it is a kind office to mankind to endeavour to <88> weaken that belief; or whether it is not the part of a good member of society, and an honest man, to consider well before he publishes to the world his singular notions, whether the promulgating them may not have a bad effect; contribute to lessen the regard to virtue, or at least the restraints from vice?

QUERY VII

Whether the works which were performed by JESUS CHRIST, to evince the truth of the doctrines he taught, are not a natural, proper and full proof of their truth in the strictest and most philosophical sense of proof or evidence; since his works bear the same relation to his doctrines, as signs or samples of their truth, that any Experiments in philosophy bear to the conclusions justly inferred from them; or in other words, since they are signs of their truth in the same sense that experiments or samples of gravity or elasticity, for instance, are signs of the reality of these properties?

QUERY VIII

Whether that kind of proof or evidence can be said to be above the reach of any one, upon which even the lowest and most ignorant of mankind daily reason and act in many instances: and whether all degrees of men do not reason and act every day upon the evidence or proof, which signs and samples afford of that quality, natural or moral, of which they are signs and samples?

The evidence therefore, upon which the truth of Christianity depends, is at the same time a strictly philosophical unexceptionable evidence, and an evidence that is obvious to every capacity, nay familiar to every one. <89>

These Queries serve to give a short view of the chief design of this EN-QUIRY; and are humbly offered to the serious consideration of all who pretend to be *Free-thinkers,* that is, accurate, impartial enquirers after truth: for free-thinking, in this only just and true sense of it, is man's duty and glory.[20]

20. Compare Turnbull's comments on free thinking above, pp. 3–4.

Appendix

I am satisfied that I have clearly proved that the Miracles of JESUS CHRIST are a proper and full proof of his doctrines in the strictest and most philosophical sense of proof or evidence; and that the preceding ENQUIRY contains as full an answer to all that is said by the *Moral Philosopher*[21] about Miracles in his first or second volume, as if it had been written on purpose to refute his false reasoning, tho' it was published several years before that performance appeared. Yet, in order to prevent as much as it lies in my power any one's being misled by that author, I shall here subjoin a chain of reasoning which appears to me absolutely certain, that necessarily leads to a conclusion about Miracles and the evidence of Christianity diametrically opposite to his.

1. All truths which directly tend to encourage and promote the practice of virtue are moral or divine truths; truths conducive to the purification and <90> moralizing of our affections and tempers; truths that strongly excite to the imitation of the divine moral perfections, and that by consequence have an immediate tendency to improve our minds to the highest pitch of moral perfection we can attain to; or, in other words, into a likeness to the divine nature: All such truths are moral, religious, or divine, in respect of their tendency.

This seems to be a self-evident proposition, and is indeed acknowledged to be true by the *Moral Philosopher.*

2. To every one who thinks well of human nature and of our Creator, or who is persuaded that man is endowed by his Maker with powers, faculties, dispositions, and affections, that are capable of being improved by our own diligence and application to a very noble pitch of moral perfection; which is the first principle, or rather the basis of natural religion: To every one who is thus persuaded, every proposition concerning the present or future state of mankind and virtue, that is not only consistent with that

21. Thomas Morgan; see note 2, p. 101.

persuasion, but directly tends to animate, support, perfect, and comfort true virtue, must at first sight appear very probable upon that very account.

Such a consistency and tendency necessarily constitute a very considerable degree of probability. These not only gain the affection of every good mind, and excite an earnest desire that such propositions may be true; but they necessarily dispose every unbiassed understanding to assent to them, in consequence of their agreement with other known truths. In other words, propositions that unite and tally with other known truths by so doing make a coherent system that is wonderfully persuasive as well as pleasing to the mind. Thus, for instance, to one who believes the fundamental principle of natural religion just mentioned, this following doctrine must appear <91> very probable, on account of its immediate tendency to promote and encourage virtue, and its exact agreement with that principle; namely, "That GOD will graciously forgive the repenting, that is, the reforming sinner, who, forsaking vice, seriously sets himself to make progress in virtue; and that such persons shall be made happy in a future state, in proportion to their advances in true reformation of heart or manners." This comfortable doctrine, which by no means gives any encouragement to vice, but on the contrary is the strongest inducement to repentance and reformation, so exactly tallies with our natural notions of GOD and of virtue, that at first sight every one who hath just apprehensions of the Deity must be powerfully disposed and inclined to assent to it; they must think it very probable.

3. Now could this proposition be proved to be true from the consideration of the divine perfections, that is, could it be inferred by necessary consequence from any known truths concerning GOD, it would in that case be a demonstrable truth. It would then be no longer only a probable one; it would be as certain a conclusion as any other in science. So intimately related and strictly connected are all truths, that, I believe, there are no truths concerning GOD's providence and virtue, that are not in the nature of things capable of demonstration, that is, capable of being inferred by scientifical reasoning from certain other truths. But truths may in the nature of things be capable of demonstration, and yet not be discoverable by certain beings, but be absolutely above their reach in the scientifick way of knowledge. And whether certain truths, as for instance that just mentioned

concerning the forgiveness of sins, *&c.* be capable of scientifick demonstration with respect to us in our present state, or not; yet such truths may be proved to be true <92> by another kind of evidence distinct from that which is properly called scientifical deduction, when the conclusion is inferred from principles that necessarily imply or involve its truth; but an evidence that is withal unexceptionable and truly philosophical; or by a very satisfactory and absolutely necessary way of reasoning not only in philosophy, but in all affairs of the highest concernment in life.

4. For if any Philosopher of good reputation should tell one he knew how to reduce by necessary consequences all the motions and appearances of the heavenly bodies to the law of gravity, with many effects of which law every one is familiarly acquainted; would not every one, who is satisfied with regard to the wisdom of the Author of nature, and the simplicity, unity and beauty of all his contrivances and administrations, and who is at the same time convinced of the capacity and integrity of the Philosopher who tells him so, be persuaded of the truth of his assertion, and acquiesce in it with great complacency and assurance upon that very account, in the same manner that one, without understanding the principles of physick, chymistry, painting, architecture, or any other art whatsoever, rests satisfied that he may safely employ one who hath given proper evidences of his skill in the art he professes, and of his integrity in his way of dealing with mankind? Do we not reason, satisfy ourselves, and act with great confidence and assurance of mind every day, in a thousand instances, in that very manner?

5. And by parity of reason, if any Being gives us a fuller account of GOD's providence and virtue, with regard to this present state of mankind, or to a succeeding state, than we have yet attained to, or are perhaps able to attain, by the consideration of truths we know in the scientifick way; an account that exactly tallies or makes a coherent system with <93> the principles of natural religion we already know; provided the Being, who gives us such an account, does at the same time give undoubted evidence of his integrity and good intention, and of his capacity to instruct us in what he pretends to instruct us, in consequence of his larger and fuller knowledge of nature; would we not in such a case have the same evidence for these truths that we have in the case of the Philosopher just mentioned, or that we act upon in the affairs of the greatest importance every day?

6. The argument in such a case must run thus. This Being, who assures us that, having a fuller knowledge of nature than we, he is sure that certain propositions are true, which propositions are very comfortable to virtue, and far from being inconsistent with what we know, are exceedingly agreeable to all we know: This Being having given full evidence of his larger knowledge of nature than we have, and full evidence of his integrity, we can have no reason not to trust to and depend upon the certainty of his information or assertions. He hath proved himself honest and worthy of credit, and capable of instructing us; and therefore not to trust to his informations is to doubt either of his honesty or of his capacity; that is, to doubt of what by the supposition is fully proved: The only question therefore, when such instruction is offered, is, whether the Instructor gave full evidence of his capacity to instruct, and of his integrity? Now what that evidence must be, I think, hath been shewn at full length in the preceding discourse.

7. There may be therefore an *extrinsick evidence* or proof that ought to satisfy us, even with regard to truths in their nature capable of demonstration in the scientifick way, or by *intrinsick evidence,* before we attain to it, or abstracted from it.[22] And whatever belongs to that *extrinsick evidence,* or tends to make it up, is a part of it, or a step in that kind of rea-<94>soning. Certain works, whether they are called *Miracles* or not, or however *Miracles* may be defined, that make up an *extrinsick evidence* of truths, belong to that kind of evidence, and are as proper steps towards the conclusion in that way as principles, from which a conclusion is intrinsically deduced, are with regard to *intrinsick* or *scientifick evidence.* To say works, from which the *extrinsick evidence* of truths is deduced, have no relation to these truths, is to say, "That the parts that make up a reasoning or an evidence do not belong to it." And to say there can be no *extrinsick evidence* of truths is to say, "That a Being, who knows more of nature than we, is not capable of informing us of what we do not know, and of giving us good reason to trust to him." But what is the proper evidence in such a case? Is it not evidence of honesty and evidence of knowledge sufficient to instruct us? And how can honesty be proved but by evidences, that is, samples of it?

22. See above, p. 143.

Or how can a fuller knowledge of nature be shewn and proved but by full, that is, proportioned samples and signs of that fuller knowledge pretended to? that is, in the same way that any kind or degree of knowledge pretended to is proved, by samples analogous to it and proportioned in quantity or moment.

8. So that of necessity the question concerning the instruction in the nature of GOD's providence and a future state, offered to us by JESUS CHRIST, comes to be, "Whether he gave a sufficient *extrinsick evidence* of the truth of his instructions, sufficient evidence of his goodness and integrity, and sufficient samples of the knowledge necessary to instruct us in these matters?" It comes then directly to this question, "What did his conduct and works prove? Did they prove goodness and sufficient knowledge? Are they full and proper samples of his honesty, and of his sufficient know-<95>ledge to instruct us; samples proportion'd to his claim in kind and moment?"

9. All the reasoning in the *Moral Philosopher* about *Miracles* really depends upon admitting this manifest absurdity, "That samples proportioned in kind and moment to a claim of knowledge or power are not proper proofs of that claim." For if that be false, it must be absurd to say, that *Miracles* or works can never be a proof of doctrines, since works not only may be samples of knowledge sufficient to instruct in certain truths; but there can be no other proof given of knowledge but by samples, and there can be no other samples given but by works. Let him therefore cease to tell us, that works can never be a proper proof of doctrines, and attempt to shew, if he can, that CHRIST's *Miracles* or works were not a proper proof of the knowledge he claimed by pretending to assert the truths he taught: And that he must do, by proving either that his works were not analogous to it in kind, or by proving that they were not proportioned to it in moment; in order to which he must prove, that samples of raising the dead, of delivering from evils of various sorts, and of conferring blessings of many different kinds, bodily and mental, are not analogous proportioned samples of knowledge and power to raise the dead, deliver from misery, and make happy; which is the same attempt precisely, as it would be to prove that samples of skill in an art are not samples of skill in that art.

10. Let me add to what hath been said, that truths, which are taught us

in this manner, are taught us in a supernatural, and yet in a natural way. They are taught us in a supernatural way, because they are taught us by a Being, who hath a fuller, a more comprehensive knowledge of Nature than we. And yet they are taught us in a natural way, for information in truths, <96> by a Being, of whose capacity of informing us, and integrity, we have no reason to doubt, is a most natural, common, familiar, sure, satisfying and necessary way of receiving information. That is to say, such information is supernatural with respect to its Origin or Author; but natural in respect of the evidences given of its credibility: Evidences by samples being a natural evidence in any proper sense of natural Evidence. And indeed, tho' our Instructor may be supernatural, yet we cannot be instructed by any other but natural evidence.

If such information be given by a Being authorised, commissioned, or ordered by GOD to instruct us, it is in that case divine information; that is, it is information given us by GOD's special command and appointment. But the capacity of our Informer to instruct us must be proved by his works, in the same way and manner, whether he pretends to come from GOD or not. And his pretension to come from GOD, depends absolutely for its evidence upon the same evidences of candour, honesty and good intention, necessary to gain our credit, whether he pretends to come from GOD or not. So that with regard to such information, whether the truths of which we are so informed, be capable of demonstration in the scientifick way or not; whether they can or cannot be proved to be true by intrinsic evidence; and whether, the teacher pretends to be commissioned by GOD or not; the only question is, whether he gave sufficient evidences of honesty and of the knowledge pretended to. And there cannot possibly be any reason to discredit an information, if it really be attended with all the proper evidences of knowledge and integrity; that is, with all the proper evidences of the qualities necessary to render an instructor credible and worthy of trust.

To sum up all therefore, the *Moral Philosopher,* when he asserts, that *Miracles* cannot make a Proof <97> with respect to Doctrines, must assert, that a Being, who knows more of nature than we do, is not capable of informing us concerning several truths that we do not know: or that no works any such pretender to instruct us, may or can produce, can possibly amount to a proof, either of his skill to instruct us or of his integrity. It would be trifling to say, works can never make an intrinsick evidence; for truths capable of intrinsic evidence may be satisfyingly proved to be true by such an external evidence as hath been described, abstractedly from all consideration of their intrinsic evidence: and works in the sense defined, do really make up the intrinsic evidence of the credibility of the information; or the intrinsic reasons of giving credit to, and putting full confidence in our Informer. All I have been asserting is indeed self-evident, namely, "That samples and specimens of doctrines, are proper proofs of doctrines": and that works, which are samples of the credibility of an information concerning facts or truths, are proper proofs of that credibility, or constitute intrinsick marks and evidences with regard to that credibility. "For if these propositions be true, it necessarily follows, that *Miracles* may be a proof of Doctrines; and that CHRIST's *Miracles* were a full and proper proof of his Doctrines." In truth, what we are called upon to prove by those gentlemen, who assert, that no *Miracles* can be a proof of doctrines, are truths no less plain and obvious than that two and two make four; such as that there is no reason not to trust to an informer, that shews himself worthy of trust and qualified to inform us: And that as experiments of elasticity and gravity, prove elasticity and gravity to be real properties or affections of matter; or as specimens and experiments of skill in physick, or any other art, prove skill in that art of which they are specimens, samples or experiments; so specimens, sam-<98>ples and experiments of power to raise the dead, assist the virtuous and make them happy, prove power to do it.

I should not have repeated the same plain simple truths so often, had not certain writers repeated the same objections, over and over again, without so much as giving them a new colouring. And I do declare, that if any one shall convince me of the falsity of any step in the foregoing reasoning, I will return him thanks, tho' at the same time, such is my opinion of the Christian doctrine, that I can never persuade myself not to wish it true; or not to wish it were *universally believed,* that it might be *universally practised.*

FINIS

Christianity Neither False nor Useless,
Tho' Not as Old as the Creation

ುೞ ುೞ ುೞ

NOTE ON THE TEXT

Christianity Neither False nor Useless was published by R. Willock in July 1732.[1] There were no further impressions or editions of this work.

---

1. See "A Register of Books publish'd in July, 1732" in *The Gentleman's Magazine* 2 (1732): 17.

CHRISTIANITY *neither false nor useless,*
tho' not as old as the Creation:

OR, AN

ESSAY

To prove the
Usefulness, Truth, and Excellency

OF THE

CHRISTIAN RELIGION;

And to vindicate Dr CLARKE's Discourse concerning the
Evidences of Natural and Revealed Religion, from the
Inconsistencies with which it is charged by the Author of
Christianity as old as the Creation.

By the Author of the Philosophical Enquiry, &c.

Εἶτα τὸν λοιπὸν βίον καθεύδοντες διατελοῖτε ἄν, εἰ μή τινα
ἄλλον ὁ θεὸς ὑμῖν ἐπιπέμψειεν κηδόμενος ὑμῶν.
Plato in Apol. Socr.[1]

LONDON:
Printed for R. WILLOCK, at Sir *Isaac Newton's*
Head near the *Royal Exchange* in *Cornhill.* 1732.
[Price One Shilling.]

1. Plato, *Apology,* 31a: "then you would pass the rest of your lives in slumber, unless God, in his care for you, should send someone else to sting you."

THE PREFACE

The design of this Essay *is to do justice to Dr* Clarke;[2] *and to shew that he has clearly proved the truth of certain principles diametrically opposite to those of the author of* Christianity as old as the Creation;[3] *and to excite impartial enquirers to compare the Doctor's reasonings with these of that author.*

The Doctor has proved; That bare reason, in fact, has never been sufficient to discover to the bulk of mankind, even the law of nature; tho' that law be founded upon the nature of things; and in that sense, is discoverable by reason; or by a rational, acurate, unprejudiced enquiry into the nature and relations of things. <vi>

And indeed what the author of Christianity as old as the Creation *asserts concerning the sufficiency of reason, or the light of nature, is true in no other sense but this one: "That all that is deducible from the nature of things, is deducible from the nature of things; Or that whatsoever can be found out by the right, and acurate use of reason, can be found out by the right, acurate use of reason." Which was never denied.*

2. That even supposing the law of nature, that is, the law deducible from the nature and relations of things, could be universally known and understood by all mankind in their present corrupt estate; bare unassisted reason cannot discover to mankind all that is necessary in their present estate to enforce suf-

---

2. Samuel Clarke's *A Discourse concerning the Being and Attributes of God, the Obligations of Natural Religion, and the Truth and Certainty of the Christian Religion* (based on his Boyle Lectures for 1704 and 1705) was one of the most widely read and influential books published in the eighteenth century. Turnbull's page references below show that he was quoting from the seventh edition of Clarke's *Discourse,* published in London in 1728. All subsequent page references will be to this edition.

3. Matthew Tindal (1657–1733), the prominent English Deist, whose *Christianity as Old as the Creation* was first published in 1730. Turnbull's page references indicate that he used the second edition of Tindal's work, published in London in 1732. All subsequent page references will be to this edition of *Christianity as Old as the Creation.*

ficiently upon them obedience to that law. And particularly, that the doubts and scruples a thinking mind must needs form within itself concerning futurity; the terms of acceptance with GOD; *and the condition of Penitents in another life, cannot be removed by meer reason. But that a divine revelation is necessary to give full satisfaction and comfort to those who, tho' conscious of their love to* GOD *and virtue, are at the same time sensible of their frequent relapses into known faults; and the imperfection of their best performances.* <vii>

And there is this remarkable difference between Dr Clarke's *way of reasoning to prove these truths, and that of the other author to establish his principles. That the later chooses, instead of enquiring what really is the state of mankind, to determine presumptuously what it must, or ought to be in consequence of the divine goodness. And thus he draws certain consequences from the divine goodness; which, if they were true, would indeed prove the real state of mankind, to be unworthy of* GOD. *A conclusion which, I perswade myself, he will own sufficient to overturn all his reasonings, if it is found to follow from them.*

The Doctor on the other hand first proves; that GOD *is infinitely wise and good; but that because we cannot comprehend the whole of things, we can only be sure in the general. That* GOD *cannot lie or deceive: That he cannot command that which is vitious or immoral in its tendency; nor indeed command tyrannically, or without an infinitely wise end and good reason. That he must will that all his rational creatures act reasonably, or according to the fitness of things. And that in judging his creatures, that is, in rewarding or punishing them, he will have due regard to their condition and circumstances. And that whatever* GOD *does is well done: And therefore, that the safest way to determine what it* <viii> *is fittest for* GOD *to do; is to know what he really does. And, in consequence of these and such like general conclusions, the Doctor proceeds to enquire what is the real state of mankind; gives a clear and true representation of it; and so from real fact infers, that a divine revelation was wanting. And then shews, that the doctrine of* JESUS CHRIST *has all the characters and marks of a divine revelation.*

In short, all that I pretend to do, is to vindicate Dr Clarke's *incomparable Discourse from the inconsistencies with which it is charged by the author of* Christianity as old as the Creation. *And if I can perswade any one to attend to the true state of the question, and to look carefully into what Dr* Clarke *hath said, I have my reward. Truth desires no more, but an impartial fair trial and comparison.* <I>

Christianity Neither False nor Useless,
Tho' not as old as the Creation

Having asserted in the strongest terms (in a *Philosophical Enquiry concerning the Connexion, betwixt the* Doctrines *and* Miracles *of* JESUS CHRIST) the *eternal, universal,* and absolutely *unchangeable* obligation of the *law of nature,* and that it is the great end of *Christianity* to excite and encourage to the obedience of that law; I think my self obliged to make a few remarks upon the *conclusions* the author of *Christianity as old as the Creation* infers, or at least seems willing should be inferr'd from that principle.

I choose to begin with his last chapter, *p. 319.* in which he pretends to shew, that Dr *Clarke, in his discourse of the unchangeable obligation of natural Religion, and the Truth and Certainty of the Christian Revelation,* is inconsistent with himself, and to refute the Doctor <2> from his own principles. The author of *Christianity, &c.* reasons thus: *p. 335.*

"These *Deists* entirely agree with the doctor, when he asserts, that some doctrines are in their own nature *necessarily* and *demonstrably* true; such as are all those which concern the obligation of plain *moral precepts:* and these neither need, nor can receive, any stronger proof from miracles, than what they have already (tho' not perhaps so clearly to all capacities) from the evidence of right reason. Other doctrines are in their own nature *necessarily false, and impossible to be true;* such as are all *absurdities* and *contradictions,* and all doctrines that tend to promote vice; and these can never receive any degree of proof from all the miracles in the world. But as to what the doctor adds, that other doctrines are in their own nature *indifferent,* or *possible,* or perhaps *probable* to be true, and those could not have been known to be positively true, but by the evidence of miracles, which prove them to be certain; here these *Deists* beg leave to differ with him as to any doctrines in their own nature indifferent, BEING THE WILL OF GOD; for that would be to suppose, what the doctor has proved to be impossible, that GOD acts arbitrarily, and out of meer wilfulness."

Now, not to mention, that no doctrine which does not concern the obligation of moral precepts can, in strict propriety of speech, be said to be the *will of* GOD: I would only ask, where it is that Dr *Clarke* says, that <3> doctrines in their own nature *indifferent* may be proved to be the will of GOD by *miracles;* and why this author has changed Dr *Clarke*'s words, and instead of *true, actually true, certain,* or some other such equivalent term, put in their place, words of his own, words never used by Dr *Clarke* on that occasion (*Being the will of* GOD)? the reason will be easily perceived, if we change our author's objection a little, and make use of Dr *Clarke*'s own words, where our author pretends to quote him; which is but doing justice to the Doctor. For then our author's objection will run thus: "Here the *Deists* beg leave to differ with him, as to any doctrines in their own nature indifferent, being proved to be *actually true;* for that would be to suppose, what the Doctor has proved to be impossible, that GOD acts arbitrarily, and out of meer wilfulness." And when the objection is set in this fair just light, it plainly has neither sense nor meaning in it: for into whose head could it possibly enter to argue thus? *Such a doctrine, considered by itself, is indifferent that is uncertain; but when other considerations are taken into the estimate (miracles for example) it may be found to be actually true: therefore* GOD *acts arbitrarily, and out of meer wilfulness.* Is GOD indeed arbitrary and wilful, because the nature of things are so stubborn and wilful, that tho' they cannot be proved in a way their nature does not admit, yet they may be proved by an evidence consonant and agreeable to their nature?

Our author goes on in this manner: "And here they would ask him, since as he owns evil spirits can do miracles, and the nature <4> of the doctrine must be taken into the consideration, how the miracles can prove a doctrine *relating to indifferent things* to be from GOD?"[4]

Here again I must beg leave to do justice to that *worthy writer* Dr *Clarke,* and instead of that phrase *relating to indifferent things,* to put in the Doctor's own Words, that we may see how our author's objection will stand

---

4. Tindal, *Christianity as Old as the Creation,* p. 335.

when this just change is made. And if instead of a doctrine *relating to in-different things,* it is said, in Dr *Clarke*'s words, a doctrine *in itself indifferent;* that is to say, as the Doctor himself explains it, *Such a doctrine, as cannot, by the light of nature and reason alone, be certainly known whether* it be true or false;[5] our author's question, or the question of those *Deists* whose cause he pleads, will be to this effect: "And here they would ask him, since as he owns evil spirits can do miracles, and the nature of the doctrine must be taken into consideration, how the miracles can prove a doctrine in itself indifferent, or that cannot be known to be true or false by reason alone, to be from GOD?"

And to the question stated in this light, I have no more to reply, but that Dr *Clarke* hath given a full, clear, and satisfactory answer to it; which it is not in our author, or his *Deist*'s power to invalidate.

Our author continues thus: "Or how there can be any such doctrines in the christian religion, if what Dr *Clarke* says be true; that <5> every one of the doctrines it teaches, as matter of truth, has a natural tendency, and a direct powerful influence to reform and correct men's lives and manners?"[6]

There cannot indeed be any doctrines in the christian religion *relating to indifferent things;* because, as Dr *Clarke* has proved, every one of the doctrines it teaches has a natural tendency, and a direct powerful influence to promote the honour of GOD, and the practice of righteousness; and these indeed are not *indifferent things.* But where has Dr *Clarke* said that there may be in the christian religion doctrines relating to indifferent things? nay, on the contrary, doth he not ever assert, that every one of the doctrines Christianity teaches, is so far from being indifferent in its nature and tendency, that there is not one of them, which has not naturally, a direct powerful influence to promote piety and virtue? and if he hath not said so, is it fair or just to represent him saying so? the Doctor hath sufficiently explained again, and again, what he means by doctrines in their own nature indifferent; and our author could not have any other reason for changing the Doctor's words, or misrepresenting his meaning; but that he could not

5. Clarke, *Discourse,* p. 380.
6. Tindal, *Christianity as Old as the Creation,* p. 335.

possibly disprove what the Doctor has so clearly proved; and therefore it was to his purpose to make the Doctor appear to say what he hath no where said. To say, that a doctrine that tends to promote the honour of GOD, and the practice of righteousness, is not *indifferent;* after the pains that Dr *Clarke* hath taken to explain what he means by *indifferent* is meer quibbling. And to prove that every doctrine which hath a tendency to pro-<6>mote virtue, piety, and righteousness, can be known to be certainly true by reason alone, and without the evidence of miracles, is undertaking a very difficult task; and yet it is what our author, or his *Deists,* must prove, or their question amounts to no more than this, "How can any doctrines which have a natural tendency to reform mens lives, stand in need of miracles to prove their truth?" which is the very question Dr *Clarke* hath answered. When the truth of a doctrine is proved to result necessarily from the consideration of the divine attributes, and the relation man stands in to GOD, that doctrine is indeed proved to be true in itself; and such a doctrine cannot receive any stronger proof from miracles. But is there not a manifest difference between saying a doctrine is demonstrable from the nature of GOD and of mankind; and saying that the belief of a doctrine naturally tends to encourage virtue, and restrain from vice? Or are indeed all doctrines, the belief of which has this tendency, for that very reason, necessarily true? But our author goes on thus, *p.* 337. "The *Deists* can, by no means, come into the Doctor's distinction between the moral part of our SAVIOUR's doctrine, and that part which evidently tends to promote the honour of GOD, and the practice of righteousness; it being manifestly a distinction without any difference."

It appears to me of such consequence to the whole of our author's argument, to overthrow that distinction hitherto so universally received; that I wonder our author should have satisfied himself with barely affirming, that it is a distinction without any difference. For my own <7> part, so different are the eyes of my understanding from his, that it hath ever appeared to me to be a distinction founded upon a clear and obvious difference in the nature of things. To be sure every doctrine that tends to promote a moral end, is moral in its tendency; and therefore in that sense all the doctrines of Christianity may be justly called moral doctrines. Yet that does not hinder, but that in accurate writing a distinction ought to be made between that part of our SAVIOUR's doctrine, in which he lays down rules for the conduct of life, evidently founded on the nature and reason of things, and consequently of eternal and universal obligation; And the other part, which affirms the truth of certain propositions; the persuasion of which has a powerful influence to promote the observance of these moral rules, or enjoins the use of certain means in order to our improvement in virtue, and our being assisted to live agreeably to the law of our natures. Because the first part is capable of proof from the nature of the things themselves; from the properties and relations of moral agents. The other part asserts certain facts, or constitutions in the Government of the world, only to be known by the testimony of him, who governs the world; and in consequence of the truth of these facts enjoins certain means which naturally tend to promote virtue and righteousness, but could not be known before these facts or constitutions were revealed; from which their fitness follows. Of this kind are the eternity of future rewards; an universal judgment; the resurrection of our bodies; the forgiveness of sins upon repentance, when seriously implored in the name of CHRIST; the <8> assistance promised to the virtuous in times of tryal and difficulty, when it is seriously demanded in our SAVIOUR's name, and according to his promise; and several others of the christian motives to honour GOD, and live virtuously, which Dr *Clarke* hath so well explained; as well as the means of improving in virtue, which result from the truth of these motives; such as prayer in the name of CHRIST; the commemoration of his death and resurrection; and other such christian duties. Several considerations, fetched from the nature of GOD, and what we are able to comprehend of his government and providence, contribute not a little to render these doctrines probable, but it is only testimony; testimony from GOD himself; or, which comes to the same thing, by his authority; that according to the very nature of things, is able to prove these doctrines to be actually true. A very little acquaintance with common *logic,* or the *doctrine* of *evidence,* will sufficiently prevent any one's being misled by arguments, which indeed have no force at all; but upon the supposition, that there is no place for a distinction, which that science clearly establishes: and therefore it is needless to insist long upon this head. Allow me only, by an example or two, to set the affair in a light suited to every capacity. 'Tis certainly the duty of every young man to live soberly and virtuously, and to improve his mind, as well as to take care of his health; suppose, therefore, a rich well disposed friend, to excite and encourage a young fellow to behave himself well, should write him a kind letter; lay before him the proper rules for his conduct and improvement; and at the same time pro-<9>mise him a plentiful estate, in ten or twenty years, if he behave himself according to these rules; and all that time maintain a friendly correspondence with him, by letters upon virtuous and useful subjects: such a proffer hath certainly a moral tendency, because, in the very nature of the thing, it must have a powerful influence to engage the young man to live wisely: the virtuous correspondence proposed is likewise a noble mean to cherish and improve the virtuous disposition to which the reward is promised: but surely it is not the virtuous tendency of the promise; nor of the proposed commerce that could render the young man secure as, to his obtaining at last the profered reward; it is only the promise itself confirmed and sealed in due valid form that could satisfy him, as to the reality and truth of this generous motive, to behave as common sense and reason tells him he should, without any such expectation of reward. In like manner, if a worthy offended father, after having justly abandoned his rakish rebellious son, moved by fatherly pity, and generous compassion, should promise his son, if he would yet reform in earnest, and give good evidence of his amendment, that he would forgive his former vitiousness; assist him in his endeavours to retrieve lost time; and improve in virtue and knowledge; and at last, after having had sufficient proof of his sincere and thorough reformation, make him as happy in every respect as his heart could wish; and should send one to deal with his son for this effect, and with full power to satisfy the son as to the sincerity and truth of the father's promise: such conduct is certainly worthy of a virtuous <10> tender hearted father; hath a fine tendency, and is in that respect moral, nay truly divine; and thus the son would have a strong additional motive and inducement to amend and correct his manners, which could not fail to have a very good effect, if there were yet remaining in his breast any sparks of humanity and gratitude unextinguished: such a motive however he could not have had, if the loving compassionate father had not condescended to give him assurances of it under his own hand and seal; and yet it must be owned, that to the thing itself he is strongly bound, without such encouragement, by all the ties of nature and of virtue, of reason and of religion.

But our author goes on thus: "And if the whole of religion consists in the honour of GOD, and the good of mankind (which Dr *Clarke* is far from denying); nothing can more effectually strike at the certainty of all religion, than the supposing, that mankind could not be certain, that whatever tended to promote the honour of GOD, and the practice of righteousness was the will of GOD, 'till they were convinced of it by undeniable miracles."[7]

Now here again, that no body may mistake Dr *Clarke*'s meaning, I must observe that our author has again misrepresented him; and that, when justice is done to the Doctor, and if we keep to his meaning and words, our author's objection will stand thus: "And if the whole of religion consists in the honour of GOD, and the good of mankind (which Dr *Clarke* is far from denying); nothing can more effe-<11>ctually strike at the certainty of all religion, than the supposing that mankind could not be certain, that a doctrine *in itself indifferent;* that is, (which could not be known by the light of nature and reason) was actually true (however moral and good its tendency may be) 'till they were convinced of it by undeniable miracles."

And when the objection is set in this fair light; every attentive impartial reader must needs be surprized what the author can mean by it. Is it striking at the certainty of all religion to say, that certain doctrines which, if proved and believed to be true, would have a powerful influence to promote piety and virtue, can only, according to the nature of things, be proved to be true by testimony and miracles; and to *shew* that GOD hath *testified* the truth of these doctrines by miracles undeniable? all the duties of Religion and morality are (as Dr *Clarke* has proved much better than our author, and with quite a different view) of everlasting and unchangeable obligation. But there are some motives, the belief of which must, in the nature of things, have a mighty influence to promote the practice of these duties, that divine testimony, confirmed by miracles, can only render certain. And how these are proved to be certain and positively true by the miracles of JESUS CHRIST, Dr *Clarke* has demonstrated beyond all exception. And if this is striking at the certainty of all religion; *demonstrating* the internal excellency and obligation of moral duties; and at the same time *confirming* other considerations, which have the most powerful tendency to promote the

7. Tindal, *Christianity as Old as the Creation*, p. 337.

practice and <12> observance of these duties, is *fighting* against religion and virtue. Sure I am it may be much more reasonably said on the other hand, that the endeavouring to destroy or diminish all regard to the motives JESUS CHRIST sets before us, confirmed by his miracles, is *striking* at the certainty of the most powerful perswasives to virtue; and under pretence of magnifying the force of the Religion of reason and nature, cutting off what has ever been found in fact to be the greatest restraint from vice.

Our author goes on thus, *p.* 338. "If no miracles can prove any indifferent thing to be the will of GOD, and all that evidently tends to promote the honour of GOD, and practice of righteousness, are *plain moral duties* (as the Doctor contends); and all such duties neither need nor can receive any stronger proof from miracles, than what they have already from the evidence of right reason. How can miracles (say these *Deists*) have any other use than to make men consider the nature and tendency of a doctrine, and judge from thence whether it be from GOD." Here again our author makes his *Deists* pervert and change the Doctor's meaning and words; for in the first place, it is true the Doctor hath often said, that moral duties can receive no stronger proof from miracles than what they have already from the evidence of right reason. But the Doctor hath no where said, that all doctrines that evidently tend to promote the honour of GOD, and the practice of righteousness are *plain moral duties;* but on the contrary he ever distinguishes between the *moral part* of CHRIST's doctrines, <13> and the *doctrines* of CHRIST which tend to promote obedience to moral precepts; being in their natures powerful motives to such moral obedience. But it seems our author thinks it allowable to reason against Dr *Clarke,* as if he had made no such distinction, because *he himself* thinks there is no foundation for the distinction; and indeed, as I have already said, the whole of our author's argument, not only in this chapter, but through all the book, depends intirely upon this single point. That there is no difference between moral duties and motives to the practice of these duties; which is just as absurd as it would be to say, that there is no difference betwixt writing good sense, and a reward for writing it. And in the next place, Dr *Clarke* has no where said, that no indifferent thing, that is, no positive institution, can be proved to be the will of GOD by miracles. I once designed to have shown at some length, in opposition to our author, that things meerly *positive* may be made by external revelation *ingredients* of religion, not only consistently with the good of mankind, as well as the honour of GOD; but effectually to prevent superstition, and all its mischievous consequences. But I have already in the *Enquiry*, sufficiently vindicated several of the positive institutions of Christianity; and find myself prevented, as to what I had further to say upon that subject, by some late writers against our author, particularly *my worthy ingenious friend Mr Wallace* in his *Remarks*.[8] Allow me only to say, that for all the author of *Christianity as old as the Creation* hath said to the contrary, it may easily be proved; That consistently with the good of mankind, and the honour of GOD, <14> to promote the most valuable and worthy of all purposes, the maintaining in human minds a steady constant sense of their absolute dependence upon GOD their Creator, and indispensible obligation to submit to his will in all things, it might have been commanded by external revelation; *That every man should once every day, hold up his hand streight for a minute or two, as a declaration of his bearing in remembrance his dependence on GOD, and obligation to obey him.* In this argument it is proper to abstract from all that is positive in Christianity, and to take for an example of a positive thing that may be made an ingredient of religion; an action the most indifferent in its own nature that can be imagined; and not ordained by any pretended revelation. Because if it cannot be demonstrated, that any action, the most positive and indifferent in itself that can be thought of, cannot be made an *ingredient of religion;* all possible objections against the *positive institutions of Christianity* must fall to the ground. Now to prove that such an indifferent action cannot be made an ingredient in religion; it must be proved, that the maintaining a constant sense of our dependence upon GOD cannot be commanded by any external revelation: that it is inconsistent with the honour of GOD, and the good of mankind, for GOD to require and command it; because common sense and reason tells us we ought to do it. Or it must be proved, that tho' GOD should command by an external revelation our maintaining and keeping in our minds a constant sense of our dependence, he cannot consistently with his honour, and the good of mankind, command us to

8. Robert Wallace, *The Regard due to Divine Revelation, and to Pretences to it, considered. A Sermon . . . With a Preface, Containing Some Remarks on a Book lately publish'd, Entitled, Christianity as Old as the Creation* (London, 1731), pp. iii–xxviii.

express the <15> sense we have of our dependence by any *outward sign:* nor command us regularly to perform any *ceremony, rite, or indifferent action,* in order to preserve upon our minds that sense; and our author has as yet said nothing to prove either the one or the other. And indeed to attempt to prove the first would be to attempt to prove, that it is inconsistent with the goodness of GOD, for GOD to take all care and pains to keep alive among mankind a sense and perswasion that naturally tends to promote his honour, and their good. And to assert the last, is to assert, that it is unworthy of GOD that men should declare the sense they have of the obligations they are under to honour and obey him: for if it is consistent with the honour of GOD, and the good of mankind, that mankind should have this sense internally, and declare it outwardly, it can never be inconsistent with the honour of GOD and the good of mankind, to appoint some *outward sign* by which it may be declared; seeing it cannot be declared *outwardly,* but by giving some *outward sign* of it. If all mankind in general, or any particular nation, should agree to perform regularly every day, any action, in itself indifferent, as a public outward declaration of the sense they have of their dependence on GOD, and obligation to obey him: such a contract or agreement could hardly be reckoned inconsistent with the honour of GOD, and the good of mankind; the end and design of this agreement being to preserve that sense of mankind's dependence upon GOD, and obligation to honour and obey him; than which nothing can have a better effect in society. Much less therefore can such an appointment by GOD <16> himself be inconsistent with the honour of GOD, and the good of mankind; seeing the performing any indifferent action, to declare the sense of our dependence upon GOD in obedience to the *divine appointment,* must have a more powerful influence to preserve that sense than the doing it voluntarily, or by human agreement. And whatever may be said, as to any society of men's having a right to appoint any thing of that kind; there can be no dispute about GOD's having a right to make such an appointment. 'Tis to no purpose to say, that it must be the main, nay the only end of an external revelation, truly divine, to promote the practice of moral duties: for that can only prove, that the end of every appointment, by external revelation, must be moral. And any sign or action that is proper to promote among mankind the sense of their dependence upon GOD, when appointed by GOD for that end, however indifferent it may be in itself, becomes in consequence of its *appointment,* in order to that end, *moral* in its tendency. And no action or sign is fit to be appointed for such an end, unless it is in its own nature indifferent. Because it is only by doing a thing in itself *indifferent,* in obedience to the divine appointment, by which we can declare the sense we have of our dependence upon GOD, and our obligation to submit to his will in all things; or indeed so effectually preserve upon our minds this sense. The doing any action in itself not *indifferent,* but of a moral and obligatory nature, could not serve this purpose so well; because such an action, being in itself moral and obligatory, could not *purely* signify and declare the sense <17> we have of our obligation to GOD, and dependence upon him: nor would such an action, to the doing which we are obliged upon many accounts, contribute so effectually to preserve that sense as the doing an action for the which there could be no reason, but the declaring outwardly our having that sense. Whatever GOD may do in a *political view* when he condescends to be a king or lawgiver to a particular people (as he did to the Jews): it is certain, that in a view *meerly religious* he cannot multiply the observance of things in themselves indifferent. But as in the former case GOD cannot be said to act *arbitrarily,* meerly because we are not able to comprehend the reasons and end of his *political laws;* but on the contrary ought, on account of his infinite wisdom and goodness, to be supposed by us ever to act for reasons worthy of himself, and of his administration: and never to have commanded any thing, without an excellent end and reason; because to act otherwise would indeed be to act tyrannically. So in the other case, GOD cannot be said to act *arbitrarily* or *without a reason* when a thing is commanded, which, tho' in itself *indifferent,* yet in consequence of its *appointment for a certain end,* becomes evidently conducive to a most noble and worthy purpose. 'Tis only the *multiplying such commands* in such a manner, as to *infringe* considerably upon human *liberties;* and so as to render the strict observance of these commands cumbersome and inconvenient, or a *real hardship;* when the end, the only end, of such commandments can be obtained by one or a few observances, not in the least troublesome or incommodious; *that can be called, acting* wilfully, or *commanding* ty-<18>rannically. Wicked priests, says our author, would soon teach the people to place all religion and virtue in the strict observance of such a positive institution. But certainly that wicked priests may pervert such an institution for their own ends, is no better reason why there never ought to be any such institution; than the abuse that has been often made of civil power, is to prove that there ought to be no such thing as civil power. I know nothing that hath not, or is not capable of being abused and perverted: and it is sufficient, with regard to all that is said by our *author and his Deists,* of the superstitious mischievous abuses that have been made of *positive institutions,* to observe, that the *abuse* of a thing will never prove that a thing is bad: and that if GOD *acts arbitrarily and wilfully* when he does any thing for mankind, that mankind may abuse; GOD *acts arbitrarily and wilfully* in bestowing upon mankind reason, philosophy, and wit, for surely these have been most manifestly abused and misapplyed to the worst, the most pernicious purposes: not only to hinder men from *hearkning* to the voice of GOD by external revelation; and to laugh them out of all regard to what he thinks fit to *command,* with the clearest marks of his *authority;* but likewise to prevent our *hearkning* to the voice of nature itself; the voice of the law of GOD within our breasts; and to perswade men that *fancy,* arbitrary whimsical *fancy,* ought to be our only guide: that we may live as we list; pursue our pleasures without remorse or fear; for GOD concerneth himself not in the matter.

Our author goes on thus, *p.* 338. "Allowing the Doctor what hypothesis he pleases <19> in relation to miracles; yet if the doctrines themselves, from their internal excellency do not give us a certain proof of the will of GOD; no traditional miracles can do it; because one probability added to another will not amount to certainty."

DR *Clarke* requires no hypothesis to be allowed him in relation to miracles, but plainly and clearly proves (Dr *Clarke's Discourse,* &c. *p.* 383.) to use his own words. "That the doctrine CHRIST taught being in itself possible, and in its consequences tending to promote the honour of GOD, and true righteousness among men; and the miracles he worked being such, that there neither was, nor could be, any pretence of more, or greater miracles to be set up in opposition to them; it was as infallibly certain, that he had truly a divine commission, as it was certain, that GOD would not himself impose upon men a necessary and invincible error."

Now if Dr *Clarke* hath proved all this; he hath not added one probability to another in order to make up a certainty: tho' undoubtedly, it is only by accumulating *probabilities,* that moral *certainty* can be produced. But to a *probability* arising from the doctrines of CHRIST considered by themselves in their natures and tendency; he hath added a *certainty* arising from the miracles which CHRIST work'd to prove his divine commission to teach these doctrines: a *certainty* founded clearly upon a *principle* as plain and true as any other in the world can be, *that* GOD *can neither lie nor deceive.* And Dr *Clarke* has clearly proved, notwithstanding <20> all our author hath said, that it is infallibly true, that CHRIST had indeed a divine mission to *assure* us of the truth of certain *propositions,* the belief of which hath a powerful tendency to promote the practice of all moral duties: and, in consequence of the truth of these propositions, to *command* the observance of certain *duties; the fitness* of which evidently appears from the truth of the *propositions* which he taught and confirmed. And to deal plainly with our author; if he would prove directly what he is manifestly aiming at, tho' indirectly, throughout the whole of his dialogue, namely, that Christianity is *false* and *useless,* he must prove that the doctrines CHRIST taught have not a strong and powerful influence to promote the observance of moral duties; obedience to the law of nature; and that the *few positive institutions* of Christianity have no tendency; no fitness to promote that end. *For if all that CHRIST taught and enjoined tends plainly to that noble end, Christianity is certainly useful, exceeding useful.* Or he must prove, that the miracles which CHRIST work'd, were not sufficient to evince his divine commission to teach these doctrines. For tho' he should prove that natural reason is able to demonstrate the truth of every doctrine CHRIST taught, as a motive to the observance of the moral law (which he will not readily undertake); it will not follow, that these doctrines may not likewise be proved to be true by extrinsical revelation and miracles; nor that such a proof of them may not be useful and fit for very noble and excellent purposes. And if Christianity properly consists in proving certain doctrines to be true, by *the extrinsic evidence of miracles;* even supposing that <21> these doctrines were capable of an internal proof and evidence, it would not follow that Christianity was as old as the Creation: unless it could be proved, that CHRIST's confirmation of these doctrines by his miracles was as antient as their internal evidence.[9] And therefore our author, even to prove the point he pretends to prove, must shew that all the doctrines CHRIST taught, as motives to the observance of the *Law of Nature,* not only have the same internal evidence that all the precepts of the *Law of Nature* have; but likewise had from the beginning of the Creation the same *extrinsic evidence* of their truth that the miracles of JESUS CHRIST give them. *For a publication or a confirmation in a certain way can never be said to be older than that publication or confirmation is.* But it is plain, that all the pains our author takes, to show that the Gospel is nothing else but a *republication* of the Religion of Nature; is designed to shew, that there never was *need* of such a *republication:* that such a *republication* would have been useless; and that there never was such a *republication* by a commission from Heaven. He hath not indeed any where directly said so; but I am much mistaken if he, or his *Deists,* will be angry with any one for taking that to be his design and intent. Let me therefore only tell him, that he hath by no means proved that point; nor so much as shewn that Dr *Clarke* is inconsistent with himself, even tho' Dr *Clarke*'s distinction between the moral part and the rest of our SAVIOUR's doctrine, should be laid aside. For, as we shall see by and by, Dr *Clarke* hath clearly proved, that a *publication* even of the Law and Religion of Nature, by <22> external Revelation and Miracles, was not only useful but necessary when our SAVIOUR appeared in the world teaching the moral law, and exhorting to the observance of it by the most powerful and perswasive motives. And our author hath not said any thing that deserves the least notice, against the sufficiency of our SAVIOUR's miracles, to prove that he taught by a divine commission: *Except that evil spirits can do miracles;* to which objection Dr *Clarke* and several others have long ago shewn, that our SAVIOUR himself gave a very satisfactory answer.[10] *And that the wise Greeks reckon miracles only fit for fools;* to which it is fully enough to answer, that while there are so many fools in the world, that can only be restrained from being knaves, by arguments fitted to their capacity and genius, that it is a very bad office to endeavour to let these fools see there is nothing at

9. On the distinction between the internal and external evidences for the truth of Christianity see above, p. 143, note 13.

10. Tindal, *Christianity as Old as the Creation,* p. 335; Clarke, *Discourse,* pp. 379–82.

all in these arguments which are such a *restraint* and *curb* upon them. While the belief of miracles is only employ'd to excite men to live honestly and righteously, and honour GOD, it is certainly doing mischief to weaken the force of that belief, tho' at the bottom there was no foundation for it but human weakness and credulity. And yet after all I may adventure to defy our author to prove, that *certain miracles* are not, in the nature of things, a fit and proper proof of certain *propositions;* and consequently a proof not to fools only, but to the wisest. But I'll say no more on that subject at present, having sufficiently clear'd that matter in the *Philosophical Enquiry concerning the connexion between the* Miracles *and* Doctrines *of* JESUS CHRIST. <23>

Our author, *p.* 339. goes on to show, that Dr *Clarke,* when he endeavours to prove the necessity of a Divine Revelation, destroys all that he had said concerning the eternal, universal, and unchangeable obligation of the Law of Nature. Now in order to see whether the Doctor does indeed contradict himself, let us enquire what the Doctor himself hath said, and not content ourselves with our author's account, or rather misrepresentation of the Doctor's argument. And indeed no more is necessary to confute the false principles our author endeavours to establish throughout the whole of his book, than to set in opposition to them the principles which Dr *Clarke* has indisputably demonstrated.

"DR *Clarke* proves first, that the same necessary and eternal different relations; that different things bear one to another: and the same consequent fitness or unfitness of the application of different things, or different relations one to another; with regard to which the will of GOD always and necessarily does determine itself to choose to act only what is agreeable to justice, equity, goodness, and truth, in order to the welfare of the whole universe; ought likewise constantly to determine the wills of all subordinate rational Beings; to govern all their actions by the same rules for the good of the public in their respective stations. That is, these eternal and necessary differences of things make it fit and reasonable for all creatures so to act; they cause it to be their duty; or lay an obligation upon them so to <24> do, even separate from the consideration of these rules, being the positive will or command of GOD; and also antecedent to any respect or regard, expectation or apprehension of any particular, private, or personal advantage, reward, or punishment, either present or future; annexed, either by natural consequence, or by positive appointment, to the practice or ne-glecting of those rules."[11] And from this principle which he demonstrates, *p.* 175, *&c.* He begins *p.* 197. to deduce in particular, the three great and principal branches of moral duties, or natural religion, from which all the other and smaller instances of duty do naturally flow, or may without dif-ficulty be derived. But to show the weakness of our author's reasoning against Dr *Clarke,* or rather against the necessity of a divine revelation, it is necessary to take particular notice of several things which the Doctor says and proves, in explaining and confirming that principle. And first of all, let us observe, that the Doctor expresly says, *p.* 184. "That what these eternal and unalterable relations, respects, or proportions of things, with their con-sequent agreements or disagreements, fitness or unfitness, absolutely and necessarily *are in themselves;* That also they *appear* to be to the understand-ings of all intelligent beings, except those only who understand things to be what they are not; that is, whose understandings are either very imper-fect, or very much depraved."[12] And therefore, *p.* 185. he says. "Negligent misunderstanding, and wilful passions, or lusts, are the only causes which can make a reason-<25>able creature act contrary to reason. For originally, and in reality, 'tis as natural and (morally speaking) necessary, that the will should be determined in every action, by the reason of the thing, and the right of the case, as 'tis natural, and (absolutely speaking) necessary, that the understanding should submit to a demonstrated truth."[13]

Secondly. He asserts and proves, *p.* 188, *&c.* "That in like manner as no one, who is instructed in Mathematics, can forbear giving his assent to every geometrical demonstration; of which he understands the terms, either by his own study, or by having had them explained to him by others; so no man, who has either patience or opportunities to examine and consider things himself; or has the means of being taught and instructed in any tolerable manner by others, concerning the necessary relation and depen-dency of things, can avoid giving his assent to the fitness, and reasonable-ness of his governing all his actions by the law or rule before-mentioned, even tho' his practice thro' the prevalence of brutish lusts, be most absurdly contradictory to that assent."

11. Clarke, *Discourse,* p. 174.
12. Clarke, *Discourse,* pp. 183–84.
13. Turnbull paraphrases Clarke, *Discourse,* pp. 185–86.

Thirdly, In answer to the only thing which can with any colour be objected against the necessity of the mind's giving its assent to the eternal law of righteousness: which is the total ignorance that some whole nations are reported to lie under, of the nature and force of these moral obligations. He replies: "All that this objection proves, supposing the matter of it to be true, is only this; not that the mind of man can ever dissent from <26> the rule of right, much less that there is no necessary difference in nature between moral good and evil. But it proves only, that men had great need to be taught and instructed in some very plain and easy, as well as certain, truths; and if they be important truths, that then men have need also to have them frequently inculcated and strongly enforced upon them. Which is very true, and is (as shall hereafter be particularly made to appear) one good argument for the reasonableness of expecting a revelation."[14]

This is a fair account, in the Doctor's own words, of what he says and proves concerning the universality and plainness of moral obligations. Let us therefore enquire whether the Doctor is justly charged with contradicting what he had said on that subject, when he afterwards asserts, *p.* 272, *&c.* "That tho' the necessity and indispensableness of all the great and moral obligations in religion be thus in general deducible, even demonstrably, by a chain of clear and undeniable reasoning: yet (in the present state of the world, by what means soever it came originally to be so corrupted) such is the carelessness, inconsiderateness, and want of attention of the greater part of mankind; so many the prejudices and false notions taken up by evil education; so strong and violent the unreasonable lusts, appetites, and desires of sense; and so great the blindness introduced by superstitious opinions, vicious customs, and debauched practices thro' the world; that very few are able in reality and effect to discover these things clearly and plainly for <27> themselves: but men have great need of particular teaching, and much instruction to convince them of the truth and certainty, and importance of these things; to give them a due sense, and clear and just apprehensions concerning them; and to bring them effectually to the practice of the plainest and most necessary duties."[15]

Or when he asserts, *p.* 281. "That tho' in almost every age, there have

---

14. Clarke, *Discourse,* pp. 196–97.
15. Clarke, *Discourse,* pp. 272–73. Turnbull has altered Clarke's wording.

indeed been in the heathen world some wise and brave and good men, who have made it their business to study and practise the duties of natural religion themselves; and to teach and exhort others to do the like; who seem therefore to have been raised up by providence as instruments to reprove in some measure, and put some kind of check to the extreme superstition and wickedness of the nations, wherein they lived; yet none of these have ever been able to reform the world with any considerably great and universal success; because they have been but very few, that have in earnest set themselves about this excellent work; and they that have indeed sincerely done it, have themselves been intirely very ignorant of some doctrines; and very doubtful and uncertain of others, absolutely necessary for the bringing about that great end; and those things which they have been certain of, and in good measure understood, they have not been able to prove and explain clearly enough; and those that they have been able to prove and explain by sufficiently clear reasoning; they have not yet had authority enough to enforce and in-<28>culcate upon mens minds with so strong an impression, as to influence and govern the general practice of the world." [16]

If these assertions are true, the conclusion the Doctor draws from them, in his seventh proposition, *p.* 304. must be inevitably so. "That for these reasons there was plainly wanting a *divine revelation,* to recover mankind out of their universal degenerate state, into a state suitable to the original excellency of their nature."

Now the Doctor proves the assertion to be true; from which this conclusion necessarily follows in the only way that *facts* must, or indeed can be proved at all, from the *history* and *experience* of all ages. The enquiry is not what GOD may, or may not permit; what is consistent, or not consistent with his divine wisdom;* but what is truth and matter of fact; and how the case, with respect to mankind, stands. And in order to show that the fact is not as the Doctor hath represented it, one must disprove all history, and flee in the face of universal experience itself. But if the facts are as they are represented in the foregoing assertions, our author's first and fundamental

---

* *For it is in a very few cases only that we are able to determine what* GOD *may, or may not permit: tho' in the general we are sure "That whatever he does, or permits, is wisely done, or permitted."*

16. Clarke, *Discourse,* pp. 281–82.

proposition is utterly false, *p.* 1. "That GOD at all times has given mankind sufficient means of knowing what he requires of them."* As is also <29> his thirteenth proposition, *p.* 208. "That the bulk of mankind, by their reason, are able to distinguish between religion and superstition."[17] And indeed all our author's reasonings, to prove these two propositions, amount to no more than this; *It seemeth to me wise and good that it should be so, therefore it must be so:* and that is a reasoning long ago exploded by philosophers in their enquiries concerning phaenomena, facts, or appearances of whatever kind, natural or moral. But not to insist upon the arrogance that is in this kind of argument, so unbecoming creatures: nor to stay to prove the wisdom of the divine moral government as it really is, because that belongs not to the present question; I shall only take notice of the chief things our author says against Dr *Clarke* upon this subject. This, says our author, *p.* 339. (after a short representation of Dr *Clarke*'s argument) "is supposing GOD had left mankind for four thousand years together, and even the greatest part to this day, destitute of sufficient means to do their duty, and to preserve them from sinking into a corrupt and degenerate state, and that it was impossible for them when thus sunk to recover themselves."[18] To this I answer, that Dr *Clarke*'s assertion, concerning the estate of mankind, does not *suppose,* but *affirm* this. But then why does the Doctor affirm it? Because as he himself tells (of his *Discourse, p.* 302.) "In experience and practice it hath appeared to be altogether impossible for philosophy and bare reason to reform mankind effectually, without the assistance of some higher principle; for tho' the bare natural possibility of the thing cannot in-<30>deed easily be denied; yet (as *Cicero* excellently expresses it)† *in like manner as in physic it matters nothing whether a disease be such, that no man does or no man can recover from it: so neither does it make any difference whether by philosophy no man is, or no man can be made wise*

---

* I. e. *As he himself explains it; All the duties of natural religion; or, that are founded on the natures of things.*

† Cicero de Natura Deorum, l. iii. [Cicero, *De natura deorum,* III.xxxii.79: "For just as it makes no difference whether no one *is* in good health or no one *can be* in good health, so I do not understand what difference it makes whether no one *is* wise or no one *can be* wise."]

17. Tindal, *Christianity as Old as the Creation,* p. 209.

18. Tindal, *Christianity as Old as the Creation,* pp. 339–40.

and good. So that (continueth the Doctor) without some greater help and assistance, mankind is plainly left in a very bad state."

But according to this supposition says our author, *p.* 340. "GOD expects impossibilities from mankind, their duty being the same after as before the fall, *viz.* either to preserve themselves from falling, or if fallen, to recover themselves." [19] Now I would gladly know how this conclusion follows; that because mankind actually are in a degenerate state; out of which it is morally impossible for them to recover themselves, that therefore GOD expects impossibilities. Sure I am Dr *Clarke* has no where said so. And as sure I am the conclusion does not follow. On the contrary it is as certain as that there is a GOD, that GOD cannot require impossibilities; and consequently that GOD cannot require that mankind should come to the knowledge of all these truths that are necessary to be known by them, in order to their effectual recovery out of a corrupt and degenerate state; which they cannot know without some greater help and assistance than bare reason. How GOD will judge men at last, belongs not to us to determine. One thing however we may be sure <31> of, that GOD is merciful and gracious, and will have a due regard, in judging mankind, to the state and circumstances men were placed in by his over-ruling providence: but in reality in this *Enquiry,* which is indeed concerning matter of fact, we are by no means obliged to determine what GOD may precisely require of men in certain circumstances, or how GOD will judge men that have been actually placed by his providence in certain circumstances. The question is, What is the *state* of mankind without a *revelation,* and whether *bare philosophy* and *reason* hath ever been able to *teach* mankind even all *moral* duties; and to *enforce* them upon their minds with due efficacy? And to determine this question, and show that there was plainly wanting a divine revelation, to recover mankind out of their universally degenerate estate, into a state suitable to the original excellency of their nature; I appeal, as Dr *Clarke* does, to history and universal experience, which only can determine this question. But surely every unprejudiced reader must needs be surprised to hear our author reasoning thus: "That if mankind be in a state of universal degeneracy and corruption, this must then be the state GOD designed they

19. Turnbull has altered Tindal's wording.

should be in: and it would seem not only to be in vain, but a crime in them, to endeavour to change that state in which GOD of his infinite wisdom and goodness thought fit to place them."[20] For the degeneracy and corruption of mankind being indisputable, is not that way of arguing an indirect accusation of an all-wise and infinitely good GOD, as if he was pleased to see his creatures in an abject degenerate state. And <32> according to this way of reasoning, of our author's (for the fact from which it is inferred is undeniable) it was a crime for *Socrates,* and other brave and wise antient moralists, to instruct their fellow creatures and endeavour to reform them. And when a nation or people is in a state of ignorance and barbarity, which is the condition of a great part of the world at this very day, it is opposing the design of Heaven; horrid thought! for any one to awaken out of that dismal universal sleep; rouse his natural powers and endeavour to become wiser himself: and still *more criminal* for any one to take pains to make his fellow citizens wiser and better.

As for what follows in the same *p.* 340. one part of it is certainly true: "That GOD will at no time command any thing not fit for him to command; or for man to do."[21] But as for what he says in the beginning of that paragraph: "If men alike at all times owe their existence to GOD, they at all times must be created in a state of innocence, capable of knowing and doing all GOD requires of them." If it proves any thing, it proves (as the schools speak) too much: no more however than is absolutely necessary to the purpose of our author's book; and without which all his reasoning falls to the ground. *That GOD is obliged by his infinite wisdom and goodness, to place all mankind at all times in such circumstances, that they may be all equally wise, equally knowing, equally good, and equally happy; and that any part of mankind's being at any time in a state of corruption and ignorance, is utterly inconsistent with the divine perfections.* <33> And if that could be demonstrated; (as indeed it cannot) considering the case of a great part of the world in all ages, and at this very time; there would be no need of disputing about a *divine revelation.*

Our author goes on thus: "The Doctor to shew the fault was not in

20. Tindal, *Christianity as Old as the Creation,* p. 340.
21. Turnbull distorts Tindal's meaning in this passage.

mankind, but in the guide GOD gave them; says, &c."²² And here I only desire any candid reader to look to what Dr *Clarke* has said; or cast his eye on what I have quoted from him in his own words; and I will leave it to him to judge of our author's fairness and integrity in his way of treating that worthy justly esteemed author, notwithstanding his pretended zeal for the universal law of righteousness; the very first principle of which is to render justice to every one. The Doctor hath in the plainest strongest terms asserted again and again "That negligent misunderstanding, and wilful passions or lusts, are the only causes which can make a reasonable creature act contrary to reason. And *that was it not for these inexcusable* corruptions and depravations it is impossible but the same proportions and fitnesses of things which have so much weight, and so much excellency in them; that the all-powerful Creator and Governor of the universe thinks it no diminution of his power to make this reason of things the unalterable rule and law of all his own actions in the government of the world; and does nothing by meer will and arbitrariness; it is impossible (saith the Doctor) if it was not for inexcusable <34> corruption and depravation, but the same eternal reason of things must much more have weight enough to determine constantly the wills and actions of all subordinate, finite, dependent, and accountable Beings."*

And is this then to say that the fault was not in mankind, but in the guide GOD gave them? The Doctor indeed says, that the light of nature and right reason was altogether insufficient to restore true piety; but not that GOD *has any where left himself altogether without a witness,* or that the difference of good and evil is to any rational being undiscernible; but because the greater part of mankind are not only unattentive, and barely ignorant; but commonly they have also, thro' a careless and evil education, taken up early prejudices, and many vain foolish notions which pervert their natural understandings, and hinder them from using their reason in moral matters to any effectual purpose. And because in the generality of men, the appetites and desires of sense are so violent and importunate; the business and the pleasures of the world take up so much of their time; and

---

* Dr *Clarke*'s Discourse, *p.* 185.
22. Tindal, *Christianity as Old as the Creation,* p. 340.

their passions are so very strong and unreasonable, that of themselves they are very backward and unapt to employ their reason upon moral matters; and still more backward to apply themselves to the practice of them. And that which above all other things, according to the Doctor, most depraves mens natural understandings, and hinders them from discerning and judging rightly of moral truths, is this; That as stupid and careless ignorance leads them into fond and superstitious opinions; and the appetites of sense overcome and tempt <35> them into practices contrary to their conscience, and judgments; so on the reverse the multitude of superstitious opinions, vicious habits, and debaucht practices; which prevail in all ages, through the greater part of the world, do reciprocally encrease men's gross ignorance, carelessness, and stupidity.

Our author says, *p.* 340. "And as tho' this was not enough, Dr *Clarke* adds, that the light of nature no where appeared." Here I beg leave to observe, that Dr *Clarke* in the place referred to by our author, is quoting *Cicero*,* and does not make *Cicero* say, that the *light* of nature no where appears, but that the *true light* of nature no where appears; tho' indeed *Cicero* himself says, *depravatis sic restinguimus ut nusquam naturae, lumen appareat;*† which is to say, that the light of nature no where appears. 'Tis certainly unfair in disputing with any man not to distinguish when he expresses himself in his own words, and when he chooses to describe a thing in the words of another. But whether Dr *Clarke* said it, or *Cicero* said it, the thing is true. "That nature has given us only some small sparks of right reason, which we so quickly extinguish with corrupt opinions, and evil practices;

---

* *Dr* Clarke's Discourse, *p.* 374. [The passage to which Turnbull refers appears on p. 275.]

† Cic. Tus. Quest. l. 3. [Cicero, *Tusculan Disputations,* III.i.2–3: "[nature] has given us some faint glimmering of insight which, under the corrupting influence of bad habits and beliefs, we speedily quench so completely that no flicker of nature's light remains. The seeds of virtue are inborn in our dispositions and, if they were allowed to ripen, nature's own hand would lead us on to happiness of life; as things are, however, as soon as we come into the light of day and have been acknowledged, we at once find ourselves in a world of iniquity amid a medley of wrong beliefs, so that it seems as if we drank in deception with our nurse's milk; but when we leave the nursery to be with parents and later on have been handed over to the care of masters, then we become infected with deceptions so varied that truth gives place to unreality and the voice of nature itself to fixed prepossessions."]

that the *true light* of nature no where appears. As soon as we are brought into the world, immediately we dwell in the midst of all wickedness, and are surrounded with a number of most perverse and foolish opinions; so that we seem to suck in error even with our nurses milk. Afterwards, when we return to our parents, and are <36> committed to tutors; then we are further stock'd with such variety of errors, that truth becomes perfectly overwhelmed with falshood, and the most natural sentiments of our minds are entirely stifled with confirmed follies. But when, after all this, we enter upon business in the world, and make, the multitude conspiring every where in wickedness, our great guide and example; then our very nature itself is wholly transformed, as it were, into corrupt opinions."[23] A livelier description indeed (as the Doctor says) of the present corrupt estate of human nature is not easily to be met with. And I have set down the passage at large as the Doctor hath translated it, because this true account of the human nature, in *Cicero*'s words, is sufficient to prove against our author and all his *Deists;* how little bare reason and philosophy is able to do; and that revelation is indeed wanting to recover mankind out of their corrupt and degenerated estate. Let me also recommend to their reading the incomparable table of *Cebes,* in which the difficulty, if not moral impossibility, in the present state of mankind, of coming even at the true philosophy, is beautifully and convincingly described.[24]

Our author goes on with his charge against the Doctor: "The Doctor, to pursue this point, and to shew that the fault was not in the creatures but the Creator, says, that even those few extraordinary men of the philosophers, who did sincerely endeavour to reform mankind; were themselves intirely ignorant of some doctrines absolutely necessary for bringing about this great end <37> of the reformation and recovery of mankind: ———— their whole attempt to discover the truth of things, and to instruct others therein, was like wandring in the wide sea without knowing whither to go, or which way to take, or having any guide to conduct them."[25]

---

23. Clarke, *Discourse,* p. 275.

24. *The Tablet* is a dialogue ascribed to Cebes of Thebes (ca. 430–350 B.C.E.) in Diogenes Laertius, *Lives of Eminent Philosophers,* II. 125. The dialogue most probably dates to the first century AD.

25. Tindal, *Christianity as Old as the Creation,* p. 341.

I need not say, that Dr *Clarke* was incapable of pursuing so *impious a point;* as to *shew* that the fault was not in the creatures, but in the Creator *must be owned* by every sober mind to be. And that the fault is in the Creator and not in the creatures cannot be inferred from any thing that the Doctor hath said, will, I believe, be easily granted; if it is found not to follow from what our author quotes from the Doctor, in order to fix this *monstruous consequence* upon him. For he that was capable of charging him with pursuing so *impious a point;* would certainly have quoted from the Doctor any passage that could most easily be so misrepresented, as to give a palpable handle for inferring such a conclusion from him. What the Doctor asserts concerning the *ignorance* and uncertainty of even those few and extraordinary *philosophers* is fact; and the Doctor proves to be so from history and experience, and the confessions of the best philosophers themselves. But how does it follow from this fact, that the *fault* is in the *Creator* and not in the *creatures?* Is that to be imputed to GOD which is manifestly owing to the corruption and degeneracy of men? Or can he be said to *ascribe* the fault to GOD, who hath clearly and evidently *shewn* that it proceeds from causes by no means imputable to him? What those causes are we have already seen. <38>

But as if Dr *Clarke* had wrote his discourse on purpose to impeach GOD; our author goes on with his charge in this manner: "And that you might be sure the fault was in the eternal universal and unchangeable law of nature, he calls those philosophers who thus wander in the wide sea, wise, brave, and good men; who made it their business to study and practice the duties of natural religion themselves, and to teach and exhort others to do the like: nay one would imagine he thought them, notwithstanding their unavoidable ignorance, *inspired,* since he says there never was a great man but who was inspired (*nemo unquam magnus vir sine divino afflatu fuit*) and for this he quotes the authority of *Cicero,* who, if the Doctor's reasoning is just, was certainly inspired."[26]

Dr *Clarke, p.* 284. shews that some of the antientest writers of the Church have not scrupled to call *Socrates,* and some others of the best of

---

26. Tindal, *Christianity as Old as the Creation,* p. 341. The passage from Cicero is cited in Clarke, *Discourse,* p. 303. Clarke's Latin is a variant of Cicero, *De natura deorum,* II.lxvi.167: "Nemo igitur vir magnus sine aliquo adflatu divino umquam fuit./No one, then, has ever been a great man without some breath of the divine." Turnbull also invoked Cicero's maxim; see above, p. 154.

the heathen moralists, by the name of Christians; and to affirm, that as the *law* was as it were a *school-master* to bring the Jews unto CHRIST; so *true moral philosophy* was to the Gentiles a *preparative* to receive the *Gospel.*[27] "And this," saith the Doctor, "was perhaps carrying the matter too far. But to be sure this much we may safely assert, (continueth he) that whatever any of these men were at any time enabled to deliver *wisely,* and *profitably,* and *agreeably* to *divine truth;* was, as *a light shining in a dark place,* derived to them by a *ray* of that *infinite overflowing goodness* which *does good* to all, even both *just* and *unjust;* from GOD the sole *author* of all <39> *truth* and *wisdom:* and this for some advantage and benefit to the rest of the world, even in its blindest and most corrupt state."[28] And in this sense these wise, brave, and good men may be said to have been *inspired;* or rather, to use Dr *Clarke's* words, to have been *raised up* by providence as useful *instruments* to reprove in some measure, and put some kind of check to the extream superstition and wickedness of the nation wherein they lived.[29] But I would have it observed, that where Dr *Clarke* quotes the authority of *Cicero, p.* 303. it is to prove, that the best and wisest philosophers ever confessed that human nature was so strangely corrupted and degenerated; that to remedy all those disorders, and conquer all these corruptions; there was plainly wanting some extraordinary and supernatural *assistance,* which was above the reach of *bare reason* and *philosophy* to procure; and yet without which the philosophers themselves were sensible there could never *truly* be any great men. But how does it follow, that the fault was in the Creator and not in the creatures; or that the fault was in the eternal and unchangeable law of nature; because the best and wisest philosophers were, as they themselves own, in ignorance and blindness, and much in the dark, not only as to the *profounder things of wisdom,* but as to such things also which seemed very capable of being in great part discovered?* nay even those things which in themselves were of all others the most manifest, (that is, which whenever *made known* would appear most obvious and evident) their natural understanding <40> was of itself as unqualified to find out

* *Dr* Clarke's Discourse, *p.* 289.
27. Clarke, *Discourse,* pp. 283–84.
28. Clarke, *Discourse,* p. 284.
29. Clarke, *Discourse,* p. 283.

and apprehend, as the eyes of bats to behold the light of the sun? Is there not a manifest distinction between saying that the eternal differences of things upon which the law of nature is founded are clearly discernible; and would necessarily force our assent; if we would but attend to them with due attention, and without prejudices: And saying, on the other hand, that in the present degenerate state of mankind, without a greater guide than bare reason; without a higher assistance than philosophy alone can afford; few, very few, are able to arrive at any tolerable degree of moral knowledge; much less at any tolerable degree of moral perfection in their practice: And that the generality of mankind must remain unavoidably in a blind ignorant state; and shew the effects of their blindness in the wickedness and depravity of their lives.

Both are true in fact; nor is there, or can there be, any inconsistency; unless truth can clash with truth; or one matter of fact be inconsistent with another. Nothing more is necessary to *vindicate* the eternal and unchangeable law of nature, or its author; than to *shew*, as Dr *Clarke* has clearly done, that the law of nature is in itself clear and manifest; and that the negligent misunderstanding, and wilful passions or lusts are the only causes which can hinder a reasonable creature from perceiving its obligation; or make him act contrary to it: And that it is owing to the corruption and degeneracy of mankind, whencesoever that originally proceeds, that the law of nature hath not that weight to determine the wills and actions <41> of all rational Beings, which it naturally and necessarily must have when duly apprehended or attended to.

"Our author says, that the Doctor's scheme outdoes that of the most rigid predestinarians; for that at all times saves the *elect*, but here are no *elect*: but all for many ages are inextricably involv'd in a most depraved, corrupted, and impious state."[30]

I find Dr *Clarke*, as hath been often said, giving a true account of the state and condition of men in all ages: but I do not find Dr *Clarke* pronouncing a *sentence of damnation* against any part of mankind: nor does it appear to me to follow from his scheme, that GOD will damn any part of mankind, for faults out of which they could not possibly extricate

---

30. Tindal, *Christianity as Old as the Creation,* pp. 341–42.

themselves. Nor indeed, according to the true scheme by which alone we can know any thing about *damnation* or *salvation* with any certainty; the *scheme of the Gospel; is the wrath of* GOD *revealed from Heaven, except against all ungodliness and unrighteousness of men; who hold the truth in unrighteousness, because that which can be known of* GOD *is manifest in them, for* GOD *hath shewed it unto them* ———— *So that they are without excuse: because that when they knew* GOD, *they glorified him not as* GOD; *neither were thankful, but became vain in their imaginations, and their foolish heart was darkened, professing themselves to be wise; they became fools; and changed the glory of the incorruptible* GOD, *into an image made like unto corruptible man.* ———— *Who changed the truth of* GOD *into a lie, and worshipped and served the creature more than the* <42> *Creator, who is blessed for ever.* ————*And even as they did not like to retain* GOD *in their knowledge;* GOD *gave them over to a reprobate mind, to do those things that are not convenient.* ———— *Who, knowing the judgment of* GOD, *(that they which commit such things are worthy of death) not only do the same, but have pleasure in them that do them.** This is the judgment of GOD; and this judgment (as the same Apostle saith in the following chapter) is according to truth.

Our author goes on thus, *p.* 342. "Tho' I pay a due deference to the Doctor's deep penetration in matters of religion, I dare not say there is the least difference between the law of nature and the gospel, for that would suppose some defect in one of them, and reflect on the author of both; who certainly was equally good, equally wise, when he gave the one as when he gave the other (if it may be called another) law. Nor dare I be so rash as to charge the light of nature with *undeniable defects,* as the Doctor presumes to do; since if that light was sufficient to answer the end designed by GOD, which was to be a competent guide to men in relation to their present and future happiness there could be no deficiency: if not, then there must be an undeniable default in the giver of it; in appointing means not sufficient to answer their designed ends, tho' both means and ends were entirely in his power." <43>

This is not only the modestest passage in our author's book, but must be owned to be something like reasoning to prove that, according to Dr

---

* Rom. i. [Romans 1.18–23, 25, 28, 32.]

Clarke's Scheme, the fault must be in the guide which GOD hath given to man. But in answer to it; let us observe first, that there is a manifest difference between the *Law of Nature* and the *Gospel;* which does not suppose any *defect* in one of them; nor reflect on the author of both. The Gospel sets before us certain truths which are powerful motives to moral obedience; that the Law, or Light of Nature, cannot discover: Not that there is any defect in the Law of Nature, but because these truths, in the nature of things, cannot be known by the Light of Nature; but can only be made known by divine testimony. And surely the Light or Law of Nature cannot be said to be imperfect; because it cannot discover that, which, according to the nature of things, is not discoverable by the Light of Nature. Far less does it reflect upon the author of the *Law of Nature,* that he hath revealed and made known to mankind by JESUS CHRIST, these motives, helps, and assistances to moral obedience, which the Light of Nature or unassisted Reason could not possibly make known.

Secondly, I would have it observed, that, according to Dr *Clarke*'s Scheme, in the degenerate corrupt state of mankind, the Light of Nature is not sufficient to recover mankind out of that estate, into a state suitable to the original excellency of their nature; but that there was plainly wanting a divine revelation to answer that end. And hence it plainly follows, that the Light of Nature was not designed by GOD <44> to answer that end; but that on the contrary, both the necessities of men and their natural notions of GOD, ever gave reasonable ground to expect and hope for a divine revelation, as the only sufficient and competent remedy to recover mankind. Our author's argument plainly depends upon this supposition; that GOD designed the light of nature to be a competent guide to men, in relation to their present and future happiness. But to this I answer, in Dr *Clarke*'s words, *p.* 303. "That indeed in the original uncorrupted state of human nature, before the mind of man was depraved with prejudicate opinions, corrupt affections, and vitious inclinations, customs, and habits; right reason may justly be supposed to have been a sufficient guide; and a principle powerful enough to preserve men in the constant practice of duty. But in the present circumstances and conditions of mankind, the wisest and most sensible of the Philosophers themselves, have not been backward to complain, that they found the understandings of men so dark and cloudy, their wills so biassed and inclined to evil, their passions so outragious and rebellious against reason; that they looked upon the rules and laws of right reason as very hardly practicable, and which they had very little hopes of ever being able to perswade the world to submit to. In a word, they confessed that human nature was strangely corrupted; and they acknowledged this corruption to be a disease of which they knew not the true cause, and could not find out a sufficient remedy. So that the great duties of religion were laid down by them, as mat-<45>ters of speculation and dispute rather than as the rules of action; and not so much urged upon the hearts and lives of men, as proposed to the admiration of those who thought them hardly possible to be practised by the generality of men. And therefore that to remedy all these disorders, and conquer all these impediments, there was plainly wanting some extraordinary, and supernatural assistance; which was above the reach of bare reason and philosophy to procure."

Indeed what GOD designs as absolutely sufficient to answer an end, must be absolutely sufficient to answer that end. But the very thing Dr *Clarke* proves from history and experience, as a fact must be proved, is, that in the present corrupted circumstances of mankind, a divine revelation is necessary to recover men out of that degenerate estate; and was not only *designed* by GOD, but actually *given* by him, to answer that end.

Our author goes on: "Nor dare I say, there are several necessary truths not possible to be discovered with any certainty by the light of nature; because GOD's means of information, will and must always bear an exact proportion to the necessity of our knowing what we are obliged to know, especially touching the nature and attributes of GOD."[31]

And here I will shew, with Dr *Clarke*, that there are *necessary truths;* not possible to be discovered, with any certainty, by the light of nature: that is, truths necessary to the great end of recovering mankind <46> out of their universal degenerate estate, into a state suitable to the original excellency of their nature. Only let it be first observed, that all the means of information and knowledge given by GOD to mankind, whether by revelation, or by the light of nature, cannot be of any use to men, if men will not make due use of them; and consequently, that even these attributes of

---

31. Tindal, *Christianity as Old as the Creation,* p. 342.

GOD, which are clearly manifested in us, and may be clearly understood by the things that are made; his eternal power and Godhead cannot be seen or understood, if men will shut their eyes against the light which shines clearly around them; and in spight of all they know, will not glorify GOD as they know he ought to be glorified. And that as wilful ignorance and blindness must produce superstition and wickedness: so superstition and wickedness must reciprocally encrease blindness and ignorance.

And passing all the idle cavils he hath gathered together against the scripture account of the original state of human nature, which have been so often refuted; I shall confine myself to the objections he makes against what the Doctor says concerning the impossibility of knowing, by the light of nature, with any certainty, what, as the Doctor saith of all other things, was of the greatest importance for sinful men to know, *viz. The method by which such as have erred from the right way, and have offended* GOD, *may yet again restore themselves to the favour of* GOD, *and to the hopes of happiness.*[32]

Our author's first argument against the Doctor amounts to this: "That Mr *Nye* and Mr <47> *Locke* say; The *one*, that if GOD be a merciful and benign Being, he will accept the payment we are able to make, and not insist upon impossible demands with his frail bankrupt creatures. The *other*, that the same spark of divine nature and knowledge which, making him a man, shewed him the law he was under, as a man; shewed him also the way of atoneing the merciful, kind, compassionate author and father of him and his being, when he had transgressed that law."[33]

To which I answer, that it is very easy to prove from Mr *Nye* and Mr *Locke*, that upon the whole, they have said no more upon this head than what Dr *Clarke* hath also said. "That from the consideration of the goodness and mercifulness of GOD, the philosophers did indeed very reasonably hope, that GOD would shew himself placable to sinners; and might be some way reconciled."* But whoever asserts, that GOD must receive returning

---

* *Dr* Clarke's Discourse, *p*. 293.

32. Clarke, *Discourse*, p. 293.

33. A paraphrase of Tindal, *Christianity as Old as the Creation*, pp. 354–55, where Tindal quotes from Stephen Nye, *A Discourse concerning Natural and Revealed Religion* (London, 1696), pp. 85–87, and John Locke, *The Reasonableness of Christianity, as delivered in the Scriptures*, edited by John C. Higgins-Biddle (Oxford, 1999), pp. 139–40.

sinners; and accept of repentance instead of perfect obedience; or that GOD is absolutely *obliged* to pardon all creatures all their sins at all times, barely and immediately upon their repenting; ought to prove it; and he who attempts to do it, will soon find it impossible. "For," as Dr *Clarke* saith, "it cannot be positively proved from any of GOD's attributes: And yet while that remains uncertain there is no sufficient comfort to sinners; but anxious and endless solicitude about the means of appeasing the Deity."[34] And all our author <48> himself says to prove that repentance must be sufficient to procure pardon, amounts to this: "That the supposing GOD had left all mankind for so many ages in a most miserable state of doubt and uncertainty about the pardon of sin, is inconsistent with the divine goodness, or he is at a loss to know what is so."[35] Is then every thing inconsistent with the divine goodness, which we cannot know how it is consistent with the divine goodness? From what we know of GOD and his perfections, we have good reason to conclude, that every thing that GOD does in the government of the world, is perfectly consistent with his goodness, and with the *great end* of his *government,* which can be nothing else but the *good of the whole.* And it is no wonder, that several facts and events appear to us, in our partial, narrow view of things very unaccountable, or rather inexplicable. We ought never therefore to reason thus; *Such a thing cannot be, because we cannot see how it is consistent with the divine goodness that it should be:* But ought with regard to the divine government to content ourselves to know what is matter of fact; and ought ever to conclude, as we have abundant reason to do, that *whatever GOD does, is wisely done,* tho' in innumerable instances we are not able to find out the wise reason for which it is done. Thus are we, particularly in this case, to reason, that GOD's having left the greater part of mankind, in a most miserable state of doubt about the pardon of sin, is not inconsistent with the great ends of the divine government; because the fact is certain. For tho' it should be granted possible for reason to prove, that GOD will forgive upon repentance; <49> yet it is indisputable, that even the *best* and *wisest* of mankind have always been in the greatest uncertainty about that point, as they themselves have owned. And here we

---

34. A paraphrase of Clarke, *Discourse,* p. 293.
35. A paraphrase of Tindal, *Christianity as Old as the Creation,* pp. 355–56.

may again apply what *Cicero* says of philosophy, in another respect, it being equally applicable in this: "In like manner as in physic, it matters nothing whether a disease be such, that no man does, or no man can, recover from it; so neither does it make any difference whether, by philosophy, no man is, or no man can, be made sure of the method, by which such as have offended GOD may again restore themselves to his favour."[36] We know indeed, that as GOD cannot command tyrannically; or without a reason worthy of himself and his administration; so neither can GOD punish in this world, or the world to come, but in a way suitable to the great end of his government; the general good of the whole. But can we, by the light of nature, fully ascertain the duration and proportions of punishments and rewards in a future life, which this end precisely makes necessary, or fit? Can we indeed find out, by reason alone, what must be the methods of divine providence in the other world? Or how the general good and happiness of the whole system of rational Beings positively requires, that the various classes and sorts even of repenting sinners should be disposed of? Is any thing more certain, than that the virtue of the best in this world is but very weak and inconstant; that reformation is often very late, and never perfect? And is it demonstrable by reason, that GOD will immediately after death make every sincere penitent eternally happy in the enjoyment of himself; <50> and that there is no degree of suffering or punishment in the other world, but for those who have lived and died in an obstinate hardened course of sin? He who saith there is no need of revelation must however shew, that reason alone is sufficient to answer every important question concerning a future state; and to set all in a clear and satisfying light that is necessary to the satisfaction of a thinking honest man. In a word, it is certain, that when we have offended, the best part we can act, is to repent: and we have reason to hope, that, if our repentance is sincere, and produces, in our after conduct, an humble strict, and lasting watchfulness, GOD of his infinite goodness will at last forgive us. But in order to prove that GOD is obliged to forgive us immediately, we must be able to point out the reason that obliges him. That his goodness obliges him to accept of the

---

36. Turnbull paraphrases Samuel Clarke's translation of a passage in Cicero, *De natura deorum,* III.xxxii.79, that appears in Clarke, *Discourse,* p. 302.

repentance of all sinners, at all times, for all sins, and to make the reformed sinner eternally happy; can never with any colour of reason be asserted; unless we can prove, *that the good of the whole* obliges him to it. For the good of the whole, is the end that infinite goodness obliges GOD to pursue; if his infinite goodness can properly be said to oblige him to any thing. And who does not see that in order to point out with any certainty what the good of the whole requires; as to that point, we must know more than creatures can possibly know, without divine instruction, or a divine revelation.

I will now sum up all that hath been already said; or that it is indeed necessary to say, in order to vindicate Dr *Clarke* from the incon-<51>sistencies with which he is charged by the author of *Christianity as old as the Creation:* or to prove, that *Christianity is neither false nor useless, tho' not as old as the Creation,* in the few following observations; all of which Dr *Clarke* has sufficiently proved.

First, That the saying the law of nature is not sufficient to recover man out of their universally degenerate estate, into a state suitable to the original excellency of their nature; is not saying, that in the original uncorrupted state of human nature right reason was not a sufficient guide; and a principle powerful enough to preserve men in the constant practice of their duty. And that it is not accusing the law of nature of any defect to say, that in the present circumstances and condition of mankind, it is not a sufficient guide; because its insufficiency to be a guide in these circumstances, proceeds from mankind's actually being in these circumstances. And mankind's being in these circumstances does not reflect upon the author of our nature, unless it is contrary to divine wisdom and goodness to have created us moral free agents.

Secondly, That in christian countries, at least where Christianity is professed in any tolerable degree of purity, the generality, even of the meaner and most vulgar and ignorant people have truer and worthier notions of GOD, more just and right apprehensions concerning his attributes and perfections, a deeper sense of the difference of good and evil, a <52> greater regard to moral obligations, and to the plain and most necessary duties of life, and a more firm and universal expectation of rewards and punishments, than in any heathen country any considerable number of men were ever found to have had.* This is true in fact; and therefore Christianity is not useless.

Thirdly, That Christianity, or the Gospel of CHRIST, makes known, or reveals, several truths not discoverable by the light of nature, the knowledge of which is absolutely necessary to recover mankind out of their degenerate depraved estate; and which have the most powerful and effectual influence, when known, to promote the honour of GOD, and the practice of universal righteousness among mankind, And that CHRIST hath confirmed by miracles his divine commission to teach these truths; given sufficient evidence of his being sent of GOD to reform mankind effectually, to restore them to the favour of GOD; instruct them in all their duties; and give them all the motives, helps, and assistances, that are necessary to enable mankind in their corrupted degenerate state, to perform all the duties which the eternal law of reason shews to be obligatory or binding upon all rational creatures. And therefore that Christianity is neither false nor useless, and yet no older than the teaching of CHRIST.

Fourthly, That in order to prove, that a divine revelation is needless, or not wanting; one must not only prove, that the light of nature is able of itself to discover to a corrupt and sinful world, all that is necessary to their effe-<53>ctual reformation; But that the law of nature was ever perfectly well understood; and ever had due weight and influence.† For if the contrary is true, as it certainly is, it follows evidently, that *revelation is wanting, nay necessary.* It is in vain to talk of a light that never enlightned; of a law that was scarcely known, and had but little influence even upon those who owned its obligation; of a remedy that never wrought a cure. Supposing it to be true, that all the obligations and motives of morality, could be discovered and explained clearly by the meer *light of nature alone;* this would not at all prove, that there is no need of revelation: while it is certain in fact, that the wisest philosophers of old were never able to do so to any effectual purpose, but always wanted some higher assistance. But on the contrary it must follow, from that matter of fact, that the Christian Revelation is so far from being *useless,* that it is absolutely necessary.

* *Dr* Clarke's Discourse, *p.* 311.
† *All that our author says about the sufficiency of the light of nature, supposes, that there is no difference between being knowable, and being actually known.*

Fifthly, From these considerations plainly follows, the exceeding great use* and necessity there is of establishing an order or succession of men, as is by CHRIST appointed, whose peculiar office or continual employment it may be, to teach and instruct the people in their duty, to press and exhort them perpetually to the practice of it, and to be instruments of conveying extraordinary assistances to them for <54> that purpose. To this excellent institution it is, that the right and worthy notion of GOD and his divine perfections, the just sense and understanding of the great duties of religion, and the universal belief and due apprehension of a future state of rewards and punishments, which the generality even of the meaner, and more ignorant sort of people among us are now possess'd of; are manifestly and undeniably almost wholly owing. Hence it follows, that such an institution is of the greatest use in society: And that friends to society and useful knowledge must be friends to such an institution.

Sixthly, That the small influence Christianity has to reform men, in proportion to what it must be owned to be naturally fitted to have; or the mischievous purposes to which it hath been misapplied; can only prove, that when all is done by providence to instruct, reclaim, or reform mankind, that could be done consistently with our natures as moral and free agents, mankind are hardly to be reformed. And to ask why Christianity was not sooner revealed, and made known, seeing it is so necessary? is really asking how comes it about, that the infinite wise ends of GOD's government did not allow that CHRIST should appear sooner in the world than he did? a question to which we need not be ashamed to own, that we can give no answer: but that so it seemed good to him who cannot err.

Seventhly, That if one, who really loves mankind, and wishes well to human society, is not seriously convinced in his own mind, not <55> only that the christian religion is false and useless, but that it is pernicious, and tends to the hurt and ruin of mankind; *seeing there must be a public religion;* he cannot possibly answer to his own conscience for endeavouring to destroy or diminish its authority and influence: Far less can he answer to his own conscience, or his natural sense of right and wrong, for his taking pains to subvert the belief of the most powerful motives and perswasives to virtue

* *Dr* Clarke's Discourse, *p.* 281.

and goodness; to the love of GOD and of mankind; and to weaken the credit of institutions which evidently tend to promote these ends. And yet of these two it is that Christianity is made up.

Eighthly, That tho' evil spirits can do miracles, it is manifestly absurd to suppose, that they would employ their powers, or work miracles to instruct men in their duty to GOD, and to enforce upon them the practice of every moral virtue; and to assure them of assistance and success in their earnest aims and endeavours to advance and improve in piety and virtue. And therefore JESUS CHRIST, by the miracles he worked, gave a full and compleat proof of his really being invested with the divine power and authority to which he pretended; that he was indeed sent of GOD, not only to republish the law of nature, the law of moral duties, which tho' deducible from the nature and reason of things, thro' the degeneracy and corruption of mankind was become of no effect; but likewise *to make known the Gospel of peace,* the *doctrine of grace and eternal consolation;* to teach the forgiveness of sins; and to call all men to repent, that they might find favour <56> with GOD, and obtain eternal life; to bring life and immortality to light; and to assure men, that if they are not wanting to themselves, but in good earnest to become virtuous; and seriously implore *wisdom* and *assistance* from GOD in his name, GOD will not *upbraid* them, but *give,* unto them that ask, *liberally;* and reward their pious and virtuous labours here with immortal glory and happiness hereafter. His miracles were not only an undeniable proof of his mission from Heaven, but, in the nature of things, compleat and adequate *specimens* or *samples* of all these doctrines, of all that he taught as our divine Instructor, and ever blessed SAVIOUR. And therefore Christianity is not only useful, divinely useful, but infallibly true; tho', in the nature of things, it cannot possibly be more antient than the *appearance* of its *Divine Author* in the world. And, upon the whole then, I may justly conclude, that he who loveth GOD and mankind, society and virtue, must like Christianity; or must have a very false or wrong notion of it. A mistake from which any one must soon be delivered, who will do common justice to Christianity; and seek for it in the discourses of our SAVIOUR and his Apostles.

FINIS

An Impartial Enquiry into the
Moral Character of Jesus Christ

ട്ടൗ ട്ടൗ ട്ടൗ

NOTE ON THE TEXT

An Impartial Enquiry into the Moral Character of Jesus Christ was initially published by the London printer and bookseller James Roberts. The date of publication is given as 1740 although the work is listed among other books published in February 1741 in *The Gentleman's Magazine.*[1] A "second edition" was published by the London publisher and bookseller Jacob Robinson in 1742. Apart from a new title page, the text of the 1742 edition is identical to that published in 1740.

1. *The Gentleman's Magazine* 11 (1741): 112.

AN

Impartial Enquiry

INTO THE

MORAL CHARACTER

OF

JESUS CHRIST:

Wherein he is considered as a

PHILOSOPHER.

IN A

LETTER to a FRIEND.

Scilicet uni Aequus virtuti, atque ejus amicis

HOR. Sat. 1. L. 2.[1]

LONDON:

Printed for J. ROBERTS, near the *Oxford-Arms* in
Warwick-Lane. Sold by A. DODD without
Temple-Bar, and E. NUTT at the *Royal Exchange.*
MDCCXL.
[Price One Shilling.]

1. Horace, *Satires,* II.i.70: "Kindly in fact only to Virtue and her friends."

An *Impartial Enquiry*, &c.

You thought, my Friend, I became grave, in a late conversation, and are, it seems, afraid you may have offended me by your freedom. I know what fired you; for that you was warm, you seem now to be convinced: But I have gained so much instruction by free conferences with you about religion, that instead of being angry at any thing that happened on your part, I long excessively for another on the same subject, between you and believers, but of a more moderate turn; should I say of a temper more like the master they pretend to be zealous for, I am sure you would join with me; for I have often heard you commend his behaviour to the Sadducees and other unbelievers, and own he never shewed anger but against hypocrisy and superstitious zeal. Indeed what I have often said to you on other occasions, I think I have now better reason than ever to affirm. 'Tis what our Saviour said to the lawyer, who having asked which was the first commandment of all, approved the answer Jesus gave to him, saying, Thou hast said the truth, for there is one God, and there is none other but he: And to love him with all the heart, and with all the understanding, and with all the soul, and with all the strength, and to love my neighbour as myself, is more than all whole burnt-offerings and sacrifices. The reply was this, Jesus when he saw he answered discreetly, said unto him, *Thou art not far from the kingdom of God*.[2] To <2> you who are firmly persuaded of this great and important truth, without which revelation hath nothing to build upon, and must therefore be an empty sound: "That the sure and sole way of pleasing God, or recommending ourselves to his favour here or hereafter, is by the sincere study and practice of virtue": To you who sincerely believe this truth, the same character is applicable, you are *not far*

---

2. Turnbull elaborates on Matthew 22.35–40 and Luke 10.25–37.

from the kingdom of heaven; you are almost a Christian, *i.e.* whether you be a Christian or not, you are a good man; you are sound in the fundamentals; for if religion be not a mere sound, that truth must be fundamental.

Was it not to this purpose you run on for some time t'other night, after we had been entertained with a great deal of panegyric upon certain modern apologists for Christianity, and very much heat, to give it no worse name, against those who resisted the evidence; for no allowance was made even to weakness of understanding, but wilful prejudiced opposition was taken for granted to be the only possible case. Was it not much to this effect you put an end to the arguments, tho' not to the zeal of your opponents. "Did Christ give any reason to prove he was sent of God or not? If he did not, I know not where we should look for, or expect to find reasons to shew he was. And if he did, why have divines taken such various routs in their very laboured and subtle reasonings about the matter? Why don't they directly produce his own argument, and shew it to be good? For my own part, I never met with any apologist for Christianity who would not be very angry if his apology was not thought intirely his own invention. This is new, says one. None hath taken this method, says another. This alone, says a third, is the true, the solid argument. Who, pray, amongst them all says this is Christ's own argument; and if it be not <3> good, in vain do we look out for any other. Divines serve revelation as philosophers long served nature. It was with the greatest difficulty the latter were at last persuaded to go to nature herself to learn from her how she operates, tho' nothing be more evident, than that all philosophy she herself does not teach and confirm by experience, however ingenious it may be, is but romance and conjecture. The case is the same with regard to the doctrine of Christ. They go to their invention, they go to Aristotle, or to Plato, they go every-where to find it but where alone it can be found. Yet it is not more certain, that philosophers cannot spin the knowledge of nature out of their brains, or get at it any other way than by studying nature herself, than it is, that if Divines do not fetch both the doctrine of Christ, and its proofs, from Christ himself, *i.e.* from those who have given us the history of his life, doctrine and works, it is by mere chance, if they hit either upon the true doctrine, or the real evidence that was given of its truth. Pray what title can I have to the name of a Christian, if I do not take both my faith, and the grounds of my faith from the teacher himself in whom I profess to believe? If you would prove

Christianity to me therefore, you must shew me which way Christ himself reasoned to prove his mission and the truth of his doctrine. I am indeed at no small loss to find out what one can gain by believing Christianity, who is already persuaded that the sincere practice of virtue is the only way of serving or pleasing God; that a revelation which places religion in any thing else, must be false; and that a true one can say no more to us about the matter. This principle being certain, I cannot easily, I say, find out what great advantage one who is persuaded of it can reap from any revelation. But however that be, if you would make a Christian of me, shew me plainly how Christ <4> himself reasoned, to evince the truth of his pretension. If his argument be good, I promise you I will yield to it; that is, I will freely own I am convinced by it. But if you can produce no reasoning that is his, why should I trouble myself with the apologies for Christianity of those who came after him, the best of which are owned to be no older than this or the last century; unless you can prove to me that one may be sent of God, and yet either offer no reason at all, or which is more unaccountable still, very bad and inconclusive arguments to prove his mission, neither of which hath any one, I think, been so absurd as to assert."

To this effect did you, Sir, express yourself. And I think the way to satisfy you is, 1. To develope to you the argument he himself brought to prove his divine mission and the truth of his doctrine: In order to which, I must first of all give you a clear view of his doctrine. 2*dly,* To shew that Christianity does not place religion in any thing else but the sincere practice of virtue, which will appear from a faithful representation of his doctrine. And yet, 3*dly,* That there are several great advantages arising from the belief of the Christian doctrine, even to those who are already persuaded of this truth, without laying which down as a first principle, there are no principles to reason from about true or false revelation, *viz.* That virtue, and it alone, can recommend us to the divine favour. All these I think I can prove. But if you can shew me what I take to be a good proof of any of them not to be so, I shall be obliged to you. For what others say of Plato, Aristotle, and other great names, I am not afraid to carry farther, and say, "Nothing is sacred to me but truth." If Christ had not good reason to say of himself, *I am the truth,* he hath no title to our regard.[3]

3. A paraphrase of John 14.6.

But you have often said, that the first question of <5> all in this enquiry
ought to be, "What was Christ's moral character." Let us therefore, before
we enter upon any of these arguments, consider Christ merely as a Philosopher, and enquire into his character as a man. In vain, certainly, is it to
talk of his coming or not coming from God with a special commission, till
we are sure he was a good man. It concerns us very little how much he
knew, or what mighty works he did, till we are fully satisfied he was a thoroughly honest, candid and benevolent person. 'Tis goodness alone that can
create or lay any foundation for trust. If he was not a most perfect example
of genuine piety and virtue, he cannot possibly be proved, by any argument
from prophecies, miracles, or whatever other consideration, to have been
entrusted by God with the declaration of his will to mankind. To imagine
so, is to fancy God could make a very odd choice of a messenger; for to say
no worse of it, it would be to make a choice that could not fail to puzle,
not to say scandalize all lovers of virtue, and all believers of providence.
Let us therefore, first of all, consider Christ merely as a man, or enquire
into his moral character, and consider his works, which are called miracles,
barely as acts of ordinary skill and power, to cure diseases, and perform
other such good offices to mankind.

Now, it is no small presumption in favour of his pretension, when it is
taken in the highest sense, that we find him reasoning in this manner himself, and telling those to whom he appeared, "That the first thing they ought
to do, when any one comes to them, boasting of extraordinary gifts, or of
a special message from heaven, is to search carefully and impartially into
his moral character."[4] He lays down this rule in general, with regard to all
pretenders to prophecy, and with respect to himself he often puts the whole
stress of his claim upon this <6> single point, the moral tendency of his
doctrine, the goodness of his life, and the beneficialness of his works.

Such language, it must be owned, hath not the air of an impostor. But
lest it should be said, impostors must talk in this strain, and counterfeit a
shew of benevolence and candour to gain a hearing; let us see whether we
can discover any one feature of a deceiver in him, any motive or view that
gives the least ground for suspicion, any cunning or chicane, any double

4. Turnbull elaborates on Matthew 7.15–20.

dealing; or any sinistrous address that favours, in the smallest degree, of any other design but that of teaching men true religion and virtue, and shewing them an example of it. Let us judge here as we ought always to judge, *i.e.* according to all appearances fairly laid together and impartially considered. For surely no reasonable person will say, he may have been dishonest, tho' there be no symptom of his not having been thoroughly honest and virtuous. We do not say so of Socrates, Confucius, or any other philosopher. And not to pronounce like conclusions in like cases, is certainly partiality.

What you use to call *the previous question,* in an enquiry about the truth of Christianity, cannot be more strongly represented to be such than it is by Jesus Christ. Let me give you his reasoning at some length, for it will at the same time serve for a specimen of his elegant and apposite use of figures, or allegory. A successful manner of instilling truth of every kind, reproof in particular, into prejudiced minds, practised by the most renowned sages of antiquity, and approved by all critics, in which Christ eminently excelled.

"Beware of false prophets, which come to you in sheep's cloathing, but inwardly they are ravening wolves."* Attend carefully to them, to their conduct <7> and to their doctrines. And ye shall know them by their fruits. Do men gather grapes of thorns, or figs of thistles? Every good tree bringeth forth good fruit; but a corrupt tree bringeth forth evil fruit. A good tree cannot bring forth evil fruit; neither can a corrupt tree bring forth good fruit. And every tree that bringeth not forth good fruit, is hewn down and cast into the fire. Wherefore, by their fruits shall ye discern impostors, who have sensual or ambitious designs, from those whose only aim is to preach the will of our heavenly Father; his eternal immutable will, even moral rectitude, or sanctity of heart and life: Without this it is impossible to please him: And he who teacheth any other doctrine, teacheth not the will of God. They who place religion in external rites and ceremonies, or in any thing else but mercy, truth, and goodness, teach for the *doctrine of God the commandments of men,* and supplant true religion, or *make it of no effect,* by their *vain traditions.* But *every plant which our heavenly Father hath not planted shall be rooted out.* I am come to root it out, and truth shall at last

* Matt. vii. 15.

prevail against falshood and error. To this purpose does our Saviour reason about true religion, and the principal test that ought to be applied to such as pretend to declare the will of God to mankind. We are, according to this rule laid down by him, to pay no regard to boasts of knowledge and power, till we have first strictly canvassed the life and character of the pretender. And accordingly, in urging his divine commission, he appeals to the daily hearers of his doctrine, and witnesses of his actions; nay, to his most inveterate enemies and opposers, in this manner: "Which of you convinceth me of sin? And if I say the Truth, why do you not believe me?"* I appeal to your own consciences, whether you do not oppose me because <8> I will not tell you lies, suit my doctrines to your lusts and passions, and flatter you in your sensual and corrupt practices, but tell you the truth, pure and spiritual truth, or the necessity of purity of heart and manners to please God. If I have done any thing that makes me unworthy of your belief; if my conduct be not strictly conformable to the piety and virtue I teach, why doth not some of you convict me of it? This would quickly put me to silence, as it would effectually destroy the principal argument I have to offer for my doctrine and mission. But on the other hand, if my doctrine be worthy of belief; if it have all the internal characters of true and reasonable, and if my behaviour be congruous to it, what reason can you alledge for not receiving and believing me? I will tell you a very plain and certain truth, *He that is of God heareth God's words: Ye therefore hear them not, because ye are not of God,*5 *i.e.* He who hath just conceptions of God, and a disposition of mind suitable to them, can easily distinguish whether a doctrine be of God or not. But ye refuse to hear me, because ye have not the sincere, candid and virtuous temper of mind which is necessary to understand and relish divine truths; and ye have imbibed false conceptions of God and of religion. Ye have been taught and inured to place religion not in spiritual worship and true goodness, but in superstitious or ritual observances: And ye will not hear me, because I tell you God is a spirit, who ought to be worshipped in spirit and in truth; and that no worship can be acceptable to him but that which comes from a pure heart. In vain do ye think to honour God by your lips,† if ye deny him by your works.

* John viii. 46.
† Matt. xv. 7, 8. &c. [A loose paraphrase of Matthew 15.7–8.]
5. John 8.47.

Upon another occasion, Jesus Christ likewise appeals to his life and actions in the most affecting convincive manner. When the Jews took up stones <9> to stone him, "Jesus said to them, Many good works have I shewed you from my Father, for which of those works do ye stone me?"* There is not only an air of composure and calmness of mind in this defence, which is truly admirable; but there is pleasant irony in it. And indeed, as we shall see afterwards, Jesus Christ greatly excelled in that irony which hath been so fully explained, and at the same time so highly commended by ancients and moderns, in drawing the character of Socrates, the best of mere philosophers.[6] The Jews falling again into a great rage, took up stones to cast at Jesus. Jesus did not run away, nor was he at all disturbed; but with the greatest presence of mind, asks them in a very pleasant manner, What just provocation have I given you, that you should thus tumultuously attempt to stone me? What work have I done among you that was not for your benefit and advantage? I have fed the hungry, I have healed the lame, I have given sight to the blind, I have cured all sorts of diseases, and I have raised the dead. For which now of these good works is it that you are so angry, that you go about to take away my life?

Thus did Jesus Christ defend himself when he was most outrageously affronted, abused and persecuted. 'Twas to his moral character, or to the goodness and sincerity of his life and actions, as well as the purity and reasonableness of his doctrine, he continually and solely appealed.

So that the rule you lay down for trying Christ by, is really Christ's own rule. It cannot be recommended or inculcated in stronger terms than it is by him on several occasions. And is not his insisting so openly, so frequently, and zealously upon this rule, this test, a very strong presumption that he was not afraid of it, a very strong presump-<10>tion that his life and character could stand the severest scrutiny, the most narrow inspection. 'Tis indeed as he expresses it, the works of darkness only that fear or shun the light, which maketh all things manifest. Truth and sincere goodness, like beauty, do not avoid the light, but cheerfully come to it. For as it detects

---

* John x. 32.

6. An allusion to Shaftesbury among the moderns. The index to Shaftesbury's *Characteristicks* contains under the heading "Raillery" the subheading "Socratick Raillery" which refers the reader to three passages in the treatise "*Soliloquy:* Or, Advice to an Author"; see Shaftesbury, *Characteristicks,* I:121–22, 123–24, and III:283.

the deformity of vice and error, so it sets forth the native charms of truth and virtue. "Every one that doth evil hateth the light, neither cometh he to the light, lest his deeds should be reproved. But he that loveth and doth the truth, cometh to the light, that his deeds may be made manifest, that they are wrought in God, that they are such as God approves."*

Having mentioned the pleasant irony for which Socrates is so highly extolled, suffer me, before I go further, to bring some other instances of our Saviour's prudent and apposite use of this admirable art. They will likewise serve to clear the point we have chiefly in view, his moral and philosophical character, in the same manner as that of Socrates is illustrated and justified, by instances of the proper moral use he made of his wonderful talent for raillery or pleasantry.

When Jesus was teaching the people in the temple,† the chief priests, pharisees and scribes, whose superstition and hypocrisy he was ever detecting and refuting, came to him, thinking to ensnare him by captious questions, and asked him by what authority he set up to be a preacher of a new doctrine, a reformer. But Jesus knowing how with a merely malicious intention these men asked this question, did not think fit to give them a direct answer, but chose rather to puzle and silence them, by retorting upon them another question. Let me, said he, ask you one thing first, that must prepare the way for answering your question: "The Bap-<11>tism of John was it from heaven or from men?"7 This question surprized and confounded them. For they reasoned thus with themselves, saying, If we shall say from heaven, he will tell us, why then believed ye him not? But if we say of men, all the people will stone us, for they be persuaded that John was a prophet. They therefore answered, that they could not tell whence it was. Upon which Jesus in like manner said to them, Neither do I, said he, tell you what authority I have to do what I do. Here certainly is an instance of that kind of defensive raillery which *is the fittest resource when the spirit of curiosity would force a discovery of more truth than can conveniently be told. As it is in some cases real humanity and kindness to hide strong truths from*

---

* John iii. 20. [John 3.20–21.]
† Matt. xxi. 23. Luke xx. 1. [Luke 20.1–8.]
7. Matthew 21.24–25 and Luke 20.3–4.

tender eyes;[8] and for this reason, we find Jesus Christ suiting his discoveries to the understandings of his disciples,* letting in light upon them in proportion to what they could bear, and hiding other things from them which were yet too hard for them; so in other cases it is true prudence to wave giving a direct answer: But to *do this by a pleasant amusement, is certainly easier and civiller, than by a harsh denial or remarkable reserve. To go about industriously to confound men in a mysterious manner, and to take advantage, or draw pleasure from that perplexity they are thrown into by such uncertain talk, is as unhandsome, in a way of raillery, as when done with the greatest seriousness, or in the most solemn way of deceit. 'Tis certainly a mean impotent dull sort of wit, which amuses all alike, and leaves the most sensible man, and even a friend, equally in doubt, and at a loss to understand what one's real mind is upon any subject.*[9] This is that gross sort of raillery which is so offensive in good company. And indeed there is as much *difference between one sort and another, as between fair-dealing and hypocrisy.*[10] But it is often necessary, it is <12> often fit, to speak in parables and with a double meaning, that the enemy *may be amused, and they only who have ears to hear may hear.*[11] Accordingly our Saviour willingly explained his allegories to those who shewed a sincere disposition to learn truth and virtue, when they found any difficulty to understand them. But the malicious and evil-intentioned, he left to their own dulness of understanding, or rather hardness of heart. This is the reason he gives for his speaking so often in parables.† And upon the occasion just mentioned, having confounded the priests and scribes by his unexpected repartee, he proceeds to tell this tale or parable, which exceedingly moved the well-affected, but cut the priests and scribes to the quick. For they perceived that it was directed against them. A certain man, said Jesus, planted a vineyard, and let it forth to husbandmen, and went into a far country for a long time. And at the time of vintage he sent a servant to the farmers to receive of them a proportion of the fruit of the

---

* Mark iv. 33.

† Matt. xiii. 9. [Matthew 13.10–17.]

8. Shaftesbury, "An Essay on the Freedom of Wit and Humour," in Shaftesbury, *Characteristicks,* I:41.

9. Shaftesbury, *Characteristicks,* I:41.

10. Shaftesbury, *Characteristicks,* I:42.

11. A paraphrase of Matthew 13.9 and 13.43; Mark 4.9, 4.23, and 7.16; Luke 8.8.

vineyard; but they, instead of rendering him his just dues, abused and beat his servant, and sent him away empty. And again he sent another servant; but they maltreated him, and sent him likewise away empty. He sent a third, and they were more outrageous. They wounded him, and cast him out in the most violent manner. At last, the owner of the vineyard seeing his servants had not authority enough to bring the husbandmen to their duty, resolved to send his own beloved son to them, thinking that surely they would reverence him. But when the husbandman saw him, they reasoned among themselves saying, This is the heir, come, let us kill him that the inheritance may be ours. So they cast him out of the vineyard and killed him. Now, said Jesus, after this enormous cruelty and wickedness, what punishment do you think the master of the vineyard, when he re-<13>turns, will inflict upon those ungrateful and rebellious husbandmen? Some answered, He will certainly destroy those wicked men, and give the vineyard unto other husbandmen, which shall render him the fruits in their season: And they said, God forbid this should be our case. But the priests and scribes seeing their own opposition to the instructions of God painted out by this allegory in a very touching manner, they were provoked, and would have laid violent hands upon him, had they not feared the people. But not daring to do this, they pursued their resolution of endeavouring to ensnare him by cunning questions, that they might take hold of his words, and have something to accuse him of to the Roman governor. In pursuance of this design, they suborned spies to follow him, and under a pretence of desiring his opinion in a case of conscience, some of these put to him such a question, on a certain occasion, as they thought he could not possibly answer, without offending either the common people of the Jews on the one side, or the *Roman* governor on the other. The question they put to him was this, "Whether the Jews, who were the peculiar people of God, and under his immediate government, ought in conscience to pay tribute to the Roman Emperor, and so acknowledge the authority of the Romans over them or not?" [12] And in hopes to entice him to give such an answer as they might interpret to a seditious sense, they prefaced their question with

12. In this long paragraph and quotation Turnbull paraphrases Matthew 22.15–22, Mark 12.1–17, and Luke 20.9–26.

a profession of their great opinion of his extraordinary integrity, courage and sincerity, and that therefore they knew he would not fear to tell them his judgment plainly. But Jesus, aware of their crafty malignant intention, said to them, Why do you think to draw me into a snare? I well know your hypocritical malice. And calling for a piece of money wherewith the tribute used to be paid, he asked them whose stamp was upon it? They answered Caesar's; which, when <14> they acknowledged to be the Roman Emperor's, he said, Render then to the Roman Emperor what ye confess to be his due; and always submit yourselves so far to the government ye are under, as is consistent with what ye owe to God, or with his laws. Not being able to make any bad handle of this judicious answer, they marvelled at his superior prudence, and left him.

But after these were gone, some of the Sadducees, who believed that men perish utterly at death, and there is no future life, came and put this question to him. "Moses in the law directs, That if a man dies and leaves his wife without children, his brother shall marry his widow, to raise up children for the continuance of the name and family of the deceased. Now there happened in a certain family to be seven brothers, whereof the eldest having married a wife, after some time died, and left no children. The second married the widow, and he also died without children. The same happened to the third, to the fourth, fifth, sixth and seventh brother. Therefore, in the other life, or after the resurrection, whose wife must that woman be, for all the seven brothers had an equal right to her?"[13] This it seems the Saducees, who had a great regard for the law of Moses, thought an unanswerable objection against a future state. Now, on this occasion, a principal article in religion being concerned in the question, our Saviour talks plainly and roundly with them, and offers an argument for a future state to them,* which they could not, upon their own principles refuse. He tells them that in a future state, there is neither marrying nor giving in <15> marriage,

---

* The word ἀνάϛαϛις ["raising the dead"] properly signifies a future life in general. See Dr. Samuel Clarke's paraphrase on this passage. [Samuel Clarke, *A Paraphrase on the Four Evangelists,* 4th ed., 2 vols. (London, 1722), 1:155 note.] The Sadducees denied the resurrection, not because they thought it impossible, but because they thought there was no future state at all, but that the soul perished at death.

13. Matthew 22.23–29.

because there will be no mortality or succession; but that those who are worthy of happiness in the other world, are equal unto the angels. And he adds, now that this is no fiction, but that there shall be another life after this; if ye had studied the scriptures ye profess to believe, ye might and ought to have collected from God's stiling himself to Moses in the bush, The God of Abraham, Isaac and Jacob, long after the death of those patriarchs. God surely is not the God of those who do not exist, but of the living. These patriarchs therefore being dead, yet live to God.

Hereupon some of the Scribes, or expounders of the law, who were present and heard this dispute, being pleased at the readiness and clearness of Jesus's answer, by which he effectually confuted and silenced the Sadducees, they could not forbear testifying their admiration and approbation, saying, "Master thou hast well said." [14] In like manner did he frequently silence those who came to entangle him by other ensnaring questions, and put them to shame publickly. And upon all such occasions, he was sure to lay open and lash severely the hypocritical superstitious zeal of the Pharisees. "Beware," says he, "of the Scribes, who affect an air of gravity and austerity, in order to be accounted wise and virtuous by the people, but under a mask of religion, conceal the oppressive injustice and covetousness of which their hearts are full. They love greetings in the markets, and the highest seats in the synagogues, and for a shew of godliness make long prayers. But look into their moral conduct; and are they not miserable oppressors of the widows and orphans, and all those who are not able to detect their frauds or oppose their violence? Surely they shall be doubly punished by the just judgment of God, both for their wickedness, and for the false varnish of religion under which they cover it." [15] <16>

But none of them durst retort any such charge against him, as willing as they were to destroy his credit and authority. When the multitude, stirred up by the priests and Pharisees, cried out, Crucify him, the governor said, What evil hath he done? And when Pilate saw that he could prevail nothing, but that rather a tumult was made, he took water and washed his hands before the multitude, saying, I am innocent of the blood of this just person,

14. Luke 20.39.
15. The quotation is a paraphrase of Matthew 23.1–32 and Luke 20.46–47.

see you to it. To mention but one other instance at present, of the prudence with which he defended himself against his wicked and malignant persecutors, without confounding or obscuring the truth to those who were of a temper fit for receiving information (for more will occur when we come to consider his doctrine) let us cast our eyes upon the subsequent part of that story we have already narrated. When the Jews took up stones to throw at him,* having pleasantly asked them, for which of his good works it was they so maletreated him? The Jews answered, "For a good work we stone thee not, but for blasphemy, because thou, being a man, makest thyself equal to God." To this Jesus replies, Does not your own scripture call men gods, and children of the Most High, only because being judges and magistrates, they acted by commission and authority from God. If then the scripture itself, which ye cannot contradict or find fault with, scruples not to call ordinary magistrates *Gods,* how unreasonable is it in you to accuse me of blasphemy for calling myself the Son of God, unless you can shew that I am not sent by him into the world, upon a much more extraordinary occasion, with other authority and with other powers, and with other testimonies of my divine commission, than was ever given to any temporal ruler or judge? If I do not give evidence of my being sent of God, and sanctified by him, <17> believe me not. But if you cannot make any solid objection against my sanctity, my doctrine, or the evidences I give of my divine commission, why call you me a blasphemer, if the scripture blasphemes not, when it calls ordinary rulers Gods, and children of God?

We have thus agreed upon the rule or test by which pretenders to prophecy and divine mission are to be tried in the first place; or rather Christ himself hath fixed and determined it for us. Let us then try him by his own rule. I think in treating of other things, his zeal for true religion and virtue, in opposition to superstition, hath sufficiently appeared, and other instances of it will occur afterwards: But it is so essential a point, even when we are considering Christ as a mere philosopher, as a Socrates, for instance, that I cannot choose but add one or two more examples of his teaching on this subject.

Jesus happened to walk through some corn-fields on the sabbath-day

---

* John x. 35. [John 10.31–38.]

with his disciples.* And as they were going, the disciples being hungry, and
knowing what they were permitted by the law in such a case to do,† plucked
the ears of corn, and rubbing out the corn with their hands, began to eat.
But the Jews, who watched all occasions of reproaching them, observing
that it was the sabbath-day when they did this, said to Jesus, See you not
how your disciples break the sabbath? Why do you not reprove them? Jesus
answered, Consider what you say; you are reflecting upon examples ye pretend to hold in great veneration, from which you may and ought to learn,
that God never intended by any positive constitution, such as the strict
judaical observation of the sabbath, to put such difficulties upon men, as
to hinder them from doing things abso-<18>lutely necessary. Have ye not
read how David behaved himself in such a case? Do ye not remember, how
when he was hungry on a journey, the priest gave him consecrated bread
out of the tabernacle, which in strictness none but the priests were allowed
to eat, and both David and they that were with him, eat of it? Now, if
David be not blameable for this, how can ye, consistently with yourselves,
reproach my disciples for doing so small a thing as plucking and eating ears
of corn on the sabbath-day? Again, do you not remember how the priests
are by the law appointed to do several sorts of works in the temple upon
the sabbath-day, and yet they are no where accused, but are reckoned blame-
less. You will perhaps say this was a case excepted, because on that occasion
the priests were employed in the temple, and about the service of God, by
God's own express command. Very true. And I might tell you, after the
proofs I have given of my extraordinary mission from God, to declare to
the world the true and acceptable religion, that in this place is one who is
greater than the temple, or whose business and employment hath a nearer
relation to God than the external decorum of the temple. But I shall only
tell you, that if ye understood the frequent declarations God has made to
you by his prophets, or had just ideas of God himself, ye would not make
this objection. For what hath God more clearly manifested by his prophets
to you, or what doth reason itself more plainly teach, than that God will
have mercy and not sacrifice, or that God prefers works of righteousness

* Deut. xxiii. 2. *When thou comest into the standing corn of thy neighbours, then mayest
thou pluck the ears with thine hand.* [Deuteronomy 23.25.]
    † Matt. xii. [Matthew 12.1.]

and charity before sacrifices, and the most punctual performance of all positive laws and outward ceremonies. Ye cannot find fault with my disciples, unless you deny this truth, and affirm that the sabbath was made to be a hindrance to man in the performance of moral <19> duties, and cannot, even in case of necessity, be dispensed with by any man.

On another sabbath-day, Jesus entered into the synagogue,* and there offered an occasion of inculcating and confirming the same doctrine. For there happened to be in the synagogue a man having a withered hand. And the Jews still lying at the catch for something they might accuse Jesus of, observed him, and asked whether he would think it lawful to heal the man on the sabbath-day? Jesus said to them, Who is there among you so foolish, as under pretence of strict regard to the sabbath-day, would not, if a beast should by any accident be in danger of its life, or of any great mischief, immediately relieve it even on the sabbath-day. But how much better is a man than a beast? Wherefore, it is lawful to do well to mankind on the sabbath-day. Upon this occasion he inculcates upon them this eternal truth, "That the sabbath was made for man, and not man for the sabbath,"[16] *i.e.* that all positive or ritual ordinances are, in the nature of things, submitted and subordinated to the great purpose of religion and virtue, the real good of man, for whose use they are appointed.

Another instance of this class is to this effect: The Pharisees and Scribes, who held it strictly as a law delivered down to them by tradition,† from their predecessors or Rabbi's, that in many cases they ought not to eat without washing their hands immediately before, when they saw some of Jesus's disciples eat bread with unwashen hands, they found fault, and asked him, "Why walk not thy disciples according to the tradition of the elders; but eat bread with unwashen hands?" To this he answers, Well hath Esaias described your character when he says, "This people honoureth me with their lips, but their heart is far from me. But in <20> vain do they worship me, teaching for true religion certain usages founded merely on the commandment of men. Neglecting the great commands of God, justice, charity and truth, ye lay the stress of your religion upon such frivolous things, intro-

---

* Ibid. and Luke vi. [Matthew 12.9–13; Luke 6.6–10.]
† Mark vii. [Mark 7.1–13.]
16. Mark 2.27.

duced by superstitious customs and traditions, as washing of hands, and pots and cups, and the like." Nay, and ye not only prefer these fooleries before the commandments of God, founded upon and discoverable from the immutable differences of things, to the neglect and omission of your duty; but ye even directly transgress and act plainly in contradiction to those commandments, when some tradition happens to be contrary to them. For instance, it is an express command of God,* that every man should honour his father and mother. This commandment is of natural obligation, and of such importance and necessity is this duty, by the law of Moses, that whoever transgresses it, is positively condemned to die by that law. Yet ye on the contrary teach, that if a man gives that money to be employed in the service of the temple, with which he ought to have relieved the necessities of his parents, that then he sins not, though he suffers his parents to want. And thus ye hinder men from relieving the wants of their parents, which yet is evidently an especial part of that honour which men are expressly required to pay to them by the law of God. By this, continueth he, and many such unjust devices and traditions, you make the laws of God of no effect; ye distinguish and subtilize away all moral obligations into mere ceremony, into an empty form of godliness. Upon this occasion, turning himself from the Scribes and Pharisees, he called to the common people to draw nigh, and to attend to a most important truth, that understanding it, they might treasure it up in their minds, as a <21> preservative against all the artful abuses of superstition and hypocritical zeal. Cleanness and uncleanness in the sight of God, consist not in outward things, such as meats and drinks, but in inward things, *i.e.* the inward dispositions and affections of the mind. A man is not rendered impure by outward accidents; but then is a man defiled, when the impure motions of his heart produce or excite to immoral and wicked actions. Whosoever is capable and desirous of instruction, let him remember and often reflect upon this verity.

This is a very obvious truth. One would imagine that none could consider it without perceiving its evidence, its reasonableness. But here we have a strong instance of the power of prejudice and wrong education, and how superstition blinds reason, and renders it incapable of understanding the

* Exod. xx. 12. Exod. xxi. 17.

plainest moral truths. His disciples themselves did not fully comprehend the meaning of this lesson. However, being desirous of instruction, when he was alone, they asked him to explain to them yet more fully the notion of cleanness and uncleanness, which he did in this manner: That which enters not into the heart but into the belly, cannot defile a man's mind, which is the seat of virtue and vice. Nothing can be called unclean, or be said to defile a man but what comes from man himself, that is, proceeds from the thoughts and designs of his heart, of which he is master. All other things are, with respect to him, external and out of his power. From within, or out of the heart proceed evil thoughts, and all evil actions, such as fornication, adultery, murder, theft, covetousness, fraud and oppression, cheating, lasciviousness, envy, pride, calumny, and in one word, all tumultuous and irregular appetites and passions. And these are the things, which proceeding from corrupt minds, make men really unclean and hateful to God. But <22> if your minds be pure, and free from these pollutions, there is no uncleanness in neglecting the superstitious washings of the Pharisees, who wash their bodies but not their hearts, who affect an external shew of purity, but are inwardly rottenness and corruption, like whited or adorned sepulchres.*

Thus did Jesus teach. And tho' you know, my friend, how highly I esteem the moral doctrine of Socrates, yet I do not scruple to assert, that no where do we find him opposing superstition with such ardour and force of argument as Christ was ever and anon doing. Nor is there any where, certainly, so plain an account to be found of the nature of true worship, than (to mention no other of Christ's discourses or conferences) in his short conversation with the Samaritan woman.† This woman being convinced by a previous conversation with him, that he was a person of very extraordinary knowledge, and might be a prophet, asked his opinion about the great dispute between the Jews and the Samaritans. We, said she, the Samaritans, contend that mount Gerazim here, where our temple is built, is the place where God ought to be worshipped with sacrifices and offerings; Abraham and Jacob having built altars here, and so this being a more an-

* St. Luke xi. 39. Matt. xxiii. 27, &c. [Matthew 23.27–28.]
† St. John iv. 20. [John 4.7–26.]

cient place for sacrifice than even Jerusalem itself. The Jews, on the contrary, contend, that Jerusalem is the only place in which God has chosen to have sacrifices offered to him: And they abhor and detest our worship as erroneous and superstitious, because it is performed in a place and manner somewhat different from theirs. Now I desire you would inform me, whether our place of worship be not as holy as theirs, and our worship as true and acceptable to God. Jesus answered her: There is the less reason to trouble yourselves now about this dispute, inasmuch as the time is at hand, when the sacrifices <23> which are offered either in Jerusalem or Gerazim shall cease for ever; and the temples themselves shall be destroyed, and so the privilege about which ye contend will be taken from you both. One thing, however, I must tell you, That as for you Samaritans, when your ancestors came first into this land, they neither knew the manner of God's worship, nor him to be the true God, but took him for some petty God of this particular country. And you owe your better instruction to the Jews, who have all along had abundant means of knowing both whom they ought to worship, and how to do it. God hath honoured Jerusalem by raising his prophets from amongst them, and never among you Samaritans; so that you have had no other means of knowing his particular revelations but by them. And which is more, according to the promises made to the fathers, of their lineage the Saviour of the world was to come, by whom God intended to give a more compleat and universal revelation of his will than ever was yet made. Light and salvation are therefore of the Jews: But what you are most concerned to observe and understand is this, That hereafter neither shall the worship of God be confined to one place, nor shall it stand in sacrifices and burnt-offerings: But they only shall be accounted the true worshippers, who, in what place soever they are, give their hearts and souls entirely to God, to love and obey him in all things. For that is the worship which always was most acceptable to God; and that doctrine is already begun to be preached, by which the great reformation is to be made. You may think this a new doctrine; but consider that it must be true, for God is a spirit, and they who would approve themselves, and offer acceptable worship to him, must worship him in spirit and in truth. You cannot reflect upon the spiritual nature and moral <24> perfections of God without perceiving this truth. For how can we please such a Being, but by adoring with pure hearts and understanding minds, his moral excellencies, and by endeavouring to imitate them in our lives.

This is indeed a truth discoverable, demonstrable by reason, from the nature of things. Nor does its being said by Socrates or Jesus, render it less or more such a truth. But tho' it be such, yet it was far from being universally known when Socrates preached against superstition, and endeavoured to bring men to the knowledge of the truth. And when Christ appeared in the world, the sense of this truth seemed to be almost universally effaced, even among the Jews. And therefore, if the Greeks were obliged to Socrates for his moral instructions, the Jews and Romans were at least equally indebted to the instructions of Jesus. Without diminishing the former, justice may be done to the latter. And whoever impartially considers the doctrines of these two instructors, will find himself obliged to own, that it was Jesus who was most full and particular in refuting superstition, and shewing wherein true religion consists.

To give but one example in this comparative way: The discourse of Socrates with Alcibiades about prayer, is full of excellent instruction.[17] There he shews, how ignorantly of true good or happiness, men go to petition or pray to the Gods, and puzles Alcibiades rather than instructs him. But Jesus in his discourses on the subject, clearly points out the true happiness of man, the unity of God, and the universality of providence, and the difference between the things that are within man's power, and by consequence, the only proper objects of his solicitude, and those which are independent of him, or without his power, and therefore the objects neither of his care nor industry, but of his resignation <25> to the divine will. Let us run over one passage to this purpose.

When one applied to Jesus in this manner,* Sir, I believe you to be an extraordinary prophet, I beseech you therefore, make use of your authority to oblige my brother, who unjustly detains from me my share of an estate, to do me right. Jesus answered, Who gave me a right to judge and divide in matters of property? I have no such right. My business is of another kind, even to instruct in the great truths of religion and morality. It would

* Luke xii. [Luke 12.13–21.]
17. Plato, *Alcibiades,* II.

be a very just ground of exception against me, if I should take upon me to determine in affairs belonging to the civil judges. Having thus refused to intermeddle in this affair, he took occasion to warn his disciples and all the people, of the evil of covetousness. "The two pursuits," says he, "which divide mankind, are external and internal goods; virtue and riches. And as no man can have two masters, so none can make virtue his chief happiness, and at the same time have his heart wholly set upon external goods. Ye cannot serve God and Mammon. Beware therefore of covetousness; and consider that the true comfort of life, or genuine and sincere, unchanging happiness, consisteth not in having many and great possessions. They are most miserably deluded, who are extremely sollicitous about outward things as their chief good, and promise themselves all happiness in the enjoyment of them. The happiness of a rational being cannot lie in perishing things, but must consist in goods which are as immortal as our souls." [18] This lesson he enforces by a parable. There was, says he, a certain rich man whose ground brought forth a very plentiful crop, so that all his barns were not sufficient to contain it. Upon this the rich man, considering with himself how he should dispose of all his wealth, came at last to this <26> resolution, that he would pull down his old granaries, and build new ones larger than the former, and that in them he would treasure up this great plenty, sufficient for many years. And then he thought, that having laid up so many goods in store for a long time to come, he might safely indulge his ease, fare deliciously every day, live splendidly and luxuriously, and not fear that any thing could deprive him of this happiness, or that so great provision could ever come to an end. He said to his soul, Take thy pleasure, eat, drink and be merry, for this is true happiness, and now have I sufficient means for every enjoyment. But what was the event, said Jesus? Observe how unthinkingly, how fatally he deceived himself. For at the very instant he was applauding himself in his own mind, promising himself much pleasure, and calling himself a very happy man, God called him suddenly into another world, whither his treasures could not follow him.[19] This is the case of him who layeth up treasures for himself on earth, and makes no pro-

18. A paraphrase of Matthew 6.24–25 and Luke 16.13.
19. A paraphrase of Luke 12.16–21.

vision for his future happiness, by enriching his mind with those virtues that are treasures which endure for ever. Let therefore your chief sollicitude be to increase in spiritual riches; to grow in wisdom and virtue, and the goods of the mind, which are everlasting as is the soul. Be not at all sollicitous about things absolutely without your power, but learn to resign the conduct and management of these to the infinitely good providence, which governeth all things. Learn to know the difference between what your sollicitude and industry can, and what it cannot do. Now, which of you, by all his anxiety, can add any thing, for instance, to his stature. But if it be vain and unreasonable to be anxious about this, it must be equally so to be anxious about other things, as much or rather more without your power. Nay, be not too careful and sollicitous even about the outward <27> things, which in some measure depend upon your industry. And for this end do ye frequently call to mind, and seriously reflect upon the all-ruling providence of God. Consider the other creatures of God, the birds, beasts and plants, things far inferior to rational beings, and of much less value in the sight of God. Consider how God, without their being able to provide for themselves before hand, or so much as to foresee their own wants, preserves and nourishes even these meaner creatures, and wonderfully furnishes things necessary for their subsistance in their several seasons. Consider this extensive care of heaven, and reflect how much more an all-wise providence will provide for you, whom he hath created with so much greater excellencies, and therefore to nobler ends. Exert your industry, without which you cannot acquire any external goods, but with resignation to God; and be not over anxious, distrustful or fearful, but make it the principal business of your lives to grow in virtue; for that, and that alone is stable happiness. Seek the kingdom of God, seek the knowledge of God's will, and those excellent dispositions of mind, which make men good subjects to God, and which alone can qualify for dwelling in his kingdom, the future kingdom of the blessed, into which nothing impure can enter. And be persuaded, that God will take proper care of those who make virtue their chief study. He best knoweth of what you have need, or what is best for you.[20]

This is the account our Saviour gives of human duty and happiness; and

20. A paraphrase of Matthew 6.26–33.

accordingly the excellent directory he gave his disciples for prayer, consists not of *informations* or *counsels* to God, but of adoration, resignation, thanksgiving, confession of sin, and generous benevolent wishes for the increase of virtue, or the spreading of his kingdom in the world, and acts of forgiveness to those who offend us, under a <28> serious impression of the need we stand in of pardon from God, and of the acceptableness to him of a charitable, meek, forgiving and beneficent temper. And surely no exercise can be more proper for perfecting us in any art or habit, than this moral exercise is for purifying our minds, subduing our irregular appetites and passions, strengthening our virtuous affections, and comforting and establishing us in the practice of true goodness, in love to God and love to mankind, which Jesus often tells us is the whole of human duty, and the way to eternal happiness, as well as in itself the most agreeable temper of mind, and by being such a present reward to itself. *Thus to ask, thus to wish more virtue is to gain.*[21]

But after having shewn what an enemy Christ was to superstition, it is by no means improper to observe, that he well knew the necessity of a public religion, in order to preserve regard to God and to virtue in the world, the great props of society, and of all that is great or good in human life; and that for this reason, there must be some ritual or positive ordinances of his appointment, and to consider whence he adapted them, and for what use. Mean time, let it just be suggested, that he came to be baptized of John, who knowing him to be the Messiah, refused to baptize him, saying, It is much more fit that you should baptize me than I you. And for what reason did our Saviour do this? It was because, as he tells John, he thought it thus became him to give an example of doing all things decently and with order. "Thus it becometh us," says he, "to fulfil all righteousness."[22] This respect we owe to outward rites and ordinances, even tho' they be not immediately of God's appointment, (as baptism was not) if they have a good meaning and intention, and however they may be abused, have in themselves an aptitude or propriety to signify the great end of worship and religion, purity of life <29> and manners. He for the same reasons eat the

21. A paraphrase of Epistle IV, line 326, of Alexander Pope's "An Essay on Man": "Since but to wish more Virtue, is to gain."

22. Matthew 3.15.

passover with his disciples; and exercised his power and authority in cleansing the temple of those who profaned it by rendering it a place of covetousness, extortion and cheating, saying,* This place was designed not for a place of merchandize, but for the service of God, according as Esaias prophesied, "That the temple of God should be an house of prayer for all people." The place he cleared, was the outward court, the court of the Gentiles, where the devout proselites of the Gentiles, who were not admitted into the inner and holier part of the temple, might worship the true God. This he found like a common market, filled with money-changers stalls, and sellers of cattle and doves, and the like, who sat there under pretence of having these things near at hand, for the convenience of those who came up to sacrifice. And from whatever motives this abuse was suffered or connived at by the priests, it was certainly fit for him to exercise his authority in rectifying it, who came to teach, that with God there is no respect of persons, but that whosoever feareth God and worketh righteousness, of whatever nation he be, is accepted of God. Nor did he, by so doing, commit any riot contrary to law, but he acted agreeably to the law, and the original intention of the place which he thus cleansed. It was therefore an example of his respect to the public order and establishment, as well as an emphatical declaration against the encroachments those who ought to have taken care of the public laws had made, or suffered to be made, on the rights of the Gentile proselites. And to add no more at present upon this head, when he had cured any person, his orders to them were, Go thy way and shew thyself first to the priest, who is to judge of your being clean, and offer the sacrifice which the law requires for your purification, that <30> ye may convince them of the reality of the cure, and yet not give them any occasion of calumny.

He had therefore good reason to say, when he laid open the corruptions that had crept into the Jewish church, by false expositions of the law of Moses, Think not because I thus correct the errors and false doctrines of your rabbi's and priests, that I am come to destroy the law or the prophets. "I am not come to destroy but to fulfil."[23] I am not come to oppose your

* Matt. xxi. [Matthew 21.12–13, Mark 11.15–17, and Luke 20.45–46.]
23. Matthew 5.17.

established religion, but to restore you to just notions of its spiritual and moral intent, and to shew you that it hath been corrupted and abused, and that now its typical signification is fully accomplished. For verily your ceremonial law shall not cease till its spiritual end is fulfilled. Indeed, setting aside all the reasons we have to think the Jewish ceremonial law was of divine appointment, hardly can so good an account be given why a Socrates paid such regard to the superstitious usages in his time, while he was declaiming so openly against false notions of religion, as why Jesus Christ opposed nothing but the misrepresentations and corruptions of the law of Moses, and submitted in every instance, with great decency and reverence to the authorised rites and usages of the Jews, took care to caution against confounding them with the *weightier matters of the law,* and placing the whole of religion in them, or imagining the most pious and virtuous could not be acceptable to God, if they were strangers to such positive ordinances. He no-where refuses the fitness* of some exterior observances, without which there can be no such thing as a public acknowledgment of God, well-knowing how necessary a general sense of religion is to public peace and good order, and that public religion cannot be upheld without some positive institutions or symbols: For publick worship must be performed <31> in an authorized regular place and manner. But he well understood, on the other hand, how liable all such are to be perverted by corrupt and crafty men. And therefore this was, so to speak, the *chief burden* of all his discourses, even to warn men against being deceived into regarding positive rites as of the same importance with moral obligations, or in any other view but as shadows of the absolute necessity of sanctity of heart and life, in order to please God, and attain to his favour. The Essenes among the Jews, like some modern mystics, thought public worship of little consequence, and laid a mighty stress upon closet contemplation and devotion. The Pharisees, on the other hand, placed the whole of religion in punctual regard to external ceremonies, and imagined they could thereby atone for irregularities in practice, nay for unrighteousness, and thus substituted certain outward formalities in the room of real virtue. And this hath been the most numerous sect in all times, partly because religion is natural to mankind,

---

* Luke ii. 42, &c. [Turnbull's reference to Luke does not make sense.] Matt. xxiii. 23.

and those who acknowledge a God, must have some plausible way of appeasing their consciences if they live in sin, and partly because superstition may be made a profitable trade at the expence of virtue, against which corrupt traffic, just notions of moral obligations are the only security. The Sadducees denied a future state, and taught that the soul is not distinct from the body, and therefore must perish with it, but yet were in their practice less dissolute, and far more benevolent than the proud Pharisees, who preached and boasted of a godliness superior to good works. Jesus Christ taught a future state of rewards and punishments in opposition to the Sadducees: The absolute necessity of virtue, and the subordination of ritual performances to morals, in contradiction to the doctrine of the Pharisees, whom he every-where represents as the most dangerous enemies to virtue, <32> there being indeed no other so effectual way of supplanting it, as by putting something very specious and solemn in its room: And in opposition to the Essenes, he set forth the spirit of ritual and positive institutions, and paid due deference to them in their spirit, or as they may be means of maintaining upon men's minds that pious veneration of God, without which, that virtue, which is the cement and ornament of present society, as well as a necessary qualification for happiness in the future life, where all the enjoyments are rational, cannot be perfect. Religion, in a word, is the firmest bond of civil society: But public worship is requisite to keep up a sense of religion: And public worship can no more take place without some external forms, than there can be language or discourse without words. Now Jesus Christ hath left us the simplest form of public worship, and the least capable of being perverted into superstition that can be imagined; tho', while there is such a thing as ambition or avarice in the world, *i.e.* while men are men, nothing is absolutely secure against corruption and wicked abuse. There is nothing that can be called wholly positive in the religion he taught, besides baptism and the supper; the intention of which rites shall be considered afterwards. And hardly can any portion of his instructions be read, which does not warn us in the strongest terms to beware of substituting any outward worship in the room of sincere virtue; for nothing can render us acceptable to God, who is perfect reason and virtue, but a well regulated mind and life; or qualify for future felicity but virtuous dispositions and habits, an improved understanding, a sanctified heart, and a truly generous and benevolent soul. This is the end of all his parables: To this scope are all his reasonings and exhortations solely directed. So that while nothing is added to the religious worship Christianity prescribes, except <33> some few necessary decencies and formalities, which it must be left to society to regulate, if reading the institutions of our Saviour make any part of divine service, there is all the security that there can be in the nature of things, against the abuses or misrepresentations of the Christian rituals, to which religious ceremonies the best chosen cannot but be liable.

What virtue doth he not recommend? And what else does he pronounce blessed, but piety towards God and benevolence towards mankind? Charity is the fulfilment of his law, or more properly speaking, the fulfilment of what he calls the will of God. According to his doctrine, virtue alone is happiness here or hereafter; or in whatever state rational and social beings are placed, they can only be happier as they are more *benevolent and kinder.* God is supremely happy, because he is supremely good. What is the purport of his discourse on the mount, but that *heighth of bliss is but heighth of charity,*[24] and that virtue's very tears yield more true satisfaction than the broadest mirth of fools.

Blessed, said he, are the modest, humble and contented, who prefer honesty and virtue to all the pomp and pageantry of this world, for theirs is the kingdom of heaven.[25] Blessed are the pious and virtuous, even when they are distressed and mourn, for virtuous consciousness, and the hope of future bliss, are the truest, the most solid comfort. These afford joys far surpassing all sensual revellings. Blessed are they who are not tormented by insatiable appetites after wordly riches or honours, which are as unsatisfactory as they are uncertain, but whose hunger and thirst are after greater perfection in knowledge and virtue, and who can derive virtuous strength and consolation to their minds, from the belief of an infinitely wise providence, and a glorious immortality after death, in which the pure in <34> heart shall attain to knowledge of God's works and government, which in comparison of the highest and clearest knowledge we can now attain, may be called *seeing God.* Let therefore the love of God and the love of mankind reign in your hearts. Give full scope to benevolence to expand itself, let it

24. Pope, "An Essay on Man," IV.360.
25. In this paragraph Turnbull paraphrases Christ's sermon on the mount in Matthew, chapters 5–7.

extend even to your enemies; for to do good, to be generous even to the unthankful, and overcome evil by good, is godlike beneficence. By such boundless love and charity alone, can we become like God, and merit to be called his children, who *makes his sun to rise on the evil and the good, and sendeth rain on the just and the unjust.*[26] Few men are so bad as not to love those that love them. And it is indeed but a very small degree of goodness to boast of, if we only pay ordinary civilities to those who deal kindly with us. This is no more than what the worst of men think themselves bound to do in common gratitude. Let therefore your charity and well-doing rise far above this common pitch. Let it extend itself universally, in imitation of the divine goodness, which is the greatest excellency and perfection of God. Be ye all love, for God is love. His exhortations every where run in the same strain. Who, according to his doctrine, are approved and rewarded at the day of judgment, or in a future state, but those who fed the hungry and cloathed the naked, those who abounded in charity and good works? And who are accused or condemned to punishment, but the selfish and hard-hearted, those who are utterly devoid of humanity and compassion, and who living in riot and luxury, are strangers to the divine pleasure, of relieving the distressed and doing good? Let me just take notice of two of his parables relating to charity and beneficence.

Jesus sitting in the court of the temple,* over against the treasury, looked upon the people, as <35> they gave in their free-will offerings into the chest for pious and charitable uses. And among the rest there came a poor widow woman, and put in two small pieces of money, making the value of a farthing. Now, when Jesus observed this, he called his disciples to him, and gave them this excellent lesson. Assuredly, said he, this poor woman has done a greater act of piety and charity than any of the rich men whom you saw cast in a great deal of money. For they gave only a small proportion out of their great estates, but she, in the zeal of her heart, has put in her whole stock. And God judges of men's actions, not by the measure of the outward work, but by the inward affection and temper of the mind. The outward means are not in our power, but the good disposition itself is.

Again, a certain lawyer, one versed in determining questions, and de-

---

* Mark xii. 41.
26. Matthew 5.45.

ciding difficulties in the law,* came to make trial of Christ's knowledge and judgment, and to observe whether he would teach any thing contrary to the law. The question he proposed to Jesus was, What do you say is *the main and principal thing,* by which a man must attain that eternal life which you discourse so much about. Jesus said, What doth the law you are so well skilled in determine in the case? What does it say about religion and duty? The scribe answered, That which the law commands is this, That we should love God sincerely and constantly, and that we should love our neighbours as ourselves. Jesus replied, You have answered well. This rule do you observe, and you shall inherit eternal life. The Scribe could not choose but approve Jesus's answer, but yet desiring to justify himself, and hoping to appear a very good man, for being kind to those that dwelt near him, of the same nation, and religion or sect, he asked Jesus farther, saying, When <36> the law commands us to love our neighbour as ourselves, whom does it mean by *our neighbour,* and how far must we extend that word. To this Jesus answered by a parable. There was, said he, a traveller going down from Jerusalem to Jericho, and in the way he was attacked by robbers, who stripped him, and not content with that, sorely wounded him, so that they left him upon the road almost dead. Now it happened that a certain priest passed by that way, who one would expect by his very place and office, professing great holiness, should have assisted the poor wounded traveller. But when he saw him, he turned off to the other side, and went on his way. A little after a levite came likewise to the same place, of whom, if not for the sake of his religion, yet at least on account of his tribe and profession, it might have been expected, that he should have had compassion on his brother, and have relieved him in his extreme distress: But this man also only looked on him, and passed by without doing any thing for him. At last a certain Samaritan passing that way saw him, and took pity on him, and tho' a stranger to the nation, and an enemy to the religion of the Jews, yet in great charity he stopped, and went to him and dressed his wounds, and set him upon his own beast, and carried him to an inn, and saw all necessary care taken of him. And the next day, being obliged to go on in his journey, he called the master of the house, and paid him for the

---

* Luke x. 25. [The paragraph that follows is a paraphrase of Luke 10.25–37.]

wounded man's lodging, and other expences, and gave him strict charge to take particular care of him till he should recover, and promised at his return to pay all the charges himself. Now said Jesus to the Scribe, which of these three men do you think was properly the poor traveller's neighbour, and did the office of a neighbour to him, the priest and Levite that passed by and neglected him, or the Samaritan, who tho' a <37> stranger both by birth and religion, yet with great charity assisted and relieved him? The Scribe said, He that charitably assisted him was no doubt his best neighbour. Then replied Jesus, Do you likewise follow this rule. If the Samaritan acted herein the part of a good man, do you go and imitate his example. Look not upon those only to be your neighbours who dwell near you, or are of the same nation, religion, or sect; but think every one such who stands in any need of your relief and assistance, however otherwise he may be a stranger to you; and so extend your charity to all mankind.

How instructive is this excellent similitude? And how, indeed, can any one impartially attend to the parables or allegories of Christ, and not admire in him what other sages of antiquity, Socrates in particular, are so highly commended for, a *certain exquisite and refined raillery, by virtue of which he could give the most cutting reproofs, without directly reproaching, and treat the highest subjects of religion and morals, and those of the commonest capacity both together, and render them explanatory of each other.*[27] His tales or fables were so many mirrors, in which his hearers could not but see their own features nicely delineated: Looking-glasses,* in which his hearers could not choose but see at once their own follies and vices, and the true beauty or virtue they ought to aspire after. It is indeed this mirror-quality of parables and fabulous narrations, in which their peculiar excellency and force, as instructors, above bare precepts and reasonings consists. And it is good for us, if we would learn our duty, and discover our imperfections, often to look into such mirrors. <38>

Whatever, therefore, may be found to be true with regard to any other pretension of Jesus Christ, his instructions must be acknowledged to be very sound, and to have been delivered in a most masterly way. And it is

---

* So St. James speaks of the Christian law, Epist. of St. James i. 24. [James 1.23–24.]
27. Turnbull elaborates on a passage in Shaftesbury, *Characteristicks*, I:121.

no wonder that he who thus taught true religion and virtue, and thus reproved superstition and vice, was heard with admiration, and owned greatly
to excel, in his manner of instructing, the Jewish doctors, who filled their
discourses with vain subtleties, and reasoned in a dry formal manner, from
the authority of rabbi's and heads of sects, or from idle traditions. The
things which he spake were great and noble; and he delivered them with a
voice of majesty and authority, of gravity and truth, and enforced them by
the most apposite striking similitudes.

All this, I think, hath been made sufficiently evident. But let us compare
his example with his preaching. Did his conduct answer to his excellent,
his most pure and virtuous doctrine?

First of all, he was most indefatigable in teaching true religion, and in
confuting errors that struck at the very vitals of morality and virtue, and
perverted godliness into a vain form, without any beneficial power or efficacy, nay, into a commutation for that which only can be of any use, and
consequently have any excellence, a benevolent and pious temper of mind,
and conformable practice. He not only avoided no occasion of doing this,
but he sought opportunities of giving these wholesome instructions. And
in consequence of this vigilance to teach truth and righteousness, he was
malitiously upbraided with liking the company of publicans and sinners,
and suffering his disciples also to associate with them.

When Jesus called Matthew to follow him,* he invited Jesus home with
him to his house. And <39> when they sat down to table, many tax-
gatherers, who were men hateful to the Jews, and many profligate persons
of their acquaintance, sat down next to Jesus and his disciples. Which,
when the proud Pharisees saw, they were moved with envy, but not daring
to provoke Jesus himself, who had formerly reprehended their arrogance,
they asked his disciples, "Why doth your master, who pretends to be a holy
and sanctified person, keep company with the worst of men?"[28] But Jesus
hearing them ask the question, gave an answer to them that is full of instruction, and not obscurely pointed out the great end he proposed to himself by his preaching, and that in the figurative way we have already com-

---

* Matt. ix. 10. [Matthew 9.9.]
28. Matthew 9.11.

mended. "They that are whole need not a physician, but they that are sick."[29] Further, saith he, I would have you who make this objection, to attend carefully to the full meaning of the saying of a prophet whose authority you own, "I will have mercy and not sacrifice."[30] For I came not to call the righteous, but sinners to repentance." The meaning of the answer plainly amounts to this. As those that are in health need not the assistance of the physician, but those that are sick, so those that are truly righteous need not my exhortations to repentance, but those that are sinners. Since therefore you account yourselves just persons, who do not need any instructions, why are ye angry with me for keeping company with such as do? And if ye account it an unfit thing, or a kind of pollution for a man to keep company with sinners, whom he may advantage by his advice, instruction and example, what think you can be the meaning of that saying of the prophet Hosea, "I will have mercy and not sacrifice?"* For my part, I think to take proper methods of reforming the wicked, and bringing them to a sense of their evil ways and of their duty, is <40> the greatest act of charity we can do. And the great design of my coming into the world, and of my preaching, was not to call the righteous, but sinners to repentance. For to the former I have nothing to say, but to exhort and encourage them to go on in the virtuous course they are already in. He preached the acceptability of true repentance, or sincere reformation to God. And nothing can indeed be more moving than the parables he employed to this purpose. I shall only mention one of them, which he spoke on the occasion that hath been taken notice of. Jesus continuing to teach and instruct the multitude,† many men of bad lives and very evil reputation, came to hear his doctrine. Whereupon the Scribes and Pharisees, men of no real virtue, but puffed up with pride and vanity, valuing themselves upon an affectation of extraordinary austerity, and despising persons of a lower character, so far as to disdain to converse with them, quarrelled with Jesus, and accused him, as if he could not possibly be a good man himself, that allowed access to such bad men to converse freely with him, and even to eat with him. But Jesus, to convince

---

* Hosea vi. 6.
† Luke xv.
29. Matthew 9.12.
30. Matthew 9.13.

them of their folly and uncharitableness, shewed them, that conversing with sinners in order to reform them, was so far from being a thing inconsistent for a good man to do, that on the contrary it was really one of the most charitable actions, and the most pleasing to God that could be done, because God truly desires the conviction of sinners, and that they may be brought by repentance into the way to happiness. And this he illustrated and confirmed to them by the following beautiful comparison. If a man, said he, has a flock of a hundred sheep, and one of them chance to go astray, and be in danger to be lost, is it not natural for him to leave the rest of his flock, and <41> run after the straying sheep, and search all the country for it? And if he be so happy as to find it, does he not bring it back with great gladness, and rejoice on this occasion with his friends and neighbours, and testify even a greater and more sensible pleasure at the unexpected recovery of that one which was like to have been lost, than at the safety of the other ninety and nine, which never went astray? Even thus, continued Jesus, when a great sinner who was running headlong in the way to destruction, is happily reclaimed, and beyond expectation is brought back into the ways of virtue and happiness, God himself is well pleased, and all the angels in heaven rejoice, and all good men here upon earth ought to be very glad, and to do all that is in their power, with the greatest condescension and meekness, to be the instruments of so happy a change.

He added several other parables to the same purpose, all of which contain the strongest incentive to repentance. For this is plainly their meaning. While men continue in their sins they are in the way to eternal perdition, in consequence of the laws of moral rectitude, which God observes in his government of rational beings. But when they forsake their evil courses, and being convinced of the folly and unreasonableness of vice, and of the beauty of holiness, they turn to God, and begin the serious study of virtue, they are restored into the paths of life and eternal happiness: God is reconciled to them, and their recovery gives joy to the angels in heaven. "There is joy, saith Christ, in the presence of the angels of God, over one sinner that repenteth."[31] And how can they who love mankind, and love virtue, not rejoice at this happy event, or not take pleasure in bringing it about?

31. Luke 15.7.

This comfortable doctrine, which without encouraging sin, is a most powerful motive to repentance, <42> is the glad tidings which Christ delighted to preach, and which constitute a great part of his gospel, as we shall see afterwards; even that God, who may as a law-giver, exact strict obedience, and rigorously punish every transgression, will forgive the penitent upon their cordial reformation, and instead of perfect conformity to his will, accept of sincerity in the inward man, and habitual endeavours to improve in virtue and moral perfection. And surely to preach this doctrine to sinners, or to take all opportunities of inculcating it upon them, in order to gain them to God, *i.e.* in the scripture stile, to persuade them into the practice of virtue, which is the way to merit the favour of God, and to obtain eternal happiness, was a noble and generous employment.

But Jesus Christ did not lead a merely contemplative, or even a merely preaching life, but a very busy active one. *He was continually going about doing good.*[32] We are not at present concerned to enquire whence he had his power, or whether it was ordinary or extraordinary. However that may be, he was continually comforting and relieving the afflicted; and to him every hour seemed lost, in which he had not an opportunity of doing some truly useful or beneficial action.

'Tis well worth our observation on this head, that he was far from being morose or sour, insomuch that he was called a glutton and a wine-bibber, a friend of publicans and sinners. But against this reproach he thus justifies himself:* Whereunto, saith he to his accusers, shall I liken the men of this generation, and to what are they like? They are like children playing together in the street in a froward and peevish humour. For as children at such a time do every thing just contrary to what their companions expect and desire, so the men of <43> this generation interpret crossly and perversely whatever we say or do; neither can any argument persuade them to hearken to instruction, nor any manner of behaviour remove their malicious prejudices against us. John the Baptist, when he came to preach repentance to them, appeared after a retired manner in the wilderness, with fasting and abstinence, with great strictness and severity of life; and they

* Luke vii. 31. [Luke 7.31–35.]
32. Acts 10.38.

said he is a madman or possessed. On the contrary, Christ comes to them
without any such austerity, conversing with all sorts of men freely, and eating all meats indifferently; and they say he is a loose prophane person, a
despiser of the law, and a companion of publicans and sinners. But wisdom
is justified of all her children, and from them alone can it expect a favourable reception. Men, in order to judge soundly or wisely of doctrines, must
be calm and unprejudiced, lovers of truth, and lovers of virtue. And to
such I fear not to appeal. Their approbation alone is worth seeking, and if
my doctrine or life deserve it, I will be sure to meet with it from such.

Again some told him, *viz.* some of John's disciples,* who had been accustomed to fastings, and greater austerities than ordinary, being somewhat
displeased at that freer way of living which Jesus seemed to allow his disciples, came to Jesus and said, How is it that you commend the holiness of
our master John the Baptist, and profess yourself to be a teacher of extraordinary piety, yet you permit your disciples to live with greater liberty,
and suffer them to omit those mortifications and austerities which both the
disciples of John, and also of the Pharisees, constantly practise, fasting often, and seting apart at least some days in every week for prayer and abstinence. Jesus answered, I do not condemn you for your constancy and abstinence in fast-<44>ings; but every thing is good only in its proper season;
and this is by no means a fit time to put my disciples upon such severities.
For as it would be unreasonable to require the friends of a bridegroom to
fast, just at the time of the wedding, and while they are with the bridegroom
at the feast; so is it by no means proper to make my disciples fast, so long
as I their master am with them. But the time will come, and that shortly,
when I shall be taken from them; and then they will have occasions enough
of mourning and fasting. And this he illustrated by several very pleasant
and suitable similitudes.

Add to this, that the first miracle Christ is said to have performed, shewed
he was no enemy to innocent mirth, and at the same time manifested his
complaisance to his relations. There was a marriage celebrated in Cana of
Galilee,† by some of Jesus's relations, and Mary the mother of Jesus was

* Luke v. 33.
† John ii. [John 2.1–10.]

present at it. Jesus himself also being at this time in Galilee, with intent to choose disciples, was invited to the feast, with as many of his disciples as had begun at that time to follow him. Now it happened that the company being great, the wine that was provided for the entertainment fell short. Upon which Jesus's mother, concerned for her friends at this solemn occasion of rejoicing, went to Jesus privately, and told him that all the wine was out, intimating her desire, that as during the time of his retired life with his parents, she had sometimes observed him to exert his miraculous power in relieving the wants of his friends, so now upon an extraordinary occasion, he would be pleased miraculously to assist them. Jesus answered, I must tell you, mother, it doth not belong to you to choose or direct when or what miracles I should do. And besides, the time is not yet come, tho' it be very near, in which I shall con-<45>firm the truth, by doing beneficent miracles indeed, for the relief of the distressed. And here really there is no such occasion. Nevertheless, I will not refuse to satisfy you in this expectation, and to do this office of civility to my kindred, in order to shew that I am no enemy to innocent festivity. Upon this, water being brought him by the servants, at his mother's orders, he immediately turned it into the purest and best wine. So that when the governor of the feast tasted it, he said to the bridegroom, Sir, we are extremely obliged to you for your generous civility. Usually men give their best wine at the beginning of a feast, and when the guests have drank a good deal, then they treat them with that which is worse. But you have entertained us all along with good wine, and that which we are now drinking is even manifestly better than any we have yet had. The bridegroom was surprized, and professed he knew nothing at all of it; till at last the servants being examined, the miracle was discovered, and Jesus's extraordinary power was made manifest to the whole company.

I am far from thinking an excellent author not to be in earnest, or to speak ironically, when he remarks, "As for our Saviour's stile, 'tis not more vehement and majestic in his gravest animadversions, or declamatory discourses, than it is sharp, humorous and witty in his repartees, reflections, fabulous narrations, or parables, similies, comparisons, and other methods of milder censure and reproof. His exhortations to his disciples, his particular designation of their manners, the pleasant images under which he often couches his morals and prudential rules, even his miracles themselves (especially the first he ever wrought) carry with them a certain festivity, alacrity and good-humour so remarkable, that I should look upon it as impossible not to be mov'd in a pleasant manner at their recital."[33] <46>

Two only of all his miracles have any appearance of ill-nature, or did any hurt. All the rest were kindly and beneficent works. These two are the blasting the fig-tree, and sending the devils into the swine.[34] And with regard to them, all we can say, till we come to consider the general end of his miracles, is, that it was by no means unnecessary, in order to gain attention to his doctrine, to give some instances of his power to curse as well as to bless; and hardly could any works proper to serve that end be less hurtful than these two. Blasting a single fig-tree in that country was no great damage. And as for the perishing of the swine, the Gergesenes deserved to be punished for keeping those beasts, which were a snare and an offence to the Jews, their flesh not being permitted to be eaten.

Certain it is, that Christ delighted not in works of cruelty, but of mercy and goodness; and employed his power in curing the diseased, and relieving the distressed. But to whom did he give the honour and glory of his power? He did not assume it to himself, but rendered it to God. His doctrine he calls the doctrine of God. And to him does he ascribe all his gifts, all his power and knowledge. He sought not his own honour, but honour to God who sent him, and whose doctrine he taught. All he desired was to be believed and honoured as the Sent of God, or as his messenger to declare and execute his will, for the general good of mankind; the messenger of God who sent him to be a light to the world, that the world might no longer lie in darkness, but have the light of life, the knowledge of the true God and true religion, and of the only way to eternal life, which is pure and sincere obedience to the laws of God: Those eternal laws of moral rectitude, which are immutable as God is, being founded upon the unchangeable nature of God himself, who is perfect truth, virtue and holiness. Thus he fre-<47>quently reasons:* "I come not to do my will, but the will of God who is in heaven. My doctrine is not mine, but his that sent me," *i.e.* The doctrine which I teach, is not indeed a doctrine of human learning and

* John vii. 16. &c.
33. Shaftesbury, *Characteristicks,* III:76.
34. Matthew 21.19; Matthew 8.28–32, Mark 5.11–13, and Luke 8.26–33.

wisdom: I have not studied or invented it, in hopes to become a celebrated preacher for pompous oratory, and learned subtilty in disputes, as the Scribes generally do, whose principal aim is the applause of men. But the doctrine which I preach is the plain doctrine of God, fitted not to please your curiosity, but to reform your hearts and lives, and communicated to me immediately from the Father, whose glory alone I seek, and not my own. Examine my doctrine impartially, and if it hath not the characters of truth, respect it not; but if it carries with it all the marks of truth and of divine approbation, then receive it for his sake from whom it comes, and not for mine; give the glory of it to him who sent me to declare it to you, and by whom I am assisted and directed in teaching it and confirming it. There are certainly marks and characters by which a candid examiner may easily discern whether a doctrine be of God or not. There is no man who lays aside partiality, and unreasonable prejudices, and who is disposed to believe whatsoever shall sufficiently appear to be the will of God, how contrary soever it may prove to men's carnal and sensual lusts, but may easily be able to judge, from the very nature and tendency of a doctrine, whether it proceeds from God or not. A deceiver aims at nothing but popular applause, or worldly honours and advantages. If one speak of himself, he seeketh his own glory, and will take all the honour to himself. But what reason can you have to suspect one of imposture, or of any end a deceiver can have in view, who seeketh not his own glory, but the glory <48> of God? Shew me any unrighteousness in my doctrine or life if you can: Any symptom of vain-glory or ambition, any worldly view in my conduct, any mark of any other aim whatsoever but the glory of God and the good of mankind, and then you effectually destroy my pretension. But take heed that ye reject not the truth, through prejudice, and contrary to all appearances. Judge righteous judgment. Look well into my doctrine; for I deliver nothing to you but what I am commissioned by God to teach,* and what God will abundantly justify and confirm. When you have vented your fury against me, and think you have effectually put an end to me and my pretensions, I tell you now beforehand, that soon after it will appear yet more evidently than it now does, that I have not gone about to deceive you, by

---

* John viii. 26.

pretending an authority which I have not; but that I have faithfully delivered a doctrine God sent me to teach.

We have already seen how he answered on one occasion, when he was
accused of blasphemy, in equalling himself to God. And we are as expresly
told, that when some gave him titles which he thought belonged to God
alone, he corrected them, saying, Why callest thou me good, there is none
good but God, the only true God. There is none good but one, that is God.*
"The Jews," 'tis said, "sought to kill him, because he had broken the sabbath, and said also that God was his Father, making himself equal to God."†
We have already observed, how solidly he confuted the first article of this
charge. And as for the latter he answered, "Verily, verily, I say unto you, the
Son can do nothing of himself but what he seeth the Father do: For whatsoever things he doth, these also doth the Son likewise. For the Father loveth
the Son, and sheweth him all things that himself doth: And he <49> will
shew him greater works than these, that ye may marvel. For as the Father
raiseth up the dead and quickeneth them; even so the Son quickeneth
whom he will. For the Father judgeth no man, but hath committed all
judgment unto the Son, that all men should honour the Son even as they
honour the Father. He that honoureth the Son, honoureth the Father that
sent him."[35] Here we have the principal doctrine of Christ, and his own
argument to confirm it. But we are not yet come to unfold and explain this
reasoning. All we would at present observe is, that Christ sought not his
own honour, but the glory of God, ascribing his doctrine, and all his power
to confirm it, to God who sent him. For, if in this way of proceeding and
reasoning, there be not all the marks of sincerity, self-denial, and true piety,
what do these qualities mean? How can they show themselves, or how can
truth distinguish itself from imposture? Can we call this selfishness, vain-
glory, arrogance, impiety? Or what is it that we would allow to be sincerity,
candour, good-will to mankind, and pious respect to truth and the God of
truth?

If the history of Christ be true, he certainly foresaw his death; and he
was daily persecuted in the cruelest manner. He neither had any worldly

* Matt. xix. 17.
† John v. 18.
35. John 5.19–23.

honours rendered to him, nor had he any prospect of them; but on the contrary, he was daily affronted and vilified; and he knew that he was to be crucified in the most ignominious manner. For so he forewarned his disciples, that they might not be offended at it. And indeed so candidly did he deal with them, that he forewarned them not only of his own sufferings, but of the sufferings they were to undergo for their adherence to him, and preaching his doctrine. He did not hide this from them, but expresly told them, "Ye shall be hated and persecuted of all men for my names sake."[36] Promise not yourselves peace and prosperity, but lay your <50> account with the sword, with the cruelest persecution on my account. Behold I send you forth as sheep in the midst of wolves. Be ye therefore wise as serpents, and harmless as doves. Ye shall be delivered up to the councils, ye shall be scourged in the synagogues, ye shall be brought before kings and governors for my sake. But in all these fiery trials, ye shall be wonderfully comforted, emboldened and assisted. They have so male-treated and will so male-treat your Master; and therefore wonder not if they so treat you his disciples. Fear them not, but consider how blessed ye shall be if ye are faithful and endure to the end; and speak out boldly all the truths I have told you in secret, for when my ministry is fulfilled, then will it be the proper time to preach my doctrines openly and fully; for then shall you have the whole of my character and history, my death, resurrection and ascension to reason from, and abundantly confirm my doctrine by. If any man resolve to follow me, let him act a wise part, and count the cost before-hand; let him not say he was seduced into it by fair speeches and flattering hopes. For I must be persecuted even unto death, and they who are to preach my gospel, or profess their faith in me, must resolve upon the severest trials, the cruelest male-treatment. They must resolve to suffer, not only to renounce all worldly comforts, but to undergo with true fortitude, the severest hardships and persecutions. Was not this fair, honest dealing?* Is it likely that an impostor would have taken this method to gain followers? Or if this conduct can be imagined to have proceeded from any other view but the religious and virtuous purpose Christ professed, what is it that could have distinguished the

* Matt. viii. 19, 20. [Matthew 10.16–39.]
36. Luke 21.17.

purest, the most disinterested, glorious design, from cunning, ambition, or hypocritical pretences to virtue, in order to carry on the more successfully, under that disguise, some very <51> opposite scheme? What could such a teacher or his followers have in their eye, but the promotion and advancement of the refined morals they taught, seeing they from the beginning laid their account with the most violent opposition, and were indeed from the beginning most barbarously used by those whose ambition, avarice and hypocrisy they detected, and to whose wicked enslaving designs, their doctrine was diametrically repugnant. For from the days of John the Baptist, the kingdom of heaven, *i.e.* the gospel, from the time when it first began to be preached, suffered violence,* and the men of power harrassed its preachers, tore it to pieces, or treated it and them in the most violent abusive manner. How can sincerity, honesty and virtue be made manifest, but by a continued course of sincere, candid and virtuous conduct? And whom can we call sincere, upright or good, if Jesus and his apostles were not such? Did they either seek power or riches? Did they not on the contrary, renounce all that the men of the world set their hearts upon, and despising poverty, calumny, persecution, the cruelest torments, persist boldly in reproving vice, and preaching righteousness and a future judgment, in which God shall render to every one according to his works, whether they be good or bad? Jesus Christ taught, that true riches, as well as true merit, consists in being rich in good works, and in greatly contemning all the pomp, pageantry and luxury of this world. This he calls being *rich to God, and laying up treasures in heaven,*[37] because 'tis only from such internal riches or treasures, that true happiness can be found in the future immortal life of our souls, when we shall be far removed from all the objects of sense. Never did any person recommend or inculcate in so strong a manner, the merit with God of public spirit and self-denial, and of true fortitude or magnanimity of mind? What was it, according to his <52> doctrine, that men ought solely to fear? It was not poverty or death, but vice, a guilty, a defiled conscience? And how powerfully doth he, on many occasions, set forth the

* Matt. xi. 12. So the passage ought to be translated. [The King James translation reads: "And from the days of John the Baptist until now the kingdom of heaven suffereth violence, and the violent take it by force."]
   37. Matthew 6.19–21.

contagious, corruptive nature of wealth. Nothing, saith he, is more difficult than for a rich man to enter into the kingdom of heaven, *i.e.* for a rich man to walk humbly and moderately, and to prefer the arduous paths of virtue, to the soft dissolving pleasures of sense. Ease and affluence inflame many lusts and passions, which adversity quite extinguishes. 'Tis therefore harder to govern the mind, and keep the appetites in due order and discipline, amidst plenty of all sensual delights, than it is to bear adversity with patience and resignation.

Such is the deceitfulness of the love of riches, saith he,* that it is an exceeding hard thing (than which scarcely can any thing be imagined more difficult) for a rich man to become a worthy disciple of Christ, and to attain that resigned disposition of mind, and readiness to part with all things for the sake of religion, virtue, and a good conscience, which God requires. This was said by our Saviour upon a very remarkable occasion. A young man, of a religious disposition, hearing that Jesus taught the strictest piety and virtue, came to him saying, Good master, what excellent or extraordinary thing shall I do, whereby I may attain the eternal life which thou preaches?[38] Jesus answered him, Why do you call me good, whom you do not know to be any other than a mere man? There is none truly good but God, who is the only author of all goodness and happiness; however, as to your question, you know what are the conditions and qualifications for eternal life: Keep the commandments of God. Then the young man asked what commandments? Jesus said, Not to commit murder, nor do wrong; not to commit adultery, nor fornication; not to steal, nor cheat and <53> defraud any man; not to accuse any one falsely, nor pervert justice; to honour and reverence your parents, and all other superiors; and to do to all men, as you would they should do to you, with equity and charity. The young man answered with great alacrity, hoping to be greatly commended by Jesus, All these commands have I obeyed from a child, what lack I yet? Jesus replied, These are the necessary duties which God hath made the indispensable conditions of eternal happiness. But if you aim at a greater degree of perfection, and will do something excellent and extraordinary,

---

* Matt. xix. 26. [Matthew 19.23–24.]
38. Turnbull paraphrases Matthew 19.16–22 in this paragraph.

then go sell all your estate, and give it to the poor, and come and follow me through afflictions and poverty, and laying aside all worldly affairs, apply yourself wholly to be a preacher of my gospel, and you shall have an extraordinary degree of reward in heaven. It does not appear but the young man might have done well, if he had gone away satisfied with Christ's first answer: So that our Saviour does not seem to have bidden him sell his estate, as a thing absolutely necessary to his *being a good man,* but only as a thing necessary *at that time,* to his being a *preacher of the gospel,* and that he might reprove his confidence, and have an occasion to represent to his disciples, the great danger and mischief of the love of riches.

Accordingly our Saviour enters immediately into the most serious reflections on the danger to virtue arising from prosperous circumstances, and the temptations which much riches occasion. Which, when his disciples heard, they seemed greatly concerned, and said, If the way of life be so very difficult, who then can be saved?[39] Jesus therefore looking upon them with a compassionate countenance, and pitying their anxiety, answered, 'Tis true that disposition of mind which the gospel requires, is so spiritual, so pure, and the provocations which affluence and prosperity minister to carnal lusts and appetites, <54> are so many and great, that, morally speaking, 'tis hardly possible, in the ordinary course of things, for a very rich man to take his affections off from sensual pleasures, and set them wholly upon God and virtue: But God favours virtuous endeavours; and therefore, if men exert themselves to make a good use of their wealth, and to overcome all temptations arising from ease and opulence, to pride, vanity, effeminacy and sensuality, they shall be enabled to make this noble conquest, and become eminent examples of virtuous self-denial, and truly disinterested benevolence.

But Jesus Christ not only taught that vice only ought to be feared, and that it is far greater to prefer virtue to all the pomp and pride of the world, than to possess the means of them in the greatest abundance. A Socrates, or an Epaminondas,[40] was not a more eminent example of true magnanim-

39. Turnbull elaborates on Matthew 19.25–26.
40. Epaminondas (d. 362 B.C.E.) was a general in the army of Thebes whose military campaigns against Sparta precipitated the disintegration of the Peloponnesian League. Compare Turnbull's comments on Epaminondas in his preface to Justin's *History of the World,* pp. 307, 313, 314, 316–17, below.

ity, and of generous contempt of all worldly riches and grandeur than Jesus
Christ? Many, indeed, imagined he was come to erect a temporal kingdom,
and followed him a while on that account. But he expresly calls the kingdom
he came to establish in the world, the kingdom of God and the kingdom
of heaven; and he took every proper occasion to correct this mistake, and
root out this prejudice. None who are acquainted with human nature can
think such prejudices may be easily eradicated. It requires great art, very
dextrous address, to enlarge gradually, narrow, contracted and prejudiced
minds, and get the better of their false notions and prepossessions, and
confirmed habits; and our Saviour took the fittest method of correcting
this prejudice, which was not to attack it directly, till he had first fully
preached the nature of God, and of true religion, and shewn the prefera-
bleness of virtue to all worldly grandeur. When his followers were prepared
for hearing of his sufferings and resurrection, then he tells them what was
to happen to him, <55> and how it behoved him to die, but that he was to
rise again from the dead. Indeed when he first discoursed to his disciples
of these things they were startled. Peter particularly, whose thoughts
seemed to be fullest of worldly glory and greatness, was so disturbed at this
discourse, that he could not forbear, but took Jesus aside, and expostulated
with him, saying, "Be it far from thee, Lord, this shall not be unto thee."[41]
But Jesus turning about to him with displeasure, said, Have I been at so
much pains to instruct you in just notions of true greatness, and do you
yet entertain such false sentiments? Canst thou yet speak to me in this carnal
strain? It grieves me. Your discourse favours not of the things of God, but
of those that be of men. Your views seem to be yet carnal and worldly, not
spiritual and divine. And upon this occasion, Jesus shewed unto them *how
he must be perfected by suffering*,[42] or the necessity of his suffering in order
to compleat his ministry, and give full evidence of his divine mission, as
well as a perfect example of virtue to the world; and plainly tells all present,
that whoever would be his disciple, must be willing to follow his example,
and to be also perfected by suffering: He must absolutely resign himself to
the will of God, and renouncing all worldly desires, resolve both to do and
suffer whatever God shall think fit to require of him. And pray, says he,

41. Matthew 16.22.
42. The link between Christ's suffering and his perfection is made in Hebrews 2.9–
10 and 5.8–9.

what comparison is there between all the things this present world can afford, if any one could possess of them all, and the saving or losing a man's soul eternally? What valuable consideration can be given for a man's soul, the salvation of which must consist in his maintaining a sound mind and a good conscience, by adhering to God and virtue, in contempt of worldly honours or sufferings?

Jesus, after he had made himself known to his disciples, charged them not to publish in plain terms that he was the Messiah, till he should give <56> them liberty to do it, when it was proper; because he would not provoke the unbelieving Pharisees to apprehend him, before he had fulfilled his ministry, and because he would not give occasion to the multitude, who entertained false notions of the kingdom he was sent to establish in the world, to come together seditiously, and attempt to make him a temporal king: But chiefly, because it was most agreeable to his design of teaching true religion, confuting superstition, and giving a perfect example of virtue, that men should infer and conclude who he was, from the whole of his doctrine and life, when having suffered, and risen from the dead, he had ascended into heaven, and from thence had effused all necessary gifts upon those who were to make the first publication of the gospel to the Gentiles. For these, and other reasons already mentioned, he forbid those upon whom he had performed miraculous cures to proclaim them, at least till they had first made the offerings the Jewish law required, upon one's restoration to health, or purification from any polluting disease. For the same reasons did he charge those who were witnesses to his glorious transfiguration, not to say any thing of what they had seen till after his resurrection. It was proper that his design should gradually open and discover itself, in proportion as men were prepared to understand and receive it. And the prerequisites to this were great regard to virtue, and spiritual notions of true grandeur and happiness. Those alone could understand or relish Christ's whole doctrine, who had first attained to just conceptions of this more essential part of it, that true happiness lies not in wealth, or outward power and splendor, but in the love of God and of mankind, and in the contempt of every thing that competes with virtue and a good conscience, or vainly promises us truer satisfaction than these can afford. Accordingly this was the doctrine our Saviour inculcated, and in proportion <57> as this spiritual doctrine gained ground, did he speak out the sufferings he was to undergo, his resurrection, and the spiritual nature of the kingdom of God he was come to establish. When after he had often preached this doctrine, he perceived that some of his disciples still entertained a notion that he would after his resurrection, at least, appear in great pomp and glory to restore to the Jews a temporal kingdom,* then he found it necessary to correct this mistake more directly. And on such occasions we find him discoursing to this purpose: My kingdom is not, as ye fondly imagine, notwithstanding of all I have said, a temporal kingdom, consisting in earthly glory and greatness; but it is a spiritual kingdom, consisting only in holiness and righteousness, and true piety, and in the spiritual rewards of these divine virtues. Places of dignity in it therefore are not to be expected by favour or affection, but are to be attained by humility, by patience and sufferings. Can ye therefore follow my example, in bearing patiently injuries, sufferings and death? Salome the wife of Zebedee, with her two sons, to whom this discourse was directed, answered, We are able. Jesus replied, ye shall indeed follow me in persecutions and sufferings, and may thereby attain a place in my kingdom, and a share of the rewards of it: But for the chief seats of dignity and pre-eminence above others, this is not mine to dispose of by any absolute favour, but must be conferred upon those persons, and according to those conditions and qualifications which God hath appointed. Now, when the other apostles heard what these two brethren had desired, they were jealous for fear they should have been preferred before them. But Jesus called them all to him, and said, Ye have all a very wrong apprehension of the matter. In the kingdoms of this world, indeed men strive ambitiously to get the dominion one over another; <58> and they who are greatest in riches and power have the greatest honour and respect paid them by others. But among you, he that desires to be great and honourable, let him seek to deserve his honour by meekness and lowliness, and let him exercise his power, not in domineering over any, but in assisting and doing good to all. He that desires to have the dignity and pre-eminence among you, let him be eminent for humility and readiness to serve all men. For I myself came not into the world to exercise power and dominion, to rule over men and

* Matt. xx. 22. &c. [Matthew 20.20–28.]

to be served by them, but to serve, and assist and do good to all men, with all humility, meekness, and gentleness, and to lay down my life for the public and general good.

And to mention no more instances on this head, "When Jesus being brought before Pilate, was asked by him to this effect: Is it true what these men lay to your charge, that you have indeed attempted to set up yourself king of the Jews? Jesus answered, Have you ever, during your stay in this province, heard any thing of me that gave you any reason to suspect me guilty of secret practices and seditious designs against the government? Or do you only go upon the present clamour that is raised against me? If so, take heed you be not imposed upon, merely by the ambiguity of a word. For to be *king of the Jews,* is not to set up an earthly kingdom, in opposition to that of the emperor; but a thing of a very different nature, Pilate answered, Am I a Jew? Can I tell what your expectations are, or in what superstitious senses you understand words? The rulers and chiefs of your own people, who are best judges of those matters, have brought you before me, as a riotous and seditious person: And if this be not the truth of the matter, pray let me know what is? Jesus answered, My kingdom is not of this world: The kingdom I have professed I would establish, is not a worldly <59> one, that any ways tends to give disturbance in the government. For if it had, my servants would have fought for me, and not suffered me to have fallen into the hands of the Jews. But to tell you the truth plainly, 'tis a kingdom wholly spiritual, consisting only in the submission of men's wills and affections to the laws of God."[43]

In the conduct of Jesus therefore, as there was no ambitious or worldly design; so neither was there any instance of the rashness and impetuosity of enthusiasm. But he opened his doctrine gradually, and prudently accommodated himself to the prejudices of mankind, in the way that was most proper for curing or changing them. We have many examples in his history, of his intrepidity in reproving vice, and in persisting to teach virtue and true religion, in spight of abuse and persecutions of the most cruel outrageous kinds. But we have none of the wilfulness, and blind precipitant warmth and zeal which is the characteristic of enthusiasm being indeed

43. A paraphrase of John 18.33–37.

inseparable from it. Besides, enthusiasts in all ages have been generally more zealous about matters of opinion and forms of belief, than about morals. But our Saviour shewed a remarkable lenity to the Sadducees, who maintained the worst of errors, denying the spirituality of the soul and a future state, because they were regular in their lives; whereas he treated the superstitious Pharisees with some severity, who made a cloke of religious zeal for rites and ceremonies to hide their corrupt practices, and tho' they believed a future state, yet placed the whole of sanctity, or at least the principal part of it in external observances. And yet 'tis for want of attending to the genius of the language in which our Saviour spoke, that we are apt to look upon some of the terms he uses in reproving them as too harsh, or which is worse, as an authority for us to abuse any who differ from us in matters of opinion and faith. For 'tis well known, that the <60> phrase *children of the devil,* in that language, means no more than being exceedingly wicked, as *works of the devil* signify works of iniquity, works of injustice and oppression, under the mask of piety in particular.[44] And our Saviour never calls any persons wicked, without specifying the wicked deeds on account of which they demerited that reproach.

We find nothing in the history of Jesus Christ, that hath the least appearance of affecting pomp or state. His whole life was a continued train of good offices to mankind, and of acts of the greatest humility. He condescended even to wash the feet of his disciples, to show them how lowly, gracious and condescending they ought to be, and how removed from pride and haughtiness.* How humble was even the only procession he made, that had the least shew of state, his journey to Jerusalem,† to mourn over it and to confirm his divine mission, by foretelling its destruction in a public manner, and in order to shew his displeasure against the profanation of the temple, and the encroachments thereby made upon the rights of the proselytes of the Gentiles, as hath been already observed. And in what did the whole solemnity of this journey consist? The disciples who came along with him from Galilee, when they drew near to the city, begun to express their joy in loud acclamations, praising God for all the mighty works they had

* John xiii. 14. &c.
† Luke xix. 30, &c. [Luke 19.28–40.]
44. See, for example, Acts 13.10.

seen. And they said, Blessed be he whom God hath sent to be our king and deliverer: Heaven prosper the kingdom of the Messiah, and establish it in peace and glory. Upon which some of the Pharisees which were in the company, said unto Jesus, Rebuke thy disciples. But he answered, If these should not give praise to God on this occasion, God would even work a miracle to raise up others to glorify his name, and acknowledge his power, and the fulfilment of the predictions of his prophets. <61>

In what a moving manner doth he weep over Jerusalem. "O Jerusalem, Jerusalem, thou wast once the holy city, and the beloved of God, but thou hast often rejected God and persecuted his servants, and slain the prophets he sent to you, and thou hast continued obstinately corrupt and impenitent; how often has God tendered to thee the offers of mercy and pardon, and entreated thee to repentance with all the tenderness a father can shew his most darling child? But thou refused to hear. Behold now therefore, the time of mercy is past, and the final dissolution of the city and temple, with the fearful destruction of the Jewish nation, is unalterably fixed. And I assure you the time will speedily come, and is now at hand, when ye shall see me no more, who sincerely loved you, and would have gathered you as a hen gathereth her chickens under her wings; and then shall ye be forced to own me whom you now despise, to be indeed the Son of God and the Messiah." [45]

How unjustly then is he accused of not having recommended patriotism, or the love of our country, who gave so strong an instance of his love to his native country, by taking so great pains to reform his compatriots from vice and superstition; and who thus wept over his country, from an affecting sense of its impending ruin: He who tho' the Jews reviled and stoned him with unrelenting fury, yet went about continually doing good to them, and exhorting them to amend their ways and turn to God: He who was a martyr to his zeal to promote their greatest good, and to their rage and indignation against every one who told them their errors and vices. How groundless and unreasonable is this charge, especially when we call to mind, that after having been persecuted during his most beneficial ministry, and at last crucified by them in the most unjust furious manner, he gave charge to his apostles, to whom he committed the preaching of his

---

45. A paraphrase of Matthew 23.37 and Luke 13.34.

saluta-<62>ry doctrine, to begin by preaching it to the Jews, his ungrateful barbarous compatriots, who had so maletreated him, and rejected his doctrine with such virulence?

Equally groundless, my friend, is that other charge against the morality of Christ, that friendship is not recommended by it.[46] For he chose but twelve persons to be his immediate and constant followers, and one of them he made his friend. John, who seems to have been by his temper peculiarly fitted above all the rest for friendship, is called the disciple whom Jesus loved, and he is regarded by the others as the person whom he always treated with the greatest intimacy and confidence, and with particular marks of that tenderness and affection in which friendship consists.

This is a sufficient vindication of our Saviour's doctrine and life, against these accusations: But it is well observed likewise on this subject, that there is generally, and there was at the time of our Saviour's appearance particularly, but little reason to insist much upon the love of one's country and friendship. For as partial attachments are generally more common than universal benevolence, insomuch that men in all ages of the world have been very apt to fancy themselves virtuous enough, when they are warm in their friendships, and have great zeal for their country, however inhumanly they may treat the rest of mankind, or however dissolute they may be in their lives: So amongst the Jews and Romans, when Christ appeared in the world, an affection for particular countries was really a nusance; it did indeed triumph over justice and humanity. The Jews were so partially fond of their own nation, that they looked upon themselves as the only favourites of heaven, and were quite unsociable to all who were not of their own religion. And as for the Romans, their love of their country was really a spirit of rapine and conquest, and had led them to spread <63> terror, ruin and slavery through the greatest part of the then known world. The proper lesson therefore to be inculcated at this time, or in such a state of things, was that universal goodness and benevolence, without which what is called zeal for one's country, is but cruel ambition and insatiable lust of universal dominion; and partial friendship is little better than the contracted, narrow,

---

46. Turnbull's target is Shaftesbury, whom he had earlier criticized in his *Philosophical Enquiry;* see pp. 149–50 above.

ungenerous union of pirates and robbers: For these public pests subsist by private confederacy, and a kind of friendship.

To all that hath been said of Christ's moral character, it may be added, that he did not teach men to extirpate their passions, as some pretenders to philosophy have absurdly done, but to moderate them. He exhorts us to rejoice with them that rejoice, and to weep with them that weep. And such likewise was his practice. He sympathised in the most affectionate manner with the distressed, and his greatest joy lay in doing good, or in making others happy; in relieving men from their distresses, or comforting them under them. Upon proper occasions he shewed his indignation against vice in the firmest manner, as we have seen. But generally his censures and reproaches were of the mildest kind, and tho' sharp, yet pleasant. He never entertained resentment, or any thoughts of revenge against his bitterest enemies: And he died expressing his compassion, and praying for forgiveness to those who had most unjustly persecuted him even unto death. How divine are his last words! "Father forgive them, they know not what they do."[47] Tho' he was not insensible of the violent pains he suffered, but was made to cry out by them, *My God, my God, why hast thou forsaken me?*[48] Yet he quickly recollected his strength of mind, and died not only resigning himself chearfully to the will of God, which he was come to accomplish, but with the most affectionate wishes for mercy to his cruelest and most inveterate persecutors. <64>

Thus, my friend, I have laid before you some of the most remarkable discourses of Jesus Christ on moral subjects, and some of the more remarkable incidents in his life, in order to point out his Moral Character, and shew that he was, at least, one of the best of Philosophers, whether with respect to teaching, or what is a more powerful and engaging instructor than mere teaching, good example. For, as Pliny says, speaking of the excellent Emperor Trajan, *Nec tam imperio nobis opus, quam exemplo, & mitius jubetur exemplo.*[49] We do not want precepts so much as patterns, and ex-

47. Luke 23.34.
48. Matthew 27.46 and Mark 15.34.
49. Pliny, *Panegyricus,* 45.6: "for example is what we need more than command." Turnbull has altered the wording of the passage. The original Latin reads: "nec tam imperio nobis opus est quam exemplo."

ample is the softest and least invidious way of commanding. I do not mean to detract from the merit of a Socrates, when I say, I think Jesus Christ was nothing inferior to him, if not far superior, either in regard to the doctrine he taught, or his life and practice. And I think an apology for Christ, in imitation of Plato's noble apology for Socrates, *i.e.* the apology he makes Socrates speak for himself to his judges, a subject worthy of some Christian Pen equal for it.[50] This I hope to find executed some day by you, my friend, when you have looked more carefully into Christianity than you have yet done; for of your impartiality I am fully convinced.

If what hath been said in answer to what you call *the previous question* with respect to Christianity, be in any degree satisfactory to you, I am willing to go on with you in the enquiry, and to develop to you what I take to be Christ's own argument for the truth of his mission and doctrine. 'Tis a very different one from that which is generally used by modern writers against Deism, as it is called. And a Person of your truly philosophical turn is such a convert to Christianity, as one who has a sincere regard to its interests cannot choose but be very desirous of gaining. *I am,* &c.

PHILALETHES

50. Plato, *Apology.*

Three Dissertations

☙ ☙ ☙

NOTE ON THE TEXT

We have been unable to establish precisely when the *Three Dissertations* was published by the London bookseller and man of letters Robert Dodsley (1703–64). It is likely that the book appeared in the late summer or autumn of 1740 because the work was reviewed in *The History of the Works of the Learned* for December 1740.[1] There were no further impressions or editions.

---

[1]. *The History of the Works of the Learned,* edited by Ephraim Chambers, 2 vols. (London, 1740), II:440–58.

THREE
DISSERTATIONS;

ONE

On the CHARACTERS of

Augustus, Horace and *Agrippa,*

With a Comparison between
His two Ministers *Agrippa* and *Maecenas,*
by the Abbe *de Vertot.*

To which is added,
Some Reflections on the Characters of *Augustus, Maecenas* and
Horace, and on the Works of *Horace,* by the Earl of SHAFTSBURY.

With a *Print* from an ancient Painting, representing *Augustus,*
Agrippa, Maecenas and *Horace.*

ANOTHER

On the Gallery of *Verres,* by the Abbe *Fraguier,*
in which many excellent Pieces of ancient Statuary,
Sculpture and Painting are described.

A THIRD

On the Nature, Origin and Use of Masks, in theatrical
Representations among the Ancients, by Mr. *Boindin.*

WITH

A Print from a fine antique Bas-relief, lately discover'd
at *Rome,* representing ancient Actors in their Masks,
with a Musician playing on the double *Tibia.*

LONDON:
Printed for R. DODSLEY, at *Tully's* Head, in *Pall-Mall.*
MDCCXL.

Plate 1

TO

RICHARD MEAD, *M. D.*

Physician to his Majesty[1]

SIR,

The Discourses I beg Leave to inscribe to you in Acknowledgment of the highest Obligations, will, I make no doubt, be reckoned by you and all good Judges of polite Literature, worthy of being translated into our Language; especially since they appear in it with Ornaments so suit-<iv>ted to the Subjects, *viz.* A Print representing *Augustus,* attended with *M. Agrippa, Maecenas,* and, as some not without Reason think, *Horace,* giving a Crown, probably to *Phraates,*

> ———— *jus imperiumque* Phraates
> Caesaris *accepit genibus minor.*
> HOR. Ep. L. I. Ep. 12.[2]

done after an ancient Painting in your curious and elegant Collection; to which, in one highly valuable Branch of Antiquity, there is none in the World equal: For no where even in *Italy,* are there now so many well-preserv'd Pieces of ancient Painting: Those, which while they adorned the

---

1. Richard Mead (1673–1754), the prominent London physician whose collection of books, manuscripts, medals, coins, antiquities, engravings, and paintings was among the most significant of its kind in eighteenth-century Europe. In 1737 Mead's fame as a collector reached its zenith when he acquired the famous fragment of an antique fresco which he believed depicted the Court of Augustus (see plate 1). In 1738 Mead pulled off another coup. The Scottish portraitist Allan Ramsay (1713–84), who was then in Italy, purchased on Mead's behalf an important book of drawings executed by Pietro Santi Bartoli (1635–1700) of ancient paintings extant in Rome and its environs. The book survives and is now in Glasgow University Library.

2. Horace, *Epistles,* 1.xii.27–28: "Phrates, on humbled knees, has accepted Caesar's imperial sway."

Palace of the *Massimi* at *Rome,*[3] were justly esteemed amongst the most curious Remains Time or Barbarity had left undestroy'd, are now, all of them, where every *Briton* who loves the Arts, will rejoice to know they are placed; being carefully preserved in a Library, to which that Character is universally acknowledged to be due, which *Cicero* gives of one of the best Collections in the World at his Time, as what render'd it truly an Honour to its <v> Master, *Sic ornata, ut urbi quoque esset ornamento.**

Another Plate exhibiting ancient Actors upon the Stage in their Masks, done from a very exact and elegant Drawing of a very beautiful Bas-relief lately discovered at *Rome,* which being well worthy of a Place in the same excellent Collection would likewise have been procured for you had it been possible.[4]

Marcus Agrippa,[†][5] whose many other great Qualities are painted out to

---

* Hujus domus est vel optima *Messanae,* notissima certe, & nostris hominibus apertissima maximeque hospitalis. Ea domus, ante adventum istius, sic ornata fuit, ut urbi quoque esset ornamento. ——— *Messanam* ut quisque nostrum venerat, haec visere solebat: omnibus haec ad visendum patebant quotidie: Domus erat non Domino magis ornamento quam civitati. *Cicero in Verrem.* 4. [Cicero, *The Second Speech against Gaius Verres,* II.iv.2 §3: "His house is perhaps the finest in Messana, and at any rate the best known, and its hospitable doors the most widely open to our countrymen. It was so full of beautiful things as to add much to the beauty of the city" (translation slightly modified); *Against Verres,* II.iv.3 §5: "When visiting Messana, all our countrymen would go to see these statues; the house was open daily to visitors who wished to see them; its beauty was for the whole town to enjoy not less than for its owner."]

† *M. Agrippa,* vir rusticitati propior quam deliciis. Extat certe ejus oratio magnifica & maximo civium digna, de tabulis omnibus signisque publicandis: quod fieri satius fuisset, quam in Villarum exilia pelli. *Pliny, L.* 35. [Pliny, *Natural History,* XXXV.ix.26: "Marcus Agrippa <was> a man who stood nearer to rustic simplicity than to refinements. At all events there is preserved a speech of Agrippa, lofty in tone and worthy of the greatest of the citizens, on the question of making all pictures and statues national property, a procedure which would have been preferable to banishing them to country houses."]

3. The Massimi or Massimo family has for centuries been one of the most prominent in Rome and is among the oldest noble houses in Europe. The Palazzo Massimo alle Colonne dates from the sixteenth century and was built to the design of Baldassarre Peruzzi (1481–1536), who was also involved in the building of St. Peter's. Members of the family were prominent patrons of the fine arts in the Renaissance and early modern periods. Cardinal Camillo Massimo (1620–77) employed Pietro Santi Bartoli to execute the book of drawings of ancient paintings later acquired by Richard Mead.

4. See plate 2 and below, p. 283.

5. Marcus Vipsanius Agrippa (ca. 63 B.C.E.–12 B.C.E.), Roman statesman and ally of the Emperor Augustus (63 B.C.E.–C.E. 14), famous for his public works program in Rome.

Plate 2

us in the First of these Dissertations by a very masterly Hand, (*L'Abbe de Vertot*)[6] was such an intelligent and zealous Patron and Encourager of the polite Arts, that he published an Oration against those pretended Admirers of them in his Time, who locking up and imprisoning *Greek* Busts, Statues, Bas-reliefs and Pictures in their Town-Cabinets and Country Villa's, and cruelly de-<vi>nying the Curious free Access to study and examine them, acted in down-right Contradiction to the chief Uses for which Persons of truly good Taste collect and preserve such Remains: *Namely,* The Ambition to excel in the Arts of Design, which sometimes were, and always may be employ'd to very useful and noble Purposes, an attentive Consideration of the Antique never fails to excite in Minds, where natural Genius only waits

6. René Aubert de Vertot (1655–1735), author of various historical works, most notably his *Revolutions romaines* (Paris, 1719). He was elected a member of the Académie des Inscriptions et Belles-Lettres in 1703.

a Call to disclose it self: Assistance to ingenious Students of these Arts in that laudable Pursuit: and to mention no more, the Helps which may be continually derived from ancient Paintings and Sculptures for the right understanding of ancient Authors; the Poets in particular, by those, who uniting Skill in History and Antiquity, and a good Taste in the Arts of Design, with Knowledge of the ancient Languages cultivate the Study of polite Literature in the surest as well as the largest and most entertaining Manner.

Pliny, not improbably, uses *M. Agrippa*'s own Phrase, when he emphatically calls that barbarous Practice, exiling the best Productions of the ingenious Arts, and robbing the Publick of the best Rouzers and Awakeners of Genius <vii> and Taste, and the best Models for perfectionating them.*
Cicero, who appears by many of his Letters to *Atticus* and other Friends, and indeed throughout all his Writings to have been an equally knowing and warm Lover of the fine Arts, and of all polite Learning, as well as deeply vers'd in the more abstruse and profound Sciences, inveighs with great Warmth and Eloquence, on several Occasions, against the Iniquity and In-

---

* *Pliny ibidem.* He has several Phrases to the same Purpose, which are very strong, *ingenia hominum rempublicam fecit,* speaking of the publick Library, established by *Asinius Pollio.* See what he says of *M. Varro, Benignissimo invento,* ——— *inventor muneris etiam Diis invidiosi, &c.* Speaking of the ancient Greek Painters, he says, *omnium eorum ars urbibus excubabat, pictorque res communis terrarum fuit.* Speaking of *Fabulus* a *Roman* Painter he calls *Nero's* Palace, *Carcer ejus artis.* Several Passages of *Cicero* in the same Strain, are quoted in the Discourse on the Gallery of *Verres.* [Pliny, *Natural History,* XXXV.ii.10: "At Rome this practice <of placing portrait statues in libraries> originated with Asinius Pollio, who first by founding a library made works of genius the property of the public"; *Natural History,* XXXV.ii.11: "The existence of a strong passion for portraits in former days is evidenced by . . . the most benevolent invention of Marcus Varro, who actually by some means inserted in a prolific output of volumes portraits of seven hundred famous people, not allowing their likenesses to disappear or the lapse of ages to prevail against immortality in men. Herein Varro was the inventor of a benefit that even the gods might envy, since he not only bestowed immortality but dispatched it all over the world, enabling his subjects to be ubiquitous, like the gods. This was a service Varro rendered to strangers"; *Natural History,* XXXV.xxxvii.118: "With all these artists their art was on the alert for the benefit of cities, and a painter was the common property of the world"; *Natural History,* XXXV.xxxvii.120: "the prison that contained his productions." Fraguier quotes extensively in his discourse from Cicero's *Against Verres* II.iv, wherein Cicero catalogs the notable statues and other precious objects that Verres had stolen. Passages cited by Fraguier paralleling the quotations from Pliny are to be found in Cicero, *Against Verres* II.iv.3.5 and II.iv.57.126.]

humanity of those, whose Fortunes enabled them to make Collections of Antiquities, if they did not allow the most favourable and gracious Admittance to all to study them, who were capable of being instructed by them, or making useful Reflexions upon them: And he often lays it down as a sure Mark and Characteristick by which one who was prompted by intelligent Love of Arts and Letters, and guided by good Taste in purchasing their best Productions, might be distin-<viii>guished from him, who does it merely for Ostentation, or to enrich and embellish his House with rare and costly Furniture; that he will be perceiv'd, by his obliging Reception of all ingenious Men, and his cordial Readiness to encourage and promote every useful or ingenious Undertaking, to have collected them purely that he might have the Pleasure to render them of publick Utility in exciting Praiseworthy Emulation, and assisting ingenious useful Studies.

That this, SIR, is your generous Motive in daily adding to one of the best chosen and most valuable Collections of Books, Medals, Busts, Statues, Paintings and Drawings that is any where to be seen, all who know you tell with Pleasure. It is not only the universal Language at Home of all among us who have any Regard for Letters or any of the ingenious Arts: But even Abroad you are amongst the first that is named, when the Conversation turns upon a Subject to which learned and ingenious Foreigners, in their great Politeness are apt to lead it; the Encouragement of Learning and Ingenuity in *England.* <ix>

I never enter into your Library without wishing most ardently, that some Person equal to the Task would give us a just Description of the many valuable Antiquities and Master-pieces of Art in it. It would furnish a very agreeable Occasion to one perfectly well acquainted with ancient Learning and the fine Arts to enter into several very pleasant as well as useful Discussions: And there cannot certainly be a more engaging or effectual Way of displaying the Beauties of the polite Arts, and shewing the chief Uses of their Productions, than by a judicious Account of a good Collection, to which every Person of Taste may have free Access as often as he pleases, to compare the Description with the Original. Had we such an Academy here for the Improvement of the *Belles-Lettres* as that at *Paris,*[7] (to which the

---

7. The Académie des Inscriptions et Belles-Lettres was founded in 1663.

Discourses I have *Englished,* were read,) to describe your's and some other Collections in *England,* would be one of their first, usefullest, and pleasantest Employments: And shall we so servilely imitate the *French* almost in every thing but their Zeal to cultivate and promote polite Literature in all its Branches, by the Establishment <x> of Academies on Purpose, not only in *Paris,* but in all their great Towns.

As none better deserves to have it in his Power, so none, SIR, is better qualified to make a good Collection, whether of Books or of Antiquities; so thoroughly conversant are you in Arts and Sciences, which yet, 'tis well known, have never been more than your Amusement. For your Time and Studies have always been, and still are principally laid out in a more important and beneficial Manner to Mankind; in adding daily to that extensive Knowledge of Nature, from which your Country daily reaps Benefits, the agreeable Accounts of which naturally lead every Friend to Mankind to give his Assent and Approbation to the Encomiums of the wise Son of *Syrach,* upon a highly honourable, because highly useful Profession, to which you are so great an Ornament: *Honour a Physician with the Honour due unto him, for the Uses which you may have of him: for the Lord hath created him. For of the most High cometh Healing, and he shall receive Honour of Kings. The Skill of the Physician shall lift up his Head,* <xi> *and in the Sight of great Men shall he be in Admiration. The Lord hath created Medicines out of the Earth; and he that is Wise will search them out: And he hath given Men Skill that he might be honoured in his marvellous Works. By such does he heal Men and take away their Pains, and send Health over all the Earth.*[8]

That your Country may long enjoy the many Advantages it daily receives from your Love of Letters, and your profound Skill in Nature and the medicinal Art, join'd with a very uncommon Goodness and Generosity of Heart, is the most cordial earnest Wish of,

SIR,
Your highly obliged
and most Obedient
Humble Servant,
GEORGE TURNBULL. <xiii>

---

8. Turnbull quotes from the apocryphal *The Wisdom of Jesus the Son of Sirach, or Ecclesiasticus,* 38.1–4, 6–8.

Preface to the Reader

L'Abbe de Vertot, L'Abbe de Fraguier, L'Abbe de Bos and Mr. *Boindin,* the Authors of the *French* Discourses, with an *English* Translation of which I now present you, are Names so well known in the Republick of Letters, that I need say nothing about them.[9] What induc'd me to publish these Dissertations in *English,* was in the first Place my having it in my Power to give the Publick, along with the Translation two very rare Pieces of Antiquity, representing the Subjects of two of them. <xiv>

A Print from an ancient Painting representing *Augustus, M. Agrippa,*

9. Turnbull translated Vertot's "Caractére d'Auguste, avec la comparison entre Agrippa & Mécénas, ministres de ce prince," *Histoire de l'Académie Royale des Inscriptions et Belles Lettres. Avec les mémoires de littérature tirez des registres de cette Académie, depuis l'année M.DCCXXV,* 5 (1729), 235–41.

Claude-François Fraguier (1666–1728) was known primarily for his work on the literature of ancient Greece. He was elected a member of the Académie des Inscriptions et Belles-Lettres in 1705, and a member of the Académie Française in 1708. Turnbull translated Fraguier's "La Gallerrie de Verrès," *Mémoires de littérature tirez des registres de L'Académie Royal des Inscriptions et Belles Lettres. Depuis l'année M.DCCXVIII. jusques & compris l'année M.DCCXXV,* 6 (1729), 565–76.

Jean-Baptiste Du Bos (1670–1742), diplomat, historian, and author of the highly influential *Réflexions critiques sur la poésie et sur la peinture,* first published in 1719. He was elected a member of the Académie Française in 1720 and became its *secrétaire perpétuel* in 1722. Turnbull translated Part 3, Chapter 12 of Du Bos's *Réflexions critiques sur la poésie et sur la peinture,* rev. ed., 3 vols. (Paris, 1733), III:184–210. His translation of this section from Du Bos occupies pp. 105–22 of the main body of the text of the *Three Dissertations.*

Niçolas Boindin (1676–1751), author of a number of comedies and historian, who was widely suspected of atheism. He was elected a member of the Académie des Inscriptions et Belles-Lettres in 1706. His election to the Académie Française was blocked because of his irreligion. Turnbull translated Boindin's "Discours sur les masques et les habits de theatre des anciens," *Mémoires de littérature tirez des registres de l'Académie Royales des Inscriptions et Belles Lettres. Depuis l'année M.DCCXI. jusques & compris l'année M.DCC.XVII,* 4 (1723), 132–47.

Maecenas, and not improbably *Horace,* could not certainly be more suitably plac'd than before *a Discourse on the Characters of these great Personages,* by the *Abbe de Vertot.* It is already *publish'd* in my Treatise on *Ancient Painting.* But every Person, whether he hath any thing of the *Virtuoso* Turn or not, will feel a Double Satisfaction, when a lively well-drawn Picture of the Mind is join'd with one of the outward Likeness: And many may be fond of having Portraits of those Great Men, who are not very curious about *ancient Paintings* in general. The *original Picture* is now in Dr. *Mead*'s Collection. The *other Print* represents *Ancient Masks;* [10] (the Subject of Mr. *Boindin*'s learned Dissertation) to render which complete nothing was wanting but such a Plate, and the *Observations on the same Subject* by the *Abbe de Bos,* in his excellent Essay on *Poetry* and *Painting,* which I have subjoined. This *Print* is done from a Drawing after an ancient Bas-relief, of exquisitely good *Taste* and *Workmanship* taken for me at *Rome* by one of the best Hands there for copying the Antique, *Camillo Paderni.* [11] This Bas-relief was but lately discovered, *and was never engrav'd before;* and therefore it must be a very acceptable Present to the *Curious;* and it sets the Observations and Conjectures of Mess. *Boindin* and *de Bos* on that Subject, beyond all doubt.

To these *Dissertations* I have added an *elegant Description* of the famous Gallery of *Verres* by the *Abbe de Fraguier,* because these few Discourses make a small *Spe-<xv>cimen* of the *ingenious Enquiries* with which the Memoirs of the Academy of *Belles-Lettres and Inscriptions* at *Paris* are filled: Enquiries which cannot be carried on either so successfully or so agreeably as by a *Society of learned Men* united on Purpose. Were there any such *Establishment* here, the Arts and Sciences which we seem generally to admire and love, would certainly soon come to greater Perfection among us, than it is *possible* for them to do without *such publick Countenance* and *Assistance;* or by single Endeavours. And what a Reproach to us is it, that

---

10. See plate 2.

11. Camillo Paderni (1720–70), an Italian artist who later served as the director of the Museum Herculanense at Portici near Naples. In 1736 he became a close friend of the Scottish portraitist Allan Ramsay while Ramsay was in Rome. Through Ramsay, Turnbull secured the services of Paderni to execute the drawings of classical antiquities that were engraved for Turnbull's *Treatise on Ancient Painting.*

a Nation where *Genius, Wit, Learning* and *free Enquiries* must of Necessity labour under very great Disadvantages, should leave us so far behind them in every Branch of *polite Literature,* that we have very little of that Kind in our Language, which is Original.

In a Country bless'd with the free Constitution we enjoy, there is no doubt that an *Academy of Literature* would be established upon a larger and freer Bottom than it can be in a *despotick enslav'd Kingdom;* and so it would quickly become an experimental Proof how much more naturally *ingenious Sciences* and *Arts* grow up to their Maturity in such a generous Soil, when they are planted in it and endow'd with the necessary Helps for their Cultivation and Advancement, than they can any where else; how ever much they may be cherish'd or flatter'd for merely *political Purposes:* An *experimental* Proof[12] that it is only under the Sun-shine of Liberty, that the *ingenious Arts and Sciences* can bring forth their best, their beautifullest, pleasantest and usefullest Fruits. 'Tis <xvi> not without Pain a Lover of Liberty hears the Glory of Arts flourishing ascribed either to an *Augustus* or to *Lewis XIV.* It was *Maecenas* who turn'd the former, a Prince naturally cruel and barbarous, to the Love and Courtship of the Muses. And it was Mr. *Colbert,*[13] a Minister, who gave the same Turn to his Master's Vanity, of whose Generosity to Men of Merit, Mr. *Rollin* mentions an Instance not to be paralleled in any Country, at least in modern Times.* Mr. *Colbert,* says he, set apart forty thousand Crowns a Year out of his own private Estate, for the Supply and Encouragement of those chiefly who had distinguished themselves in any Art or Science: And he charged Mr. *Perrault* and some others, whom he had entrusted with the Care of making ingenious

---

* *La maniere d' etudier les Belles Lettres.* [Charles Rollin, *The Method of Teaching and Studying the Belles Lettres, or, An Introduction to Languages, Poetry, Rhetoric, History, Moral Philosophy, Physicks, &c.,* 4 vols. (London, 1734), III:291.]

12. Turnbull here as elsewhere uses the term *experimental* in the more general sense of "experiential."

13. Jean-Baptiste Colbert (1619–83), Louis XIV's most powerful minister. Colbert was the Controller General of Finances from 1665 and the Secretary of State for the Navy from 1668, and held other lesser government positions. He was a member of the Académie Française, and he was instrumental in the founding of the Académie des Inscriptions et Belles-Lettres, the Académie des Sciences (1666), the Académie Royale d'Architecture (1671), the Académie Royale de Musique (1671), and the French Academy at Rome (1666).

Men known to him, that he might reward them, in the solemnest Manner, to make Conscience of discharging their important Commission faithfully and diligently; telling them, "That if any Person of Merit was in Distress or pinching Circumstances throughout *France,* whom he could relieve, the horrid Guilt must lie upon them; they must answer for it." Is it any wonder to find the Arts and Sciences thriving under a *publick Minister,* who was such an intelligent Lover of them, and so generous a Rewarder, so zealous a Distinguisher of Merit; and whose Maxim and Study it was to make an arbitrary Government, he could not change, as light and easy to the Subjects, as could possibly be done.

Foreigners have indeed Reason to wonder, that an Establishment so requisite, as that of Academies of *Belles Lettres, Painting, &c.* to do Justice to Merit, to ren-<xvii>der Collections of Antiquities of extensive Use; and to promote good Taste and laudable Emulation to excel in ingenious Arts, should be wanting in a Country where there are such noble Collections of Books, Pictures and Antiquities; in a Country which bears so great a Character all the World over for encouraging Learning and Ingenuity; and where there are very few of Birth and Fortune who have not taken the Trouble of a Journey through *Italy* on *purpose* to visit *classick Ground,* and see the Remains of *ancient Arts.*

The Design of the Discourse on the Gallery of *Verres,* is not to celebrate the infamous *Verres,*[14] but the Masterpieces of ancient Art, which his *Vanity and Avarice** had amassed by Methods diametrically *opposite* to that *generous and humane Temper* which is the natural Concomitant of *good Taste;* and which, if the *polite Arts* do not produce, they indeed fall far short of their *principal Aim* and best Effect: That noble Tendency to *humanize the Mind,* whence they anciently took their Name *(Literae hu-*

---

* Haec Scipio non intelligebat homo doctissimus atque humanissimus, tu sine ulla bona arte, sine humanitate, sine ingenio, sine literis intelligis & judicas. *M. T. Cic. in Verrem.* 4. 44. [Cicero, *Against Verres,* II.iv.44 §98: "that an educated and cultivated man like Scipio had no understanding of such things, whereas an utter savage like yourself [Verres], uncivilized and stupid and illiterate, can understand and appreciate them."]

14. Gaius Verres served as the Roman *propraetor* or governor of Sicily from 73 to 71 B.C.E. His abuse of power was attacked in Cicero's *Verrine Orations.*

*maniores)** to which I have often regreted there should be none for them in our Language *strictly or adequately correspondent.* Perhaps that Appellation was given them to signify likewise that it is by the Arts of ingenious Composition, whether by the *Pen,* the *Pencil* or *Chizzel,* that Men are most remarkably *superior* to the Brute Creation. They *are the Arts of Men.* 'Tis not *Verres* but <xviii> the *Bas-reliefs* and *Statues* in his Gallery he commends, and by his elegant Description of *many wonderful Pieces of Art,* (or rather *Cicero*'s, for it is collected from his Descriptions of them in his Pleadings against *Verres*) [15] he makes us feel what is due to the *ingenious Arts;* and to those who generously collect and preserve their best Productions, in order to *recommend, animate, assist* and *promote good Taste and laudable Emulation to excel in Arts,* which sometimes have been employed to very noble and truly useful *Purposes;* ever may; and always shine most when they are so: I mean, by *perpetuating* the Memory of great Men and great Actions, to *excite and support truly Praise-worthy Ambition* to rival such glorious Examples: And in Subordination to that *principal End,* by transmitting to Posterity true Representations of certain more remarkable Customs and Usages among the Ancients *civil and religious,* to give Satisfaction to a Curiosity that naturally *springs up in great Minds;* and which if it does not become their *chief Employment,* but holds only the Place of an ingenious Amusement is no ignoble or unworthy Passion. The very Amusements of *Man* ought to be *manly* and *ingenious,* and far removed from *Vice.*[†]

The justly celebrated Earl of *Shaftsbury*'s Observations on the *Augustan* Age, and the Characters of *Augustus, Marcus Agrippa* and *Maecenas,* are so

---

* Humanitas—politior humanitas literae humaniores—quae ad humanitatem pertinent intelligis artes quibus ad humanitatem animus informari solet. *Cicero pro Archia Poet.* [Cicero, *Pro archia poeta.* The wording of the passage in Turnbull's footnote does not appear in Cicero's text. Turnbull has taken two phrases from Cicero, "quae ad humanitatem pertinent" (i.2) and "quibus ad humanitatem animus informari solet" (iii.4), as the starting point for his paraphrase.]

† Solebat Plato, quoties e schola descederet, dicere: Videte, pueri, ut ocio ad honestam aliquam rem utamini. *Plato de Sanitate tuenda.* [Plutarch, "Advice about Keeping Well," *Moralia,* 135 D: "He <Plato> used to say, in dismissing them from their class, 'Watch my lads, how you use your leisure time. Put it to some worthy business.'"]

15. Cicero enumerates these art works at length in Book IV of *The Second Speech against Gaius Verres.*

agreeable to the Pictures, the *Abbe Vertot* has drawn of them; that I could not choose but join them together. And no where is there to be found such a just Idea or Character of *Horace* and his Writings as that which his Lordship has given <xix> us, not all at once indeed, but in different Parts of his admired Works. The *Reflections* upon some *beautiful Passages* of *Horace,* which I have selected out of many scattered thro' his Lordship's Writings, as they stand in them, are so incidental, and environed with so many Beauties more essential to his main Design, that they are generally not sufficiently attended to, to have the Effect, they cannot, I think, fail to have, when they are presented to one by themselves, or in an *united View,* as Pieces of truly rational and useful Criticism.[16] And therefore I thought that *gathering* and *uniting* them together, might be of use to shew what *true Criticism* ought to do; and to what important and profound Reflections *Homer, Virgil, Horace,* and other *ancient Authors,* lead those who read them with *Intelligence,* and are capable of entering into their *Spirit:* For in *them* and all *good Writers,* to use a Phrase of one who well deserves to be placed among the Ancients, *More is meant than meets the Ear.** In order to this, one must not merely be Master of *dead Languages,* which it can never be worth while to learn, if one is to learn *nothing else* by them: But he must be very well acquainted with *Antiquity* and *History,* with *ancient Philosophy,* with *Mankind;* and with that *true* and *solid Criticism* which deduces all its *Maxims* and *Rules* from *Human Nature* and the *Knowledge* of the *World.* This plainly *appears* from *these few Reflections* on *ancient Authors,* on *Horace* in particular, we have selected from that *incomparable Writer* on Purpose to evince it. And he who *understands* and *relishes* <xx> them, will *heartily* give his *Assent* and *Approbation* to what his *Lordship* says on the *Subject* of *Polite*

---

* Milton, il Penseroso. [Milton, Il Penseroso, l. 120: "Where more is meant than meets the ear."]

16. "A Character of Augustus, Maecenas and Horace: With some Reflections on the Works of Horace, by the Earl of Shaftesbury" (which occupies pp. 20–67 of the main body of Turnbull's text) is based on passages taken from Shaftesbury, *Characteristicks,* I:8–9, 48, 64–67, 89 note–90 note, 118–24, 128–30, 136, 149–57, 167 note, 172–73, 202; III:14–15, 23–24, 123 note–24 note, 151–54, 159 note–62 note, 188–89.

Scholarship, and the *Common Methods* of *Modern Education,* in a *Passage* I can't choose but transcribe here, so *greatly* does it deserve our *Attention.*

"It seems indeed somewhat improbable that according to modern Erudition, and as Science is now distributed, our ingenious and noble Youths should obtain the full Advantage of a just and liberal Education by uniting the Scholar Part with that of the real Gentleman, and Man of Breeding. Academies for Exercises so useful to the Publick, and essential in the Formation of a genteel and liberal Character, are unfortunately neglected. Letters are indeed banished, I know not where, in distant Cloysters and unpractis'd Cells, as our Poet has it, confined to the Commerce and mean Fellowship of bearded Boys. The sprightly Arts and Sciences are sever'd from Philosophy, which consequently must grow dronish, insipid, pedantick, useless and directly contrary to the real Knowledge and Practice of the World and Mankind. Our Youths accordingly seem to have their only Chance between two widely different Roads; either that of Pedantry and School-learning, which lies amidst the Dregs and most corrupt Part of ancient Literature; or that of the fashionable illiterate World which aims merely at the Character of the fine Gentleman, and takes up with the Foppery of modern Languages and foreign Wit. The frightful Aspect of the former of these Roads makes the Journey appear desperate and impracticable. Hence that Aversion so generally conceiv'd against a learn'd Cha-<xxi>racter wrong-turn'd, and hideously set out, under such Difficulties, and in such seeming Labyrinths and mysterious Forms; as if a *Homer,* or *Xenophon* imperfectly learn'd in raw Years, might not afterwards in a riper Age, be study'd as well in a capital City, and amidst the World, as at a College or Country Town! Or as if a *Plutarch,* a *Tully* or a *Horace,* could not accompany a young Man in his Travels, at a Court, or (if Occasion were) even in a Camp! The Case is not without Precedent. Leisure is found sufficient for their reading of numerous modern Translations and worse Originals of *Italian* or *French* Authors, who are read merely for Amusement. The *French* indeed may boast of some legitimate Authors of a just Relish, correct and without any Mixture of the affected or spurious Kinds, the false Tender or the false Sublime, the conceited Jingle or the ridiculous Point. They are such Genius's as have been form'd upon the natural Model of the Ancients, and willingly owe their Debt to those great Masters. But for the rest, who draw from another Fountain, as the *Italian*

Authors in particular, they may be reckon'd no better than the corrupting of true Learning and Erudition; and can indeed be relish'd by those alone whose Education has unfortunately denied them the Familiarity of the noble Ancients, and the Practice of a better and more natural Taste."[17]

The Criticism, of which a few Samples are here given from this Noble Author, is of a Kind not to be met with almost in any of that *insipid Race of voluminous Writers called Commentators on ancient Authors* (for so he often very justly characterizes them.) If our *Gataker,* the Ca-<xxii>*saubons* and a very few more are excepted, *there is none of the Tribe whom it is not pernicious to have read.*[18] It is Criticism of a Kind sadly wanting in the more ordinary Course of what is called *classical Education:* For which Reason young Gentlemen have no sooner acquired with *great Drudgery,* some small Acquaintance with *Greek* and *Roman* Words, than they throw aside the Authors from whom they would quickly receive an abundant Reward for all that Toil, *were they but once directed into the right Taste, and the profitable Manner of reading them,* which are so charmingly delineated to us by this *instructive elegant Master,* in his Advice to an Author, *in particular.*[19] This is so much the more to be wondred at, that we have had for some Time a *System of Notes* in our own Language, on *Homer,* (for the Translation is *Homer* still) that is a *most perfect Model of true and useful Criticism;*[20] and plainly *points* out to those who are concerned in the Education of Youth, in what Channel their Lectures on *ancient Authors* ought chiefly to run, if they would *form* or *improve* a good Taste of them; and instead of giving *young Gentlemen* a *very idle Turn* (to say no more of it) toward *merely verbal*

17. Shaftesbury, "Soliloquy: Or, Advice to an Author," in Shaftesbury, *Characteristicks,* I:205–6 note.

18. Compare Shaftesbury, *Characteristicks,* I:65 and 77. Thomas Gataker (1574–1654) was a noted English clergyman and distinguished classical scholar who prepared a widely admired edition of Marcus Aurelius. See above, pp. 104–5, note †, for Isaac Casaubon. His son Meric (1599–1671) was a Church of England clergyman who also published scholarly editions of classical texts, as well as learned polemics against the Catholic Church and an attack on religious enthusiasm.

19. Shaftesbury, "Soliloquy: Or, Advice to an Author," in Shaftesbury, *Characteristicks,* I:95–224.

20. Homer, *The Iliad,* translated by Alexander Pope, 6 vols. (London, 1715–20); Homer, *The Odyssey,* translated by Alexander Pope, 5 vols. (London, 1725–26).

Criticism, inspire them early with that *just Relish for Manly Science,* and *useful Reflections* on *Men, Manners,* and *Things,* which if *Education* be not *adapted* to *produce,* it is *any thing* else but what it assumes the Name of. Were these *Notes* translated into a Language *Foreign Pedants* could read, *Criticism perhaps* might take a *better Turn* among them; or, at least, cease to *corrupt* and *spoil good Books* and *good Taste.* <xxiii>

I have no more to add but that I thought it not *improper to give the principal Authorities* from which the *Abbe de Vertot's* Characters of *Augustus, M. Agrippa* and *Maecenas* seem'd to me to be taken, in the Margin by way of Notes, One pretty large Note concerning the Education of *Augustus* and *Maecenas,* well deserves its Place, because it shews us what Notion the *Ancients* had of *truly liberal Education;* or of the different Parts, which being rightly *coalited* constitute a *proper Institution* for the Youth of higher Rank. I have taken the same Care *with regard* to the Description of *Verres's* Gallery, having inserted in the Margin the Passages scattered through *Cicero's* Orations against *Verres; from which* it is fetch'd. As for Mr. *Boindin,* he is so full and exact in his References to the Authorities on *which* he founds his Opinion, that there *was* nothing more left to me to do, but to add the Observations of Mr. *de Bos* on the same Subject published *afterwards,* and the curious Print prefixed to those Discourses, which all the Lovers of Antiquity *will* be glad to see. With regard to Re-searches of this Sort *allow* me to conclude in *Cicero's* Words.

———— *Quod si non hic tantus fructus ostenderetur, & si ex his studiis delectatio sola peteretur: tamen ut opinor hanc animi adversionem humanissimam ac liberalissimam esse judicaretis.*[21]

Of such Amusement it may be said,

> ———— *Vires instigat alitque*
> *Tempestiva quies, major post otia virtus.*
>
> Statius Sylv. *l. 4.*[22]

21. Cicero, *Pro archia poeta,* vii.16: "But let us for the moment waive these solid advantages; let us assume that entertainment is the sole end of reading; even so, I think you would hold that no mental employment is so broadening to the sympathies or so enlightening to the understanding."

22. Statius, *Sylvae,* IV.iv.33–34: "Timely rest stimulates and fosters strength, energy is greater after ease."

The History of the World Translated from the Latin of Justin

ာ ာ ာ

NOTE ON THE TEXT

Turnbull's translation of Justin's *Epitome of the Philippic Histories* of Pompeius Trogus, which Turnbull has styled *The History of the World* (after the Latin title *Historiae Philippicae et totius mundi origines et terrae situs*), was published twice before his death in 1748. The first edition, entitled *Justin's History of the World Translated into English,* was published by the London bookseller and publisher Thomas Harris in December 1741 (see above, p. xv). The title page merely states that the translation and editorial matter were done "By a Gentleman of the University of Oxford" and there is no indication that Turnbull was responsible for the translation, annotations, or the "Prefatory Discourse." The second edition, entitled *The History of the World Translated from the Latin of Justin,* was published by the London booksellers Samuel Birt and Benjamin Dod in 1746. This edition bears a reworded title page which names Turnbull as the editor and translator. The text of the body of the work is essentially the same, apart from the insertion of a list advertising books printed by Birt and Dod in what in the first edition was a blank space in the page at the end of Turnbull's "Prefatory Discourse."

THE

HISTORY

OF THE

WORLD

Translated from the LATIN of

JUSTIN:

WITH

Some necessary REMARKS by way of *Notes;*

AND A

PREFATORY DISCOURSE,

Concerning the *Advantages* that ought chiefly to be
had in view, in reading this or any ancient Historian.

To this new Translation is subjoined, an exact
CHRONOLOGICAL TABLE
of the Affairs of the WORLD, from the
CREATION to the Birth of *CHRIST.*

The Whole very useful for all Readers of HISTORY;
Beginners more especially.

By *G. TURNBULL* LL.D.
The SECOND EDITION.

LONDON:
Printed for S. BIRT, and B. DOD, both in *Ave-Mary Lane.*
M.DCC.LXVI. <iii>

A Prefatory Discourse,

*Concerning the Advantages Masters ought chiefly to
have in view, in reading any ancient Historian, Justin
in particular, with young scholars*

Good Translators of ancient authors are useful in a double capacity. First,
to supply the want of acquaintance with Greek and Latin, to those whose
more useful employments do not leave them time to study these languages,
though they now and then afford them leisure hours for reading books in
their own tongue. And indeed, as, to bring the experiences, the observations, the discoveries, the sentiments of ancient sages, about men and
things, and, what is chief, the history of ancient times within the compass
of those, who, being busied in carrying on the arts and traffic which are
the supports of human life, have no other resource for their instruction and
improvement, but their native language, is one of the best offices, one of
the greatest services the learned can render to such; so it is a compensation,
a tribute the learned owe to them, in return for the exemption from bodily
labour, and the agreeable freedom and leisure of study they enjoy. In
fine, if the trading or working, which is by far the more useful part of a
na-<iv>tion, hath a right to knowledge, to acquaintance with ancient history, from which they may reap not only amusement in hours of ease and
recess from business, but very profitable instruction and information: or if
any service be due from the learned to them, they have a right, if not to
exact, yet to expect the labour of translating useful ancient books, from
those who give themselves up to the study of the ancient languages. And
accordingly, the learned of this class have thought themselves obliged to
render this service to the public.

II. Another use of Translations, which hath no small influence in en-

gaging the learned to take the trouble of translating ancient books, is fa-
cilitating the learning of the dead languages to young scholars, whose circumstances afford them the advantage of a liberal education; that they may
not be disgusted at study, by the difficulty of making progress in any of
the learned languages, without such help; and that as little of their precious
time as possible may be wasted upon the mere acquisition of words. But
the use of literal Translations hath been fully evinced by the very ingenious
Mr. *John Clarke,* in the preface to his *JUSTIN,* and his other tracts upon
the education of youth in grammar schools; and therefore I shall not insist
longer upon this head.[1]

This Translation of *JUSTIN* is designed to serve both these purposes;
and for that reason it is as literal as the idiom of our language permits. The
author's transitions and connexions, and the general turn of his phrases are
preserved as much as could be done, without rendering the translation a
very unpleasing piece of English. Nay, I won't venture to say, that a delicate
English ear may not now and then be offended at certain harshnesses of
style in it, which might easily have been avoided, had the Translator proposed no other end to himself, besides the information of an English reader:
but these will very readily be pardoned, for the sake of the learners of Latin
to whom a looser translation of these passages would not be of great benefit,
by all who think giving proper assistances to them, a purpose not to be
sacrificed to mere melody. We need not recommend *JUSTIN* to the schools;
this author hath long had his proper place there: but it can never <v> be
unseasonable to put youth in mind of what they ought chiefly to attend
to, and impress upon their minds in reading historians. And I wish there
was no occasion to tell masters, that they ought to have something of more
importance in their view, than the mere explication of words and syntax
in all their lessons. For the sake of beginners therefore in the study of his-

---

1. John Clarke, *An Essay upon the Education of Youth in Grammar-Schools,* 2nd ed.
(London, 1730), pp. 30–33; *Justini Historiae Philippicae. Cum versione Anglica. Ad verbum, quantum fieri potuit, facta. Or, the History of Justin. With an English Translation, as
literal as possible,* 2nd ed. (London, 1735), esp. pp. iv–xiii; *A Dissertation upon the Usefulness of Translations of Classick Authors, both Literal and Free, for the Easy Expeditious
Attainment of the Latin Tongue* ([London], 1734). John Clarke (1687–1734) was a widely
read educational theorist who served as the master of the Hull Grammar School from
1720 to 1732.

tory, *JUSTIN* being one of the first authors such will be directed to, I shall here prefix some remarks upon the principal advantages of that study. And indeed the following considerations will shew it to be the most useful and important of all studies: a study, which young people, those of birth and fortune more especially, ought early to be guided into the right method of carrying on; and a study, to the profitable pursuit of which, the direction and assistance of persons of experience and acquaintance with history and the world, is absolutely necessary.

Every one who understands that by history is meant a register of human affairs, in which great actions are traced to their motives or springs, and the characters of their authors are developed, will forthwith give his assent and approbation to all the eloges bestowed upon this kind of writing: such as these of Cicero, who calls it, "the light of all times; the faithful depository of events; the impartial witness of truth; the source of prudence and good counsel; the rule of life and conduct; the school of manners."[2] "Without its aids we would," says Seneca, "during our whole life, remain shut up within the limits of the age and country in which our lot falls; be confined within the narrow circle of our own particular experiences and observations; and so continue all our lives in a sort of infancy, quite strangers to the rest of the universe, and in profound ignorance of all that preceded our existence, and all that environs us. What is that small number of years (saith he) which composes the longest life? What is the largest extent of country we can occupy, or run through upon this globe? What are they, but imperceptible points, in respect of the vast regions of the universe, and of that long <vi> succession of ages, which hath been in a constant flux since the origin of the world? yet to these almost imperceptible points is our knowledge limited, if we do not call history to our assistance, which opens to our view all the ages and countries of the world, and brings us into acquaintance and commerce with all the great men of antiquity; which sets

---

2. A very loose paraphrase of Cicero, *De oratore,* II.ix.36: "And as History, which bears witness to the passing of the ages, sheds light upon reality, gives life to recollection and guidance to human existence, and brings tidings of ancient days, whose voice, but the orator's, can entrust her to immortality?" Turnbull's discussion here and in subsequent paragraphs follows Charles Rollin, *The Method of Teaching and Studying the Belles Lettres, or an Introduction to Languages, Poetry, Rhetoric, History, Moral Philosophy, Physicks, &c,* 4 vols. (London, 1734), III:1–8.

before our eyes all their actions, all their enterprizes, all their virtues, and all their failures or vices; and which, by the sage reflexions it suggests to us, or leads us into, procures us, in a very short time, a prudence, or foresight, that anticipates experience, far superior to the lessons of the ablest masters."[3]

We may say, that history is the common school of mankind, equally open and useful to great and small, to princes and to subjects; but much more necessary to the Great, than to others. For amidst that crowd of flatterers, with which they are besieged on all hands, who are ever admiring and praising them, *that is,* corrupting and empoisoning their minds, how can modest truth find admittance to them, or make its humble voice to be heard amidst such a tumult and confused noise? How can she take the courage to tell them the duties and obligations of grandeur and power, and shew them wherein true glory consists; let them see, that if they will take the trouble of tracing their dignity to its original, they cannot choose but clearly perceive, that *they are made and appointed for the people, and not the people for them,* as Cicero speaks?[4] How dare she discover their faults to them, or unfold by anticipation, the just judgment posterity will pronounce upon

3. The quotation elaborates on Cicero, *Orator,* xxxiv.120: "To be ignorant of what occurred before you were born is to remain always a child"; Seneca, *De consolatione ad Marciam,* xxi.1–2: "All things human are short-lived and perishable, and fill no part at all of infinite time. This earth with its cities and peoples, its rivers and the girdle of the sea, if measured by the universe, we may count as a mere dot; our life, if compared with all time, is relatively even less than a dot; for the compass of eternity is greater than that of the world, since the world renews itself over and over within the bounds of time"; and Seneca, *De brevitate vitae,* xiv.1–2, "By other men's labours we are led to the sight of things most beautiful that have been wrested from darkness and brought into light; from no age are we shut out, we have access to all ages, and if it is our wish, by greatness of mind, to pass beyond the narrow limits of human weakness, there is a great stretch of time through which we may roam . . . Since Nature allows us to enter into fellowship with every age, why should we not turn from this paltry and fleeting span of time and surrender ourselves with our soul to the past, which is boundless, which is eternal, which we share with our betters?" Compare Rollin, *Method of Teaching and Studying the Belles Lettres,* III:1–2.

4. The quotation is in fact a paraphrase of Seneca, *De clementia,* I.xix.8: "Oh, surely a man so fortunate would owe it also to himself to live; to that end he has shown by constant evidences of his goodness, not that the state is his, but that he is the state's." The whole of this paragraph is taken from Rollin, *Method of Teaching and Studying the Belles Lettres,* III:2–3.

them, and thus dissipate that thick delusive mist, with which their intox-icating grandeur and power over clouds their minds?

Truth cannot render these important, these so necessary services to the great and powerful, without the aids of history; which alone is in possession of the right of speaking to them with due liberty; and which carries this right to the point of passing a sovereign sentence upon the actions even of kings. In vain are their mental abilities boasted of; in vain is their wit, the com-<vii>prehension of their judgment, their courage admired; or their exploits and conquests celebrated; if all be not founded upon truth and justice, history will treat them as they deserve, and set them forth to show in their genuine colours. And how doth it consider or regard the greater part of renowned conquerors, but as public scourges, enemies of mankind, destroyers of nations; who, pushed by blind and restless ambition, carried desolation through the world, like a fire, or an innundation? It exhibits a Philip, an Alexander the Great, a Caligula, a Nero, a Domitian, who were so loaded with flattering praises in their lives, as become, after their death, the horror and execration of mankind: whereas we find by it, that an Epam-inondas, a Pelopidas, a Titus, and an Antonin, are yet mention'd in the world with pleasure and delight, because they never employ'd their power, but in doing good.[5] History, even while princes and great men are alive, is,

5. Philip II (382–336 B.C.E.), King of Macedon, under whose leadership Macedonia challenged the military and political preeminence of Athens; Alexander III (356–323 B.C.E.), King of Macedon, son of Philip II and styled "the Great" because of his military exploits in expanding the empire of the Macedonians into Asia Minor and India; Caligula (C.E. 12–41) or, more properly, Gaius Iulius Caesar Romanicus, Emperor of Rome (37–41), known to posterity for his moral corruption and hunger for power even though he was initially a popular ruler and an effective governor; Nero Claudius Caesar (37–68), Emperor of Rome (54–68), whose murder of his mother Agrippina in C.E. 59 led to his gradual political downfall and suicide in the face of unrest in Gaul and Spain and censure by the Roman Senate; Titus Flavius Domitian (51–96), Emperor of Rome (81–96), who was praised by the poets Statius and Martial but who was bitterly opposed by the Senate, in part because of his autocratic style of rule; Epaminondas (d. 362 B.C.E.), a Theban general who helped liberate Thebes from Spartan rule in 379 and who campaigned against the Peloponnesian League, winning famous victories at Leuctra (371 B.C.E.) and Mantinea (362 B.C.E.), where he was killed in battle by the Spartans; Pelopidas (d. 364 B.C.E.), a Theban general and friend of Epaminondas who also fought against Sparta; Titus Flavius Vespasianus (C.E. 39–81), Emperor of Rome (79–81), the widely respected son of the Emperor Vespasian (C.E. 9–79) and conqueror of Jerusalem (C.E. 70) to

in some degree, to them, in lieu of that tribunal among the ancient Egyptians, before which, princes as well as private persons, were cited after their death; and shews them by advance, the impartial sentence which shall render their infamy indelible for ever. In fine, 'tis history, as a very celebrated historian (Tacitus) expresses it, that stamps the seal of immortality upon truly good and great actions, and burns flagitious ones with a mark of ignominy, that no length of time can efface.[6] Unknown or mistaken merit, and oppressed virtue, expect redress and justice from this incorruptible tribunal, and appeal to it; and it will render them abundant compensation for the iniquitous treatment they suffered from their contemporaries; for, without respect of persons, being no longer awed by power that is no more, it never fails to condemn, with inexorable severity, every unjust abuse of authority and power.

There is no age or condition of mankind which may not draw equal advantages from history:[7] and what hath been said of princes and conquerors, extends, in certain proportions, to all persons in high stations; to ministers of state, generals of armies, magistrates; superiors of all kinds, civil or ecclesiastical; fathers and mothers in <viii> their own families; masters and mistresses in their little domestic republics: in a word, to all in authority over others. For it often happens, that persons in a very narrow inconsiderable elevation, have more pride, arrogance, and capriciousness, than kings, and push their arbitrary humour to a greater height. 'Tis therefore highly expedient that history should give useful lessons to all sorts of persons; and hold before them, with an unsuspected hand, a faithful mirror, in which they may behold their faults, and at the same time, discern their duties and obligations.

---

whom Pliny the Elder (C.E. 23/4–79) dedicated his *Natural History;* Antoninus Pius (C.E. 86–161), Emperor of Rome (C.E. 138–61), whose character and reign were celebrated in the *Meditations* of his adopted son, Marcus Aurelius (C.E. 121–80).

6. Tacitus, *The Annals*, 3.65: "It is not my intention to dwell upon any senatorial motions save those either remarkable for their nobility or of memorable turpitude; in which case they fall within my conception of the first duty of history—to ensure that merit shall not lack its record and to hold before the vicious word and deed the terrors of posterity and infamy." The reference and much of the paragraph are taken from Rollin, *Method of Teaching and Studying the Belles Lettres,* III:3–4.

7. This paragraph is taken from Rollin, *Method of Teaching and Studying the Belles Lettres,* III:4–5.

History therefore, when it is well taught, becomes a school of morality to mankind, of all conditions and ranks.[8] It discovers the deformity and fatal consequences of vices, and unmasks false virtues; it disabuses men of their popular errors and prejudices; and despoiling riches of all its enchanting and dazling pomp and magnificence, demonstrates by a thousand examples, which are more perswasive than reasonings, that there is nothing truly great or praise-worthy, but untainted honour and probity. From the esteem and admiration which the most corrupt cannot with-hold from the great and good deeds she sets before them, history obliges us to conclude, that virtue is man's true good, and that alone which can render any one truly great and estimable. History teaches us to respect virtue for its own sake, and to discern its intrinsic beauty through the thickest veils, poverty, adversity, obscurity, or even obloquy and defamation, may cast over it. As, on the other hand, it inspires into us a thorough contempt, hatred, and abhorrence of vice, however richly it may be bedeck'd and adorn'd; even tho' it should happen to be cloathed in regal purple, seated upon a throne, and holding a scepter in its hand.

But to keep within the bounds of my present design, I look upon history as the first master we ought to give to youth; being equally fit to amuse and to instruct them; to improve their understandings and their hearts, by conveying into their minds an infinity of facts, no less agreeable and entertaining, than edifying.[9] Nothing is so proper for awakening and piquing their curiosity, <ix> and thereby begetting a taste for study; which is the first point to be gained in education, and is indeed the chief thing. Accordingly, with relation to the institution of youth, it hath been looked upon by the considering, in all times and ages of the world, as a fundamental maxim, that the study of history should go first, and prepare the way for the other sciences. Plutarch informs us, that Cato the elder, that famous censor of Rome, whose virtue hath done so great honour to that republic, and who took particular care of his son's education himself, and would not entrust it in any other hands but his own, composed, for his use, a choice collection of beautiful pieces of Roman history, on purpose, said

8. This paragraph is taken from Rollin, *Method of Teaching and Studying the Belles Lettres,* III:5–6.

9. This paragraph is taken from Rollin, *Method of Teaching and Studying the Belles Lettres,* III:6–7.

he, that this infant, without going out of his father's house, might contract an acquaintance with the greatest men of his country, and be enabled to form himself upon the ancient models of probity and virtue.[10]

But it is not necessary to insist longer upon proving the utility of history: 'tis a point none calls into question: the great affair is to know how to reap real advantage by this study; or what ought to be observed and done for this effect. And this is what I am now to *attempt* to offer some observations upon.

In order to profit by history, one must be prepared, taught and inured to distinguish what is worthy of admiration and esteem, from what merits our contempt, or at least our indifference.[11] History abounds with shining actions, which are not virtuous or praise-worthy: and readers, guided by their own passions, or false prepossessions, may take for an action to be imitated, whatever is conformable to their humours and notions: but if we would render history a school of morality, due care must be taken to lead students, by proper reflections upon actions and events, to just notions of characters and enterprizes; and to secure them against the corrupt influence of outward pomp and splendour, by accustoming them to penetrate, beyond outward appearances, into the intrinsic nature and value of things, and to distinguish between the gaudy or glittering, and solid, substantial, and abiding worth. The great lesson in morals, and, consequently, the great lesson to be <x> learned from history, is to form a just judgment of external wealth and power, of riches, magnificence, splendour, luxury, conquests, fame, glory; and likewise of the internal abilities, talents, and virtues of the mind; and to be able to discern wherein true glory and solid happiness lies; where, and where alone, unallay'd contentment can be found. In the age we live in, every thing conspires to insinuate early into young minds the desire of riches, as that which makes the chief joy and honour of life; and a dread and contempt of poverty, as that alone which makes miserable, or brings disgrace and shame. Avarice is now the universal passion: ambition is no more. But 'till the mind is fortified against this fatal error, none of the great virtues can grow up in it. Such a prepossession will choak them

10. Plutarch, *Plutarch's Lives*, "Marcus Cato," xx.5.
11. Turnbull's argument in what follows (pages 310–15) is drawn from Rollin, *Method of Teaching and Studying the Belles Lettres*, III:9–39.

in their first budding, if perchance there are any seeds of them in the soul. Now the ancient history of Greece and Rome furnishes us with noble examples for correcting this false prejudice, and instructing young minds in the true use, and in the vile abuse of wealth. We find in antiquity a whole state revolting against a representation of riches as the most desirable object in human life. Euripides had put into the mouth of Bellerophon a magnificent speech in praise of wealth, which ended in this sentiment; "riches are the sovereign good of mankind, and they justly excite the admiration of gods, and of men." This saying shocked the whole Athenian audience, and raised their indignation to such a pitch, that they unanimously rose up against the poet, and would have expelled him out of the city, if he had not entreated them to wait for the result of the piece, in which this adorer of wealth miserably perished.[12] However extraordinary this instance may appear in modern times, antiquity affords us yet stronger examples of generosity, public spirit, and what is inseparable from it, contempt of private riches. In those ancient and heroic times (when men thought that to be necessary which was virtuous) the nobility of Athens having the people so much engaged in their debt, that there remained no other question among them, than which of them should be king, no sooner <xi> heard *Solon* speak, than they quitted their debts, and restored the commonwealth; which ever after held a solemn and annual feast, called the *Sisactia,* or *Recision,* in memory of that action.[13] Nor is this example the phoenix; for at the institution by Lycurgus, the nobility having estates, as ours here, in the hands of Laconia, upon no other consideration than the model of the commonwealth proposed by him, threw them up, to be parcell'd by his Agrarian.[14] The whole history of Sparta is one continued instance of the glorious influences of true magnanimity, which makes, not private fortune, but justice and public good, the rule of its conduct, and looks down with detestation upon the most redundant riches vice can offer; and of the fatal effects

12. Seneca, *Epistles,* CXV.14–16.

13. Solon's law of *seisachtheia* (the "shaking off of burdens") freed those who had been enslaved for their debts and prohibited the future enslavement of debtors.

14. Turnbull has taken his discussion of Solon and Lycurgus almost verbatim from James Harrington, *The Commonwealth of Oceana,* in Harrington, *Political Works,* p. 241. Compare Diogenes Laertius, *Lives of the Eminent Philosophers,* I.45, and, especially, Plutarch, *Plutarch's Lives,* "Solon," xv.2–xvi.3, and "Lycurgus," viii.1–4.

of prevailing avarice to public states. Amongst the Romans, in their best times, the same noble sentiments prevailed almost universally. "Every one (says *Valerius Maximus*) sought, not to enrich himself, but his country; and chose rather to be poor in an opulent state, than to be rich themselves in a poor republic."[15] And we may soon see, from history, that to the prevalence of those generous sentiments, Rome owed its power and glory; and to their decline, its fall. It was in this school, and in the bosom of poverty, as Horace tells us, that the Camilli, the Curii, the Fabricii, and all the ancient Roman heroes, were formed.[16] And while the Roman republic was in its greatest glory, it was usual for the great men in it to die, without leaving enough behind them to portion their daughters, or even defray the expences of a decent burial. I might mention many noble examples in ancient history, which furnish abundant occasion for inculcating upon youth the beauty of generosity, and the vileness of avarice; and for arming them against all the enchanting charms of wealth on the one hand, and all the horrors of poverty on the other. Cimon, the Athenian general, we are told by Plutarch, made no other use of his riches; he thought they were given by providence for no other end, but that he might thereby have the god-like satisfaction of relieving the distressed, dispelling misery, and spreading happiness far and wide, in proportion to <xii> the deserts of his fellow-citizens.[17] Aratus, the Achaean general, gained universal love, and saved his country, by applying the rich presents he received from kings, in composing and calming the dissentions which reign'd in it; in paying the debts of some, and in supplying the necessities of other fellow-citizens; in ransoming captives; and in every act of generosity and beneficence.[18] Philopoemon, commonly called by historians, the last of the Greeks, *i.e.* the last in whom the true Grecian public spirit prevailed, in that degree to which Greece owed its liberty, glory, and fame, employed all he had taken from the enemy, in fur-

---

15. Valerius Maximus, *Memorable Doings and Sayings,* IV.4.9: "For everybody was eager to increase the country's wealth, not his own, and would sooner live a poor man in a rich empire than a rich man in a poor one."

16. Turnbull conflates Horace, *Epistles,* I.1.64, and Valerius Maximus, *Memorable Doings and Sayings,* IV.4.11.

17. Plutarch, *Plutarch's Lives,* "Cimon," x.1–8.

18. Plutarch, *Plutarch's Lives,* "Aratus," ix.2, xi.2, xiv.1–3, xix.1–3.

nishing his fellow-citizens with horses and arms, and in redeeming the prisoners of war.[19]

To mention no more instances, let young gentlemen, when they read the character of Epaminondas, which is so well drawn by Justin,[20] be asked what they think of such an example, when compared with those narrow souls, who live as if they were born for themselves only; and who, employing their wealth to gratify their appetites and passions, to pamper their bellies, or flatter their vanity, are of no advantage to their neighbours, relations, or friends; and seem not to feel the ties of blood, of friendship, or of gratitude; nor to be sensible of any obligations upon them to their family, their country, or to merit. Let them oppose these pictures one to the other, and by the contrast, the beauty of virtue will appear with a force that cannot fail to make its way into young hearts very speedily, and to leave impressions there, not to be easily erazed.

Young minds are now so accustomed, from their infancy, to admire outward show, that representations of external magnificence in history are very apt strongly to attract their attention, and to strike them with wonder, that is quickly followed with emulation. But let masters take occasion from history, to correct the false ideas of external ornaments, that are, without attention to the consequences of them, too often instilled into youth, even by virtuous parents, at the time that the greatest care ought to be had of the notions and <xiii> habits which are excited and formed in their minds. Let them be taught to reflect, that dress, equipage, and other such outward trappings, have nothing truly great or estimable in them; because they make no part of us, but are without us, and absolutely foreign to us. It is in such things the greater part of mankind place their grandeur, as if they were incorporated, so to speak, with every thing that environs them: these things greaten them in their own fancy, and they imagine they likewise greaten them in the eyes of others. But let us set apart the glittering of dress and equipage, and search into the real character of such persons; and what are they but, in comparison, as dirty walls hung with fine tapistry, as Seneca

19. Plutarch, *Plutarch's Lives*, "Philopoemen," i.4, iv.3, vii.4.
20. For Justin's "character" of Epaminondas see the *History*, Bk. VI, chap. viii.

expresses it;[21] under this splendour and magnificence lurks littleness and meanness of soul. We shall find all the great men of antiquity despising ostentation, gawdery, and pageantry. And let the youth learn from the history of Epaminondas, Philopoemon, Scipio,[22] and many others, not to judge of men by the exterior, but to look through the outside into the heart and character of the man. What can be more simple or obvious than this reflection; that uncommon merit may lie hid under a very mean dress, as a very costly and shining garment may cover a very base and flagitious heart. Do we judge of horses by their trappings? We read even of women, in ancient times, who were proof against all the dazling lustre of jewels and finery. One very remarkable instance of this kind is worth mentioning. The famous Cornelia, the mother of the Gracchi, is a very distinguished name in history.[23] There was not a more illustrious family, or a richer at Rome. Valerius Maximus tells us, that a lady of Campania came to see her, and staying all night, took an opportunity of displaying, with no small ostentation, all her ornaments, all her jewels, rings, bracelets, and other shining gew gaws, which the ancients called *Mundum Muliebrem*.[24] Cornelia dextrously prolonged the conversation, 'till her children, who were at school, came in; and when they were returned, pointing to them, she said, "These are my jewels, my ornaments."[25] One needs only attend to what he feels <xiv> upon comparing these two women, to discover how much the noble simplicity of the one is above the vain magnificence of the other. And in-

21. Turnbull here summarizes the argument of Seneca, *Epistles*, LXXVI.32 and LXXX.

22. Cornelius Scipio Aemilianus Africanus (185/84–129 B.C.E.), renowned for his military prowess and a friend of Marcus Porcius Cato (234–149 B.C.E.), known as Cato the Censor, and the historian Polybius (ca. 200–ca. 118 B.C.E.). Scipio was much admired by Cicero; see Cicero, *De officiis*, III.i.1–4.

23. Cornelia (life dates unknown) was one of the most learned and politically influential women in ancient Rome. The daughter of Cornelius Scipio Africanus the Elder, she married Tiberius Sempronius Gracchus and had twelve children. Of the three children that survived, her sons Tiberius Sempronius Gracchus and Caius Sempronius Gracchus both played prominent political roles in the Roman republic. See Plutarch, *Plutarch's Lives*, "Tiberius and Caius Gracchus." On Cornelia compare Rollin, *Method of Teaching and Studying the Belles Lettres*, III:38–39.

24. *Mundus muliebris*, a Latin phrase meaning the items in a woman's toilet.

25. Valerius Maximus, *Memorable Doings and Sayings*, IV.4.preface: "These are *my* jewels."

deed, what merit is there in purchasing precious stones, and other ornaments, to make a vain shew of them, and in being able to discourse of
nothing else but dress? And, on the contrary, what nobleness of mind was
it for a lady, of the first quality more especially, to contemn all tinsel, and
to place her honour and glory in the good education of her children; to
spare no expence to obtain that end; and thus to shew, that greatness of
mind is not the property of one sex. What hath been said concerning for-
tifying young minds against the allures of wealth, pomp, and finery, may
easily be applied to table-luxury, and sumptuous palaces. But not having
time to insist upon every thing in a short Preface, we shall only add to what
hath been said, some reflections upon the use that ought to be made of
history, to prevent or extirpate false notions of birth or nobility, dignities
and honours; and above all, of conquests.

It must be acknowledged, that there is in nobleness of extraction, and
the antiquity of families, some powerful charm that attracts esteem and
regard.[26] The respect which it is natural to pay to those of noble descent,
is a kind of homage that we think ourselves obliged to render to the memory
of their ancestors, on account of their eminent services to the public. It is,
as it were, the continuation of the payment of a debt which we could not
fully discharge to themselves, and which, for that reason, ought to be acquitted to their posterity. But besides the gratitude which engages us not
to confine our respect for great men to their lives, whose generosity was not
limited within these narrow bounds, but extended by them to the remotest
ages; the public interest demands that we should pay to their offspring a
tribute of honour, which may be, with relation to them, an obligation to
maintain and perpetuate in their family the reputation of their progenitors,
and to pique themselves upon perpetuating also the virtues which rendered
their forefathers so illustrious. But that this honour we render to noble
birth, may be real homage, <xv> it must be voluntary, and proceed from
the heart. If any one pretends to exact it as a debt, or to force it, he loses
all the right he had to it, and becomes contemned and hated. The self-love,
natural to man, rebels against such pride and arrogance. And is it indeed

26. The first half of this paragraph is taken from Rollin, *Method of Teaching and
Studying the Belles Lettres,* III:62–64.

so great a glory to be able to count a long race of forefathers, eminent by their virtues, if we bear no resemblance to them? Can the merit of others become ours? The only true source therefore of nobility, is virtue and merit.[27] We have seen nobles dishonour their birth by base actions; and we have seen persons of ignoble extraction, exalt and ennoble their family by their glorious virtues. It is praise-worthy to support the glory of ancestors by actions conformable to their reputation; but it is also glorious to leave a title to our posterity, which we did not derive from our progenitors, but purchase by our own merit. Pride on account of their birth, is the disease to which, as *Salust* remarks, the nobility have ever been very incident; and therefore history ought to be employ'd to correct this vanity, than which there is not a greater obstacle to laudable ambition, and all valuable improvements.[28] But what period of history doth not afford instances for chastising, for shewing the ridicule of this vice? How absurd would it be, to make a shew with borrowed riches? But sure it is not less so, to expect honour and esteem on account of the merits of our forefathers, which upbraid our degeneracy, and render our baseness and wickedness at once more conspicuous, and more shameful? As for dignities, or high offices in the state, and the honours annexed to them; surely there is no merit in possessing them, if one be not qualified for them, or does not exerce them for the great and sole purpose of authority and power, the public good. They do not confer merit, they only give occasion of displaying it; and where there is no virtue, they bring forth to view the weakness or vileness that might otherwise, being less hurtful, have been less observed. With regard to them, how amiable, how great, how truly noble, was the conduct of Epaminondas, according to the character our author gives of him! " 'Tis uncertain (saith he) <xvi> whether the man or the general were more to be esteemed in him; for if he aspired after empire, it was not for his own, but for his country's advantage. So little covetous was he of money, in the whole course of his life, that he left not enough to defray the expences of his funeral. Neither was he more desirous of honours than of wealth; for all

27. Juvenal, *The Satires*, VIII.20: "Virtue is the one and only true nobility."

28. Sallust's most notable attack on the pride of the Roman nobility occurs in the speech given by Marius to the Senate in *The War with Jugurtha*, LXXXV; see especially LXXXV.17–25.

the offices he so worthily sustained, were forced upon him; and he so well acquitted himself in every station, that he did not receive, but give a new lustre to the greatest employments."[29] None can read this passage without feeling wherein solid glory consists, and what is true ambition. Let not masters therefore pass such examples in history, 'till they have fully rivetted upon the minds of their scholars, a just notion of the end of civil dignities; a true idea of glory; and fired them with an ambition of qualifying themselves for being useful in the world; which will never cause any of those disturbances false ambition does, its aim being public tranquility and good, whereas the aim of the other is power and wealth, cost what it will to those, for whose benefit a truly great mind will sacrifice every private enjoyment. Above all, it is necessary to guard young minds against the false and hurtful notions the encomiums given to military courage and prowess may engender in young minds. Let them be taught to examine with due coolness and indifference, impartially, and with eyes enlighten'd and guided by reason, into the real merits of those famous heroes of antiquity, that make such a figure and noise in history; and they will find, that those illustrious conquerors, who are set forth in such a pompous dazling light by flattering panegyrists, have ever been regarded, by the wiser part of mankind, as savage destructive monsters; and were indeed actuated in all their enterprizes by vanity, cruelty, or avarice. Those conquerors of the world, whose exploits raise the admiration of the vulgar, were miserable slaves to their own passions; the meanest, the basest of passions. What else but madness can we call the impetuous fury which pushed Alexander into remote and unknown countries, to ravage them? A pirate, as Cicero informs us, told <xvii> him the truth, when he asked him, what right he had to infest the seas; for he answered with undaunted freedom, "The same you have to pillage the universe. But because I rob in a small ship, they call me a pirate; and because you rob with a large fleet, they call you a conqueror."[30] Every man, whose mind is not quite over-run with passions, that bear down within his breast all the sentiments of humanity natural to man, and therefore very strong in young minds, if they have not had a very bad education, and very per-

29. Justin, *History,* p. 71.

30. Cicero, *De re publica,* III.24. Cicero's pirate is also mentioned in St. Augustine, *The City of God against the Pagans,* IV.iv.

nicious examples before their eyes from their tenderest years; every one who reads the lives of the illustrious Greeks and Romans, in Plutarch, or Justin's compendious view of all the more celebrated personages of antiquity, and their exploits, if he examines himself, will find, at the bottom of his heart, that 'tis not to a Philip, an Alexander, or a Caesar, he gives the preference above others; that they are not, in his sentiment, the greatest and most accomplished persons, or such as have done the greatest honour to human nature; that 'tis not them he judges worthy of his esteem, love, and veneration, or of the high praises some have given them. But that youth may be able to form a just and sound judgment of these famous conquerors, it is necessary to teach them to distinguish and separate their justly estimable qualities, from those that are blameable. While they render justice to their courage, their activity, their address and dexterity in public offices, their prudence and foresight; they should be led into regret, that they knew not the use they ought to have made of these great talents; and that they should have misemployed them in the service of vice: qualities highly valuable in themselves, but designed by nature to serve virtue or benevolence; and only glorious, when they are applied to do the great good that may be done by the proper exertion of them. For this end, this is the maxim that must be strongly enforced upon young minds, "*Nihil honestum esse potest quod justitia vacat*";[31] and that if it is self-interest, and not public good, that rouzes to encounter dangers, such a disposition does not merit the name of courage, but of savage ferocity; and that true for-<xviii>titude of mind consists in looking upon vice, as a greater evil than poverty or death. So even Horace teaches, lib. 4. od. 9.

> *Duramque callet pauperiem pati,*
> *Pejusque letho flagitium timet:*
> *Non ille pro caris amicis*
> *Aut patria timidus perire.*[32]

---

31. Cicero, *De officiis,* I.xix.62: "nothing that lacks justice can be morally right."
32. Horace, *The Odes,* IV.ix.49–52: The truly happy man is one who learns "to endure hard poverty, and who fears dishonour worse than death, not afraid to die for cherished friends or fatherland."

Let them be taught to regard probity, bold and undaunted probity, directed by prudence, as true glory; and to look not only upon beauty, strength of body, and other outward embellishments, but even upon mental accomplishments and improvements, such as extensive knowledge, eloquence, courage, and the like, as only meritorious in proportion to the good use made of them; and to attend, in particular, how much modesty adds to their price and beauty. Let them learn early, from proper examples, wherein true glory consists: that whatever is exterior to a man, whatever may be common to the good with the bad, does not render a man truly estimable: and that it is by their hearts we ought to judge of men. From hence flow great designs, great actions, great virtues: solid greatness, which cannot be imitated by pride, nor equalled by arrogance, resides in nobleness of sentiments and disposition. To be good, liberal, beneficent, generous; to put no other value upon wealth, but as it is the means of doing great good; nor upon dignities, but as they are opportunities of serving one's country; nor upon power and reputation, or credit, but as they raise one to a capacity of abashing and repressing vice, and of encouraging and rewarding virtue; to be truly good, without affecting merely to appear so; to support poverty with magnanimity; to bear injuries and affronts with patience; to stifle revenge, and render all sorts of good offices to an enemy one hath in his power; to prefer the public good to every thing; to be able to sacrifice to it his estate, his life, and even his reputation, if times require it: ——— This is to be truly great. Doth not Alexander appear more great in his humane, generous treatment of Darius's <xix> family, than in any of his conquests? Or what action in the story of Scipio, whose life was a continued scene of great exploits, raises him higher in our admiration, than when we behold him not only giving lectures of continence and prudence to a young prince who had forgot his duty, with great gentleness and mildness; but surmounting a passion which conquers almost all mankind, and thus giving a noble example to youth of chastity, generosity, and self-command? I think, the regard that Alexander shewed to the writings of Homer, and in the sack of Thebes, to the memory of Pindar, have procured him more reputation than all his victories: and he is more worthy of admiration, when laying aside all his pomp and royalty, he held familiar conferences with the celebrated painters and sculptors of his age, than when marching at the head of an army, he spread terror all around him.[33] The love of praise is a passion deeply fixed in the mind of every extraordinary person; and those who are most affected with it, seem most to partake of that particle of the Divinity which distinguishes mankind from the inferior creation. 'Twas an excellent observation, "That we then only despise commendation, when we cease to deserve it."[34] 'Tis therefore the great business of education, to form early in minds a just notion of glory; and to strengthen in them a passion for honour, that will not only preserve them from every thing that is mean and dishonouring, but be continually pushing them to great and good deeds.

Our natural sense of shame and honour is the proper handle to be used in the formation of youth, for moulding their minds into a right temper and frame: and history is ever affording occasions either for exciting our aversion, or raising our emulation. Some very sage observers of human nature have thought it best to begin in education by raising the aversion of young people to what they ought to hate, and thus weaning the mind from the pursuits it ought to fly. Others have thought, that the desire of imitation may be a greater incentive to the practice of what is good, than the aversion we <xx> may conceive at what is blameable. History furnishes means for employing both arts, by giving representations of the bright side of human nature, as well as the dark and gloomy. And indeed, the one immediately directs us what we should do, whilst the other only shews us what we should avoid. Mr. Locke, in his excellent treatise of education, hath shewn the disadvantages of hiding the vices and corruptions of mankind from youth; and the fitness, the absolute necessity of shewing them the world as it is, as they will soon find it to be: that they, upon their entrance into the world, may neither be tempted to think they were not fairly dealt with by their

33. Darius III (d. 330 B.C.E.), King of Persia, was defeated by Alexander the Great in a series of battles and was killed by his own men while trying to escape capture by Alexander. Alexander had earlier captured members of Darius's family after the battle of Issus (333 B.C.E.) but spared their lives. See Plutarch, *Plutarch's Lives*, "Alexander," esp. VIII.2, XI.6, XXI, XXVI.1–4, XXX.1–3, and Arrian, *Anabasis of Alexander*, I.9.10, I.12.1–2, II.11.8–9, II.12.3–8, IV.19–20. On Scipio, see Livy, *From the Founding of the City*, XXVI.xlix.11–l.14, and Polybius, *The Histories*, X.2–5, X.18.7–19.7, and X.40.1–9.

34. *The Spectator*, no. 467, Tuesday, 26 August 1712.

instructors; nor be, thro' their ignorance of vice, and simplicity of heart, dupes to the knaves that are ever lying in wait for such a prey.[35] Now History shews us the world as it is; it conceals none of the bad passions or wickednesses of men from us: and a skillful teacher will, in reading history with his pupils, have full opportunity of teaching them what they are to expect in the world, and to prepare them against the various shelves and rocks, to which they will be exposed during the whole voyage of life; but more especially at their first launching out into this dangerous ocean. As a sea-chart to the sailor, so is history to life; and as such, ought it to be considered and treated by instructors of youth. It shews all the different courses and bearings men may take or pursue, and all the various dangers that lie in the different steerings and navigations of life: and therefore one duly instructed in history is qualified for being his own director; and those who are not, are mere novices in the world, utter strangers to its perils and snares, and to the whole conduct of life. What pity is it then, that the philosophy of life, and History, which must go hand in hand, being as inseparable as rule and example in any other science, should not have a larger share than they commonly have in education; and that much more time should be bestowed upon the explication of certain authors, which, in the opinion of the better ancient pagan masters, ought not to be read to young people, than upon such useful arts! The great end of education <xxi> is to fit and prepare one for life: and therefore the whole course of education ought to be a course of moral lectures, illustrated and confirmed by proper examples from History, for that effect.[36] And that history may be a compleat moral school, teachers ought to trace actions to their springs and motives in the human breast: and to shew, I. That the differences amongst mankind are not owing to different original passions, but to the different spheres and circumstances of action, in which the same passions are placed; and, II. That all appetites and passions inlaid by nature into the human frame, are of the highest use to us. As by such teaching youth will learn how appetites and affections, in themselves good and useful, degenerate, and take a vitious

35. John Locke, *Some Thoughts concerning Education,* edited by John W. and Jean S. Yolton (Oxford, 1989), §§ 70 (p. 129) and 94 (pp. 152–55).

36. Compare George Turnbull, *Observations upon Liberal Education, in All Its Branches,* edited by Terrence O. Moore Jr. (Indianapolis, 2003), pp. 331–34, 345–46.

turn, or are misled into very hurtful and base passions; so they will likewise learn not to think ill of human nature, or its Author, on account of the corruptions and vices which have been so prevalent in all ages of the world; since none of the passions, whose perversions create the greatest disturbances in human society, could have been with-held from us, without rendering us incapable of very great virtues, and several truly noble pleasures. Besides, it is only by engaging youth to attend to the affections natural to the human mind, their connexions, dependencies, and bearings, and their various workings in different situations that youth can be prepared for entering into the characters of men, and for tracing actions to their causes; without which (as *Polybius,* who shews us, by reflections on proper examples at full length, what this study means) [37] history may exhibit an agreeable or entertaining show to us; but it cannot be an useful lesson: it may satisfy our curiosity, but it is of no consequence with relation to life and conduct. These reflections, it may be said, are too deep for young minds. But doth not, must not every science advance gradually from simpler to more sublime and complex truths? and 'till education hath rendered capable of such observations, what hath it done to fit one for life? In truth, the minds of youth open and enlarge, in proportion to the proper culture bestowed <xxii> upon them: and, generally speaking, we are late of attaining to true and useful knowledge, merely because we are thought incapable of such instruction, 'till we are arrived to years at which we may learn from history, that the Greek and Roman youth were equally qualified for the bar, the cabinet, and the field. There is evident danger in treating youth too long in a trifling way, as mere infants, and delaying to communicate to them, in a rational way, truly solid instructions; but there is none in taking proper methods early to expand, fortify, and enrich their minds. According to the common course of education, the habits of trifling and idling, not to mention worse ones, are fixed during the first seven years; and then some sort of teaching is thought of; as if habits could be easily undone, or good lessons have any success, 'till such habits are quite destroyed. As the soil

37. Throughout *The Histories* Polybius emphasized the importance of the search for the causes of both human behavior and the rise and fall of empires; see Polybius, *The Histories,* I.1–4, II.38.4–10, III.1.3, III.6, III.7.4–7, III.31–32, VI.2.8–10, XI.19a.1–3, XII.25b, XII.25d–i, XXII.18, XXIX.5, XXXVI.17.

must be duly prepared before the seed be thrown into it, otherwise the best seed will be lost; so the first and most early part of education ought to be to dress the soil of the mind, or to form those habits and affections in it, which render it a proper soil for receiving and fructifying good seed; the love and desire of knowledge, the patience of thinking, docility, pliableness, modesty, regard to truth, and such like dispositions, upon which the noblest virtues may easily be grafted, and from which good seed cannot fail of producing a rich crop of the most valuable fruits in human life. The reflections that have been just mention'd, are not the first that young minds ought to be led to; they are above their reach, 'till they have been for some time inured to more simple and easy ones; and much more so are enquiries into the national effects of different political constitutions; to which, however, the education of the better sort ought gradually to proceed, or it will fall far short of the liberal institution that alone can qualify for public service in the higher stations of civil society. But the observations upon morals, with which we began this discourse, will prepare them for these other more profound speculations: and they are not beyond the reach of youth; <xxiii> or at least, 'till they are understood, one is indeed in a state of childhood, and absolutely unfit for the most common offices of life. The simplest truths in morals may indeed be perplexed with verbal subtleties; but if they are preserved pure from this sophistication, and exhibited to undebauched minds in their native simplicity and beauty, they never fail at once to captivate the assent of the understanding, and the approbation of the heart. The principles of morality have a character of truth, which touches and perswades more than that of the principles of other human sciences: for whereas the principles of other sciences, and the particular truths which depend upon them, are only the objects of the mind, and not of the heart, the first principles of morals, and the particular rules essential to those principles, have a character of truth, which every body is capable of knowing, and which affects the mind and heart alike. The whole man is penetrated by them, and more strongly convinced of them, than of the truths of all the other human sciences. And if the mind be once tinctured with a just notion of the beauty and excellence of virtue, it will soon be able to attend to the rise and progress of those vices which have pulled down the mightiest states, and to those political methods of forming and supporting the virtues by which alone states can attain to or preserve liberty and greatness: which is one of the most useful instructions that can be inculcated from history; and is indeed a truth, that the history of all ages and nations abundantly confirms. I have already got beyond the bounds of a Preface, and yet have but lightly touched several very material things. I shall only add, that masters ought not to neglect or pass by several errors in *JUSTIN* unobserved: two in particular; his account of Cyrus, and his account of the Jews.[38] And in both these matters, as well as upon other occasions, it will be of great use to read with scholars *Rollin*'s excellent Summary of ancient history, from whose discourses on the method of teaching the *Belles Lettres,* many of the preceding remarks are taken; and whose discourses upon solid Glory, and the proper method of reading History, sacred and profane, cannot be too warmly recommended to the frequent, serious perusal of <xxiv> youth.[39] Let me finish this discourse with a maxim often repeated by that excellent writer. "He who hath not learned at school, or from his masters, to live, whatever else he may have learned, hath miserably lost his time."[40]

38. Justin, *History,* Bk. I, chaps. v–viii and Bk. XXXVI, chaps. ii–iii. Justin's accounts of King Cyrus the Great (d. 530 B.C.E.) of Persia and the early history of the Jews were at odds with Turnbull's Christian reading of history. Compare the comments on Cyrus in Charles Rollin, *The Ancient History of the Egyptians, Carthaginians, Assyrians, Babylonians, Medes and Persians, Macedonians, and Grecians,* 10 vols. (London, 1734–36), I:xii–xvi, where Rollin emphasizes that Cyrus was a tool of divine providence rather than the secular hero depicted in Greek and Roman sources.

39. Rollin, *Method of Teaching and Studying the Belles Lettres,* vols. 3 and 4; Rollin, *Ancient History.* Turnbull had earlier praised Rollin in his *Observations,* pp. 339–40.

40. We have been unable to locate the quoted passage in Rollin's *Method of Teaching and Studying the Belles Lettres* or his *Ancient History.* Turnbull may be alluding to Seneca, *Epistles,* CVI.12: "It is clearly better to use literature for the improvement of the mind, instead of wasting philosophy itself as we waste other efforts on superfluous things. Just as we suffer from excess in all things, so we suffer from excess in literature; thus we learn our lessons, not for life, but for the lecture-room."

A Treatise on Ancient Painting

ဆာ ဆာ ဆာ

NOTE ON THE TEXT

The gestation of Turnbull's *Treatise on Ancient Painting* was long and complex. On 29 April 1737 he submitted a formal proposal requesting the support of the Society for the Encouragement of Learning to publish "a book intitled, *An Essay concerning the antiquity and progress of painting amongst the Greeks and Romans, and the opinion, which the ancient philosophers had of that art, and its influence on education.*"[1] A week later, he again met with the Society's managing committee in the hope of persuading them to underwrite the publication of the work. The Society's minutes record that he showed them two copies of ancient paintings that he presumably acquired in Rome and that "his MS. Treatise on the painting of the Ancient Greeks & Romans was near finished but that none of his Copper plates were as yet Engraved." He apparently also suggested that the text and the engravings could be published separately, but the committee rejected this idea.[2] Nothing further is heard of the proposal in the months following, even though he continued to attend the meetings of the Society. Meanwhile, he was trying to resolve the problem of the engravings and turned to the portrait painter Allan Ramsay for help. In the autumn of 1737 Ramsay secured for Turnbull the services of the Italian artist Camillo Paderni, who executed a set of drawings for Turnbull that were later engraved in London by James Mynde.[3] By late January 1738 Turnbull had received at least eighteen of

1. "Memoirs of the Society for the Incouragement of Learning taken from the Register of their Meetings, and Minute Books of the Committee," British Library, Add. Mss 6185, 38. See also "Minutes of the Society for the Encouragement of Learning," BL Add. Mss 6187, 109, where Turnbull is said to have shown the managing committee of the Society a detailed summary of the contents of the book.

2. "Minutes," BL Add. Mss 6187, 111.

3. Iain Gordon Brown, "Allan Ramsay's Rise and Reputation," *Walpole Society,* 50 (1984): 234–35.

Paderni's drawings, for on 20 January 1738 he displayed them to the committee members of the Society and requested the "Liberty from time to time to shew them [his] Work and have their opinion thereof as it advanced, which desire was unanimously complied with." Significantly, he now referred to the work as "his Treatise on Ancient painting"; that is, he used its published title.[4] He was clearly still hoping that the Society would finance the publication of his manuscript, but he subsequently alienated the managing committee by soliciting subscriptions for his projected book. At a meeting held on 24 February 1738 the committee were told by the Society's secretary, the Scottish antiquarian Alexander Gordon, that Turnbull "hoped the proposals he had published for a Subscription of his Essay *on the Rise, Progress, and decline of painting amongst the Greeks and Romans &c.* did not preclude his having the Typographical part of the Said work printed by the Assistance of this Society." The committee responded by instructing Gordon to inform Turnbull "that his having now published Proposals for a subscription for both the Copper-plates, and Typographical part together, without any distinction, has put it out of the Committee's power to print the Said Essay."[5]

Without the financial backing of the Society, Turnbull was forced to launch a sustained advertising campaign in May 1738 to attract subscriptions for his "Essay." The campaign was evidently successful enough for him to proceed, and he initially set a publication date of 25 March 1739.[6] The project was, however, significantly delayed. Although the publication of the *Treatise* by the Scottish bookseller and publisher Andrew Millar was recorded in *The Gentleman's Magazine* for October 1739, advertisements that appeared in various London newspapers indicate that the book only became available to subscribers and prospective buyers in early December 1739, which explains why the title page carries a 1740 imprint.[7]

4. "Minutes," BL Add. Mss 6187, 155.

5. "Minutes," BL Add. Mss 6187, 172.

6. *Common Sense: Or, the Englishman's Journal,* no. 67, Saturday, 13 May 1738. The same ad appeared in the next number of the paper dated Saturday, 20 May.

7. *The Gentleman's Magazine* 9 (1739): 556. Advertisements appeared in early October 1739 stating that the book would be delivered to subscribers on 15 October but it would seem that there was some delay; see, for example, *Common Sense: Or, the Englishman's Journal,* no. 140, Saturday, 6 October 1739. A new set of advertisements for the *Treatise* subsequently appeared beginning in early December 1739, stating that "This Day is pub-

Based on an entry in the catalog of the library of Dr. Richard Mead, Vincent Bevilaqua suggests that the *Treatise* may have appeared in a smaller format than the folio size of surviving copies. This is unlikely.[8] When Turnbull first launched his subscription drive for the book he stated that "The Work will consist of 72 Sheets in Folio, besides the fifty Prints, on Superfine Royal Paper," and there is no reason to think that either he or Millar subsequently printed copies in a different format.[9] The text of the *Treatise* was not reprinted in Turnbull's lifetime. But he did reissue the plates along with new prefatory material in *A Curious Collection of Ancient Paintings, Accurately Engraved from Excellent Drawings, Lately Done after the Originals, by one of the Best Hands at Rome. With an Account where and when they were found, and where they now are; and several Critical, Historical, and Mythological Observations upon them,* which was published by Millar in May 1741.[10] Turnbull undoubtedly wanted to reissue the plates because he was seriously in debt due to the expense of publishing the *Treatise*. Writing to Alexander Cunyngham in August 1740, Allan Ramsay reported that Turnbull owed Camillo Paderni £15, "and I am afraid . . . [he] will never be in a capacity to pay him."[11] However, the text of the *Curious Collection* also registers the growth of his historical and antiquarian interests during the 1730s that was stimulated by his travels on the Grand Tour and his contact with Mead and other virtuosi in London.

---

lish'd, (Beautifully printed on superfine Royal Paper) and ready to be deliver'd to the Subscribers, A Treatise of Ancient Painting," and these ads were carried in the papers through December and into the new year; see, for instance, *London Evening Post,* no. 1881, Saturday, 1 December 1739, and *The Daily Post,* no. 6376, Thursday, 14 February 1740.

8. See Bevilacqua's editorial introduction to George Turnbull, *A Treatise on Ancient Painting, 1740* (Munich, 1971), pp. viii–ix.

9. *Common Sense: Or, the Englishman's Journal,* no. 67, Saturday, 13 May 1738.

10. *The Gentleman's Magazine* 11 (1741): 280.

11. *Curiosities of a Scots Charta Chest, 1600–1800. With the Travels and Memoranda of Sir Alexander Dick, Baronet of Prestonfield, Midlothian Written by Himself,* edited by the Honourable Mrs. Atholl Forbes (Edinburgh, 1897), p. 144. Alastair Smart has calculated that Turnbull's debt was roughly equivalent to £1000 in modern currency; Alastair Smart, *Allan Ramsay: Painter, Essayist and Man of the Enlightenment* (New Haven and London, 1992), p. 75.

Notes to facing page.

1. Cicero, *De oratore,* III.vi.21: "there is also the truth enunciated by Plato, which you, Catulus, have undoubtedly heard, that the whole of the content of the liberal and humane sciences is comprised within a single bond of union; since, when we grasp the meaning of the theory that explains the causes and issues of things, we discover that a marvellous agreement and harmony underlies all branches of knowledge."

2. From the introductory section of Book I of Philostratus the Elder, *Imagines,* 1.1–5 (294 K.): "Whosoever scorns painting is unjust to truth; and he is also unjust to all the wisdom that has been bestowed upon poets—for poets and painters make equal contribution to our knowledge of the deeds and the looks of heroes—and he withholds his praise from symmetry of proportion, whereby art partakes of reason."

A

TREATISE

ON

ANCIENT PAINTING,

CONTAINING

OBSERVATIONS

ON THE
RISE, PROGRESS, and DECLINE of that Art
amongst the *Greeks* and *Romans;*

THE
High Opinion which the Great Men of Antiquity had of it; its
Connexion with POETRY and PHILOSOPHY; and the Use that may be
made of it in Education:

To which are added
Some REMARKS on the peculiar Genius, Character, and Talents of
Raphael, Michael Angelo, Nicholas Poussin, and other Celebrated
Modern Masters; and the commendable Use they made of the
exquisite Remains of Antiquity in PAINTING as well as SCULPTURE.

The Whole illustrated and adorned with
FIFTY PIECES of ANCIENT PAINTING;
Discovered at different times in the Ruins of Old *Rome,* accurately
engraved from Drawings of *Camillo Paderni* a *Roman,* lately done
from the Originals with great Exactness and Elegance.

By GEORGE TURNBULL *LL. D.*

———— *Est etiam illa Platonis vera, & tibi Catule, certe non inaudita vox, omnem
doctrinam harum ingenuarum, & humanarum Artium, uno quodam* Societatis
*vinculo contineri, ubi enim perspecta vis est rationis ejus, qua causae rerum, atque
exitus cognoscuntur, merus quidam quasi omnium consensus doctrinarum, con-
centusque reperitur.*   Cicero de Oratore, *Lib.* 3.[1]

Ὅστις μὴ ἀσπάζεται τὴν ζωγραφίαν, ἀδικεῖ τὴν ἀλήθειαν, ἀδικεῖ δὲ καὶ
σοφίαν, ὁπόση ἐς ποιητὰς ἥκει – φορὰ γὰρ ἴση ἀμφοῖν ἐς τὰ τῶν ἡρώων εἴδη
καὶ ἔργα – ξυμμετρίαν τε οὐκ ἐπαινεῖ, δι᾽ ἣν καὶ λόγου ἡ τέχνη ἅπτεται.
Philostrati Imagines.[2]

LONDON:
Printed for the AUTHOR; and sold by A. MILLAR, at *Buchanan's* Head,
over-against St. *Clement's* Church, in the *Strand.*
M.DDC.XL.

To

The RIGHT HONOURABLE

HENRY

Lord Viscount *Lonsdale,* &c.[3]

This TREATISE is humbly dedicated

By his LORDSHIP's
Most Devoted,
and Obedient Servant,

GEORGE TURNBULL. <v>

---

3. Henry Lowther (1694–1751), third Viscount Lonsdale and Lord Lieutenant of Cumberland and Westmorland.

An Epistle

To the Right Honourable the Lord Viscount
Lonsdale, Upon Education, and the Design of this
Essay on Painting, &c.

My Lord,

I Should not have adventur'd to dedicate this Essay to your Lordship did it aim at nothing higher (as some may imagine from the Title) than merely to recommend to our Youth a Taste in Painting as an ingenious and innocent Amusement. That Art is indeed discoursed of at great length in this Treatise; but in such a manner as affords me full room to give my Sentiments, or rather the Sentiments of some of the greatest Men of Antiquity concerning Education. A Subject, my Lord, of the highest Importance, and to the mature Consideration of which your real Love of Mankind, and sincere Concern for their Happiness, must have often led your penetrating Mind.

In shewing wherein the real Excellence of Painting consists, and the happy use that was or might be made of it in forming Youth to Virtue and a good Taste of all the Arts; I am naturally led to animadvert upon several Mistakes in Education; and to shew the necessity of combining in it all the Liberal Arts and Sciences, in order to accomplish most successfully its acknowledged End; which is to form and improve betimes in young Minds the Love of true Knowledge, and the Love of Society, Mankind, and Virtue; and to instil into them at the same time a right Notion of the better ways of explaining, recommending, embellishing or enforcing upon the Mind any Truth, or any Virtue; one or other of which must be the End of *Language* of whatever sort; that is, of every Art that pretends to instruct or move us.

335

So thoroughly, my Lord, am I convinced of the Usefulness of the Design that runs throughout the whole of this Essay, which is humbly offered to your Lordship by a Heart that often indulges itself with the highest delight in admiration of Parts and Virtues united together, which I am not here allowed to be so particular upon as I could wish: So fully, my Lord, do I feel the Importance of the Scope that is chiefly kept in view throughout the following Treatise, that I would gladly take advantage of the noble Image now before me; and entering upon that Subject here, make an Experiment on myself of a Rule prescribed by many ancient Writers as verify'd in their own Experience. Would you, say they, attain to a kind of Inspiration in handling any Subject; imagine you are speaking <vi> or writing to one who thoroughly understands it; has it fully at heart; and like whom you would chuse to be able to think and express your Sentiments: And then let your Thoughts flow freely, as you are warm'd and directed by that pleasing, elevating Fancy. I am sufficiently authorised, my Lord, by ancient Examples to set forth the Moment of my Design, and the Truth of the Principles upon which it is built, in this kind of Dedication: And I dare not presume to address your Lordship in the modern way of Panegyrick, though I am sure every one will say, that in order to draw the most amiable Character, all that is necessary on this occasion is to hit the Likeness, and to paint a true one.

'Tis impossible, my Lord, to reflect one moment upon Human Nature without perceiving, that its right or wrong State depends as necessarily upon Education, as that of a Plant upon proper Culture. Though Man be essentially different from every merely mechanical Being that never acts, but is in all cases passive, or moved by Springs and Causes absolutely independent of it; because Man hath an active Principle in his Frame, and a certain Sphere of Power or Dominion assigned to him by Nature, in virtue of which, many Operations and Effects, both within and without his Mind, are dependent as to their Existence or Non-existence upon his own Will: Tho' this be as certain as Consciousness can render any Fact; yet our acting well or ill, the right or wrong Exercise of our several Powers must depend upon the Principles and Habits we have early imbib'd and contracted, for these make us what we are; these constitute our Temper and Disposition; by them we are moved and influenced in all our Choices and Pursuits.

Wherefore not to think of modelling these aright in Education, is to neglect the only End it pretends to have in view, which is to mould us into a good Form or Temper. To give a wrong Cast to them by Education is to employ the forming Art to mishape, and deform or deprave us. The Business of Education is by cultivating and perfecting all our Powers and Affections, all our Faculties, and all the Movements by which we are set to work, to make Man such as he ought to be; that is, such as his greatest Dignity and Happiness require he should be: Or, in other words, to instil into him such Principles, and to form within him such Desires, Affections and Habits as will lead him right in all his Pursuits and Employments; and to inure him to such Exercises of his Powers and Faculties as will render them most vigorous; most serviceable to himself and to Society on every occasion.

RIGHT Education, if it be not the one thing needful, it is at least absolutely necessary to private or publick Happiness. The best Laws without proper care about it are Mockery: They may ensnare Men, but they can go but little way in restraining them; and none at all in forming or mending them: Whereas proper Education would in a great measure prevent the necessity of Laws and their Sanctions, by framing betimes a right Disposition in us that would naturally, and as it were necessarily produce what good Laws can only command. If the moving Powers, or Springs of Motion, and all the Wheels be sound and right, all must go well in moral Nature as well as in Mechanism.

EVERY one who hath the Perfection and Happiness of Mankind so sincerely at heart as your Lordship, must have often reflected upon the great End of Education, and the proper Methods of gaining that End; and consequently must have wondered to find a very powerful and exceeding useful Principle in our Make intirely overlooked in it, as if it had no-<vii>thing to do with our Constitution; and that is, the Influence of Habits early formed. This is the more surprizing, because the Reality and Strength of this Principle in our Natures is so universally acknowledged, that in every Nation it is and always has been a vulgar Proverb, That Custom is a second Nature. The Power of Habit is readily owned by all: But what is done, my Lord, in the forming Art that is sounded upon this Principle; or what proper means are used conformably to this acknowledged Truth, early to establish good Habits in young Minds, either in respect of Instruction or Discipline?

THE Whole of Education must consist in the Formation of right Habits: For what we call Temper is nothing else but natural Propensions formed by repeated Exercises into strong and lasting Habits. Every Affection, every Power, and every Propension must be originally of Nature: Art cannot create: All it can do is to cultivate and perfect what Nature hath planted: But 'tis Art and repeated Exercise that work natural Powers into Strength, or natural Affections into Temper. Some proper Discipline or Regimen is therefore necessary to accomplish the principal Scope of Education, if to produce virtuous Habits be such. And what can be justly called cultivating and improving Understanding or Reason, but forming one by proper Exercise into the considerative Temper, or the Habit of deliberating and computing before one chuses or acts? 'Tis certainly Pleasure and Pain that move us: Nothing can be the Object of Affection or Desire but Pleasure; or, on the other hand, the Object of Aversion and Dislike but Pain. Pleasures of Sense, of Contemplation, of Sentiment, of Self-approbation, and their Opposites, are all but so many different sorts of Pleasures and Pains. And let Metaphysicians debate and wrangle as long as they will, this must necessarily be true, and be no more than an identical Proposition, that what is pleasing is pleasing, and that Pleasure alone can be pleasant. But it is Reason's Business to examine, compute and ballance Pleasures and Pains of all kinds: And then is Reason well formed; or formed into a really useful Principle, when the Mind hath acquired the Habit of computing before it acts; and of computing readily as well as truly: Which Habit or Temper can only be attained by inuring the Mind betimes to think and reason before it acts, that is, to compare and ballance Pleasures and Pains before it chuses.

Now in forming this Habit, which not only constitutes the wise but the free Man, there are two things to be taken care of. One is to inure Youth to reason, or compute from Experience only; that is, from Facts ascertained by Observation, and not from abstract, imaginary Theories and Hypotheses. The other is to inure them to imploy their Reason chiefly about those Objects and Connexions in Nature, which have the nearest relation to human Life and Happiness. In order to both which 'tis manifest, that they ought to be taught to take a just View of human Nature, and to consider Man as he really is, neither as a merely sensitive Being, nor as a merely moral one; but as a compound of moral and sensitive Powers and Affections. For in the human Make those Powers and Affections are so blended together, that it is impossible to avoid Errors concerning Man's Duties or Interests, if any of them are considered separately, that is, independently of the rest.

IT were easy, my Lord, to point out several false Doctrines that take their Rise from dividing those constituent Parts of our Frame from one another, which are really inseparable in the Nature of things. To mention <viii> no other Instance at present: Hence, I think, it is that some have railed in such a vague, undetermined manner against Luxury, as if all Pleasures ought to be despised by wise and good Men, and therefore banished from human Society, but those that are absolutely necessary to our Subsistence; or those that produce Enjoyment and Satisfaction of the very noblest kind. In the general, confused way of declaiming against Luxury, all the Pleasures of Imagination, and all the ornamental Arts are damn'd as absolutely super-fluous, and as unworthy of our Attention in any degree: Nay Cleanliness, not to say, Elegance, is condemned and interdicted, as if Nature had given Man Eyes, Ears, and other Senses, with a natural Taste and Relish of Pro-portion, Beauty, and Harmony, to no purpose.

THE happy Consequence of inuring Youth to reason from Experience alone; and to reason first and chiefly about those things that have the nearest relation to Life, and with which it is therefore our Interest to be very early acquainted, would be, that the natural Desire of Knowledge, which is im-planted in us on purpose to impel us to seek after that Science, which is as necessary to guide our Conduct, as Light is to shew us our Road, would not be misled into a way of gratifying itself by Enquiries quite remote from the practice of the World. And I am apt to imagine, my Lord, that more are ignorant of Life, and quite Strangers to the World and human Affairs, in consequence of employing their Minds about Objects that have little or no concern with Men and Things, than through mere Stupidity or Want of Capacity. It is false Learning that is the most dangerous Enemy to the true, or that most effectually supplants it. Nothing therefore is of greater Importance in Education, than to render Youth betimes capable of distin-guishing useful Enquiries, from those that ought only to have the place of Amusements, like a Game at Chess or Piquet: And for that reason it would be of more consequence to exercise young People in often reviewing, with attention, a well-calculated Table of Arts and Sciences, in respect of their different degrees of Utility, than any other Categories or Arrangements of Ideas whatsoever, that are called Logick in the Schools, though such likewise may have their use.[4]

BUT at the same time that the Habit of reasoning well and readily is formed by inuring Youth to Reason; the Faculty of expressing known Truths clearly and strongly may be likewise acquired. It is necessary that a Teacher should take the most gradual, regular, clear, and full Method of explaining and proving Truths; or that he should proceed step by step with his Scholars: And therefore that didactick Art will of course be learned by them at the same time that Knowledge itself is acquired in that way. But there is an *Eloquence* of another kind that ought not to be neglected in the Formation of Youth; and that would soon be attained by them, were but this one Rule observed in Education, to inure Students after they have been led to the Knowledge of any Truth in the didactick way, to find out the properest Methods of expressing it concisely and strongly; or of giving a convincing, emphatical View of it in few Words. This last would be teaching them the Language in which Men ought to speak to Men about the same Truths that can only be conveyed into raw, unformed Minds in a more slow and tedious manner. After young People understand any Truth, it is neither unpleasant nor unprofitable; but on the contrary it is very fit to employ them in considering how several celebrated Authors have chosen to represent it in different Lights, each according to his own Genius; or in order to adapt it to some particular Cast of Understanding; and then in vying with them in finding out other ways of <ix> expressing the same Truth with due Force and Perspicuity. But we commonly begin in Education with Words, as if there were any other way of trying or judging Words and Phrases, or Signs of any kind, but by examining whether they are proper Expressions of the Truths they are intended to signify; whether they are equal, superiour, or inferiour to other Expressions of the same Truths in respect of the sole End of Language, which is to convey Senti-

4. Compare George Turnbull, *Observations upon Liberal Education in all its Branches,* edited by Terrence O. Moore Jr. (Indianapolis, 2003), p. 385. Much of what Turnbull says about education in this dedicatory epistle reappears in a more elaborate form in the *Observations upon Liberal Education,* which appeared in 1742.

ments with Clearness and Efficacy. The chief thing indeed is to have just
or true Sentiments; that is, to have right Apprehensions of Nature: But that
Knowledge may take fast hold of our Minds, dwell with us and afford us
variety of delight; and that we may be capable of imparting it to others, so
as to render it the Source of manifold Entertainment, as well as of Information to them; the various proper ways of proving, embellishing, and
enforcing Truths must be taught and studied. And therefore in proportion
as one acquires Knowledge, he ought likewise to learn Languages; or to be
made acquainted with all the better ways of evincing and impressing any
Truths on the Mind.

I may be thought by some perhaps to take Language in a very uncommon
Sense. But that I have used it in its justest, as well as its most comprehensive
Meaning, will be obvious to every one who but reflects, that there can be
but two Objects of human Inquiry, Truths themselves, that is, real Con-
nexions in Nature or Facts; and the various manners of making Truths
understood and felt. Whence it plainly follows, that the didactick Style,
Oratory, Poetry, and likewise all the Arts of Design, Painting, Statuary and
Sculpture, fall properly under the Idea of Language. And therefore if right
Education ought to teach and instruct in Truths, and in the various good
Methods or Arts of conveying Truths into the Mind; no sooner is one led
into the Discovery of any Truth, than he ought to be imploved in comparing and examining several different ways by which it may be unfolded,
proved, embellished, and enforced by Oratory, Poetry, or Painting. For to
apply this general Observation to Painting, which is commonly reckoned
so remote from Philosophy; nothing is more evident than, that Pictures
which neither convey into the Mind Ideas of sensible Laws, and their Effects and Appearances, nor moral Truths, that is, moral Sentiments and
corresponding Affections, have no Meaning at all: They convey nothing,
because there is nothing else to be conveyed. But, on the other hand, such
Pictures as answer any of these Ends, must for that reason speak a Language,
the Correctness, Strength, Purity and Beauty of which it must be well
worth while to understand as a Language: More especially since there is
indeed no other way of trying the Propriety, Force and Beauty of a poetical
Image, but by considering the Picture it forms in the Imagination, as a
Picture.

ALL the instructing or moving Arts considered in this light, that is, as so many Methods of conveying Truths agreeably or strongly into the Mind; or of exciting our Affections by means of Ideas fitted to move them, must belong to Education, and ought to be employed by Philosophy every step it makes. For several such Arts being compared together, must naturally conspire to give a juster Notion of the supreme Beauty and Excellence of any Language, in consequence of the sole End common to all Languages, than can be acquired by any of them, if separately studied: And being combined, they must necessarily have a multiplied Force in impressing any piece of Knowledge on the Mind. <x>

ONE great Error then in modern Education consists in imagining that Philosophy, Rhetorick, Poetry, and the other Arts ought to be taught separately; whereas in reality it is Philosophy or the Knowledge of Nature that ought to be taught; and the proper way of giving a just Notion of Oratory, Poetry, and the other Arts of illustrating, embellishing and impressing Truths, is by shewing every step Philosophy advances, what these Languages have done, or may do to exhibit and enforce any Truth with all its Effects and Consequences. And this, my Lord, is what I have endeavoured to illustrate in the following Essay.

BUT, my Lord, if to separate the instructing or moving Arts from Philosophy be a very detrimental mistake in Education, since it divides Languages from Things; must it not be yet a more pernicious one to sever moral from natural Philosophy; or not to carry on our Enquiries about Man and his Relations and Connexions in Nature (which is moral Philosophy) in the same manner, and conjunctly with our Enquiries into the Laws and Connexions of the sensible World, (the Knowledge of which is called natural Philosophy) as one continued Research into Fact and Truth, or into real Connexions in the same united System: And that with a practical View, or in order to observe what useful Maxims and Rules for human Life and Society may be inferred from any Discovery made in that Science? On the one hand, every Discovery in Nature that may be rendered subservient to the Use or Ornament of Society really adds to Man's Property and Dominion in Nature: And whatever Knowledge is conducive to the good of Mankind, is in effect moral Science. On the other hand, every Enquiry about the Constitution of the human Mind, is as much a question of Fact or natural History, as Enquiries about Objects of Sense are: It must therefore be managed and carried on in the same way of Experiment; and in the one case as well as in the other, nothing ought to be admitted as fact, till it is clearly found to be such from unexceptionable Experience and Observation. He who hath the real good of Society ever before his Eyes in his Studies, certainly imploys his Understanding to a very useful Purpose, and from a very laudable Motive: Such a one will let no Truth, he may find out, escape him, without enquiring most strictly what advantage may be derived from it to Mankind; and he will value his Discoveries proportionably. And Man being a compound Creature, *nexus utriusque mundi*,[5] (as he is called by some Philosophers) the Knowledge of the natural World is not less requisite to his Happiness than that of the moral. All the Necessities and Conveniencies of Life and Society require the Science of natural Connexions as well as of moral ones. Nay, to study human Nature can be nothing else but to enquire into that nice blending and intermingling of natural and moral Parts by which it is constituted: And Conclusions deduced from moral Powers and Affections, considered apart from sensitive ones, cannot make *Human Morality,* if Man really is a moral Being, intimately related to and connected with the Laws of the sensible World. An exact Theory of Morals can only be formed from a full and accurate Review of the various natural Principles or natural Dispositions of Mankind, as these stand related to one another, and to surrounding Objects. And indeed one cannot reflect upon the great Improvements that have been made in Philosophy, in all its Parts, since it hath been cultivated in the obvious and only way of pursuing it, without promising to one's self a very happy Enlargement of moral Philosophy, so soon as it shall be pursued in the same manner; that is, as Philosophers shall endeavour in the later, as they have done in the former, to find out from Experience, Analogies, Agreements and Harmonies of Phaenomena; or, <xi> in other words, to reduce Appearances to

5. Literally, "a binding of both worlds," namely the material and immaterial, or physical and spiritual; compare Turnbull, *The Principles of Moral and Christian Philosophy,* I:118. For a use of the phrase known to Turnbull that well illustrates its meaning in the early eighteenth century see *The Spectator,* No. 519, 25 October 1712, p. 349; this issue of *The Spectator* was subsequently republished in Joseph Addison, *The Evidences of the Christian Religion* (London, 1730), where the phrase appears on p. 125.

general Laws. That the Knowledge of Nature, of human Nature in particular, is yet so very imperfect, is certainly owing to dividing or severing natural and moral Philosophy from one another; or to our not giving due Application to collect from Experience the general Laws to which Phaenomena of the moral sort are reducible, in like manner as several Phaenomena of the sensible World have been reduced to a few simple general Laws, which have at the same time been found to be wisely and fitly established in respect of the Good and Order they produce; for all Phaenomena of whatever sort can only be explained or accounted for in that way: All that Explication of Phaenomena can mean, is the reducing them to some general Law or Principle: And therefore all other Attempts towards the Advancement of real Knowledge are to no purpose.

IN consequence of the View that hath been briefly delineated of Philosophy and Languages, it is manifest, that the right way of teaching true Philosophy, must be teaching at the same time Science and Languages: And therefore it must be forming at the same time Reason, Imagination, and Temper. 'Tis plainly forming Reason to discover or prove Truths, and Imagination to embellish and enforce, that is, to paint them. And that it is forming the Temper, is no less obvious, since Temper means nothing else but certain Affections worked into Habits, or become as such the Bent and Disposition of our Mind. But Affections can only be wrought into Habit or Temper by being often exercised and worked; and the Exercisers or Workers are Sentiments duly conveyed and enforced by Reason and Imagination.

THIS is yet more evident when we consider, that what is principal with respect to Reason in Education, is, as hath been said, to form betimes that deliberating, computing Temper by which the Mind becomes Master of itself, and able to resist all the most inviting Promises and Solicitations of Objects, till their Pretensions have been fairly canvassed. This Temper is what is properly called Virtue or Strength of Mind: without it one must be feeble and unsteady, unable to act a reasonable or becoming part in Life; nay, the Sport of contradictory Passions and Appetites. It is by it alone that one can attain to that Harmony and Consistency of Affections and Manners which create Peace and Joy within, and command Respect and Love from all around; even from the most Dissolute and Vitious; for Nature can never be rendered quite insensible to the Beauty and Charms of wise and good Conduct.

A due Consideration of those Maxims will naturally lead every thinking Person to discover Absurdities of many kinds in Education, that no doubt have frequently come a-cross your Lordship's Mind. Hence we may see the Error of the famous *Lycurgus,* since his manner of Education neither served to produce a right Temper, nor a sufficient variety of Genius, or consequently of Happiness in Society; but, on the contrary, tended to make Men savage and ferocious, and at the same time cunning and deceitful; and to exclude from human Life many excellent Virtues and agreeable Affections, as well as Philosophy, and all the fine Arts.[6]

HENCE we may see, on the other hand, the Error in *Athenian* Education; the Youth there being more employed about Languages than Things. Whence it was that *Athens* was so over-run with that Deluge of Sophistry, which *Socrates* was continually opposing; and that too many <xii> applied themselves to the embellishing Arts, or the Arts of Imagination, in proportion to the number of those who applied to the Study of Nature; or to drawing Consequences from the real Knowledge of Nature for use and practice in Life, and to be the Objects of the imitative and ornamental Arts. Whence proceeded in a great measure the fatal Abuse, Degeneracy and Corruption of the fine Arts among them, before the *Romans,* who had these Arts from *Greece,* gave any attention to them.

HENCE likewise appears the necessity of treating Morals in another way than *Puffendorf, Grotius,* and most other celebrated modern Doctors of moral Philosophy have done;[7] since their Conclusions (tho' they be

6. On the system of education in the ancient republic of Sparta compare Turnbull, *Observations upon Liberal Education,* pp. 95–96. Turnbull's view of Lycurgus echoes that of Charles Rollin, who in turn was indebted to Plato and Aristotle. See Charles Rollin, *The Method of Teaching and Studying the Belles Lettres, or an Introduction to Languages, Poetry, Rhetoric, History, Moral Philosophy, Physicks, &c.,* 4 vols. (London, 1734), III:325; Plato, *Laws,* esp. 666e–667a, and Aristotle, *Politics,* 1271b, 1333b–1334b 7, 1338b.

7. Hugo Grotius (1583–1645) and Samuel Pufendorf (1632–94), whose works on natural law provided the framework for the teaching of moral philosophy in the Scottish universities during the late seventeenth and eighteenth centuries. Turnbull here criti-

generally true) are neither deduced from a right, that is, a full View of the human Constitution, and our Relations and Connexions in Nature; nor are moral Doctrines explained and enforced in their Writings by the properest Terms of Expression: On the contrary, all insinuating, beautifying, and captivating Lights in which moral Truths may be represented, that at once enlighten and warm the Mind, are rather avoided by them. I can't help, my Lord, observing one thing farther on this Subject, that if one may reason at all from Authorities in Morals, as those Writers chiefly do, the properest way of reasoning from Authorities about Morals would be by shewing; that almost all the Truths which relate more immediately to human Life and good moral Conduct are so evident, that in all Ages and in all Countries they have been converted into Proverbs or familiar Sayings; and, which is very surprizing, they have been expressed very nearly by the same Images in all Countries, notwithstanding all the Diversities of Genius, Temperament, and Language that have prevailed in the World. Whence it would appear how common, how universal good Sense is, and always hath been.

ANOTHER Error in Education is no less manifest from what hath been said, which is, that it is not contrived in order to explore, and give free Scope and suitable Culture to all different Genius's. Education is generally carried on in the same uniform way, without any regard to the natural variety of Genius amongst Mankind; as if it were done on purpose to disappoint the kind Intention of Nature in diversifying Men's Dispositions and Talents: At least, proper Measures are not taken in Education to invite different Genius's to disclose themselves; or after they are known to give suitable Culture to each that appears, in order to improve it to its natural Perfection and useful End. Diversity of Genius amongst Men is however no less necessary to the Enlargement of human Happiness and Perfection in the Sum of things, than variety of Herbs and Plants is to the Beauty and Utility of the sensible World. And sure it is not more absurd to propose one way of training and forming all young People, than to think of one sort of Culture for all kinds of Vegetables.

---

cizes the manner in which he was obliged to teach moral philosophy while he was a regent at Marischal College Aberdeen.

THERE is another Diversity among Mankind that is as little attended to in forming Youth as that just mentioned; the remarkable variety amongst us in respect of different Propensities to certain Affections. And yet this later Diversity, if it be not quite inseparable from the former, is no less requisite than it to the End of Nature in making Man, which is the general Good of the Kind. Some are naturally hot and fiery, others are cold and phlegmatick; some are prone to Anger, some to Love, some to Ambition, and others to Quiet and Ease; some, in one word, to one Passion, and some to another: And all these Varieties are so many different Seeds that require each its peculiar Culture; and which might, each by <xiii> proper Methods of Education, be improved into that useful Temper of which it is the natural Seed or first Principle. Nature doth nothing in vain, whether in the material or moral World: Whatever Foundations it hath laid for Art to work upon, are well intended. And as Art and Culture can only perfect what Nature hath begun; so the Improvement of natural Faculties and Dispositions being wisely left to ourselves, to neglect the due Culture of any Power, Quality, or Affection Nature hath formed in human Breasts, is to despise, or at least to over-look its kind and generous Provision for our extensive Happiness in the best way of providing for us; which is by furnishing us with a proper variety of Materials and Talents for our own Cultivation and Improvement into Goods.

FROM what hath been said, it is sufficiently evident in general, what ought to be the chief Aim of Instruction; and how it ought to be managed in order to perfect our Faculties of Reason and Imagination, and to produce betimes in our Minds good and useful Habits. And at the same time it is obvious, that teaching cannot be sufficient, but that some early Discipline or Regimen is absolutely necessary to gain the principal End of Education; since it is by proper practice alone that any Virtue can be rendered habitual to the Mind; or be early confirmed into Temper.

HAVING thus, my Lord, laid open some Errors in Education, I wish I were able to propose a proper Scheme of it: But that requires a masterly Projector, a very expert moral Architect. All I am capable of doing is to throw aside some Rubbish; and shew the Foundations upon which the noble Building must be raised: [8] That Building which would effectually make human Society happy; or at least without which it is impossible, Men can arrive at that Perfection and Happiness Nature plainly intended them for; but left to themselves to build, that they might have the Satisfaction of considering it as their own Acquisition. We are certainly designed by our Maker for whatever Dignity and Happiness we are qualified to attain to by the proper Exercise of our natural Powers and Affections. And as that alone, which is so acquired, is moral Perfection, Virtue or Merit, and alone can afford the Pleasure of Self-approbation; so Mankind's being made able to arrive at their highest Perfection and Happiness only by their united Force, is the necessary Basis of social Union, and of all the noble Enjoyments resulting from social Intercourse and well-form'd Government.

IF any one thinks meanly of our Frame and Rank, let him seriously consider the Riches and Fullness that appears in Nature as far as we can extend our Enquiries; and how every Being in the Scale of Life within our Observation rises in due degree: Let him then consider how necessary the Existence of such a Species as Man is to the ascending Plenitude of Nature; to its *Fullness and Coherence;* and let him impartially examine our Constitution, and the Provision made for our Happiness; the Excellence to which our natural Powers and Dispositions may be improved and raised by good Education and proper Diligence; or the Dignity and Felicity to which we may attain by the Study of Wisdom and Virtue, especially in well-regulated Society; for he will plainly see, that though there be good reason to think that there are various Orders of rational Beings in the Scale of Existence, the lowest of which is superiour to Man, yet he is crowned with Glory and Honour, is well placed, and hath a very considerable Dominion allotted to him: Let him attentively consider several glorious Characters <xiv> in History: Or rather let him turn his Eyes with me towards a living Example of Worth and Greatness, to have a place in whose Esteem is indeed Merit, that cannot be reflected upon, without

8. An echo of "The Epistle to the Reader" in John Locke, *An Essay concerning Human Understanding,* edited by Peter H. Nidditch (Oxford: Clarendon Press, 1975), pp. 9–10. Turnbull went on to provide such a scheme in his *Observations upon Liberal Education.*

feeling a noble Ambition more and more to deserve it; nor declared to the Publick without bringing one's self under the strongest Obligations to take particular care of one's Conduct. I am,

My Lord,

Your Lordship's

Most Obedient,

Humble Servant,

London, Ap. 25.
1739.

George Turnbull. <xv>

A Preface, concerning Education, Travelling, and the Fine Arts

A Preface is now generally expected, and I fall in more readily with that established Custom, because it gives me an opportunity of premising something to the following Treatise that is by no means improper or unnecessary.

THOUGH one of the principal Ends I proposed to myself in this *Essay on Painting,* &c. be to prepare young Travellers for seeing Statues, Sculptures, and Pictures to better advantage than they can possibly do if they have not previously turned their Thoughts a little that way; Yet I am far from thinking it the chief Design of Travel to examine the Productions of the Fine Arts even with the greatest Accuracy, or in the most intelligent, philosophical manner; and much less in order to become an *Antiquary* or *Virtuoso,* in the common Acceptation of that Character; or to see the Remains of ancient Arts very superficially, and to set up for a Critick of them upon so slight a Foundation.

THERE are Subjects of a more important Nature than Paintings and Sculptures, in whatever light they are considered, that ought principally to employ the Thoughts of a Traveller, who has it in his View to qualify himself for the Service of his own Country, by visiting foreign ones. But one Point aimed at in this Treatise is to shew how mean, insipid, and trifling the fine Arts are when they are quite alienated from their better and nobler, genuine Purposes, which, as well as those of their Sister Poetry, are truly philosophical and moral: that is, to convey in an agreeable manner into the Mind the Knowledge of Men and Things; or to instruct us in Morality, Virtue, and human Nature. And it necessarily follows, that the chief Design of travelling must be somewhat of greater moment than barely to learn how to distinguish an original Medal from a counterfeit one, a *Greek* from a *Roman* Statue, or one Painter's Hand from another's; since it is here proved, that even with regard to the Arts of Design that kind of Knowledge is but idle and trivial; and that by it alone one has no better title to the Character of a Person of good Taste in them, than a mere verbal Critick hath to that of a polite Scholar in the Classicks.

LET us consider a little the pretended Reasons for sending young Gentlemen to travel: They may be reduced to these two. "That they may see the Remains of ancient Arts, and the best Productions of modern Sculptors and Painters"; and "That they may see the World and study Mankind."

NOW as for the first, how it should be offered as a Reason for sending young Gentlemen abroad, is indeed very unaccountable, when one considers upon what footing Education is amongst us at present; unless it could be thought that one may be jolted by an *Italian* Chaise into the Knowledge and Taste that are evidently prerequisite to travelling with advantage, even in that view; or that <xvi> such Intelligence is the necessary, mechanical Effect of a certain Climate upon the Understanding; and will be instantaneously infused into one at his Arrival on Classick Ground. For in our present Method of educating young Gentlemen either in publick Schools or by private Tutors, what is done that can in any degree prepare them for making proper and useful Reflexions upon the fine Arts, and their Performances? Are not the Arts of Design quite sever'd in modern Education not only from Philosophy, their Connexion with which is not so obvious, or at least so generally acknowledged; but likewise from classical Studies, where not only their Usefulness must be readily owned by all who have the slightest Notion of them, but where the want of proper Helps from ancient Statues, Bas-reliefs and Paintings for understanding ancient Authors, the Poets in particular, is daily felt by Teachers and Students? It is not more ridiculous to dream of one's acquiring a strange Language merely by sucking in foreign Air, than to imagine that those who never have been directed at home into the right manner of considering the fine Arts; those who have no Idea of their true Beauty, Scope, and Excellence (not to mention such as have not the least notion of Drawing) that such should all at once so soon as they tread *Italian* Soil become immediately capable of understanding these Arts, and of making just Reflexions upon their excellent Productions. And yet this is plainly the case with regard to the greater part of our young Travellers.

And for that reason I have endeavoured in the following Essay to lead young Gentlemen and those concerned in their Education, into a juster Notion of the Fine Arts than is commonly entertained even by the Plurality of their professed Admirers; by distinguishing the fine Taste of them from the false Learning that too frequently passes for it; and by shewing in what respects alone the Study of them belongs to Gentlemen, whose high Birth and Fortune call them to the most Important of all Studies; that, of Men, Manners and Things, or Virtue and publick Good. And this I have attempted to do by setting to view the Opinions which some of the greatest Men of all Ages have had of their truest Excellence and best Scope; and not by Arguments of my own Devise; or for which I have no better Authority than my own Judgment.

As for the other principal End of Travel, commonly comprehended under the general Phrase of seeing the World, and acquiring the Knowledge of Mankind, it is a Subject that requires a much more comprehensive Knowledge of the World than I can pretend to, to treat it as it ought to be. Having however in the following Discourse on Painting shewn, what Notions some very great Men, of ancient Times in particular, entertained of that Art; and having made the best use I could of their Sentiments and Reasonings about the fine Arts, to set them in a due light; I shall just remark here, with regard to travelling, that ancient Philosophers, Legislators, Patriots and Politicians thought Travel necessary, and accordingly travelled. But why did they travel; or at what time of Life did they set about it? They travelled after they were Men of Reading and Experience; and they travelled to see different States and to acquire more Experience in human Affairs; or a more extensive Knowledge of Mankind. And indeed he who hath been in the World, and rightly understands what knowing the World means, he, and he alone is qualified for travelling. Seeing the World is a very familiar Phrase; it is almost in every one's mouth. But how few distinctly comprehend its full Import and Signification? The Ancients travelled to see different Countries, and to have thereby Opportunities of making solid Reflexions upon various Governments, Laws, Customs and Policies, and their Effects and Consequences with regard to the Happiness or Misery of States, in order to import with them into their own Country, Knowledge founded on Fact and <xvii> Observation, from which, as from a Treasure of Things new and old, sure and solid Rules and Maxims might be brought forth for their Country's Benefit on every Emergency. For this is certain, that the real Knowledge of Mankind can no more be acquired by abstract Speculation without studying human Nature itself in its many various Forms and Appearances, than the real Knowledge of the material World by framing imaginary Hypotheses and Theories, without looking into Nature itself: And no less variety of Observations is necessary to infer or establish general Rules and Maxims in the one than in the other Philosophy. But how can one be supposed fit for such serious and profound Employment, before he hath very clear and distinct Ideas of Government and Laws, and of the Interests of Society; or who by previous Education hath not been put into the way of making Reflexions on those useful Subjects?

I have often heard a very young Nobleman[9] (the Advantage of whose uncommon Parts, and equal Virtues, may his Family, his Friends, and his Country long continue to enjoy) remark abroad, "That though all our young Gentlemen of Fortune are sent to travel at a certain Age, promiscuously or without distinction; yet it is very easy to find out whether one be fit for travelling or not; since he alone is so, who takes pleasure in reading History, not merely for his Amusement, but in order to lay up in his Mind truly useful Knowledge; and who, after having been inured for a considerable time to such a serious and profitable Train of deep-thinking about Men and Things; and having thus conceived a clear Notion of the things to be observed and enquired into in his Travels in any foreign Country, is able to form to himself a proper Plan of Travels, in order to accomplish some manly, rational Design." Such only are qualified to travel: Before such a Turn of Mind be well established by Reading, Conversation, and some Practice in the World, it is as absurd to send one abroad to study Mankind, as to think of coming at Perfection in any Science without the Knowledge of its Elements or first Principles. It is really like employing one to measure without a Standard, or count without Arithmetick.

IN order to travel with Advantage through any foreign Country, one ought to have not only a very full Knowledge of the Laws, Constitution,

9. Probably Thomas Watson (1715–46), who subsequently became the 3rd Earl of Rockingham; see above, p. xiii.

History and Interests of his own Country, (which is seldom the case); but he ought likewise to have as full and thorough a Knowledge of that foreign Country he intends to visit, as can be learned at home from Books and Conversation: And he ought certainly to have very just and well-digested Notions of Government, and civil Policy, and its Ends: Otherwise he goes indeed abroad not knowing whither he goes, or what he goes to see; without any Scheme; and absolutely unqualified to compare, or make right Judgments of Men and Things.

IF Parents send their Sons so young abroad, for no other reason but merely that they may be for some time out of their sight, (I wish it could be likewise said, that they sent them out of Harm's way) in such a case is it to be wondered at, that young Gentlemen go abroad without any other view but to make use of their Distance from all Checks, to fling themselves headlong into Pleasure, and give full swing to their Appetites; and that thus they bring back with them broken Constitutions, and a worse Habit of Mind?

IF young Gentlemen are early sent abroad for any of the inferiour Parts of Liberal Education, there must be great Defects in our own at home, which ought <xviii> to be remedied, in order to put an end to a Necessity so risquous, in whatever View we take of it. If the Exercises are so necessary to compleat Education, that young Gentlemen are sent very young into *France* on that account, (and certain genteel, manly Exercises are undoubtedly requisite to form a fine Gentleman) why have we them not in our own Schools and Universities in their proper Place and Season? [10]

IT cannot be said, that it is to learn Good-manners and a polite Mien and Carriage, that our young Gentlemen must be sent so early into *France,* without doing injustice to our own Fair Sex, by Conversation with whom they would quickly be polished into a Behaviour far preferable to that contracted abroad. 'Tis no doubt owing to our sending our Youth to be polished in *France* into genteel, pretty Behaviour (as it is called) a Complement that has been paid to that Nation by the *British* in particular, too, too long, that the *French* are the only People in the World who have the very extraordinary

---

10. On the importance of such "exercises" as fencing, dancing, and horse riding for a liberal education see Turnbull, *Observations upon Liberal Education,* pp. 293–300.

Politeness to tell all Strangers, that they alone understand *Le sçavoir vivre;*[11] and the *Commerce de la vie.*[12] That surely cannot be the reason for sending young Gentlemen betimes into Country-Towns in *France,* since it is well known how awkward the People of the best Fashion at *Caen, Angers,* or *Besançon,* for instance, appear to the Court-bred at *Versailles* or *Paris,* the Center of *French* Politeness. 'Tis the Fair Sex in every Country that is the Source of good Breeding, and that regulates genteel Manners: And thanks to our untravelled Ladies for their better Notion of a fine Gentleman; since it is chiefly by their means that any of our young Travellers who return from *France* Fops and Coxcombs, are ever recovered from their *French* Fluttering, Volatility, and Impertinence, and restored to that native Plainness and Seriousness of the *British;* of which, if ever we become generally ashamed, all that is Grave and Great amongst us, and that exalts us above every slavish Country, must be on the Brink of Ruin.

If it is said, that they are sent early into *France* to learn the *French* Language, that they may have a Tongue to travel with afterwards; I shall only say, that very many have acquired in consequence of a right Education at home, not only *French* but *Italian,* to a very great degree of Perfection, without having neglected Languages of greater Usefulness, by the Help of which they may early imbibe Sentiments much better becoming a free People, than they can from *French* or *Italian* Authors: Sentiments that will best serve to maintain Love of Liberty and publick Spirit in that due Vigour necessary to uphold a free Constitution. And there are, on the other hand, but few Examples of very great Progress made abroad in *France* in the *French* Language, by such as had not made considerable Advances in it before they left their own Country.

Tho' it appears from what hath been said, who alone are qualified to travel; and that very few young People can be so, at least till sound Politicks, and the Knowledge of the World have a greater share in our Education; yet it is with the highest Satisfaction I say it, that I have met with some very young Gentlemen abroad who travelled to very great advantage. I have already mentioned a very just Remark of one in his Travels; and I would

11. "To know how to live." For Turnbull and his contemporaries the phrase referred to the cultural ideal of polite sociability.

12. "The commerce or business of life," meaning the exchanges or transactions involved in society.

name him and a great many more, did I not fear to offend their Modesty. One very extraordinary Instance I cannot chuse but relate, to shew young Travellers what Disposition of Mind is necessary to travelling profitably. A Nobleman who set out to travel very young, not satisfied with having very well digested the Plan of his Travels before he left *England,* upon his Arrival in ———— sat down seriously to review his past Education; <xix> and to consider what remained for him to do, to fit himself for being serviceable to his Country in the high Station to which his Birth entitled him. Having then for some time maturely weigh'd the chief Ends of travelling, and considered the Preparation it requires, he wrote, by way of Directory to himself, an excellent Performance, in Imitation of the ancient Fable of *Prodicus* concerning the Choice of *Hercules.*[13] Wisdom and Pleasure accost him as they did *Hercules.* The latter courts him to fling himself into her soft Arms, and to give full Scope to every Fancy and Appetite that promises him pleasure, without being at the trouble of examining its Pretensions. But Wisdom advises him to think of Virtue and true Honour; of his Country and its Good; and to travel in order to qualify himself for worthy Pursuits and Employments at home. He by asking Wisdom what Design one ought chiefly to propose to himself in travelling, puts her upon pointing out to him the chief Purposes and Advantages of Travel, and the Qualifications necessary for gaining these Ends: Upon which he resolves to bestow some time at the University; where he then was, upon History, the Laws of Nature and Nations, and other such previous Studies; and then to travel on condition that Wisdom would go along with him, keep his Country ever in his Heart and Eye, and preserve him from the contagious Vices of the World. He was able to form to himself in this manner an excellent Scheme of travelling, and having pursued it as one could not but expect from such rare Virtue and Prudence, his Country now reaps the happy Fruits of his Knowledge and Integrity. If one would be great and amiable, let him imitate ***, and be happy by so doing.

THE World is sufficiently stuffed with Books of Travels, but in almost

13. Xenophon, *Memorabilia,* II.i.21–34. The subject of the judgment of Hercules had been made popular in early-eighteenth-century Britain by Shaftesbury's "A Notion of the *Historical Draught* or *Tablature* of the Judgment of *Hercules,* According to Prodicus, *Lib.* II. *Xen. de Mem. Soc.* With a Letter concerning Design"; see Shaftesbury, *Characteristicks,* III:211–39.

all of them I have been able to get into my Hands, the main End of travelling is over-looked; and as if the Knowledge of Mankind had nothing to do with it, every thing else is treated of in them but that alone.[14] The greater part of them are filled up with general Notices of Buildings, Statues, Basreliefs and Pictures, that are to be seen in *Italy* in particular, which do not even supersede the necessity of having recourse to the very defective Originals from which they are taken, that are to be found in every Town, under the Title of *a Guide to Foreigners,* for that place. Mr. *B——* has wrote a Book, from the Title of which one would naturally expect a Treatise upon the principal Purposes and Ends of travelling, and the right Method of accomplishing these Ends.[15] But tho' he calls it *An Essay on the Utility of Travel,* after telling us, that it is fit to carry good Maps with us of the Countries we intend to visit, and giving us some other such-like profound Advices, he immediately falls into learned, or rather advent'rous Discussions about Medals, Gems, and Talismans, as if collecting such Rarities were to be a Gentleman's chief Employment abroad; and the Knowledge of Men and Things were quite foreign to his purpose. Hardly will any one of our Travellers say, that *M——* is a sufficient Guide, or that he with all his commendable Zeal against Popery; all his ridiculous Anecdotes of Priests, Friars, and Nuns, and all his sage Counsels about carrying with us Bed-Linen, Knives, Forks, Spoons, a Blunderbuss, *&c.* has quite exhausted the Subject.

But tho' we still want something more full upon the chief Purpose of travelling, than hath been yet written, for the Direction and Assistance of our young Travellers; Lord *Bacon* hath a Chapter upon it in his moral Essays, that well deserves to be often read, and maturely pondered before one sets out, and to be frequently returned to, and read over and over again abroad.[16] In Mr. *Addison*'s Travels there are some excellent Observations upon Men and Things; but his Remarks will chiefly serve to shew, how <xx> well versed in the Classicks one ought to be, in order to have agreeable

14. On the purposes of travel compare Turnbull, *Observations upon Liberal Education,* pp. 290–91, 418–21.

15. Unidentified.

16. "Of Travel," in Francis Bacon, *The Major Works,* edited by Brian Vickers (Oxford, 2002), pp. 374–76.

Entertainment in seeing the Scenes of celebrated Actions, and the Remains of ancient Arts.[17]

LORD *MOLESWORTH* in his Preface to his Account of *Denmark,* shews what advantage one who thoroughly understands the Value of a free Constitution, and hath withal a humane, generous Soul, will reap in enslaved Countries, by seeing, or rather feeling the miserable Effects of lawless Power.[18] Travelling into such Kingdoms he thinks necessary to those who are born in free Countries; because as one is in danger of forgetting the Value of Health, whilst he enjoys an uninterrupted Course of it; so amidst the happy Fruits of Liberty, a Sense of its inestimable Worth may be lost, or at least considerably impaired. But, on the other hand, if one hath not very just Notions of Government; and a very benign, as well as penetrating Mind, may he not be dazzled by the glaring Pageantry and false Magnificence of the Courts of Tyrants; and become enamoured of the Worship paid by a slavish Commonalty to the Nobles, and think the Homage and Submission they are obliged to render in their turn to their despotick Lord, sufficiently compensated by the Power left them to tyrannize over their Inferiours.

LORD *MOLESWORTH*'s Account of *Denmark* points out to Travellers the Things that ought to be inquired into abroad: And those who having read that excellent Treatise, Sir *William Temple*'s Account of the United Provinces, *Busbequius*'s Epistles, and some other such Books, have learned what they ought principally to endeavour to know in foreign Countries;[19] and have already taken the properest Methods of getting satisfaction about all these Matters with regard to their own Country; those alone are fit to

17. Joseph Addison, *Remarks on Several Parts of Italy, &c. in the Years 1701, 1702, 1703* (London, 1705).

18. Robert Molesworth, *An Account of Denmark. With Francogallia and Some Considerations for the Promoting of Agriculture and Employing the Poor,* edited by Justin Champion (Indianapolis, 2011), pp. 7–25; Molesworth's *Account* was first published in 1694.

19. Sir William Temple, *Observations upon the United Provinces of the Netherlands* (London, 1673); A. G. Busbequius, *The Four Epistles of A. G. Busbequius, concerning his Embassy into Turkey. Being Remarks upon the Religion, Customs, Riches, Strength and Government of that People. As Also a Description of their Chief Cities, and Places of Trade and Commerce* (London, 1694).

travel; and such can't fail to return from abroad freighted with very useful Knowledge. But such, as far from being prepared for those important Enquiries, have not so much as the least Taste of the fine Arts before they travel; what else can be expected from them, but that they should entirely give themselves up abroad to shameful, ruinous Pleasures, to Dress, Gallantry and Play; and that amongst People not of the higher Rank: not merely because it is easier to have access to the lower; but rather because they meet amongst them with more of that vile, pernicious Flattery and Cringing, by which they were corrupted at home, not by Servants and Parasites alone.

I have only mentioned these few things about Travel, lest any one should imagine, that having wrote upon Painting chiefly for the Use and Assistance of young Travellers, I looked upon it to be the principal Design of travelling to get acquainted with Antiquities, or with the Hands and Pencils of Painters. And having sufficiently declared my Sentiments on that head, I shall now take advantage of another received Custom in Prefaces, and give some short Account of the following Essay. A Reader now-a-days as naturally expects that in a Preface, as one does an Advertisement, where there is any Rarity to be seen, with some general Information of the Entertainment offered for his Money. And this is so much the more necessary, with regard to this Treatise, because it is impossible to express fully in the Title of it a Design so new and comprehensive: And some may have imagined that it is only a Treatise for Painters.

THE Design of the *Essay on the Rise, Progress, and Decline of Painting among the* Greeks, *&c.* is to set the Arts of Design in a just Light; and to point out in particular the excellent Use that may be made of them in Education. <xxi>

IN the first Chapter it is observed, that the Arts of Design are very ancient; more ancient than the Fables concerning *Apollo, Minerva, Vulcan,* the *Muses* and *Graces,* and consequently than the Story of *Daedalus.* But whatever may be determin'd with respect to their Antiquity in practice, *Homer* certainly had very perfect Notions of them in all their Parts and Qualities; and a very high Idea of their Power, Extent and Usefulness, not only to charm and please, but to instruct in the most important Points of Knowledge. *Virgil* likewise has not scrupled to suppose not only Sculpture but Painting as anciently in use as the Siege of *Troy;* and he had the same

Opinion of their Dignity, Utility, and Excellence. The best ancient Philosophers entertained the same Sentiments concerning those Arts; their Fitness in particular, to teach human Nature; to display the Beauties of Virtue
and the Turpitude of Vice; and to convey the most profitable Instructions
into the Mind in the most agreeable manner. Accordingly they employ'd
them to that noble purpose, frequently taking the Subjects of their moral
Lessons from Paintings and Sculptures with which publick Porticoes at *Athens,* where the Philosophers taught, were adorn'd. Some Moderns of our
own Country, who are own'd to have come nearest to the best Ancients in
agreeable as well as useful Writing, have earnestly inculcated the like Notion
of the polite Arts, and recommended them together with the manly Exercises as necessary to complete a truly Liberal Education. Thus the Conclusion, that is principally aim'd at in this Essay, comes out with a considerable degree of Evidence in the first Chapter.

IN order to give a just View of the Excellence and Usefulness of the fine
Arts, it is requisite to give a fair Representation of the Perfection to which
they have been improved at any time. Some may suspect, that Men of fine
Imaginations have carry'd these Arts further in Speculation than they have
ever been actually brought to, or than they can really be advanced. Those
who have conceiv'd, whether from Descriptions of Poets, or from seeing a
few good Pictures, some Idea of what they may be really able to perform,
if duly cultivated and improved, will naturally be desirous of knowing what
Progress they had made in ancient Times; and by what Means and Causes
that chiefly happen'd. And in truth it is hardly possible to set their Power,
Extent, and Merit in a better light, than by shewing what they have actually
produced. Now this is attempted in the second Chapter.

BUT before I entered upon the History of the Art, it was proper to observe in an Essay, chiefly intended to shew the Usefulness of Painting and
its Sister Arts in Education, That tho' the more ancient Treatises on Paintings are lost; insomuch that we have nothing preserv'd to us that was expressly written on that Subject, except what is to be found in *Pliny* the Elder,
and the two *Philostratus*'s Works;[20] yet such was the ancient Manner of

---

20. Pliny the Elder (C.E. 23/24–79), who discusses the fine arts in his multivolume
Natural History; Philostratus the Lemnian (also styled the Elder) and his grandson, who
both authored works entitled *Imagines* which dealt with ancient paintings.

Education, and of explaining any particular Art or Science, that in their Discourses upon Poetry, Eloquence, Morals and other Subjects, many excellent Remarks are made for the Illustration of these Subjects upon the different Talents and best Performances of ancient Painters; the essential Qualities of good Painting, and the Rise, Progress and Decline of that Art: which Observations when laid together in proper Order, will be found to furnish not only a very full History of the Art, but a just Idea of its Usefulness in Education; or for the Improvement of the Heart as well as of the Imagination and Judgment. Accordingly the first Chapter ends with an Observation to that purpose upon the Authorities from which the following Account of ancient Painting is brought, and upon the ancient Manner of uniting all the Arts and Sciences in Liberal Education. <xxii>

IN the second Chapter an Account is given by way of Parallel, of the chief Talents and Qualifications of the more remarkable Painters in the two most distinguish'd Ages of the Art, that of *Apelles* and that of *Raphael;*[21] in which it is shewn by what similar Means and Causes it advanced to so like a degree of Perfection at both these Periods. The Analogy between those two Ages of Painting in many Circumstances is indeed surprising; but it is well vouch'd, and not imagined; and therefore abstractly from all other Considerations, it is, by itself, a Phaenomenon well worth a Philosopher or Politician's Attention. This History is given by way of Parallel; because it was thought it would not be disagreeable to see two Ages of the Art, as it were, at one View; but chiefly because it is very difficult to convey clear Ideas of the Talents of Painters merely by Words; and those who are at a loss to understand any ways of speaking that are used in describing the Abilities of any ancient Painter, will be best satisfied by having recourse to the Pictures (or good Prints of them) of those Masters among the Moderns, to whom the like Qualifications are ascribed. In this double History frequent Opportunities occur of setting to view the Connexion of the polite

21. Apelles (active in the 4th century B.C.E.), the most famous painter of classical antiquity, who executed portraits of Philip II of Macedon and his son Alexander the Great among other works cited in ancient sources; and Raffaelo Santi (1483–1520), commonly known as Raphael, who was widely regarded in the early modern period as the greatest painter in the European tradition and whose works appealed to the eighteenth-century taste for the antique. Turnbull's parallel lives of Apelles, Raphael, and other ancient and modern artists were modelled on the format of Plutarch's *Lives.*

Arts with true Philosophy, and their Serviceableness in shewing the Beauties and Deformities of Life and Manners, and in leading to just Notions of Nature, and of all the Arts, and likewise of good moral Conduct; more particularly in drawing the Characters of *Apelles, Pamphilus, Euphranor, Nicias* and *Metrodorus;*[22] and in commenting upon some Passages of *Cicero* and *Quintilian,* concerning the like Progress of Painting and Oratory among the *Greeks,* and some of the Causes and Means of their Improvements.

THIS Essay is divided into Chapters, because it is necessary to return again and again to the same Subject, in order to set it in various Lights and Views.

AND in the third the same Subject is resum'd, but pursu'd in another manner. It is likewise about the Progress of Painting among the *Greeks.* In it some of the best Pictures of the most celebrated ancient Artists are consider'd, such as seem'd most proper to shew the Perfection at which Painting in all its parts had arriv'd in *Greece;* to evince the Excellence of the fine Arts; and to confirm the Conclusion that is principally aim'd at, the Connexion of Painting with Poetry, and of both with Philosophy: which in the end of that Chapter is illustrated by a Paraphrase on what the two *Philostratus's* have said on that Subject in their Books of Pictures. To which Reflexions a few others are added upon the equal Extent of Painting with Poetry, and the similar Diversity both those Arts admit of, that do likewise no less plainly follow from the Examples of ancient Painting describ'd in this Chapter.

IN the fourth, after some Observations upon the Colouring and Drawing of the Ancients, and their Knowledge of Perspective; some of the most essential Qualities of good Painting; such as Truth, Beauty, Greatness, Ease and Grace are more particularly consider'd. And for this end, two Dialogues of *Socrates,* one with a Painter, and another with a Statuary, are examin'd and commented upon at great length. After which several Passages of

---

22. Pamphilus (4th century B.C.E.), painter and teacher of Apelles; Euphranor (fl. ca. 370–330 B.C.E.), painter, sculptor, and writer on the art of painting; Nicias (life dates unknown), a painter said by Pliny the Elder to be especially known for his portraits of women; Metrodorus (life dates unknown), a practitioner of the art of memory mentioned by Pliny the Elder and Cicero. In discussing these and other figures Turnbull drew heavily on the writings of Cicero and the *Institutio oratoria* of the Roman rhetorician Quintilian (ca. 35–ca. 90).

Aristotle, Cicero, Quintilian, and other Authors, relative to these Qualities of good Painting, are explain'd. And in discoursing on them, Painting having been all along compar'd with Poetry, in order to give a right Idea of both, the Chapter ends with a short View of the principal Questions, by which, in the Sense of ancient Criticks, Pictures as well <xxiii> as Poems ought to be try'd and examin'd; which shews the Consideration of both to be a very improving and truly philosophical Employment.

In the fifth Chapter, an Enquiry is made concerning the Progress of Painting among the *Romans;* in which it being quickly found out, that Painting never came to so great Perfection among them as in *Greece;* some Reflections are made upon the moral Causes, to which the Progress and Decline of all the Arts, of Painting in particular, are ascrib'd by ancient Authors. Some had been already mentioned in the second Chapter, relating to the Talents and Characters of Painters, and the Encouragement of that Art; but several others of more universal Concern are here touch'd, such as the mutual Union and Dependance of all the Arts, and their Connexion with Liberty, Virtue, publick Spirit and true Philosophy.

The sixth Chapter sheweth the excellent Uses to which the *Greeks* chiefly employ'd the Arts of Design; and the high Opinion which some of the greatest Men of Antiquity entertain'd of their real Dignity and Excellence, on account of their Tendency to promote and encourage Virtue, and to give Lustre, Beauty and Taste to human Life. After which there is some Reasoning to shew how necessary the fine Arts are to the truest Happiness of Man and the real Grandeur of Society. And last of all the Objections made against the polite Arts are remov'd: Such as, that *Plato* banish'd them from his ideal Republick; and what is said by others of their Tendency to soften and effeminate Men, and of their having been one principal Cause of the Ruin of the *Roman* State.[23]

But all these Enquiries being chiefly intended to prepare the way for a

23. In Chapter 6 Turnbull cites and responds to Plato, *Republic,* esp. bk. X, and the Roman historian Velleius Paterculus, *Compendium of Roman History,* I.xiii.5: "Yet I do not think, Vinicius, that you would hesitate to concede that it would have been more useful to the state for the appreciation of Corinthian works of art to have remained uncultivated to the present day, than that they should be appreciated to the extent to which they now are, and that the ignorance of those days was more conducive to the public weal than our present artistic knowledge."

philosophical Consideration of the fine Arts; in the seventh Chapter it is shewn, that good Taste of Nature, of Art, and of Life, is the same; takes its Rise from the same Dispositions and Principles in our moral Frame and Make; and consequently that the most successful way of forming and improving good Taste, must be by uniting all the Arts in Education agreeably to their natural Union and Connexion. To illustrate this more fully, our Capacity of understanding Nature, delighting in it, and copying after it, either in Life and Conduct; or by the imitative Arts; is shewn to arise from our natural Love of Knowledge; our Sense of Beauty natural and moral; our publick and generous Affections, and our Love of Greatness; to improve and perfect which Dispositions is certainly the principal Scope of Education. Then the properest way of teaching Oratory, Poetry, Logick, natural or moral Philosophy is enquired into; and Painting is prov'd to be requisite to the most agreeable as well as profitable Method of explaining and teaching all these Arts and Sciences. Whether Education is consider'd with respect to the Improvement of Imagination, of Reason, or of the Heart, Painting is shewn to be of excellent use. In considering the Nature and End of Philosophy, Pictures are prov'd to be proper Samples or Experiments either in natural or moral Philosophy; and they are shewn to be as such, of admirable Efficacy to fix our Attention in the Examination of Nature, the sole Object of all Knowledge, the Source of all Beauty, and the Standard of all the imitative Arts. To confirm this some moral Pictures are describ'd. And after having remarked, that in reading and explaining the Classick Authors to Pupils, Sculptures and Pictures ought for many reasons to have their place, and to be often referr'd to; this Chapter concludes with observing, that this Scheme of Education only requires, that Drawing be early taught, which, as *Aristotle* long ago asserted, is not only necessary to Liberal Education, but to that of Mechanicks.[24] <xxiv>

THE last Chapter points out some other very useful and entertaining Enquiries about Pictures, besides those that regard Truth and Beauty of Composition. For though that be the main thing in Painting as well as in Poetry; yet so like are these Arts in every respect, that some other Researches are equally pleasing and profitable with respect to both: Such as how the

---

24. Aristotle, *Politics,* 1338a 40–1338b 4.

distinguishing Genius of a Painter, as well as that of a Poet, appears in all his Works; and what use modern Painters have made of the Antique, in like manner as the best modern Poets have done of the ancient ones.

THESE Enquiries are recommended as being not merely about Hands and Styles, but about Men and Things, and for that reason they are not barely suggested; but in order to put young Travellers into the way of them, some Observations are offer'd with respect to the distinguishing Talents, Genius and Characters of several of the most famous modern Masters, and the happy and laudable Use they made of the exquisite Remains of Antiquity in Sculpture and Painting.

THIS Work concludes with some few Remarks upon the fifty Pieces of ancient Painting now engraved with great Exactness and Elegance from excellent Drawings. Several Observations are made on them in the preceding Chapters; but here some Reasons are given for publishing them. It is a part of Antiquity that deserves to be made known, and that must therefore be very acceptable to all Lovers of Antiquity. Which is more, they serve to prove that the Accounts given in this Essay of ancient Painting, from ancient Authors, may be depended upon, or are not exaggerated. But they are publish'd chiefly in order to excite those, who are concern'd in Education, to make a proper use of the ancient Remains of Antiquity in Painting and Sculpture, in explaining ancient Authors to their Scholars; and to induce Travellers instead of republishing Statues and Bas-reliefs that have been often well engraved, to enquire after such as have not yet been made publick, by which either the Taste of Art may be improv'd, or any light may be given to ancient Authors. Some Account is added of the Originals, their Sizes, where they were found, and where they are, &c. It never was my Intention to enter in this Essay upon any mythological or classical Discussions about any Remains of ancient Arts; yet some few Passages of the Classicks that occur'd to me upon considering some of these ancient Paintings, are inserted, for the sake of those, who perhaps may never have thought of the mutual Light which ancient Authors and ancient Pieces of Art cast one on the other, though that hath been taken notice of by many Writers. And I am exceedingly glad that I can tell the Publick, that one much fitter for that learned, as well as polite Task, has far advanced in such a Work, which cannot fail to be of great use to Teachers and Students of

Poetry, History, Sculpture, and Painting; and in particular to Travellers, as far at least as Improvement in good Taste of the fine Arts is concern'd in Travel, so equal is the Undertaker to that useful Design.

ALL I have further to add is, that I am exceedingly indebted to a late excellent Commentary in *French* on *Pliny*'s Book of Painting; as likewise to the same Author's Notes in *French,* added to a very correct Edition of the *Latin* Text;* and that I have not scrupled to make use of such *English* Translations and Paraphrases upon several Passages of ancient Authors relative to my Subject, as seemed to me to do justice to the Originals: But all that I have borrowed of that, or of any kind, is acknowledged in the marginal Notes; where the more important Passages of ancient <xxv> Authors commented upon in the Text, are also inserted for the most part at full length, and in the original Languages. Mr. *Pope*'s Observations on the Shield of *Achilles* make a great part of the first Chapter.[25] And indeed as an Essay on the Antiquity of Painting would have been very imperfect without taking notice of the fine Ideas *Homer* had of that Art; so it would have been vain and arrogant to have attempted any thing on that Subject after so masterly a Performance upon it. 'Tis very difficult not to indulge one's self in praising when the Heart is full of Esteem. But it very justly would have been accounted presumptuous and assuming in me, to do more than mention Mr. *Pope* when I quote any part of his Writings. It belongs to those of established Fame to dispense it, and to me to endeavour to merit it.

I have received very little assistance from any of the few Writers upon ancient Painting, (for they do little more than copy from *Pliny*) except *Junius,*† and to him I frankly own I owe so much, that had he not obliged

---

* *By Mr. D. D. London 1725.* [*Histoire de la peinture ancienne, extraite de L'Hist. Naturelle de Pline, LIV.XXXV* (London, 1725), compiled by the exiled French Protestant clergyman David Durand (1680–1763).]

† *Franciscus Junius de Pictura veterum.* [Franciscus Junius, *De pictura veterum libri tres* (Amsterdam, 1637); translated by Junius into English as *The Painting of the Ancients, in Three Bookes: Declaring by Historical Observations and Examples, the Beginning, Progresse, and Consummation of That Most Noble Art* (London, 1638).]

25. Turnbull quotes extensively from Pope's "Observations on the Shield of Achilles" and "The Shield of Achilles divided into its several Parts," in *The Iliad of Homer,* translated by Alexander Pope, 6 vols. (London, 1715–20), V:1442–66.

the World with his very learned Performance, I should never have attempted what I have done. But at the same time those who have read that Author will immediately perceive from the Account already given of this Essay, that I have pursued quite a different Scheme; and that I can have but very little in common with him except certain Authorities from ancient Authors. And with regard to those he quotes, I have left out not a few, as having very little relation to my Subject; many I have made a very different use of from what he does; and very many Passages of ancient Authors are to be found in this Treatise, which had either escaped him, or did not fall within his Plan. To give a just Idea of truly Liberal Education is my principal view throughout the whole; or by explaining the Relation of Painting to Philosophy, which is generally reckoned so remote from it, and its Usefulness in Education, to unfold at full length the Truth and Importance of that Saying of *Plato:* "That all the Liberal Arts and Sciences have a strict and intimate Affinity; and are closely united together by a certain common Bond; and that they cannot be sever'd from one another in Education, without rendering any of the Arts that is taught very defective and imperfect; and Education very narrow and stinted, and incapable of producing that universal good Taste which ought to be its Aim."[26] And that is quite a different Subject from what *Junius* had in view, tho' he likewise occasionally takes notice of this natural and inseparable Connexion and Union of all the Liberal Arts and Sciences.[27] As I have no right to give any Advice to Artists; so I have no where attempted to do it, or assumed any higher Character to myself than that of a Collector from the Ancients. Yet if any Artists should think or say that Artists alone can judge of their Performances, I would just ask such, for whom they paint, if it is for Artists only. They surely have no reason to complain, when one not of the Profession

26. Turnbull elaborates on Cicero, *De oratore,* III.vi.21: "there is also the truth enunciated by Plato, which you, Catulus, have undoubtedly heard, that the whole content of the liberal and humane sciences is comprised within a single bond of union; since, when we grasp the meaning of the theory that explains the causes and issues of things, we discover that a marvellous agreement and harmony underlies all branches of knowledge." Compare Turnbull, *Principles of Moral and Christian Philosophy,* I:457–58, and Turnbull, *Observations upon Liberal Education,* p. 417.

27. Franciscus Junius, *The Painting of the Ancients,* edited by Keith Aldrich, Philipp Fehl, and Raina Fehl (Berkeley, Los Angeles, and Oxford, 1991), p. 42.

endeavours to the utmost of his power to do justice to their Art, and to shew what excellent useful Entertainment it is capable of affording to all who will but consider it as a Species of Poetry, as it ought to be. All however I pretend to, is to have acted the part of a Compiler, and to have digested into the best Order I could the Sentiments of ancient Authors about Painting, that are scattered thro' many of their Treatises on other Subjects: But in doing so, I did not think myself obliged merely to translate, I have oftener commented or paraphrased.

LET me just subjoin, that I flatter myself the virtuous Intention with which this Work is wrote, will atone with my Readers for many Imperfec-<xxvi>tions in it, besides those in Language, with regard to which I can't forbear saying, that I have ever had the same Idea of too great nicety about Style, as of over-finishing in Pictures. I need not make any Apology for inserting so many Passages from ancient Poets in the Text, since the practice is common; those who like the original Authors from which they are quoted, will be pleased to find them applied to proper purposes; and very few Translations of ancient Poets are so equal to the Originals as that of *Homer,* that I could adventure to make the same use of them I have done of it. I return my most hearty Thanks to all those who have generously encouraged this Work; and I hope they will not blame me for its not being published precisely at the time mentioned in the Proposals, since (not to say that very few Authors have so exactly kept to their time as I have done) I can assure them, the Hindrances that retarded this Work were absolutely inevitable. Not having leave to mention those Gentlemens Names who were pleased to take the trouble of revising my Papers, and to favour me with their Animadversions upon them, all I can do is to assure them, I reckon myself exceedingly obliged to their very friendly Corrections and Amendments. <129>

CHAPTER VII

Observations on the Sameness of good Taste in all the Arts, and in Life and Manners; on the Sources and Foundations of rational Pleasures in our Natures, and the Usefulness of the fine Arts in a liberal Education

The chief Design of this Essay. — WHAT hath been hitherto observ'd concerning the Arts of Design, Painting in particular, is chiefly intended to prepare the way for shewing their Usefulness in Education, by pointing out their Foundation in our Nature, and their Connection with true Philosophy; that true Philosophy which explains the τὸ καλὸν,[28] or Beautiful in Nature, in Conduct, and in Arts, and shews it to be the same in them all. Now as in giving an Account of the Rise, Progress, and Decline of Painting amongst the Ancients, and the Causes to which these Effects are principally ascribed, I have only commented and enlarged a little on some Testimonies of ancient Authors; so even in this more philosophical Part of my Plan, my Design is merely to set the Sentiments of the better Ancients concerning good Taste and liberal Education in the clearest Light I can, by reasoning from their Principles and Maxims.

A Summary of the Doctrine of the better Ancients, concerning the Sources of our noblest Pleasures. — THE Doctrine of the best ancient Philosophers concerning our Powers and Faculties, true Happiness, good Taste, and right Education, amounts briefly to this.

THE Pleasures of the Mind are far superiour to those of the Body: We have, (say they) by our Frame and Constitution but a very scanty Provision

28. "The fine" or "the beautiful."

370

for Enjoyment in the way of Sense and common Appetite; but we have a very noble and ample one for rational Happiness; since even our Senses in that respect make a very proper and useful part of our Stock or Furniture; whereas considered abstractly from our intellectual Powers and Capacities, or otherwise than as Ministers to them, they are a most mean and narrow Pittance. A very slight Review of our Make and Contexture is sufficient to convince us, that the chief Enjoyments our Senses are capable of affording us, are those which they administer to us, as Inlets of Materials for Imagination, Reason, and our inward Sense of Beauty, natural and moral, to work upon and employ themselves about: And that if we were not indued with these superiour Faculties, all the barely sensual Gratifications our outward Organs can receive or convey, would constitute but a very low degree of Happiness. Our highest Pleasures are those which accompany, or result from the Exercises of our moral Powers; the Pleasures of Imagination, Understanding, Virtue, and a moral Sense: Otherwise indeed those Powers which distinguish a Man from the lower Herds of Animals could not be called his most noble and honourable Faculties; or be said to raise him to a higher Rank and Dignity in Being.[a] But what are the Objects adapted to

---

a. Compare what *Cicero* says *De finibus Bonorum, lib.* 2. N° 33, & 34. Quod vero a te disputatum est majores esse voluptates, & dolores animi quam corporis ——— Ad altiora quaedam & magnificentiora nati sumus: Nec id ex animi solum partibus, in quibus inest memoria rerum innumerabilium, inest conjectura consequentium, non multum a divinatione differens, inest moderator cupiditatis pudor, inest ad humanam societatem justitiae fida custodia: Inest in perpetiendis laboribus, adeundisque periculis, firma & stabilis doloris mortisque contemptio. Ergo haec in animis: Tu autem membra ipsa sensusque considera: Qui tibi ut reliquae corporis partes, non comites solum virtutum, sed ministri etiam videbuntur, &c. [Cicero, *De finibus bonorum et malorum*, II.xxxiii.108 and II.xxxiv.113: "As for your contention that mental pleasures and pains are greater than those of the body—We were born for higher and more splendid things than this, Torquatus, believe me. I say this not merely because of our mental faculties, among which is memory of innumerable things—in your case a boundless memory, calculation of consequences scarcely differing from prophecy of the future, a sense of modesty that controls our desires, and faithful observance of justice for the preservation of human society; there is also a contempt of pain and death that remains firm and steadfast in enduring trials and facing danger. These are our mental faculties. But consider also our actual limbs and senses; like other parts of the body they will appear to you to be not merely the companions of our virtues, but also their agents, etc.] *De Nat. Deor. lib.* 2. N° 58, & 59. Omnisque sensus hominum multo antecellit sensibus bestiarum. Primum enim oculi in iis artibus quarum judicium est oculorum, in pictis, fictis, caelatisque for-these Faculties, or how do they employ themselves about them? What is it the Understanding delights to know; Fancy to describe, or Art to imitate? Is it not Nature? And what is it that Virtue emulates? Is it not likewise the Benevolence, the Beauty and Harmony of Nature? Nature being therefore the sole Object of Knowledge, and of Imitation whether in Arts or Life; all our greatest Pleasures and Enjoyments, all our noblest and worthiest Exercises must be very nearly allied. It is the same Stock of Powers and Faculties that capacitates us for them all: They have the same Object, Rule, Measure and End: And consequently good Taste in Science, in Arts, and in Life, must be the same; that is, it must be founded on the same Principles; lead to the same Conclusions; and be improveable in the same manner. Accordingly, the Perfection of our Understanding, does it not consist in as full and compleat a Knowledge of Nature as we can obtain by Study and Contemplation; <130> or in a just Comprehension of its Order, Wisdom, Beauty, and Greatness in all its Operations? The Perfection of Life and Manners, does it not consist in conforming our Affections and Actions to that beautiful Model of Simplicity, Consistency, Greatness, and Goodness, which a right understanding of Nature sets before us for our Imitation? And the Perfection of all the Arts of Imagination, in what else does it con-

---

mis, in corporum etiam motione atque gestu multa cernunt subtilius. Colorum etiam & figurarum venustatem atque ordinem, & ut ita dicam decentiam oculi judicant: atque etiam alia majora, nam & virtutis & vitia cognoscunt: Iratum, propitium, &c. ———— Auriumque item est mirabile quoddam artificiosumque judicium, &c. [Cicero, *De natura deorum*, II.lviii.145 and 146: "Every human sense is far superior to the senses of the beasts. For first the eyes have a finer perception in those arts in which judgments are made by the eyes, in painting, sculpture and engraved figures, as well as in bodily movements and gestures. It is the eyes that judge the beauty and arrangement of colours and shapes and what I might call their appropriateness, as well as much more important matters; for they also recognize the virtues and vices, anger, friendliness, etc. The ears are likewise marvellously skilful organs of discrimination."]

The whole Design of *Marcus Antoninus*'s Meditations is to shew, that we are made not merely for the Pleasures of Sense, but for those of Reason, Virtue, and Religion. There are several Discourses of *Socrates* in the memorable things by *Xenophon* to the same purpose. See in particular *l.* 4. *cap.* 5. [Xenophon, *Memorabilia*, IV.v, esp. 3–11.] See to the same effect a beautiful Passage of *Plato* quoted by *Longinus, de Sublimitate, sect.* 13. as an instance of *Plato*'s sublime way of Writing. [Longinus, *On the Sublime*, 13.1, which quotes from Plato, *Republic* IX, 586a–b.]

sist but in emulating the Beauty, the Harmony, the Grandeur, and Order of Nature, in Systems or Works of our own Invention and Formation?[b]

MAN, say the Ancients, is made to contemplate and imitate Nature, and to be happy by so doing.[c] His Dignity, his Duty, his Happiness, principally consist in these two. The Dignity, Duty, and Felicity of a Being, must be but different Names signifying the same thing; they cannot be really different: And how can they be ascertain'd or determin'd, but from the Consideration of the highest and noblest End, to which the Frame and

Another View of the same Doctrine concerning Man, and the Improvement of his best Powers and Faculties.

b. *Cicero* tells us, that, according to the Doctrine of *Plato,* all the liberal Arts and Sciences are strictly united, and gives this as the Reason for it, that Nature their Object is one throughout all her Works. *De Orat. lib.* 3. N° 6. Ac mihi quidem veteres illi majus quiddam animo complexi, multo plus etiam vidisse videntur quam quantum nostrorum ingeniorum acies intueri potest: Qui omnia haec quae supra & subter unum esse & una vi atque una consensione naturae constricta esse dixerunt. ——— Est etiam illa Platonis vera, omnem doctrinam harum ingenuarum, &c. [Cicero, *De oratore,* III.v.20–III.vi.21: "And in my opinion the great men of old formed a conception of something grander; they seem to have had much greater insight than the discernment of our intellects can achieve. For they declared that all things above and below are one; they are bound together by a single force; they are in a single harmony. There is also truth in that remark of Plato's that all the teaching in these liberal [arts], etc."] See *de finibus, lib.* 4. N° 21. Physicae quoque non sine causa tributus idem est honos; propterea quod qui convenienter naturae victurus sit, ei & proficiscendum est ab omni mundo & ab ejus procuratione. Neque vero potest quisquam de bonis aut malis vere judicare nisi omni cognita ratione naturae, & utrum conveniat necne natura hominis cum universa, &c. [Cicero, *De finibus bonorum et malorum,* III.xxii.73: "The same dignity is attributed also to Physics, and not without reason; for he who is planning to live in accordance with nature, must start from the whole world and its governance. Nor can anyone make sound judgements about goods and evils without first gaining knowledge of the whole system of nature . . . and whether the nature of man is in harmony with universal nature, etc."] Compare with this *De Leg. lib.* 2. N° 22, & 23, and the Passages that are afterwards quoted. [Cicero, *De legibus,* 2.22–23. This reference makes no sense. It may be that Turnbull meant to cite *De legibus,* I.xxii–xxiv, where Cicero discusses the scope and various branches of philosophy or "the love of wisdom."]

c. *Cicero de Senect.* N° 21. Sed credo Deos immortales sparsisse animos in corpora humana ut essent qui terras tuerentur, quique coelestium ordinem contemplantes imitarentur eum vitae modo, atque constantia. Nec me solum ratio impulit ut ita crederem, sed nobilitas etiam summorum philosophorum & auctoritas, &c. [Cicero, *De senectute,* xxi.77: "But I believe that the immortal Gods sowed souls in human bodies, so that there would be beings who would protect the earth and in contemplating the order of the heavens would imitate it in the regularity and consistency of their lives. And it is not only reason that led me to believe this but also the renown and authority of the greatest philosophers, etc."] *De Nat. lib.* 2. N° 56. ——— Qui primum eos humo excitatos celsos

Constitution of a Being is adapted? That is, from the Consideration of that End, towards which its Powers, Faculties, Instincts, and Affections consider'd, as making by all their mutual Respects one Whole, or one certain determinate Frame and Constitution, are fitted to operate.[d] Now if the Frame of Man be thus consider'd, we shall find that he is made, chiefly, to contemplate and imitate Nature: Because his Senses, Powers, Faculties, Instincts, and Affections qualify him for that end; and the highest and noblest Pleasures he is capable of, arise from these Sources. Every other inferiour Exercise or Gratification, in the way of ordinary Appetite, rather terminates in Dissatisfaction and Nauseating, than in solid and pure Pleasure.

& erectos constituit ut Deorum cognitionem coelum intuentes capere possent. Sunt enim e terra homines non ut incolae atque habitatores sed quasi spectatores superarum rerum atque coelestium quarum spectaculum ad nullum aliud genus animantium pertinet, &c. [Cicero, *De natura deorum,* II.lvi.140: "First, [nature] raised [humans] from the ground and made them stand tall and erect, so that they might receive knowledge of the Gods from gazing on the sky. For men are from the earth not as natives and inhabitants but as spectators so to speak of higher, heavenly things, the contemplation of which is available to no other kind of living creature, etc."] And again in the same Book, Ipse homo ortus est ad mundum contemplandum & imitandum. [Cicero, *De natura deorum,* II.xiv.37: "Man himself came into being to observe and imitate the world."]

    d. *Cicero de Nat. Deor. lib.* 2. N° 13. Neque enim dici potest in ulla rerum institutione non esse aliquid extremum atque perfectum. Ut enim in vite, ut in pecude, &c. [Cicero, *De natura deorum,* II.xiii.35: "For it cannot be denied that in every system of things there is a final and perfect state. As in vines or in cattle, etc."] *De Leg. lib.* 1. N° 7. Animal hoc providum, sagax, multiplex, memor, plenum rationis & consilii, quem vocamus hominem praeclara quadam conditione generatum esse a supremo Deo, &c. [Cicero, *De legibus,* I.vii.22: "this animal which we call man, endowed with foresight and intelligence, versatile, possessing memory, fully capable of reason and deliberation, has been created by the supreme God in an excellent condition."] *Acad. lib.* 2. N° 41. Est enim animorum ingeniorumque naturale quoddam quasi pabulum consideratio, contemplatioque naturae: Erigimur, elatiores fieri videmur, humana despicimus: Cogitantesque supera atque coelestia haec nostra ut exigua & minima contemnimus, &c. [Cicero, *Academica,* II.xli.127: "For the consideration and contemplation of nature is a kind of natural food for our minds and intellects. We are lifted up, we seem to take a broader view, we look down upon human affairs; and in thinking on higher and heavenly things, we despise our own affairs as small and petty."] See his elegant Description of Philosophy, *Tusc. Quaes. lib.* 5. N° 2. O vitae philosophia dux, &c. [Cicero, *Tusculan Disputations,* V.ii.5: "O philosophy, guide of life, etc."] Compare, with these Passages, the Reasoning in the 5th Book *de Finibus,* N° 9. to shew how the ultimate End of any Being may be determin'd, *Ergo Instituto veterum, &c.* [Cicero, *De finibus bonorum et malorum,* V.viii.23: "Therefore following the practice of the ancients, etc."]

IF therefore it be the great Business of Education, to improve the Capacity and Taste of those Employments and Satisfactions, which are the remotest from all Grossness and Disgust, and yield the highest and most lasting delight; Education ought, by consequence, to aim chiefly at improving those natural Powers, Capacities, Affections, and Senses, by which we are capable of contemplating and imitating Nature; that is, at bringing to perfection that Sense of Beauty, Order, Harmony, Goodness and Greatness, by which alone we can enjoy Nature in Contemplation; and which alone fits for imitating it in Arts and Manners; or for receiving Satisfaction from Conformity with it in Speculations and Imitations of whatever kind.

NOW this 'tis evident must be but one Work; for from what hath been said it necessarily follows, that good Taste of Beauty, Order and Greatness in Nature, transferred to Life and Conduct, or to the Arts, must produce an equally good Taste in them, and reciprocally good Taste of Order, Beauty, and Greatness, transferred from the Arts, or from Manners to Nature, must produce a good Taste of Nature. A sound and thorough Sense of Beauty, Greatness, and Order in Nature, in Life, or in the fine Arts, will therefore be best form'd, by such a Course of Instruction and Education, as exercises the Mind in passing from Nature to Imitations, and reciprocally from Imitations to Nature; and in observing that the Beauty and Perfection of Arts, of Life, and of Nature, is the same.[e]

THE End of Philosophy, is it not to form a good Taste of what is beautiful and admirable in Nature, orderly in Life, Conduct and Society, and true and perfect in Arts? But that Philosophy must be one, into whatever different Parts it is branched <131> and divided; or, all the Sciences which conduce towards this End, must be very strictly and intimately related; and have a very close Union and Connection; because the Transition from Beauty and Truth, in any one kind, to Beauty and Truth in any other kind, is not only very easy and natural; but Beauties of different kinds being

e. Such Philosophy or Education may (as *Junius* observes *de Pictura veterum, l. 1. c. 4.*) be rightly called φιλοσοφία ἐκ παραδειγμάτων, philosophiam salubrium exemplorum intuitu spectantium oculos conformantem. [The Greek phrase translates as "philosophy by examples," while the Latin translates as "philosophy which educates the eyes of the viewers by the contemplation of wholesome examples." The quoted material appears as a marginal note only in the Latin version of the text; see Franciscus Junius, *De pictura veterum libri tres,* rev. ed. (London, 1694), p. 30.]

compar'd and brought to the same common Standard, must mutually illustrate and set off one another to great advantage. And it is indeed impossible to give a just and adequate Notion of Truth and Beauty, whether in Nature, in Manners, or in Arts, otherwise than by shewing from proper Examples, that wherever it is found, it is the Result of the same settled Laws and Connections in Nature, together with the Constitution of our Mind, as it is adjusted by Nature to these Laws and Connections. Our Reasonings upon Truth and Beauty of whatever sort, if they do not proceed in this manner, must be not merely very narrow and confined, but very lame and defective; we cannot have a clear and full Idea of Truth and Beauty in any Subject, without comparing it with Truth and Beauty in many, or rather in all Subjects; for it is by means of Opposition and Comparison that Truth and Beauty are display'd to the best advantage.

The chief Points of this Doctrine more fully illustrated.

THIS is the Sum of what the better Ancients have said of the natural Union and Connection of all the Sciences which form good Taste, and of the Design of Liberal Education.

BUT it is well worth while to set this important Doctrine in a fuller and clearer Light, by inquiring more particularly, what is meant by contemplating and imitating Nature; and by considering those Faculties, Instincts and Affections, by which we are qualify'd for contemplating and imitating Nature.

Of the Contemplation of Nature, and how we are qualify'd for it.

THE Study of Nature, is nothing else but that accurate impartial Enquiry into Nature itself, by which the general Laws it observes in all its Productions, may be investigated and determin'd. Physiology consists in reducing all particular similar Effects to general Laws. 'Tis too obvious to be insisted upon, that the Laws of Nature cannot be found out otherwise than by attending to Nature itself; by diligently tracing its Operations, and comparing Appearances with Appearances. Nor is it less evident, that if Nature did not observe general Laws in its Productions, but work'd in a desultory, inconstant manner, it could not be the Object of Science: It would be an unintelligible inexplicable Chaos. Did not Nature always speak the same Language, it would be absolutely incomprehensible; that is, were not its Connections fix'd, steady, and uniform, we could not know by any Marks or Signs what Qualities are co-existent, or what Effect would be produc'd in any given Circumstances; we could not know, for instance, when Fire would give a pleasant degree of Heat, and when it would burn and destroy: We could not know when to plow and sow, nor indeed what it was safe to eat or even to touch. On the other hand, Nature, by observing general Laws, and operating always uniformly, or according to the same settled Rules and Connections, becomes orderly and the Object of Science; it is regular, and therefore it may be studied, traced and understood. A Phenomenon is then said to be fully explained in a physical way, when it is reduced with several other like Effects to a uniform general Law of Nature. For those are justly concluded to be general Qualities, Laws or Connections, which are found to work steadily and uniformly; and to which many Effects being analogous are reducible. And indeed what else doth or can the Analogy or Likeness of Effects mean, besides their similar Method of Production, or Nature's analogous manner of Operation in producing them? Thus, for instance, it is reasonably concluded, that Gravity is a general Law of Bodies prevailing throughout our mundane System, because every Body gravitates; no Body is found devoid of that Quality, and many very distant Operations are reducible to it as their physical Cause, because of their Likeness to Effects of the same nature, that fall more immediately under our Cognizance.

NATURAL Philosophy is, then, nothing else but the Knowledge of the general Analogies and Harmonies which take place in Nature, to which particular Appearances are reducible.

BUT how are we fitted and qualify'd by Nature for this Science; or for finding out the general Laws and Connections, the Harmonies and Analogies, which constitute the Order of the sensible World? Is it not by our natural Sense of Beauty arising from Regularity and Order, or, in other words, from Uniformity amidst variety? 'Tis this natural Sense improv'd and cultivated by Exercise, that chiefly distinguishes the natural Philosopher from the common Herd of Spectators; all his Satisfactions arising from the Contemplation of Nature's Unity, Beauty, and Harmony, are owing to this Sense; that is, they belong as properly to it as those of hearing to the Ear, or of tasting to the Palate. For as without the Organ of Hearing we could not perceive Sounds, or <132> without the Palate, tastes; so no more could we perceive Unity, Beauty, Simplicity, and be pleased with these Perceptions, without a Sense and Disposition adapted to them.

By our natural Love of Order, Analogy, Unity amidst variety, or of general Laws.

This Taste serves to put us into the right way of discovering Truth, and satisfying our natural desire of Knowledge.

THERE is indeed implanted in our Natures a strong desire after Knowledge; Light is not more sweet and agreeable to the Eye, than Truth to the Understanding: The Mind of Man is naturally curious and inquisitive about the Reasons and Causes of Things; it is impatient to understand and comprehend every thing; what is dark to it or hid from it, gives it Uneasiness and Disquiet; whereas what we know, we look upon ourselves as in some degree Possessors and Masters of, and so far we are easy and contented. But besides the Satisfaction Knowledge gives to our Curiosity, and the Pleasure that attends the Exercise of our reasoning Faculty, there is another Enjoyment arising from the Perception of Beauty and Unity; which, as it is exceedingly agreeable to the Mind, so we are directed and guided by our natural Love of it, delight in it, and desire after it, to that right Method of enquiring into the Nature and Order of Things, that alone can satisfy our Thirst after Knowledge. For by it we are led to search after Harmonies and Analogies; to compare Effects with Effects, and to reduce like ones to like Causes; which is the only way of coming at the Knowledge of Nature. We are delighted with Analogy; we are exceedingly charm'd with Unity amidst variety; and hence we are determined to seek after Unity and Regularity, or, in one word, settled Analogies and general Laws. And this we soon find to be an equally pleasing and profitable Employment, leading us very successfully into the Knowledge of Nature, and giving us higher and higher delight the further we advance. Thus it is that Nature points out to us the Method of coming at the Knowledge of its Operations and Orders. How Men ever came to pursue the Knowledge of Nature, in any other way than this to which we are so strongly directed and invited by Nature, or by our internal Sense of Beauty, is a Question that would lead us into too long a Digression. 'Tis sufficient to our present purpose, to have observed how we are qualify'd by Nature for physical Knowledge, and the Pleasures attending it.

We are by our moral Sense dispos'd to inquire after moral or final Causes, and to delight in the Contemplation of Good.

BUT this is not all: We have likewise by Nature a moral Sense, or we receive Pleasure and Satisfaction from Effects that produce Good and Happiness in Nature: Not only are we pleased with the Contemplation of Effects, Laws, and Causes, that tend to our own Good; but we are delighted with the Perception of Good and Happiness wherever we observe or behold it; though no other Portion of that Good and Happiness should fall to our share, besides the Pleasure which the View of it affords us. Now by this moral Sense, we are naturally led to inquire into the good Effects of the general Laws of Nature. In consequence of it we are not contented with the barely physical Explication of Appearances; but are chiefly prompted to search after the moral Ends or final Causes of Effects, or rather of the general Laws from which Effects result. We perceive high delight in contemplating natural Beauty and Uniformity; but it is moral Beauty that is most satisfactory and delighting to our Mind: For thus, together with Unity of Design, Goodness and Benevolence are perceived; and therefore, at the same time that our natural Sense of Beauty is entertain'd, our natural Love of generous Intention is gratify'd; and all our benign, social Affections are most agreeably exercised.

We shall not now inquire how it ever came about, that investigating, moral, or final Causes hath been at any time excluded from Philosophy; but certainly those who content themselves with reducing Effects to their physical Causes, without any Reflections upon the Wisdom, Goodness, and Benevolence, that appear in the Laws of Nature, deprive themselves of the highest Satisfaction the Study of Nature affords. For can there be a more refin'd Joy than to range at large through Nature, perceiving every where not only Unity of Design, Harmony, and Analogy; but Beneficence, Kindness, Bounty, and Goodness? Now for this Satisfaction we are qualify'd by our moral Sense. These Pleasures do as necessarily pre-suppose it, as Light and Colours do the Sense of seeing; or Musick, the Capacity of distinguishing Harmony and Discord in the Combination of Sounds.

Thus then we are fitted to receive Pleasure from the Study of Nature, by our Curiosity, or Thirst after Knowledge; by our Sense of Beauty arising from Unity of Design, or Uniformity amidst Diversity; and by our moral Sense, or our Sense of Beauty and Fitness resulting from the Pursuit of Good; or, in other words, from our Disposition to delight in the Happiness of Beings, and in the Contemplation of the Good of a Whole, steadily pursued by excellent general Laws, or by wisely and generously contrived Analogies and Harmonies. <133>

But there is yet another Source of Pleasure to our Minds, in the Contemplation of Nature, that deserves to be consider'd, depending on our natural Sense of Greatness, or our Disposition to be struck with pleasing Admiration by the Greatness of Objects, or by the Greatness of the manner

Another Source of Pleasure to our Minds in the Contemplation of

Nature, is our natural Sense of Greatness, or our Disposition to admire great Objects, or Greatness in the manner of Objects.

in which they exist and operate.[f] The Mind of Man is naturally great and aspiring: It hates every thing that looks like a Restraint upon it: It loves to expatiate and dilate itself, prove its Force and range unconfin'd. And therefore it is wonderfully pleas'd with every thing that is noble and elevated, that fills it with lofty and sublime Ideas, and puts its Grasp to the trial. Hence an inexhaustible Source of Entertainment to the Mind in the Contemplation of Nature: For there is an Immensity every where in Nature,

f. The Passages of antient Authors relating to our Sense of Beauty in natural Objects, and our Sense of moral Beauty, shall be quoted afterwards when I come to speak of Virtue. Let it only be observ'd here, that the Nature of this Discourse does not allow me to enlarge more fully upon the reality of these Principles in our Natures, far less to answer the Objections that have been made against the Writings in which they are explain'd: Let those who desire to be satisfy'd upon this head, have recourse to the *Characteristicks, Traité de Beau,* par M. *Crousaz,* Mr. *Hutchinson's* Enquiry, and his Illustrations on a moral Sense. [Shaftesbury, *Characteristicks;* Jean-Pierre de Crousaz, *Traité de beau: ou l'on montre en quoi consiste ce que l'on nomme ainsi, par des examples tirez de la plupart des arts & des sciences* (Amsterdam, 1715); Francis Hutcheson, *An Inquiry into the Original of Our Ideas of Beauty and Virtue* (London, 1725); Francis Hutcheson, *An Essay on the Nature and Conduct of the Passions and Affections, with Illustrations of the Moral Sense* (London, 1728).] As for this Principle of Greatness, see *Longinus de Sublim. sect.* 35. Ut multa alia omittam, hoc eos praecipue intuitos existimo: Naturam non humile nos quoddam, aut contemptum animal reputasse: Verum cum in hanc vitam, & in hunc universum terrarum orbem, ceu in amplissimum quoddam nos mitteret amphitheatrum, invictum una simul & insuperabile mentibus nostris omnis magnae rei, & humanam conditionem excedentis, adeoque divinioris, ingeneravisse desiderium. Atque hinc fieri, ut humanae mentis contemplationi conjectuique ne totus quidem orbis sufficiat; sed ipsos saepenumero ambientis omnia coeli terminos immensa animi agitatione transcendat: Quare si quis undequaque vitam hanc omnem consideraverit, & quantum quod grande est & excellens in cunctis rebus pulchro nitidoque praevaleat, intelliget e vestigio, cui nos rei nati simus. Itaque instinctu illo ducti naturae non exiles miramur rivulos, ———— verum ad conspectum vel Danubii vel Rheni resistimus attoniti; maxime omnium autem ad ipsius intuitum Oceani. Ad eundem modum non igniculum aut flammulam, &c. [Longinus, *On the Sublime,* 35.2–4: "Beside many other things, I think that they particularly had this before their eyes, that Nature has not reckoned us to be some low or despised animal; but when she sent us into this life and into this great world, as into some vast amphitheatre, she at the same time implanted in our hearts an invincible and unquenchable longing for everything that is great and exceeds the human condition and is therefore divine. And that is why not even the whole universe satisfies the thought and contemplation of the human mind; but man, with the measureless activity of his mind, frequently passes beyond the very limits of the heaven which encircles all things. Therefore anyone who has reflected on this whole life of ours on every side, and recognized how very much that which is grand and excellent in all things surpasses the

that flings the Mind into a most agreeable Astonishment, not only in the greater Prospects it affords in contemplating the Orbs that compose the vast and mighty Frame of the Universe, amidst which our Earth is so small a point; but even in considering those Objects, which in respect of our Senses are called minute: In every Insect, for instance, there is an endless Source of Wonder and Amazement, or Marks of Wisdom and Contrivance of an astonishing unmeasurable Greatness.

THIS must be allowed to be a just Account of the Contemplation of Nature, or of natural Philosophy, and the Pleasures which it yields. *Socrates* long ago found fault with those pretended Enquirers into Nature, who amused themselves with unmeaning Words, and thought they were more knowing in Nature, because they could give high-sounding Names to its various Effects; and did not inquire after the wise and good general Laws of Nature, and the excellent Purposes to which these steadily and unerringly work.g My Lord *Verulam* tells us, that true Philosophy consists in

This is a true Account of natural Philosophy, and the Pleasures arising from the Study of Nature, according to Socrates, Lord Bacon, and Sir Isaac Newton.

---

pretty and elegant, will immediately understand what we are born for. Under the influence of this natural instinct, we do not admire small streams, . . . but when we view the Danube or the Rhine, we stand astonished, and most of all at the sight of the Ocean itself. At the same time it is not a small fire or flame, etc."] So *Cicero. Est id omnino verum, nam omnium magnarum artium sicut arborum altitudo nos delectat. Ad M. Brutum Orator.* N° 43. [Cicero, *Orator,* xliii.147: "And it is completely true, for as in the case of trees it is the loftiness of all the great arts that pleases us."]

g. See *Platonis Phaedo, Edit. Steph. tom.* I. *p.* 97. *At cum ego aliquando audirem aliquem legentemque ex quodam libro, ut ipse dicebat, Anaxagorae, mentem esse quae omnia ordine disponat regatque omniumque sit causa: Hac nimirum causa delectabar, mihique illa quodammodo recte comparata esse videbatur, mentem nimirum omnium rerum esse causam: Et ita apud me statuebam, si ita res habeat, confici mentem illam gubernatricem atque dispositricem omnia ita disponere, itaque res singulas eo in loco collocare ubi fuerint rectissime constitutae.* ———— *Cum haec in animo meo reputarem, cum magna voluptate arbitrabar me praeceptorem comperisse, qui me ex animi mei sententia rerum causas edoceret, illumque mihi explicaturum, primum an terra lata sit an rotunda: Illisque rebus expositis adjuncturum etiam copiosiorem explicationem causae & necessitatis: Id est, ecquid melius, & cur ita omnino melius fuerit.* ———— *A mirifica tamen illa spe, crede mihi, excidi: Quandoquidem cum ulterius in illorum lectione progredear, hominem video nec mente quidem nec judicio ullo utentem, neque ullas causas ad rerum compositionem ordinemque commodi assignantem sive digerentem: At aëras quosdam & aetheras, aliaque multa & absurda quaedam pro rerum causis collocantem. Et mihi quidem videtur idem omnino illi contingere ac ei qui diceret, quicquid agit Socrates, mente & ratione agit: Deinde instituens explicare causas singularum rerum quas agam, diceret me primum quidem hic sedere, quia corpus meum ex ossibus & nervis*

gathering the Knowledge of Nature's Laws from Experience and Observation. And Sir *Isaac Newton* hath indeed carried that true Science of Nature to a great height of Perfection; of which he himself thus speaks in his Opticks,

"LATER Philosophers[h] banish the Consideration of such a Cause out of natural Philosophy, feigning Hypotheses for explaining all things mechanically, and referring other Causes to Metaphysicks: Whereas the main Business of natural Philosophy is to argue from Phenomena without feigning Hypotheses, and to deduce Causes from Effects, till we come to the very first Cause, which certainly is not mechanical; and not only to unfold the Mechanism of the World, but chiefly to resolve these and such like Questions. What is there in Places almost empty of Matter, and whence is

---

constet: Ossa vero sint solida & firma & juncturarum discrimina seorsim a se invicem habeant: ——— Cum ergo ossa in suis commissuris elevantur nervi qui modo laxantur, modo intenduntur, efficiunt ut membrorum incurvandorum inflectendorumque habeam facultatem, atque hac de causa hic sedeam incurvus, *&c.* [Plato, *Phaedo,* 97b–98d: "But when one day I heard someone reading from a certain book which he said was by Anaxagoras, and when I heard him say that it is mind that sets all things in order and governs them and is the cause of all things, I was naturally delighted with this cause, and it seemed to me that it was in some way right to regard mind as the cause of all things. And I reflected that, if this is the case, mind is the governor and disposer which organises all things and therefore sets every individual thing in the place where it is right for it to be. As I revolved these things in my mind, I was very happy to think that I had found a teacher, who would give me explanations of the causes of things that I would be happy to accept. He would explain to me first whether the earth is flat or round, and having done that, he would also give me a more elaborate account of the reason and the necessity of it; that is, which one is better, and why it is absolutely better so. But believe me, my wonderful expectations were disappointed. For as I continued reading these things, I saw that the man made no use of the mind or judgment, and did not offer or suggest any reasons of advantage in the organisation and ordering of things, but posited certain airs and ethers and many other absurdities as the causes of things. And it seemed to me that he was in exactly the same position as a man who should assert that whatever Socrates does, he does by mind and intelligence, then later when he sets himself to explain the causes of my individual actions, says first that I sit here because my body consists of bones and muscles, and bones are solid and hard and have joints that separate them from one another. So since the bones are free in the joints, the muscles, which are sometimes limp and sometimes tensed, give me the ability to flex and bend my limbs, and this is the cause why I am sitting here with my legs bent, etc."]

h. Opticks by Sir *Isaac Newton, Book* 3. *p.* 345. [Query 28 in Sir Isaac Newton, *Opticks: Or, a Treatise of the Reflections, Refractions, Inflections, and Colours of Light,* 4th ed. (London, 1730), p. 344.]

it that the Sun and Planets gravitate towards one another, without dense Matter between them? Whence is it that Nature doth *nothing in vain;* and whence arises all that *Order* and *Beauty* which we see in the World? To what end are Comets, and whence is it that Planets move all one and the same way in Orbs concentrick, while Comets <134> move all manner of ways in Orbs very excentrick; and what hinders the fix'd Stars from falling upon one another? How came the Bodies of Animals to be contrived with so much Art, and for what Ends are their several Parts? Was the Eye contrived without Skill in Opticks, and the Ear without Knowledge of Sounds? *&c.*"

I shall only observe farther on this Head, that if this be the right Method of improving and pursuing natural Philosophy, it must necessarily follow, that the Knowledge of the moral World ought likewise to be cultivated in the same manner, and can only be attain'd to by the like Method of enquiry: By investigating the general Laws, to which, if there is any Order in the moral World, or if it can be the Object of Knowledge, its Effects and Appearances must in like manner be reducible, as those in the corporeal World to theirs; and the moral Fitness of these general Laws, or their Tendency to the greater Good of the whole System to which they belong. A little Reflection upon the Constitution of our Minds, or our intellectual and moral Powers, will shew us, that general Laws obtain with regard to these, as well as in the sensible World.

What we may infer from this Account of natural Philosophy, concerning the right Method of improving moral Knowledge, or the Science of the moral World.

FOR, to name but two Instances; there is, with respect to us, a Law of Knowledge as fix'd and uniform as the Law of Gravity; in consequence of which, Knowledge is acquir'd by Experience and Application, in proportion to our Situation for taking in Views, and to our Assistances by social Communication.

AND there is also a Law of Habits, in consequence of which, repeated Acts produce a Propensity to do, and a Facility of doing; and, in consequence of which, we can acquire the Mastership of ourselves, or the Habit of acting deliberately, and with mature Examination.

NOW the many Effects that will soon be found on Reflection, to be reducible to these two excellent general Principles or Laws of our Nature, must convince every thinking Person, that were moral Philosophy studied and pursued in the same way as natural Philosophy hath been for some time, we should quickly see another kind of it produc'd, than what hath hitherto appear'd. This is perhaps what Sir *Isaac Newton* means, when he says, "And if natural Philosophy in all its Parts, by pursuing this Method shall at length be perfected, the Bounds of moral Philosophy will be also enlarged. For so far as we can know by natural Philosophy what is the first Cause, what Power he has over us, and what Benefits we receive from him, so far our Duty towards him, as well as that towards one another, will appear to us by the Light of Nature."[i]

Of the Imitation of Nature, and the Pleasures accruing from that Source.

BUT having thus briefly shewn by what Faculties, Powers, and Senses Man is fitted for the Contemplation of Nature, and directed to the right Method of acquiring natural Knowledge; let us next consider what is meant by the Imitation of Nature, and the Pleasures arising from it, and how we are qualify'd for them.

NATURE may be imitated two ways, by ingenious Arts; and in Life and Manners. And Man will be found fitted for both these kinds of Imitation by the same Powers, Faculties, and Senses that render him capable of contemplating and understanding Nature.

How we are fitted for the Imitation of Nature in Life and Conduct, by the same natural Powers and Senses, or Tastes above mention'd.

MAN is impelled to imitate Nature in the Regulation of his Affections and Actions, and fitted for it by his Sense of Beauty and Regularity; his publick Sense, or Delight in publick Good, and in the Affections and Actions that pursue it; and his Magnanimity, or Sense of Greatness. And accordingly, all the Virtues and Excellencies of human Life are reducible to these four; Prudence, Benevolence, Fortitude or Magnanimity, and Decency, or orderly and beautiful Oeconomy.

THESE virtuous Affections are pleasant and agreeable in the immediate Exercise, because we are so made and constituted as to receive Pleasure from them by our inward Senses, in the same manner as Light is pleasant to the Eye, or Harmony to the Ear. And they afford a yet higher and nobler Pleasure upon Reflection, in consequence of our Capacity of reviewing our Conduct, and approving it when it is perceiv'd to be becoming the Dignity of our Nature, and conformable to the Temper and Disposition of Nature's all-governing Mind.

i. Opticks by Sir *Isaac Newton, Book* 3. *p.* 381. *The fourth Edition.* [Query 31 in Newton, *Opticks,* p. 381.]

THE Cardinal Virtues are reduced by *Cicero* to these four above mentioned, because there are four Principles in our Natures, which exalt us to the Rank and Dignity of Being we hold above merely sensitive Creatures. The Desire and Love of Knowledge; our social Feeling, Love of Society or Delight in publick Good; Greatness of Mind, or a Desire of Power and Perfection; and a Sense of Beauty and Decorum in Characters and Actions. All the Virtues, Duties or Excellencies of human Life can be nothing else <135> (saith he) but those our principal Powers, Faculties or Senses operating, conjunctly each with proper force, towards the Perfection and Happiness of our Minds, and the Beauty and Regularity of our Conduct. All these mix'd with Art and confin'd to due Bounds, make and maintain the Ballance of the Mind; and by their well-accorded Contrasts produce a lovely Harmony and Consistency of Life and Manners. *Cicero* shews us in many different parts of his Writings, that all the Virtues are these Powers and Principles duly regulated, or mixing and combining with well-proportion'd Strength to give Nerves, Beauty, and Grace to Life. The Whole of Virtue consists (according to that Philosophy) in living agreeably to Nature; agreeably to what we perceive by our moral Sense and Conscience to be suitable to the Dignity of our Nature; agreeably to what we perceive, by the same Sense and the Study of Nature, to be the End appointed to us by Nature; agreeably to the End pursued by Nature itself in all its Works.[j]

Cicero's Account of the Virtues corresponding to the distinguishing Principles in human Nature.

j. See *Marcus Antoninus's* Meditations, *Collier's* Translation, *p.* 140. *c.* 26. Pleasure and Satisfaction consists in following the Bent of Nature, and doing the things we are made for. And which way is this to be compass'd? By the practice of general Kindness, by neglecting the Importunity and Clamour of our Senses, by distinguishing Appearances from Truth, and by contemplating Nature and the Works of the Almighty. All this is acting according to kind, and keeping the Faculties in the right Channel, *&c.* And *p.* 77. *c.* 21. Among all things in the Universe direct your Worship to the Greatest; and which is that? 'Tis that Being which manages and governs all the rest. And as you worship the best thing in Nature, so you are to pay a proportionable regard to the best thing in yourself: You'll know it by its relation to the Deity, *&c.* [*The Emperor Marcus Antoninus His Conversation with himself,* translated by Jeremy Collier (London, 1701), pp. 76–77, 140–41.] *Cic. de Off. lib.* 1. N° 4. Homo autem quod rationis est particeps, per quam consequentia cernit, causas rerum videt, earumque progresslus & quasi antecessiones non ignorat, similitudines comparat, & rebus praesentibus adjungit, atque annectit futuras: Facile totius vitae cursum videt, ad eamque degendam praeparat res necessarias: Eademque natura, vi rationis hominem conciliat homini & ad orationis & ad vitae societatem ———— In primisque hominis est propria veri inquisitio atque investigatio. Itaque ———— cog-

Virtue
necessarily
pre-supposes
a Sense of
moral Beauty
and Perfec-
tion, and
Greatness of
Mind.

HAD we no Sense of moral Beauty and Perfection, no Sense of Harmony and Decorum in Life and Manners; no moral Sense, shewing us the Subordination in which all the inferiour merely sensitive or animal Appetites and Affections ought to be maintain'd, we could not be capable of Virtue, we could not approve or disapprove Affections and Manners. Without a Sense of Beauty and Harmony, Greatness and Becomingness of Affections and Actions, we could no more have any Sense of the Dignity of

---

nitionemque rerum aut occultarum aut admirabilium, ad beate vivendum necessariam ducimus. Ex quo intelligitur, quod verum, simplex, sincerumque sit, id esse naturae hominis aptissimum. Huic veri videndi cupiditati adjuncta est appetitio quaedam principatus, ut nemini parere animus bene a natura informatus velit, nisi praecipienti, aut docenti, aut utilitatis causa, juste & legitime imperanti: Ex quo animi magnitudo existit, humanarumque rerum contemtio. Nec vero illa parva vis naturae est, rationisque quod unum hoc animal sentit quid sit ordo, quid sit quod deceat, in factis dictisque qui modus. Itaque eorum ipsorum, quae adspectu sentiuntur, nullum aliud animal pulchritudinem, venustatem, convenientiam partium sentit, quam similitudinem natura, ratioque ab oculis ad animum transferens, multo etiam magis pulchritudinem, constantiam, ordinem in consiliis factisque conservandum putat: ———— Omne quod honestum est, id quatuor partium oritur ex aliqua. Aut enim in perspicientia veri, solertiaque versatur: aut in hominum societate tuenda, tribuendoque suum cuique & rerum contractarum fide, aut in animi excelsi, atque invicti magnitudine ac robore; aut in omnium quae fiunt, quaeque dicuntur, ordine & modo, in quo inest modestia & temperantia. Quae quatuor quanquam inter se colligata atque implicita sunt, tamen ex singulis certa officiorum genera nascuntur, &c. [Cicero, *De officiis,* I.iv.11–16: "But because man participates in reason— by which he discerns consequences, sees the causes of things, and is not ignorant of their developments and what we might call their antecedents, compares similarities, and connects and associates future events with present events—he easily sees the course of human life, and prepares what is necessary for leading it. Nature also by the power of reason brings people together to share both speech and life together. Above all, the search and inquiry after truth is man's special quality. Therefore we think that the discovery of things that are obscure or admirable is necessary for a happy life. From this we infer that everything true, simple, and genuine is most fitted to the nature of man. To this desire to see the truth is united a certain ambition for primacy, so that a mind well-formed by nature is unwilling to be subject to anybody except a person who instructs and teaches, or one who governs in justice and legitimacy for everyone's benefit. This is the source of greatness of mind and contempt for human affairs. Further it is no insignificant property of nature and reason that this animal alone perceives what order is, what is fitting, and what moderation is in word and deed. This is why no other animal apprehends the beauty, grace, and propriety of the parts of the things that sight perceives; nature and reason transfer it by analogy from the eyes to the mind, and holds that a much greater beauty, regularity, consistency, and order should be maintained in one's deliberations and actions. Everything that is morally good [*honestum*] arises from one of four parts. For either it is concerned with intelligence and the perception of truth; or with preserving

our Natures, and of acting a right part, than a blind Man can have of Colours. 'Tis in consequence of moral Conscience, or of our moral Sense of the Beauty, Dignity, Worth, and Merit of Characters, Affections and Actions, that though we may be brib'd or terrify'd into the doing a base Action; yet we can neither be brib'd nor terrify'd into the Approbation of it. It is in consequence of it that we are able to form any other Idea of an Action, besides that of the Quantity of sensible Pleasures it may bring, and that

---

society among men by giving to everyone his due and keeping faith in agreements; or with the greatness and strength of a lofty and unconquered mind; or with order and moderation in everything that is done and spoken, in which lie modesty and temperance. And although these four are bound and implicated with each other, nevertheless certain duties arise from each one of them individually, etc."] See *Cicero de Oratore, lib.* 1. Nº 3, 4, & 5. [Cicero, *De oratore,* I.iii–v.] *De Partitione Oratoria,* Nº 22, & 23. Est igitur vis virtutis duplex, aut enim scientia cernitur virtus aut actione. Nam quae prudentia quaeque gravissimo nomine sapientia appellatur, haec scientia pollet una. Quae vero moderandis cupiditatibus, regendisque animi motibus laudatur, ejus est munus in agendo, cui temperantiae nomen est. ——— Quae autem haec uno genere complectitur magnitudo animi dicitur: Cujus est liberalitas in usu pecuniae: simulque altitudo animi in capiendis incommodis & maxime injuriis: ——— Custos vero virtutum omnium est verecundia, &c. [Cicero, *De partitione oratoria,* xxii.76: "Virtue therefore has two thrusts; for it is seen either in knowledge or in action. For the virtue which is called prudence and that which is called by the most solemn name of wisdom count as a single form of knowledge. But the virtue that is applauded for moderating the passions and governing the emotions, its task is in action, and its name is temperance"; xxii.77: "The virtue which embraces these in one kind is called magnanimity; to it belong generosity in the use of money and also greatness of mind in handling setbacks and especially injustices"; xxiii.79: "And the guardian of all the virtues is a sense of shame."] *De fin. Bon. & Mal. lib.* 2. Nº 14. Honestum igitur id intelligimus quod tale est ut detracta omni utilitate sine ullis praemiis, fructibusque per seipsum possit jure laudari. ——— Homines enim etsi aliis multis tamen hoc uno a bestiis plurimum differunt, quod rationem habeant a natura datam mentemque, & acrem & vigentem quae causas rerum, &c. ——— Eademque ratio fecit hominem hominum appetentem, cumque his natura & sermone, & usu congruentem, ut profectus a caritate domesticorum ac suorum, serpat longius, & se implicet primum civium deinde omnium mortalium societate: ——— Et quoniam eadem natura cupiditatem ingenuit homini veri inveniendi, &c. His initiis inducti omnia vera diligimus, id est fidelia, simplicia, constantia, &c. Eadem ratio habet in se quiddam amplum, atque magnificum ad imperandum magis, quam ad parendum accomodatum: Omnia humana non tolerabilia solum, sed etiam levia ducens: Altum quiddam & excelsum, nihil timens, nemini cedens, semper invictum. Atque his tribus generibus notatis, quartum sequitur, & in eadem pulchritudine, & aptum ex illis tribus; in quo inest ordo & moderatio. Cujus similitudine perspecta in formarum specie; a dignitate transitum est ad honestatem dictorum atque factorum, &c. [Cicero, *De finibus bonorum et malorum,* II.xiv.45–47: "By moral goodness [*honestum*] we mean that which is such that

we are capable of framing to ourselves general Rules of Life, by the Study and Observance of which, Life is render'd uniform, consistent, regular and beautiful; and of delighting in that moral Harmony and Beauty.

THUS it is evidently the same Senses, Dispositions, and Powers, which fit and qualify us for contemplating Nature with satisfaction; and for imitating in our Conduct the moral Perfections of its Creator and Governour, which are clearly manifested by the Frame, Constitution and Laws of Nature. And then it is that the Study of Nature must afford the highest Joy, when we feel the same Temper and Disposition prevailing <136> in our own Minds which Nature displays; and we are conscious of our earnest Endeavours to transplant into our Minds and Lives, all the moral Beauties that appear in it; the Benevolence, the Harmony, the Simplicity, the Truth, and Greatness that reign throughout universal Nature; and to become like to our Creator the all-perfect Mind, who made, upholds, and governs all.

We can only know whether we have these Powers or Principles, and Dispositions inherent in our Natures, by turning our

WHETHER we have those Senses that have been mention'd, is a matter of Experience; it can only be known by Consciousness. And therefore in speaking of them, an Appeal must be made to what we feel and perceive. It is the same with regard to all our other Faculties and Perceptions: There can be no other way of convincing one that he hath certain Powers, Ideas and Feelings, but by endeavouring to make him turn his Eyes inward, look attentively into his own Mind, and observe what passes in it. Mean time

---

it may rightly be commended for itself apart from any advantage, without any rewards or profits. Though men differ from the beasts in many ways, they do so most of all in this one thing that they possess reason and a sharp and vigorous intelligence given to them by nature which the causes of things, etc. Reason has also made man desirous of the company of other human beings, and has made him adapted to them in nature, speech and habit, so that starting out from love of his family and household, he may advance further and attach himself to the society first of his fellow-citizens and then of all human kind. And since nature has also implanted in human beings a passion for discovering truth, etc. Prompted by this instinct we love everything that is true, that is, everything that is faithful, simple, constant, etc. Reason also has something grand in itself and magnificent, better suited to commanding than obeying; it regards all the accidents of human life not merely as tolerable but as insignificant; it is lofty and elevated, fearing nothing, yielding to no one, never overcome. Now we have noted these three kinds, a fourth follows, possessed of the same beauty and following from those three; and in it is order and moderation. Having seen the analogy with this in the appearance of outward forms, we pass from the dignity to the moral goodness of words and deeds, etc."] Of Greatness of Mind, see Cicero de Off. lib. 1. N° 20. Of Beauty or Decency, ibid. 28, & 29. [Cicero, De officiis, I.xx, xxviii–xxix.]

'tis certain, that if we had not these Faculties and Dispositions, Nature could not please us by its Unity, Regularity and Beauty; or by its steady pursuance of universal Good; nor could we be delighted with amiable, lovely, and praise-worthy Characters and Actions. These would necessarily be to us as Harmony to one who has no Ear. Unity, Beauty and Grace would be empty, insignificant Sounds to us. For it must be true in general, that every Gratification or Pleasure necessarily pre-supposes an Affection, Appetite, or Disposition suited to it: And that without natural Affections, Dispositions and Appetites, no one thing could please us more than another.

THIS also is certain, that if Beauty, Harmony, Unity of Design, Regularity, and wise generous Administration, are real things in Nature, they must be so in our Conduct; or reciprocally, if they are real Qualities, and not Words without any Meaning with regard to our Conduct and Manners, they must likewise be real with respect to the Oeconomy of Nature. 'Tis impossible to have a Sense of them in one of these, without transferring them to the other. To own their Reality in the one case, and deny it in the other, is a Contradiction in terms: For how can Order, Beauty, Goodness, and Greatness belong to certain Affections and Actions; to the Character of one rational Being, or to any moral Object; and not likewise as necessarily belong to all analogous Affections, Actions, and Characters, or to every like moral Object? If the generous Pursuit of publick Good be laudable and excellent in Nature; it must likewise be valuable and praise-worthy in us, and its contrary be hateful and base: And, on the other hand, if benevolent generous Affection be amiable and commendable in us, and its opposites be mean, ignoble, and unworthy; the same must likewise be true with regard to the Administration of Nature, and the Temper and Disposition of its Author and Governour.

BUT there will be occasion to carry this Reasoning yet farther, in considering the imitative Arts, to which I now proceed. Man is not only capable of imitating Nature in Life and Manners, but likewise by several Arts. All Arts are Imitations of Nature, or Applications of its known Laws to the Uses and Purposes of human Life; as of Gravity, Elasticity, &c. But the Arts that are more properly called imitative, are those of Fancy and Genius, such as Poetry, Painting and Sculpture. Now 'tis the same Senses, Dispositions, Instincts and Powers, that render us capable of contemplating Na-

[margin:] Eyes inward, and by reflecting on our own Minds, and their Operations.

Yet it is certain that our Capacity of contemplating Nature with delight, or of imitating it by the Study and Exercise of Virtue, pre-supposes these Principles. Every Pleasure pre-supposes a corresponding Appetite, Affection, or Disposition.

Of the Imitation of Nature by ingenious Arts, and the Pleasures arising from that Source.

ture, and of imitating its Order, Beauty, and Greatness in Life and Manners; that likewise fit and qualify us for the Imitation of Nature by those ingenious Arts.

THERE is implanted in our Minds not only a strong desire of understanding Nature's Methods of Operation, and all its various Appearances; but also a very strong Disposition to imitate Nature, emulate it, and vie with it; and thus to become as it were Creators ourselves. Hence the Origin of Poetry, Painting, and of all the noble and aspiring, imitative Arts: Hence all the bold Efforts of the human Mind to add as much as it possibly can, to our Happiness by our own Invention, Genius, and Industry. Man is very wisely made by his Creator, an imitative Being; this Propensity to copy after Nature, and to emulate it, is indeed a Principle of wonderful use in such a Constitution as ours is. But to what purpose could it serve; or what could it produce that is great and excellent, were we not at the same time indued with the other Faculties and Senses that have been described, to guide and assist it in the Imitation of Nature; that is, with a Sense of Beauty, Order, and Greatness, and with a moral Sense, or a social, affectionate, generous Disposition? The chief Qualities of good Imitation by Poetry, Painting and Sculpture, that have been already enumerated and explained, do they not all of them evidently pre-suppose these Faculties and Dispositions in order to relish them, or indeed to have any Notion of them? What else is it that could prompt us to pursue and endeavour after Truth, Beauty, Consistency, Decorum, Greatness and Grace in Compositions of any kind; or that could be delighted and charmed by these Qualities when they are attained to in any human Production, but a natural Sense of Beauty, Unity, Decorum, Grace and Greatness? In like manner, if we had nothing of Sympathy, Compassion, <137> Benevolence and Generosity in our Frame, could we think of calling forth such Affections into Action, and giving them agreeable Exercise by moving and interesting Representations: Or could we be delightfully touched and affected by the imitative Arts in a tender social manner, without any Disposition or Principle in our Nature fit to be worked upon? Nothing can be more ridiculous than to speak of perceiving any Quality, without a Sense qualified to perceive it: Beings can neither desire nor relish any Entertainment for which they are not fitted by Nature, or for which, so to speak, they have no natural Appetite. On the one hand

We are qualify'd for that by the same Powers and Dispositions already mention'd.

therefore, if Truth, Beauty, Greatness and Grace, and all the other Qualities
that are ascribed to the fine Arts, as constituting their Perfection, are not
mere Sounds without a Meaning, we must have naturally implanted in us
those Faculties and Dispositions that are requisite to comprehend and enjoy
them. And, on the other hand, if we really are possess'd of Faculties and
Senses qualify'd to understand and taste these Qualities, the chief Excellence of the imitative Arts must necessarily consist in their being able to
give suitable Entertainment to such noble Faculties and Senses: Or their
Productions can only be excellent in proportion to the Satisfaction they are
able to afford to them.

THAT it is the very same Faculties and Dispositions which qualify us for
understanding and relishing the Beauty and Perfection of Nature, the
Beauty and Perfection of moral Conduct, and the Beauty and Perfection
of the imitative Arts is so evident, that it is indeed unaccountable how any
who pretend to Taste or Intelligence of these Arts, can doubt of the Reality
and Naturalness of Virtue, and of a moral Sense in our Make and Frame;
or entertain wrong Conceptions of Nature, and doubt of the moral Sense
and good Disposition of our Contriver and Author.

BUT since it is no rare thing to meet with Virtuosi or professed Admirers
of the fine Arts, who call into question all other Beauty but that of their
beloved Arts, I cannot chuse but call upon them to reflect, that they must
either give up the reality of the Taste upon which they so highly value themselves, and which is indeed a very fine Accomplishment; or they must of
necessity own the reality of Virtue and of a moral Sense, and consequently
acknowledge the Wisdom and Goodness of our Maker, the Creator and
Upholder of all things, who hath inlaid it into our Natures, and made us
capable of receiving such noble Entertainment from it in various ways.

So strictly are all Truths bound and united together, that having first
established a right Idea of Virtue, and of those Faculties that capacitate us
for perceiving and delighting in it; or of Nature's wise and regular Oeconomy in pursuing the general Good of the Whole; it is very easy by obvious
Consequences to deduce and establish a just Notion from thence, of the
fine Arts and their principal Excellencies: And, on the other side, if we begin
by settling a true Idea of the Excellencies of the fine Arts, and of those
Faculties and Dispositions in our Minds which qualify us for pursuing

them, and receiving pleasure from them, it is very easy by natural consequences from these Principles to fix the true Notion of Virtue and moral
Excellence, whether in the Government of our own Affections and Actions,
or in the Administration of Nature. For if the Perfection of Nature consists
in working unerringly towards the Beauty and Good of the Whole by simple consistent Laws; and the Perfection of Life and Manners consists in
acting in concert with Nature, and in pursuing steadily the Good of Mankind by well-poised, regular and generous Affections; then must the Perfection of the imitative Arts consist in like manner in making regular and
beautiful Systems, in which every part being duly adapted and submitted
to what is principal, the Whole hath a great, noble, and virtuous Effect upon

the Mind: And reciprocally, if the Beauty and Perfection of the imitative
Arts is acknowledged to result from a due Subordination of Parts to the
main End, and from Harmony and a noble virtuous Tendency in the
Whole; then must our Conduct and the Administration of Nature be beautiful and perfect, only in proportion to the just Subordination, Harmony
and good Tendency that prevails in the Whole.

IF Unity, Decency, Truth and Greatness are acknowledged in the imitative Arts, they must likewise take place with regard to Nature, for Nature
itself must be capable of affecting us in the same manner. And they must
likewise take place in Life and Manners, in Affections, Actions and Characters; for these must be capable of touching and affecting us in the same
manner in real Life as in Imitation. The Artist derives all his Ideas from
Nature, and does not make Laws and Connexions agreeably to which he
works in order to produce certain Effects, but conforms himself to such as
he finds to be necessarily and unchangeably established in Nature: All his
Attempts pre-suppose certain Dispositions implanted in the Breasts of
Mankind originally by Nature itself, which he cannot produce if wanting,
but may suit himself to and work upon in the way that Nature hath appointed, and thereby render his Works exceeding pleasing and agreeable.
If therefore the imitative Arts are really capable of producing beautiful,
great, and noble Effects upon us, there must be something beautiful, great
and noble in our Minds, the Improvement of <138> which is necessarily
our Excellence and Perfection, for which we could not have been suited,
but by a Mind of superiour Beauty, Nobleness and Greatness, whose Perfection consists in producing Beings capable of noble Ends and Pursuits,

and in framing and adapting each kind of Beings in every respect as may best suit to the highest Perfection in the Whole.

To acknowledge a real Excellence and Beauty in any imitative Art, without confessing a real Excellence and Beauty in Nature, and the real Excellence and Worth of Virtue, is absurdly to ascribe a Power and Influence to Copies which the Original hath not: It is the same as to assert, that a real Object of which an exact Copy is taken, would not have the same effect upon us by its real Qualities, which those Qualities have upon us in the Imitation: It is to assert not only that the Artist can form Ideas which have no Foundation in Nature itself, or are no wise suggested to him by it; but that he can give Powers and Qualities to Objects which he copies from Nature, that are quite independent of all Nature's Laws and Establishments, and in which Nature hath no part or share.

BUT this way of reasoning may appear to some too abstruse and metaphysical; and therefore I shall endeavour to set the Analogy between the moral Virtues and Graces, and the Beauties and Graces of the fine Arts in another light, by suggesting briefly a few Observations of the Ancients upon this Subject: For, according to them, to illustrate, prove and enforce this inseparable necessary Connexion, (of which I am now treating) between the reality of Beauty, Unity, Order, Grace and Greatness in Nature, and their reality in the Conduct of our Affections and Actions, and in all ingenious Imitations of Nature by Arts, is the chief Scope of true Philosophy, the fittest Method of forming betimes in young Minds an universal good Taste; and therefore it is the proper Business of Education. It is only such Philosophy that deserves to be called the Guide of Life,[k] the Discerner of Excellence, and the Source of all truly manly, rational, and pure Happiness: Or that can produce a right Taste of Life, and of Man's best Pursuits, Employments and Diversions. And therefore it is this Philosophy that the Formers of Youth ought to have ever in their View throughout the whole of Education.

Farther Illustrations upon the Foundations of the Arts, and of good Taste in our Natures, and the proper ways of cultivating it.

k. So *Cicero* addresses true Philosophy, O philosophia vitae dux, O virtutum indagatrix, expultrixque vitiorum? Quid modo non nos, sed omnino vita hominum sine te esse potuisset? &c. *Tus. Quaest. l.* 5. N° 2. [Cicero, *Tusculan Disputations,* V.ii.5: "O philosophy, O guide of life, discoverer of the virtues and enemy of the vices! What would we have been without you? What would human life itself have been?"]

A strict
Connection
and Analogy
between our
Sense of
natural and
our Sense of
moral Beauty.

THE Ancients have often observ'd, that there is a strict Analogy between our Sense of Beauty in sensible Objects, and our moral Sense, or our Sense of Beauty in Affections, Actions and Characters. So nearly are these related, or so intimately are they blended together in our Natures, that he who hath any Taste of Beauty in sensible Forms, any Notion of Harmony, Regularity and Unity in Bodies, must necessarily be led to transfer that Sense to moral Objects: And therefore if such a one is dissolute or irregular in his Conduct, he must live at continual variance with himself, and in downright contradiction to what he delights in and highly admires in other Subjects. So strictly, so nearly are those two Senses allied to one another, that it is hardly possible to speak of moral Objects in any other Language, than that which expresses the Beauties of the other kind. Hence it is that the best Authors of Antiquity speak of the Measures and Numbers of Life; the Harmony, Unity and Simplicity of Manners; the Beautiful, the Decent in Actions; the Regularity, the Order, the Symmetry of Life; the Proportions, the Graces of the Mind; Truth, Sublimity, Greatness, and Consistency of Manners. Such is the Style of the best ancient Moralists.[1] And in explaining

---

1. See the Passages already quoted, at the Beginning of this Chapter, about the Contemplation of Nature, and those just now quoted concerning the Decorum. So *Horace,*

Sed verae numerosque, modosque ediscere vitae.

> Epist. l. 2. Ep. 2. [Horace, *Epistles,* II.ii.144:
> "But to master the rhythms and measures of a true life."]

Est modus in rebus; sunt certi denique fines,
Quos ultra, citraque nequit consistere rectum.

> Sat. l. 1. Sat. 1. [Horace, *Satires,* I.i.106–7:
> "There is measure in all things; there are, in short,
> certain limits beyond which or short of which right cannot stand."]

Quid verum atque decens, curo & rogo, & omnis in hoc sum.
Aesluat, & vitae disconvenit ordine toto.

> Ep. l. 1. Ep. 2. [Horace, *Epistles,* I.i.11, 99:
> "My great care is to inquire what is true and fitting,
> and I am totally devoted to this. . . . He seethes,
> and is at odds with himself in his whole manner of life."]

Qui quid sit pulcrum, quid turpe quid utile, quid non.

> Ep. l. 1. Ep. 2. [Horace, *Epistles,* I.ii.3:
> "What is fine, what is foul, what is useful, what not."]

So *Plato, Cicero,* and all the best Philosophers are ever speaking of the τὸ καλὸν [the fine], the τὸ πρέπον [the fitting], the *pulcrum* [the fine], the *decens* [the fitting], the

these moral Qualities, they are constantly referring to those which are analogous to them in sensible Forms, and in the Productions of Fancy and
Genius in Imitations of Nature. On account of this Affinity and Analogy,
they have justly concluded, that the Admiration, and Love of Order, Harmony and Proportion in whatever kind, must be naturally improving to
the Temper, advantageous to social Affection, and highly assistant to Virtue,
which is itself no other than the Love of Order and Beauty in Society: That
all the Arts which have Truth, Order and Beauty for their Object and Aim,
must have a Tendency to advance the Love of moral Beauty in Life and
Conduct, and to check Disorder and Irregularity: But chiefly the Contemplation of the Order of Nature, from which all our Ideas of Order and
Beauty are originally copied. One of the most pleasant and entertaining
Speculations in Philosophy is the universal Analogy that prevails throughout Nature: The Analogy between the natural and moral World in every
respect. 'Tis this Analogy that lays the Foundation (as it hath been frequently observed by many Authors) for what is principal in the Works of
Genius, the cloathing moral Objects with sensible Images, or the giving
them Bodies, Shapes, and Forms in Description, Sculpture, and Painting. <139>

BUT this Analogy between the natural and moral World reaches much
farther; and indeed if it did not, Man would necessarily be incapable of
one of his noblest Pleasures; for unless there was such a Similitude or Analogy between the natural and moral World, that all Objects of the later sort
may be painted under Images taken from the former, we could not at all
have any Intercourse or Communication with one another about moral
things. It hath been often remarked, that the greater part of the Words
denoting Affections and Operations of the moral kind, do in their original
Signification express sensible Perceptions. But the truth of the matter is,
that if inward Sentiments, Affections, and Actions could not be pictured
to us by means of some things analogous to them in the sensible World,
Language and Discourse could not extend any farther than to the Objects
perceivable by our outward Senses, and those of the moral kind could not
be described or conveyed at all. But not to dwell longer on that Reflexion,

---

honestum [the morally good], convenienter naturae vivere [living in agreement with na-
ture], &c.

though it well deserves the Attention of those who are concerned in Education, and naturally leads to a juster Notion of the most profitable as well as agreeable Method of teaching Language, or explaining Words, than is commonly entertained: It is sufficient to the present purpose to observe, that Beauty in its first Meaning signifies a Satisfaction which certain visible Objects are adapted to give to the Sight; and it is fitly applied to denote a similar Satisfaction which certain moral Objects are equally adapted to give to the Understanding or Eye of the Mind, because of the Similarity of the Pleasures perceived, and because of their Analogy in all other respects. For as by Induction, in the former case it is found to be the Regularity of Objects that gives that Satisfaction; or, in other words, that whatever Object of Sense gives it is a regular Whole, that hath Variety amidst Uniformity; and it is also found, that Usefulness is always connected with Regularity and Beauty: So in the later case by Induction it is likewise found, that the same Connexions take place with regard to every moral Object that is pleasing and agreeable to our Contemplation: These also are regular Objects, or have Variety with Unity, and are in like manner profitable or useful. The Perception of Pleasure called Beauty in both cases is distinct from the Reflexion upon Utility, or upon Regularity and Unity; it is perceived immediately, or at first sight previously to all Consideration of these Concomitants. These Connexions between Beauty, Regularity and Utility, are found out afterwards by Enquiry; and it is because they are discovered to take place in many Examples, and no contradictory Instance appears, that it is established into an universal Canon by Induction, agreeably to all the Rules of Philosophy and good Reasoning; that whatever is beautiful in the moral, as well as in the natural, or sensible World, is regular, hath Unity of Design, or Variety with Uniformity, and is useful. It is upon this Connexion between Beauty and Utility, that the Ancients have greatly insisted.

The inseparable Connexion of Beauty and Truth with Utility and Advantage.

THEY have often remarked, that as in Nature, so in all the Arts, Beauty, Truth, and Utility are inseparably connected, or more properly are one and the same. Beauty and Truth are plainly join'd with the Notion of Utility and Conveniency, in the Apprehension of every ingenious Artist; the Statuary, the Painter, the Architect: And for what reason, but because it is so in Nature? The same Shapes and Proportions, which make Beauty, afford advantage, by adapting to Activity and Use. The same Features which occasion Deformity, create Sickliness and Disease. The proportionate and regular State is the truly prosperous, sound, and natural one in every Subject. Health of the Body is the just Proportion, Ballance and regular Course of Things in a Constitution. And what else is Health or Soundness of Mind but the harmonious State, or true and just Ballance of the Affections: Or what else is it that produces Deformity of the moral kind, but something that tends to the Ruin and Dissolution of our mental Fabrick?[m] *Cicero* and *Quintilian* have illustrated this Truth (*nunquam veri species ab utilitate dividitur*)[29] by a variety of Examples; from the Structures of animate and inanimate things; the Fabrick of the human Body, and the Beauty of the human Mind; and then by analogous Instances from Architecture and all

m. Et ut corporis est quaedam apta figura membrorum cum coloris quaedam suavitate: Eaque dicitur pulchritudo, sic in animo, opinionum, judiciorumque aequabilitas, & constantia, cum firmitate quadam & stabilitate virtutem subsequens, aut virtutis vim ipsam continens, pulchritudo vocatur. Itemque viribus corporis, & nervis, & efficacitati similes, similibus verbis, animi vires nominantur. Velocitas, sanitas, morbi, &c. Cic. *Tuscul. Quaest. lib.* 4. N° 13. [Cicero, *Tusculan Disputations,* IV.xiii.31: "And as the body may have a becoming shape of limb together with an attractive complexion which is called beauty; so in the mind, the term beauty is applied to a calmness and consistency in opinions and judgments, combined with a certain steadiness and stability, which is consequent upon virtue or contains the very force of virtue. Similarly, the strength of mind that is analogous to strength of body, to its muscles and powers of action, is called by similar words. Swiftness, health, sickness, etc."] *De Off. lib.* 1. N° 28, & 36. [Cicero, *De officiis,* I.xxviii, xxxvi.] Every thing is at ease when the Powers of it move regularly and without interruption. Now a rational Being is in this prosperous Condition, when her Judgment is gain'd by nothing but Evidence and Truth; when her Designs are all meant for the advantage of Society. When her Desires and Aversions are confined to Objects within her power, when she rests satisfied with the Distributions of Providence: for which she has great reason, since she is a part of it herself. And with as much propriety, as a Leaf belongs to the Nature of the Tree which bears it, *&c. Marcus Antoninus*'s Meditations, *Collier*'s Translation, *p.* 134. [Turnbull's transcription of this passage from Collier's translation is not absolutely faithful to the original.]

29. Quintilian, *Institutio oratoria,* VIII.iii.11: "In fact true beauty and usefulness always go hand in hand." Compare Cicero, *De oratore,* III.xlv.178: "But in oratory as in most things nature itself has wonderfully ensured that those things which have the greatest utility, should have the greatest dignity and often too the greatest charm."

the Arts.[n] And hence the Ancients have laid it down as an universal Maxim
in Life and Manners, in Nature and <140> in all the imitative Arts; That
what is beautiful is harmonious and proportion'd, what is harmonious and
proportion'd is true; and what is at once both beautiful and true, is of con-

n. *Cicero Orator. lib.* 3. 45, 46. Sed ut in plerisque rebus incredibiliter hoc natura est
ipsa fabricata: Sic in oratione, ut ea, quae maximam utilitatem in se continerent, eadem
haberent plurimum vel dignitatis, vel saepe etiam venustatis. Incolumitatis, ac salutis
omnium causa, videmus hunc statum esse hujus totius mundi atque naturae ————
Haec tantam habent vim ut paulum immutata cohaerere non possint: Tantam pulchritudinem, ut nulla species ne excogitari quidem possit ornatior. Referte nunc animum ad
hominum, vel etiam ceterarum animantium formam, & figuram. Nullam partem corporis sine aliqua necessitate affictam, totamque formam quasi perfectam reperietis arte
non casu. Quid in arboribus, in quibus non truncus, non rami, non folia sunt denique,
nisi ad suam retinendam, conservandamque naturam? Nusquam tamen est ulla pars nisi
venusta. Linquamus naturam, arteisque videamus. Quid tam in navigio necessarium
quam latera, quam carinae, quam mali, quam vela, quam prora, quam puppis, quam
antennae? Quae tamen hanc habent in specie venustatem; ut non solum salutis sed etiam
voluptatis causa inventa esse videantur. Columnae, & templa, & porticus sustinent. Tamen habent non plus utilitatis quam dignitatis. Capitolii fastigium illud, & ceterarum
aedium, non venustas sed necessitas ipsa fabricata est. Nam cum esset habita ratio, quemadmodum ex utraque tecti parte aqua delaberetur: Utilitatem templi, fastigii dignitas
consecuta est: Ut etiam si in coelo statueretur, ubi imber esse non posset nullam sine
fastigio dignitatem habiturum fuisse videatur. Hoc in omnibus item partibus orationis
evenit ut utilitatem, ac prope necessitatem suavitas quaedam ac lepos consequatur, &c.
[Cicero, *De oratore,* III.xlv.178–III.xlvi.181: "But in oratory as in most things nature itself
has wonderfully ensured that those things which have the greatest utility, should have
the greatest dignity and often too the greatest charm. We see that this is the case with
the whole of this world and nature for the sake of the security and safety of all things.
These things have so much power that they would not cohere if they were changed by
only a little bit and they have so much beauty that no sight could even be imagined which
was more attractive. Turn your thoughts now to the form and figure of human beings
or even of other living things. You will find no part of the body fashioned without some
need for it, and the whole form as it were perfected by art and not by chance. What of
trees, where neither trunk nor branches nor foliage exists but to retain and preserve their
nature? Yet nowhere is there a part which is not attractive. Let us leave nature, let us look
at the arts. What is so essential in a boat as the sides, the keels, the masts and sails, the
prow, the stern and the yardarms? But they are all so graceful in appearance that they
seem to have been devised not merely for safety's sake but for pleasure. Pillars support
both temples and porches. Yet they have as much grandeur as usefulness. It was not
aesthetic considerations that raised the roof-ridge of the Capitol and other great structures. For when thought was given to how water would run off both sides of the roof,
the grandeur of the roof-ridge was a consequence of its usefulness to the temple. And
so even if it were built in a climate where there could not be any rain, it seems that it

sequence agreeable and good. And accordingly, Affections, Manners, and all the Arts are to be judged by this Rule.° That which in Art is not useful to the Whole, cannot be beautiful; all Ornaments which do not naturally rise out of the Subject, and tend to support and maintain it, and promote the design'd Effect of the Whole, are, for the same reason that they are an Incumbrance, not merely superfluous, but noxious and hurtful with regard to the proposed End and Effect of the Whole.

THIS *Cicero* illustrates particularly by Architecture, which one is apt to consider at first sight as a merely ornamental Art; and so does *Vitruvius* more fully. *Cicero* and *Quintilian* shew it to be so in Oratory; and 'tis evidently so in Painting and Sculpture: For is not the Truth and Beauty of every Figure measured in these Arts, from the Perfection of Nature, in her just adapting of every Limb and Proportion, to the Activity, Strength, Dexterity, Life and Vigour of the particular Species or Animal design'd? And in a Whole consisting of many Figures relative to one main End, doth not that spoil the Unity, Simplicity and Correspondency of the Whole, which hath no necessary or proper Connection with its principal Scope, but distracts the Eye, and diverts the Attention from what is chiefly intended.

ALL Pieces of Art, like all Pieces of Nature, must make one Body, sound and well-proportion'd in its Parts, without any cumbersome Excrescencies, or without Parts of another kind, and not belonging to it as one particular Whole, however beautiful these may be consider'd apart. We cannot indeed advance the least in any Relish or Taste of Symmetry and Proportion, without acknowledging the necessary Connection betwixt the Useful and the Beautiful. And as no Reflection on Nature, and on Arts is of larger Extent,

---

would have no dignity without a roof-ridge. Thus too in all the parts of a speech, a kind of pleasantness and charm attends utility and even necessity, etc."] See *Vitruvius, lib.* 4. *c.* 2. [Vitruvius, *On Architecture,* IV.ii.5–6.] The Passage was already quoted. *Quintilian, lib.* 8. *c.* 3. where he treats the same Subject at great length, particularly towards the end of that Chapter. Nam ipsa illa ὑφέλεια simplex & inaffectata, &c. [Quintilian, *Institutio oratoria,* VIII.iii.87: "For even unaffected simplicity of style, etc."] See likewise *Cicero, Orator.* N° 25. Nam sic ut in epularum apparatu, &c. [Cicero, *Orator,* xxv.83: "For just as in the arrangements for a banquet, etc."]

o. Compare with the Passages already quoted, what *Cicero* says of the *Utile* in the 3d Book of his Offices. [See esp. Cicero, *De officiis,* III.vii.34–ix, xix, xxviii.101, xxxiii.]

so none can have a better, or more benign and wholesome Influence upon the Mind. 'Tis by it chiefly, that the Mind is improv'd to perfect good Taste in all the Arts; confirm'd in its Love and Admiration of the beautiful and useful Order that prevails throughout Nature; and kept steady to Virtue, or the Pursuit of moral Beauty in Life and Manners. And therefore a great part of moral Philosophy, in the ancient way of treating it, is justly taken up in shewing the Connection of Virtue with Interest; or, that Virtue is private as well as publick Good; and Vice, on the other hand, private as well as publick Misery; and that Nature pursues Beauty and Utility by the same excellent Laws and Methods of Operation.

In what Sense ingenious Imitations, or Works of Imagination and Genius are Imitations of the Whole of Nature.

IN the third place, another Method of explaining the Beauty of Works of Genius, of Painting in particular, among the Ancients, is by considering them as good Imitations, not of a part of Nature, but of Nature in general.

THE Meaning of this is, that as Nature is in itself a beautiful Whole, in which all is subordinate to the general Good, Beauty and Perfection of the Whole, (and therefore Perfection is not to be look'd for in any particular Part separately, but in the Whole; the Perfection of single Parts being only pursued by Nature so far as the general Good permits;) so ought it also to be in Pictures: Every Picture ought to be a perfect Whole by itself, and its Beauty ought to result from the whole Composition; not from the Perfection of single Parts, but from the Subserviency of all the Parts to one main beautiful and great End. The Artist cannot bring all Nature into his Piece; he must therefore imitate the Whole of Nature in his Work, by chusing a noble, a great, or beautiful Plan, and by adapting and disposing every particular part of his Piece in the manner that may best suit to the main End of the Whole. He therefore ought not to paint Deformity, for the sake of expressing or representing Deformity; but as Nature in the Whole is beautiful, so ought his Works to be; and the Deformities in single Parts, ought, as in Nature, to serve as Foils or Contrasts to set off some principal Beauty to the greater advantage. In one word, whatever particular parts are consider'd by themselves, the Whole ought to be harmonious and beautiful: And as in Nature, so in Imitations, it must only be to the greater Beauty of the Whole that any particular part is submitted; and that so far only as the greater Beauty of the Whole requires it. <141>

THIS is the Meaning of what they say, of gathering from the various Parts of Nature to make a beautiful Whole. This is particularly the Meaning of what *Cicero* says in the Place already quoted; where he tells us, that *Zeuxis,* from the Consideration of many Beauties, formed his Idea of a perfect Beauty: "Because Nature pursues the Beauty, and Good or Perfection of the Whole, and not of particular Parts."P The Sum of this Observation amounts briefly to this, That what is called properly Shade, is not more necessary to set off the enlighten'd Parts, in respect of Colouring, than something which, being analogous to it, may likewise be called Shade, is requisite, with regard to the Choice and Disposition of the Subject, or to poetical Composition in Painting. And it must be so in copying from Nature, since 'tis so in Nature itself: Whatever is heightened, or hath Relief, whether in the natural or moral World, is raised, distinguished, or made strong and conspicuous by Shade or Contrast.

BUT in the fourth Place, 'tis obviously our moral Sense, and our social Affections, which afford the Mind the most agreeable Touches of Joy and Satisfaction. Let one examine himself narrowly and impartially, and he shall find that the largest Share, even of all those Gratifications which are called sensible Pleasures, is owing to a social Principle deeply inlayed into his Nature. What are Riches, Titles, Honours, a Table, Dress, and Equipage, abstractedly from all Regard to Society? What is even Love itself, without the *Spes animi credula mutui?*[30] And if we attend to the Pleasures which Arts and Imitation yield, these are a sufficient Proof of the Tenderness and Humanity, so to speak, of our Make and Frame. For whence else is it, that where a Succession of the kindly Affections can be carried on, even thro' Fears and Horrors, Sorrows and Griefs, the Emotion of the Soul is so agreeable; or, that when the Passions of this kind are skilfully excited in us, as in a Tragedy, we prefer the Entertainment to any one of Sense? 'Tis certainly, because exerting whatever we have of social Affection and generous Sympathy in our Natures, is of the highest Delight, and produces a greater Enjoyment in the way of Sentiment, than any thing besides can do in the way of mere Sense and vulgar Appetite.

The chief Pleasures produced or excited in us by ingenious Imitations of human Life, presuppose a moral and publick Sense. And reciprocally, from the Reality of a moral and publick Sense, it may be inferred, that our chief Pleasures, arising from Imitations or Fictions, must be of a moral and social kind.

p. *De Invent. Rhetor. lib.* 2. *ab Initio.* [Cicero, *De inventione,* II.i.1–3.]
30. Horace, *Odes,* IV.i.30: "trustful hope of love returned."

'Tis the same with respect to the Designing Arts: Whatever touches our publick Sense, and calls into Action our generous, tender, and kind Affections, is that which most agreeably detains our Mind, and employs it. Representations of such Subjects, so soon as they are set to our View, immediately attract us, working upon us in the most pleasing, because in the most humane and social Manner.

SOME have said, that Works of Genius and Fancy please us, because they employ the Mind, which naturally delights in Exercise; and this is undoubtedly true: But 'tis not merely because they employ us, that they please us; for tho' the human Mind be naturally active, and made for Exercise, yet all kinds of Exercise do not equally please and delight. If we attend to our own Feelings, it will evidently be perceived, that of all Exercises the social and affectionate, or the Operations of the social Affections, are the most satisfactory and lasting. Who was ever cloy'd by Acts of Friendship, Generosity, and a publick disinterested Spirit? Or did ever the Workings of good and kind benign Affections, when excited by artful Illusion, leave Remorse, Bitterness and Disquiet behind 'em?q Some have ascribed all the Pleasure arising from the Imitative Arts, to the Power of Illusion, as if we were only pleased, because we are deceived into imagining a Representation real. But hardly does any one absolutely forget, that it is Imitation

q. See what is said on this Subject by the Author of the *Reflexions sur la Poesie & sur la Peinture, T.* 1. *Sect.* 1. La representation pathetique du sacrifice de la fille de Jepthe enchassée dans un bordau dorée, fait le plus bel ornament d'un cabinet qu'on a voulu rendre agreable par les meubles, on neglige pour contempler ce tableau tragique, les grotesques, & les compositions les plus riantes des pientres galands. ——— En fin plus les actions que la poesie & la peinture depeignent, auroient fait soufrir en nous l'humanité, si nous les avions vues veritablement, plus les imitations que ces arts en presentent ont de pouvoir sur nous pour nous attacher. & *Sect.* 3. [Abbé Du Bos, *Critical Reflections on Poetry, Painting and Music. With an Inquiry into the Rise and Progress of the Theatrical Entertainments of the Ancients,* translated by Thomas Nugent, 3 vols. (London, 1748), I:2: "The pathetic representation of the sacrifice of *Jeptha*'s daughter, set in a frame, is one of the most elegant ornaments of a sumptuous cabinet. The several grotesque figures, and most smiling compositions of painters of the gayest fancies, pass unobserved, to attend to this tragical picture. In short, the more our compassion would have been raised by such actions as are described by poetry and painting, had we really beheld them; the more in proportion the imitations attempted by those arts are capable of affecting us."]

he beholds in Dramatick Pieces, or in Pictures, and fancy the Objects before him real. Or, if he should, yet the Pleasure he feels while he imagines so, cannot be owing to this Deceit: Such Pleasure must be posterior, and can then only take Place, when the Mind reflects, that what it took to be real, was merely Imitation; and wonders at the Dexterity by which it was deluded. If, therefore, Fictions are capable of entertaining the Mind, previously to such Reflection, that Pleasure must be owing to some other Disposition or Sense within us, upon which the Objects represented are fitted to work. And a little Reflexion upon the Fictions or Representations which affect us most agreeably, or give us the greatest Pleasure, will shew us, that it is those which excite our social Affections, and call forth generous Sentiments, that yield us the highest and most satisfactory and lasting Entertainment. In fine, we may reason in this manner about the Constitution of our Mind, and Imitations fitted to delight or please our Mind; if those Imitations, which call forth our Pity and Compassion into Exercise, and interest us in behalf of Virtue and Merit, are indeed the Representations that give us the highest Satisfaction, it must be confessed that we are qualified by Nature to receive high <142> Pleasure from social Affections, and virtuous Exercises; and that our Frame and Constitution is social and virtuous, or deeply interested by Nature itself in behalf of Worth and Merit. Reciprocally, if our social Affections, and a publick Sense, are the Sources of our highest Satisfactions in real Life, then must those Fictions or Representations which are suited to them, afford us the highest Pleasure, the best and most agreeable Exercise. On the one hand, if we consult our natural Dispositions, as these discover themselves on other Occasions, we must quickly be led to a right Judgment, concerning the Imitations which, in Consequence of our Frame, must needs be most acceptable and pleasant to us: On the other hand, if we attend to the Effects of Imitation on our Minds, we must immediately perceive the Reality of Virtue; or that there is a natural Disposition in us to be delighted by social and publick Affections, in a Degree far superior to all the Enjoyments of mere Sense. Thus the Excellence and Naturalness of Virtue may be inferred from the Excellencies that belong to the fine Arts; and if the former is owned, there can be no Dispute wherein the latter consist.

Man is so
made as to
be highly
delighted
with what-
ever presents
him with an
Idea of the
Perfection to
which human
Nature may
be advanced
by due
Culture.

To these Observations it may be justly added, that there is a very great Pleasure in reflecting on Arts and Works of Genius and Fancy, as the skilful Productions of human Invention. For so great, so noble, and aspiring hath our Creator made the human Mind, that whatever gives it a high Idea of human Power and Perfection, or of the Force of our intellectual Faculties, to rise to noble Productions, fills it with a most transporting Satisfaction: It exalts the Mind, makes it look upon itself with laudable Contentment, and inspires it with worthy Ambition. We are so framed as to be highly delighted with what may be considered as our own Acquisition, or the Product of our own Powers, that we may be thereby impelled to exert and improve ourselves. And hence it is that we cannot consider the Works of human Genius, the great Actions of Men, or the useful Arts discovered and perfected by them, without saying to ourselves, with a secret kind of Joy, Such Works are Men capable of performing, if they take suitable Pains to improve the Faculties Nature hath kindly conferred on us!

Some
Conclusions
drawn from
the preceding
Principles:
Man is fitted
and qualified
for a very
noble Degree
of Happiness.
Not for
sensitive,
but rational
Happiness.

HAVING thus briefly suggested the chief Sources of our highest and noblest Pleasures, of whatever kind; may we not justly conclude, that Man is fitted by Nature for a very great and noble Share of rational Happiness and Perfection, by being made capable of contemplating and imitating Nature? When we consider the Pleasures the Senses are able to afford us, in the way of common Gratification, as our chief Provision and Allowance; then it is no Wonder, the Men arraign Nature, and complain of her Niggardliness. But all that can be said of the Impossibility of attaining Happiness by sensual Enjoyments; what does it prove, but that our Happiness lies not in these low Pleasures, and must be derived from another Source? It was truly kind in Nature, to accompany those Exercises of our Senses, which are requisite to uphold our organical Frame, with certain Degrees of rewarding Pleasure, and those that tend to hurt or destroy it, with certain Degrees of admonishing Pain. But our Senses are chiefly noble and dignifying, as they are suited to furnish Materials, and give Employment to Imagination, Invention, Art, Reason, and Virtue. Our Eyes and Ears, says *Cicero,* are superior to those of the Brutes; because there is in our Minds a Sense of Beauty and Harmony in sensible Objects, by means of which these outward Senses may be improved into Instruments, or rather Ministers, of several beautiful, highly entertaining Arts.ʳ 'Tis our intellectual Powers, Tastes, and Senses that truly ennoble us; because, in Consequence of these, our outward Organs may be made, as it were, rational Sources of pure, reasonable, and uncloying Pleasures, far beyond the Reach of merely sensitive Beings. It may be said, That if our chief Happiness does indeed consist in Enjoyments of the rational kind, then are Mankind upon a very unequal Footing with regard to Happiness. I answer, That some Inequalities amongst Mankind, even in respect of rational Powers, are as absolutely necessary to the General Good, Perfection, and Beauty of the kind, as Shades in a Picture, or Discords in a musical Composition. But not withstanding these necessary Inequalities, all Men may have the Pleasures of Virtue and Religion in a very high Degree.

Happiness not unequally distributed by Nature, upon Supposition that our chief Happiness is from Reason and Virtue.

> *Take Nature's Path, and mad Opinion's Leave,*
> *All States can reach it, and all Heads conceive;*
> *Obvious her Goods, in no Extreme they dwell;*
> *There needs but thinking right, and meaning well!*
> *And mourn our various Portions as we please,*
> *Equal is common Sense, and common Ease.*
>
> Essay on Man, Epis. 4.[31]

SECONDLY, their having the Pleasures of natural Knowledge, or those the fine Arts afford, chiefly depends, as the Happiness of a System of rational Beings must do, upon Government rightly modelled; upon a Constitution, Laws, and Policies that have the Publick Good for their End, and are duly adapted to obtain it. But in such Society, or under <143> good Government, the People will not be artificially kept in Darkness, but will be generously provided with all the necessary Means of Education, with publick Teachers to instruct them in that wise and good Administration of Providence, which they ought to approve, adore, and imitate, in order to be happy; and to recommend themselves to the Divine Favour here or

In a good well constituted Government, even the lower Ranks of Mankind will have the Pleasures arising from Knowledge, and from the fine Arts, in a very considerable Degree.

---

r. *De Nat. Deorum, lib. 2. No. 56. 57. 58. & 59. De fin. bon. lib. 2. No. 34.* [Cicero, *De natura deorum,* II.lvi.140–lix.149; Cicero, *De finibus bonorum et malorum,* II.xxxiv.III–15.]
31. Pope, *Essay on Man,* IV.29–34.

hereafter. In such a State Ignorance will not be look'd upon, either as the Source of Religion, or of civil Submission and Obedience; and consequently, its Subjects will not be hood-wink'd, or deny'd the Advantages of Instruction in Virtue, the Rights of Mankind, and true Happiness.

IN the third Place, where the Arts are duely encouraged and promoted, in the manner that hath been already suggested, even the common People, like those of *Athens,* will be no Strangers to the Pleasures which the fine Arts are qualify'd to give, by their Power to teach and reward Virtue, and to reproach and stigmatize Vice, while all publick Places are adorn'd with proper Works of that Nature.

Another Conclusion concerning the Benignity of the Divine Mind, the Creator, Governor, and Upholder of All.

THE Ancients had likewise good Reason to conclude, from this View of the human Nature, and of the Pleasures for which we are principally fitted by our Frame, that the Author of Nature could not have implanted a Sense of Beauty, Order, Greatness, and Publick Good in us, were he not possessed of it himself in the highest and most perfect Degree. Not only is it necessarily true, said they, that the first independent Mind can have no Malice, because such a Mind can have no private Interest, opposite to or distinct from that of the whole, his own Creation: But a malignant Mind, an Enemy to Order, Beauty, Truth, and Goodness, could not possibly be the Author of those noble and generous Dispositions which he hath so deeply inlaid into our Constitution, to be improved into Perfection and Happiness by due Culture.⁵ Far from being capable of pursuing throughout

---

s. See *M. Antoninus's Meditations, Collier's Translation, p.* 52. *c.* 27. Now can any Man discover Symmetry in his own Shape, and yet take the Universe for a Heap of Rubbish? *&c.* ——— So *p.* 57. *c.* 40. and *p.* 85. *book* 6. As Matter is all of it pliable and obsequious, so that Sovereign Reason which gives Laws to it, has neither Motion nor Inclination to bring an Evil on any thing. This great Being is no way unfriendly or hostile in his Nature. He forms and governs all things, but hurts nothing. ——— That intelligent Being that governs the Universe, has perfect Views of every thing: his Knowledge penetrates the Quality of Matter, and sees through all the Consequences of his own Operations. ——— This universal Cause has no foreign Assistant, no interloping Principle, either without his Jurisdiction, or within it. [*Marcus Antoninus His Conversation with Himself,* pp. 83–84, 85.] And see what he quotes from *Plato, p.* 121. ["That when we consider the State and Condition of Mankind, we should place our Imagination upon some lofty Pyramid, or *Observatoire;* and from thence take a Prospect of the World, and look it over as it were at one View. Here we may see how Mortals are drawn up into Towns,

all his Works, Order, Wisdom, and the greatest Good of the whole System, he could not have disposed and fitted us for delighting in the Contemplation and Pursuit of Beauty, Order, and publick Good. Without such a Disposition in his own Nature, he could not have implanted it in his Creatures; because he could not have had any Motive to implant it in them, but what must be supposed to proceed from the like Disposition in himself: Nay, he could not have produced it, because he could not have had any Conception of it. It was thus the better Ancients reasoned concerning the all-governing Mind; and consequently, they considered the Contemplation of Nature as his Workmanship; due Affection towards him, and the Imitation of his Perfections and Works, as the principal Sources of human Happiness; as the Exercises and Employments that constitute our supreme Dignity and Perfection.[t]

---

and Armies in one place, and dispers'd for Husbandry in another! Here are abundance of Things to be seen together, Marriage and Confederacy treated by Nations and Families, Births and Burials, Feasting and Jolity at one House, and all in Tears at another. Here they are in a mighty Hurry at the Bar, and there up to the Ears in Trading and Merchandize. Towards the end of the prospect, it may be you see a great deal of Barren, and Uninhabitable Wilderness, with variety of Barbarous People beyond it. Take it altogether, 'tis a strange medly of Business, Humour, and Condition; And yet if you consider it throughly, you will find the Diversity and Disagreement of the parts contribute to the Beauty of the whole"; *Marcus Antoninus His Conversation with Himself,* pp. 121–22.] See how *Socrates* writes to the same Purpose. *Xenop. Apomn. Soc. p.* 4. *c.* 4. [See Xenophon, *Memorabilia,* I.iv, where Xenophon represents Socrates as celebrating the evidence of divine design in nature.]

    t. Compare with the Passage quoted from *Antoninus, Cicero de Nat. Deorum, lib.* 2. *No.* 6. Si enim est aliquid in rerum natura quod hominis mens, quod ratio, quod vis, quod potestas humana efficere non possit; est certe id quod illud efficit, homine melius. Atque res coelestes, omnesque eae, quarum est ordo sempiternus, ab homine confici non possunt. Est igitur id quo illa conficiuntur, homine melius. ——— Et tamen ex ipsa hominum solertia esse aliquam mentem, et eam quidem acriorem, et divinam existimare debemus. Unde enim hanc homo arripuit? ut ait apud Xenophontem Socrates ——— Rationem, mentem, consilium, cogitationem, prudentiam, ubi invenimus? unde sustulimus? ——— Quid vero? tanta rerum consentiens, conspirans, continuata cognatio, quem non coget ea comprobare? ——— Haec ita fieri omnibus inter se concinentibus mundi partibus profecto non possent, nisi eo uno divino, & continuato spiritu continerentur. [Cicero, *De natura deorum,* II.vi.16–vii.19: "If there is anything in nature which the human mind and human reason, strength, and power cannot bring about, that which brings it about is certainly superior to man. There is therefore something superior to

Other Con-
clusions more
nearly relat-
ing to the
present
Design
concerning

BUT the Conclusions that belong more immediately to our Design, are those that may be drawn from the preceding Account of human Nature, its Powers and Capacities, with respect to Education and the polite Arts. Had not then the Ancients good Ground to infer, from the Principles that have been explained, that it ought to be the great End of Education, to

---

man by which those things are produced . . ." "And yet from the very intelligence of human beings, we must infer that there is some mind, a mind that is more acute than ours and divine. For whence did man derive this mind, as Socrates asks in Xenophon?" [Xenophon, *Memorabilia,* I.iv.8.] "Where did we discover reason, intelligence, counsel, foresight? Where did we take it from?" "But what? such an harmonious, consistent, pervasive relationship, whom will it not compel to accept this?" "This could certainly not be so, with all the parts of the world in harmony together, if they were not held together by one divine and pervasive spirit."] *No.* 10. Natura est igitur, quae contineat mundum omnem, eumque tueatur, & ea quidem non sine sensu atque ratione. Omnem enim naturam necesse est, quae non solitaria sit, neque simplex, sed cum alio juncta atque connexa, habere aliquem in se principatum, ut in homine mentem, in bellua quiddam simile mentis. Itaque necesse est illud etiam, in quo sit naturae totius principatus, esse omnium optimum, omniumque rerum potestate dominatuque dignissimum, *&c.* [Cicero, *De natura deorum,* II.xi.29: "It is nature therefore that holds the whole world together and preserves it, and a nature that is not without sense and reason. For it is necessary that every natural object which is not solitary or simple but joined and connected with another thing should have some leading element within it, like the mind in man and something akin to mind in beasts. Hence it is necessary that the element also in which the leading principle of the whole of nature lies should be the best of all things and the most worthy of power and dominion over all things, etc."] *No. 35.* Hi autem dubitant de mundo, casune ipse sit effectus, aut necessitate aliqua, an ratione ac mente divina: Et Archimedem arbitrantur plus valuisse in imitandis sphaerae conversionibus, quam naturam in efficiendis, praesertim cum multis partibus sint illa perfecta, quam haec simulata solertius. Atque ille apud Attium pastor, qui navem nunquam ante vidisset, ut procul divinum, & novum vehiculum, e monte conspexit. ——— Ex iis enim naturis quae erant, quod effici potuit optimum effectum est; doceat aliquis potuisse melius. Sed nemo unquam docebit: Et siquis corrigere aliquid volet, aut deterius faciet, aut id quod fieri non potuit desiderabit, *&c.* [Cicero, *De natura deorum,* II.xxxv.88–89 and II.xxxiv.86–87: "But these thinkers suggest a doubt about the world as to whether it has been brought about by some chance or necessity, or by divine reason and intelligence. And they think more highly of Archimedes for copying the revolutions of the firmament than nature for creating them, although they are many times more cleverly made than these imitations. But the shepherd in Accius who had never seen a ship before, as he viewed from a hillside afar off the god-built new vessel [*Argo*] . . ." "For from the natures that existed, the best that could be produced from them has been produced; let anyone show that it could have been better. But no one ever will; and if anyone should attempt to improve anything, he will either make it worse, or will be desiring something that could not have been, etc."]

improve our natural Sense of Beauty, Order, and Greatness, and so to lead to just Notions of Nature, Conduct, and Arts: And that good Taste in all these must be the same, and can only be cultivated and perfected by uniting all the liberal Arts and Sciences in Education, agreeably to their natural Union and Connexion? All the Arts, said they, however divided and distributed, are one; they have the same Rule and Standard, <144> tend to the same End, and must therefore be mutually assistant to one another, in promoting and improving that good Temper and good Taste, the Foundations of which Nature hath laid in our Minds, but hath left to Education and Culture to finish and bring to Perfection; that Men may be early wise, good, and virtuous, capable of the best Pursuits and Employments, disposed to seek after them, and averse to every Pleasure and Amusement that sinks and degrades the Man. If Education and Instruction are not in the least calculated to fit for Life and Society, or to give a just Notion of Pleasure, Worth, and Happiness, what is its Business; or what Name can be given to its Designs and Pretensions? But if this be really the Scope it ought to aim at, how can that End be more effectually accomplished, than by exercising our Reason and our Sense of Truth and Beauty about a Variety of proper Objects; and by observing the Sameness of Truth and Beauty in every Subject, throughout Nature, Life, and all the Arts?[u]

Education, and the best Method of improving Virtue and good Taste.

u. Compare the Passages of *Cicero* already quoted, concerning the natural Union of the Sciences, with what he says, *De fin. l. 4. No.* 13. where Education is compared to the Art of *Phidias.* Ut Phidias potest a principio instituere signum, idque perficere: Potest ab alio inchoatum accipere ac absolvere: Huic est sapientia similis. Non enim ipsa genuit hominem, sed accepit a natura inchoatum. Hanc intuens debet institutum illud quasi signum absolvere. Qualem igitur natura hominem inchoavit? Et quod est munus, quod opus sapientiae? Quid est, quod ab ea absolvi ac perfici debeat, si nihil in eo quidem perficiendum est, praeter rationem? Necesse est, huic ultimum esse, ex virtute vitam fingere. Rationis enim perfectio est virtus. Si nihil nisi corpus: summa erunt illa, valetudo, vacuitas doloris, pulchritudo, &c. Nunc de hominis summo bono quaeritur. Quid ergo dubitamus in tota ejus natura quaerere quid sit effectum? [Cicero, *De finibus bonorum et malorum,* IV.xiii.34–35. "Phidias can begin a statue from scratch and complete it himself or he can take something over from someone else and finish it off; wisdom is like the latter. For she did not herself create man, but received him in an unfinished state from nature. With nature in view, she has to finish off the work begun, like the statue. What sort of a man therefore did nature begin to fashion? And what is the task which is the work of wisdom? What is it that has to be completed and perfected by her, if there is nothing in him that needs to be perfected except reason? The ultimate thing for him

Illustrations of this, by considering how several liberal Arts and Sciences were taught by the Ancients, or ought to be taught.

THE Ancients considered Education in a very extensive View, as comprehending all the Arts and Sciences, and employing them all to this one End; to form, at the same time, the Head and the Heart, the Senses, the Imagination, Reason, and the Temper, that the whole Man might be made truly virtuous and rational. And how they managed it, or thought it ought to be managed, to gain this noble Scope, we may learn from their way of Handling any one of the Arts, or of Discoursing on Morals: Whatever is the more immediate Subject of their Enquiries, we find them, as it hath been observed, calling upon all the Arts and Sciences for its Embellishment and Illustration. Let us therefore consider a little the natural Union and close Dependence of the liberal Arts, and enquire how these were explain'd by the Ancients.

Oratory, how philosophical an Art, and its relation to Poetry and Painting.

IF we suppose teaching Oratory to make one principal Part of liberal Education, as it was justly considered at *Athens* and *Rome* to do, while these States were free; ought it not to be taught, as ancient Authors handle it, by tracing and unfolding the Foundations of that Art in our Natures, in the Texture and Dependence of our Affections, in our Sense of the Beautiful, the Sublime, and the Pathetick in Sentiments; and in our Sense of Harmony, even in Sounds, Phrases, and the Cadences of Periods? Ought not the Teachers of Oratory to distinguish true Ornaments, and the native, genuine Embellishments and Graces of Speech, from the false, affected, and unnatural; the Force which Sentiments give to Language, when it is elevated by them, from the pompous and swelling, that is empty Sound? Is it not his Business to criticise the various Sorts of Evidence and Argu-

---

must be to fashion a life on the basis of virtue. For virtue is the perfection of reason. If there is nothing but body, the highest things will be health, freedom from pain, beauty, etc. But as a matter of fact the question is about the highest good of man. Why therefore do we hesitate to inquire what has been accomplished in his whole nature?"] See likewise what he says of the Pleasures of the Body, *De fin. lib.* 2. *No.* 33. Fluit igitur voluptas corporis, et prima quaeque avolat, saepiusque relinquit causas poenitendi, quam recordandi. ——— Ad altiora quaedam et magnificentiora, mihi crede, Torquati, nati sumus, &c. [Cicero, *De finibus bonorum et malorum,* II.xxxii.106 and II.xxxiv.113: "The pleasure therefore of the body is fleeting, and each pleasure passes away in turn and more often leaves reasons for repentance than recollection. We were born for higher and more splendid things than this, believe me, Torquatus, etc."]

mentation; and to teach to discern Sophistry, artful Chicane, and false Wit, from true, clear, solid Reasoning, Strength of Argument, and Wit that is able to stand the Test of grave Examination? Now, must he not, for that End, compare Oratory with Poetry, and both with the simple didactick Manner of Teaching; and enter profoundly into the Structure of the human Mind, and into the Nature of Truth and Knowledge, as *Aristotle, Cicero,* and *Quintilian* have done? And are not the properest Subjects for the Exercises that are requisite to form the Orator, as they have likewise shewn, truly philosophical and moral; such as regard Nature, Society, Virtue, Laws, and the Interests of a State, that of one's own Country in particular? The whole Art is therefore truly philosophical, and it cannot be taught without having Recourse to the other Sciences, in order to explain its Rules, or set its Beauties in full Light. It must be ever borrowing from moral Philosophy, that is often called by *Cicero,* for that Reason, *The Fountain of Oratory.*[32] And it hath been already remarked, that we owe our Knowledge of the Painting and Sculpture of the Ancients, in a great measure, to the excellent Use ancient Writers on Oratory and Poetry have made of the former in explaining the latter.[v]

IF the Art of Poetry ought to be taught, must not the Teacher proceed in the same manner, by tracing its Foundations in our Nature; shewing its best Subjects, and properest Ornaments, its various Kinds, and the respective Provinces and Laws peculiar to each Sort? And can this be done more agreeably or advantageously, than by comparing Poetry, which gave Rise to Oratory, with its own Offspring, and the other Sister-Arts Painting and Sculpture, as *Aristotle* hath done.[w] <145>

Poetry, how philosophical an Art, and its relation to Oratory and Painting.

v. This is *Aristotle*'s, *Cicero*'s, and *Quintilian*'s Method. See likewise *Longinus, Sect.* 39. Harmoniam non modo natura ad persuadendum delectandumque esse accommodatam, sed ad implendos generoso quodam celsoque spiritu, *&c.* [Longinus, *On the Sublime,* 39.3: "Harmony is suited by nature not only to persuade and delight us but to fill us with a kind of noble and elevated spirit, etc."]

w. See his *Poeticks,* and *Andreas Minturnus de Poeta,* his best Commentator. [Aristotle, *Poetics,* esp. 1448b 4–1449b 20; Antonio Sebastiano Minturno, *Antonii Sebastiani Minturni de poeta, ad Hectorem Pignatellum, Vibonensium Ducem, libri sex* (Venice, 1559).]

32. Cicero, *De oratore,* III.xxxi.123. Compare Quintilian, *Institutio oratoria,* XII.ii.6.

Painting and Sculpture, how nearly related to all the other Arts, and how they may be taught by the by, in explaining Oratory or Poetry. Of teaching History, and how the Study of it comprehends Philosophy, &c.

THE two last may therefore be taught, as it were by the by, in explaining the other Arts. But if one was to discourse on them, or teach them by themselves, it hath already appeared, that they may make Reprisals upon Oratory and Poetry; or that the properest Similitudes and Illustrations in that Case must be brought from these Arts.

'TIS certainly one main End of Education, to form betimes a Taste for reading History with Intelligence and Reflection, and not merely for Diversion: Now what else is this but teaching or inuring Youth to make useful Remarks, in reading Histories, upon Men and Manners, Actions, Characters, and Events; the moral Springs and Causes of moral Appearances; the Beauty of Virtue, and the Deformity of Vice; the good Consequences of the one, and the bad Effects of the other? And is not this true Philosophy, sound Politicks, and the Knowledge of Mankind? But what could have a greater Influence in attracting the Attention of young Minds, or impressing remarkable Passages of History upon their Memories, than to shew them how the Poets have described the same or like Actions, and how the Pencil also hath, or may do it; and to accustom Students to entertain themselves in reading History, with Reflexions on the different Methods, the several Arts, Philosophy, History, Poetry, and Painting, conspiring to the same End, take to instil the same useful important Lessons? To this we may add; that, in reading History, the Progress or Decline of Arts ought not to be slightly passed over; since these afford sure Symptoms of rising or falling Liberty in any Country, that well deserve the maturest Consideration.

The true Design of Logick is to point out the common Union, Dependence, and Connexion of all the Arts and Sciences.

IF Logick is taught, what else is its Province, but to examine the Powers and Faculties of our Minds, their Objects and Operations; to enquire into the Foundations of good Taste, and the Causes of Error, Deceit, and false Taste; and for that Effect to compare the several liberal Arts and Sciences with one another, and to observe how each of them may derive Light and Assistance from all the rest? Its Business is to give a full View of the natural Union, Connexion, and Dependence of all the Sciences, and so to complete what I have been now attempting to give an imperfect Sketch of, and as it were to draw the first Outlines.[x]

x. See the Passages referred to in the Preliminary Remark. *Milton* particularly in his Essay on Education. [John Milton, *Of Education,* in Milton, *Works,* II:362–415, esp. pp. 374–75, 402–3.]

But if we consider what Philosophy is, we shall yet more fully perceive what excellent Use may be made of the Arts of Design in Education; if teaching either natural or moral Philosophy in the properest Manner be any Part of its Aim and Scope. Philosophy is rightly divided into natural and moral; and in like manner, Pictures are of two Sorts, natural and moral: The former belong to natural, and the other to moral Philosophy. For if we reflect upon the End and Use of Samples or Experiments in Philosophy, it will immediately appear that Pictures are such, or that they must have the same Effect. What are Landscapes and Views of Nature, but Samples of Nature's visible Beauties, and for that Reason Samples and Experiments in natural Philosophy? And moral Pictures, or such as represent Parts of human Life, Men, Manners, Affections, and Characters; are they not Samples of moral Nature, or of the Laws and Connexions of the moral World, and therefore Samples or Experiments in moral Philosophy? In examining the one, we act the Part of the natural Philosopher; and in examining the other, our Employment is truly moral; because it is impossible to judge of the one, or of the other, without comparing them with the Originals from which they are taken, that is, with Nature: Now what is Philosophy but the Study of Nature? And as for the Advantage of studying Nature by means of Copies, 'tis evident: For not only does the double Employment of the Mind, in comparing a Copy with the Original, yield a double Satisfaction to the Mind; but by this comparing Exercise, the Original is brought, as it were, nearer to our View, and kept more steadily before us, till both Original and Copy are fully examined and comprehended: The Mind is pleased to perceive an Object thus doubled, as it were, by Reflexion; its Curiosity is excited narrowly to canvass the Resemblance; and thus it is led to give a closer and more accurate Attention to the Original itself.

IF Pictures of natural Beauties are exact Copies of some particular Parts of Nature, or done after them, as they really happened in Nature; they are in that case no more than such Appearances more accurately preserved by Copies of them, than they can be by Imagination and Memory, in order to their being contemplated and examined as frequently and as seriously as we please. 'Tis the same as preserving fine Thoughts and Sentiments by Writing, without trusting to Memory, that they may not be lost. This is

The Usefulness of the Designing Arts illustrated more fully, by shewing their relation to natural and moral Philosophy; Pictures being Samples or Experiments either in the one or the other. The Advantages of studying Nature with the Help of Imitations.

Landscapes or Views of Nature's visible Beauties are Samples or Experiments in natural Philosophy, whether they

certainly too evident to be insisted upon. On the other hand, if Landscapes are not copied from any particular Appearances in Nature, but imaginary; yet, if they are conformable to Nature's Appearances and Laws, being composed by combining together such scattered Beauties of Nature as make a beautiful Whole; even in this case, the Study of Pictures is still the Study of Nature itself: For if the Composition be agreeable to Nature's settled Laws and Pro-<146>portions, it may exist: And all such Representations shew what Nature's Laws would produce in supposed Circumstances. The former Sort may therefore be called a Register of Nature, and the latter a Supplement to Nature, or rather to the Observers and Lovers of Nature. And in both Cases Landscapes are Samples or Experiments in natural Philosophy: Because they serve to fix before our Eyes beautiful Effects of Nature's Laws, till we have fully admired them, and accurately considered the Laws from which such visible Beauties and Harmonies result.

THO one be as yet altogether unacquainted with Landscapes (by which I would all along be understood to mean all Views and Prospects of Nature) he may easily comprehend what superior Pleasures one must have, who hath an Eye formed by comparing Landscapes with Nature, in the Contemplation of Nature itself, in his Morning or Evening Walks, to one who is not at all conversant in Painting. Such a one will be more attentive to Nature, he will let nothing escape his Observation; because he will feel a vast Pleasure in observing and chusing picturesque Skies, Scenes, and other Appearances, that would be really beautiful in Pictures. He will delight in observing what is really worthy of being painted; what Circumstances a good Genius would take hold of; what Parts he would leave out, and what he would add, and for what Reasons. The Laws of Light and Colours, which, properly speaking, produce all the various Phaenomena of the visible World, would afford to such an inexhaustible Fund of the most agreeable Entertainment; while the ordinary Spectator of Nature can hardly receive any other Satisfaction from his Eye, but what may be justly compared with the ordinary Titillation a common Ear feels, in respect of the exquisite Joy a refined Piece of Musick gives to a skilful, well-formed one, to a Person instructed in the Principles of true Composition, and inured to good Performance.

NOR is another Pleasure to be passed by unmentioned, that the Eye formed by right Instruction in good Pictures, to the accurate and careful Observance of Nature's Beauties, will have, in recalling to mind, upon seeing certain Appearances in Nature, the Landscapes of great Masters he has seen, and their particular Genius's and Tastes. He will ever be discerning something suited to the particular Turn of one or other of them; something that a *Titian,* a *Pousin,* a *Salvator Rosa,* or a *Claud Lorrain,* hath already represented, or would not have let go without imitating, and making a good Use of in Landscape.[33] Nature would send such a one to Pictures, and Pictures would send him to Nature: And thus the Satisfaction he would receive from the one or the other would be always double.

IN short, Pictures which represent visible Beauties, or the Effects of Nature in the visible World, by the different Modifications of Light and Colours, in Consequence of the Laws which relate to Light, are Samples of what these Laws do or may produce. And therefore they are as proper Samples and Experiments to help and assist us in the Study of those Laws, as any Samples or Experiments are in the Study of the Laws of Gravity, Elasticity, or of any other Quality in the natural World. They are then Samples or Experiments in natural Philosophy. The same Observation may be thus set in another Light: Nature hath given us a Sense of Beauty and Order in visible Objects; and it hath not certainly given us this or any other Sense, for any other Reason, but that it might be improv'd by due Culture and Exercise. Now in what can the Improvement of this Sense and Taste consist, but in being able to chuse from Nature such Parts, as being combined together according to Nature's Laws, would make beautiful Systems? This is certainly its proper Business and Entertainment: And what else is this but Painting, or a Taste of Painting? For Painting aims at visible Harmony, as Musick at Harmony of Sounds.[y] But how else can either the Eye or the

---

33. Tiziano Vicello (ca. 1487–1576), known as Titian, the great Venetian painter; Nicolas Poussin (1593/94–1665), the leading exponent of classicism in seventeenth-century France; Salvator Rosa (1615–73), an Italian artist widely admired in Britain; Claude Lorraine (1600–1682), the painter whose landscapes shaped eighteenth-century British taste.

y. These Reflexions I owe to *Plutarch:* Haud omnibus idem est judicium videndi: Etenim visus visu, ut auditus auditu, vel natura perfectior est, vel arte exercitatior ad pulchri explorationem. Ad harmonias nimirum & modulos musici, ad formas vero & species judicandas pictores ingenio sensuque plus valent. Quemadmodum aliquando Nicomachum respondisse ferunt cuidam idiotae, qui Helenam minime pulchram sibi videri

Ear, the Sense of visible or audible Harmony, be formed and improved to Perfection, but by Exercise and Instruction about these Harmonies, by means of proper Examples? Pictures, therefore, in whatever Sense they are considered, have a near Relation to Philosophy, and a very close Connexion with Education, if it be any Part of its Design to form our Taste of Nature, and Improve our Sense of visible Harmonies and Beauties, or to make us intelligent Spectators and Admirers of the visible World.

Historical or moral Pictures are Samples or Experiments in moral Philosophy; and the Usefulness of such Samples in teaching Morals.

BUT I proceed to consider historical or moral Pictures, which must immediately be acknowledged, in Consequence of the very Definition of them, to be proper Samples and Experiments in teaching human Nature and moral Philosophy. For what are historical <147> Pictures, but Imitations of Parts of human Life, Representations of Characters and Manners? And are not such Representations Samples or Specimens in moral Philosophy, by which any Part of human Nature, or of the moral World, may be brought near to our View, and fixed before us, till it is fully compared

---

dixerat, Sume oculos meos, & dea tibi videbitur. *Ex Plutarcho de Amore Stobaei, sermo 61, de Venere & Amore.* ["On Sex and Love," in Joannes Stobaeus, *Florilegium,* edited by Thomas Gaisford, 4 vols. (Oxford, 1822), II:463: "We do not all have the same visual discrimination. For one person's sight is either more perfect by nature than another's, as one person's hearing is to another's, or it is better trained by practice in the exploration of the beautiful. By native talent and sensibility musicians are better at judging harmonies and rhythms, and painters at judging forms and appearances. Compare the reply that they say Nicomachus once gave to some amateur who said that his Helen did not look very beautiful to him: 'Take my eyes, and she will appear to you a goddess.'"] *So Plutarch, de genio Socratis, ab initio,* speaking of a Painter: Aiebat rudes & artis ignaros spectatores similes esse eorum, qui magnam simul turbam salutant; scitos autem & artificii studiosos, eorum, qui singulatim obvios compellant. Illos nempe non exacte in artificum opera inspicere, sed informem quandam operum concipere imaginem. Hos autem cum judicio partes operis perlustrantes, nihil inspectatum, nihil inobservatum relinquere eorum qui vel bene vel male ficta sunt. Prorsus quemadmodum communis quispiam auditus dici recte queat, qui tantum voces valet discernere: qui vero sonos, non jam amplius communis, sed artificiosus. [Plutarch, "On the Sign of Socrates," in *Moralia,* 575B: "He used to say that spectators who are laymen, ignorant of art, are like those who greet a large company with a single greeting, but connoisseurs who have made a study of artistry are like those who have a private word of welcome for each man they meet. That is, the former do not look carefully at the works of the artists, but conceive a kind of unformed image of the works. The latter however, thoroughly inspecting every part of the work with judgment, leave nothing unexamined, nothing unobserved, of the things which have been well or ill executed. Further, just as any hearing which can only make out voices may rightly be called common, but a hearing which discriminates the sounds is no longer a common but a critical hearing."]

with Nature itself, and is found to be a true Image, and consequently to point out some moral Conclusion with complete Force of Evidence? Moral Characters and Actions described by a good Poet, are readily owned to be very proper Subjects for the Philosopher to examine, and compare with the human Heart, and the real Springs and Consequences of Actions. Every one consents to the Truth of what *Horace* says on this Subject:

Trojani belli scriptorem, maxime Lolli,
Dum tu declamas Romae, Praeneste relegi:
Qui, quid sit pulchrum, quid turpe, quid utile, quid non,
Plenius ac melius Chrysippo & Crantore dicit.

Hor. Ep. L. 1. Ep. 2.[34]

But moral Pictures must be for the same Reason proper Samples in the School of Morals: For what Passions or Actions may not be represented by Pictures; what Degrees, Tones, or Blendings of Affections; what Frailties, what Penances, what Emotions in our Hearts; what Manners, or what Characters, cannot the Pencil exhibit to the Life? Moral Pictures, as well as moral Poems, are indeed Mirrours in which we may view our inward Features and Complexions, our Tempers and Dispositions, and the various Workings of our Affections. 'Tis true, the Painter only represents outward Features, Gestures, Airs, and Attitudes; but do not these, by an universal Language, mark the different Affections and Dispositions of the Mind? What Character, what Passion, what Movement of the Soul, may not be thus most powerfully expressed by a skilful Hand? The Design of moral Pictures is, therefore, by that Means, to shew us to ourselves; to reflect our Image upon us, in order to attract our Attention the more closely to it, and to engage us in Conversation with ourselves, and an accurate Consideration of our Make and Frame.[z]

---

34. Horace, *Epistles*, I.ii.1–4: "While you are declaiming the poet of the Trojan War in Rome, Lollius, I have been rereading him at Praeneste; he tells us what is fine, what foul, what is useful and what is not, better and more fully than Chrysippus or Crantor."

z. Considering what has been so often said, upon the Union of the Sister Arts with Philosophy, it may not be amiss to refer my Readers to the Confession of one of the greatest and most learned of the Moderns, upon this Head. See therefore *Isaaci Casauboni liber commentarius in Theophrasti notationes morum, in prolegomenis:* Enimvero morum conformandorum, quod ethicus philosophus praerogativae jure quodam quasi proprium sibi assumit, non una est a veteribus sapientibus inventa & exculta ratio. Nam

As it hath been observed, with respect to Landscapes, so in this Case likewise, Pictures may bring Parts of Nature to our View, which could never have been seen or observed by us in real Life; and they must engage our Attention more closely to Nature itself, than mere Lessons upon Nature can do, without such Assistance; nothing being so proper to fix the Mind, as the double Employment of comparing Copies with Originals. And in general, all that hath been said to shew that Landscapes are proper Samples or Experiments in natural Philosophy, as being either Registers or Supplements to Nature, is obviously applicable to moral Pictures, with relation to moral Philosophy. We have already had Occasion to remark, that it is because the Poet and Painter have this Advantage, that whereas the Historian is confined to Fact, they can select such Circumstances in their Representations as are fittest to instruct or move; that it is for this Reason *Aristotle* recommends these Arts as better Teachers of Morals than the best Histories, and calls them more catholick or universal.[35] I shall only add upon this

---

idem hic, si propius attendimus, et ethici philosophi, et historici, & poetae finis est. ———— Quare tendunt quidem eodem omnes quodammodo, sed diversis tamen itineribus. ———— Omnis enim poeta μιμητὴς, ait Plato. ———— Fit autem hoc a Theophrasto magna ex parte μιμητικῶς. ———— Mores hominum ita hic olim erant descripti, ut liceret tanquam in speculo hinc virtutis splendorem et pulcherrimam intueri faciem, &c. [Isaac Casaubon, ΘΕΟΦΡΑΣΤΟΥ ἠθικοὶ χαρακτῆρες. *THEOPHRASTI NOTATIONES MORUM. Isaacus Casaubonis recensit, in Latinum sermonem vertit, & libro commentario illustravit. Editio ultima recognita, ac infinitis in locis ultra praecedentes aucta & locupletata, atque paulò ante auctoris obitum recognita* (Lyon, 1617), first published in 1592. The Latin passages appear on pages 86–88 of Casaubon's *Isaaci Casauboni ad Theophrasti Characteres Ethicos Liber Commentarius* (which has a separate title page within the work): "There is not just one method discovered and developed by the wise men of old for shaping morals, though the moral philosopher claims it for himself by a kind of prerogative right. For the purpose, if we look more closely, of the moral philosopher and of the historian and the poet is the same. And therefore they are all somehow going in the same direction, though by different routes. For every poet is an imitator, says Plato. It is done by Theophrastus for the most part by imitation. Men's characters were so set out here that one was able, as in a mirror, to look upon the splendour and beautiful face of virtue."] Compare with this his Preface to his Commentary on *Persius*. [A reference to the unpaginated "Prolegomena" in Casaubon's *Isaaci Casauboni in Persii Satiras Liber Commentarius* which is included in *Auli Persii Flacci Satirarum Liber. Isaacus Casaubonis recensuit, & commentario libro illustrauit. Ad virum amplissimum D. Achillem Harlaeum Senatus Principem* (Paris, 1605).]

35. Aristotle, *Poetics,* 1451b 5–10.

Head, that as certain delicate Vessels in the human Body cannot be dis-
cerned by the naked Eye, but must be magnified, in order to be rendered
visible; so, without the Help of Magnifiers, not only several nice Parts of
our moral Fabrick would escape our Observation, but no Features, no
Characters of whatever kind, would be sufficiently attended to. Now the
Imitative Arts become Magnifiers in the moral way, by means of chusing
those Circumstances which are properest to exhibit the Workings and
Consequences of Affections, in the strongest Light that may be, or to
render them most striking and conspicuous. All is Nature that is represented, if all be agreeable to Nature: What is not so, whether in Painting or Poetry, will be rejected, even by every common Beholder, with
Quodcunque ostendis mihi sic, incredulus odi.[36] But a Fiction that is consonant to Nature, may convey a moral Lesson more strongly than can be
done by any real Story, and is as sure a Foundation to build a Conclusion
upon; since from what is conformable to Nature, no erroneous or seducive
Rule can be inferred.

THUS, therefore, 'tis evident that Pictures, as well as Poems, have a very
near relation to Philosophy, a very close Connexion with moral Instruction
and Education.

THE chief Advantage which Painting hath above Poetry, consists in
this: <148>

*The Advan-
tages of
Painting
above Poetry.*

> *Segnius irritant animos demissa per aurem,*
> *Quam quae sunt oculis subjecta fidelibus, et quae*
> *Ipse sibi tradit spectator.*[37]

36. Horace, *Ars poetica,* line 188: "Whatever you thus show me, I discredit and
abhor."

37. Horace, *Ars poetica,* lines 180–82: "Less vividly is the mind stirred by what finds
entrance through the ears than by what is brought before the trusty eyes, and what the
spectator can see for himself."

And of
Poetry above
Painting. POETRY, on the other Hand, hath a very great Superiority over Painting, because it can give proper Language to each Character and Personage, according to a very ancient Apophthegm:aa

Pictura est poesis muta, poesis pictura loquens.[38]

BUT without entering into the Dispute about Pre-eminence between the two Sister Arts, that are both so excellent, each in its Province, 'tis worth while to observe, with regard to both, that human Nature may be better and more securely learned from their Representations, than from mere Systems of Philosophy, for a Reason that hath not yet been mentioned; because both Poets and Painters exhibit Affections and Characters as they conceive, or rather as they feel them, without suffering themselves to be byassed by any Scheme or Hypothesis. They follow the Impulse of Nature, and paint as she dictates: Whereas the Philosopher has often a favourite Supposition in View, and is thereby tempted to strain and redraw every Appearance into a Congruity with, if not a Confirmation of his peculiar System.

How they are
mutually
assistant one
to the other. AND let even that be as it will, it is obvious, from what hath been said of the Affinity between Poetry and Painting, that the Imagination, by being conversant with good Pictures, must become abler to keep Pace with the Poet while he paints Actions and Characters; and on the other hand, Acquaintance with the Works of good Poets must add mightily to one's Pleasure in seeing good moral Paintings; since by that Means the proper Sentiments each Figure seems disposed, as it were, to speak, in a good Picture, will readily occur to the Spectator, in the properest and most affecting Language. The same will likewise hold with regard to Landscapes: For, on the one side, as a poetical Description of any natural Beauty will be better rel-

aa. *Plato de Rep. Arist. Poet. Plutarch. in Simonide.* So likewise *Horace: Mutum est pictura poema.* [Among the works cited, Turnbull's maxim appears only in Plutarch, "On the Fame of the Athenians," in *Moralia,* 346F: "Simonides . . . calls painting inarticulate poetry and poetry inarticulate painting"; see also *Moralia,* 18A, where Plutarch writes of the "oft-repeated saying that 'poetry is articulate painting, and painting is inarticulate poetry.' For a slightly different formulation see [Cicero], *Rhetorica ad Herennium,* IV.xxxviii: "A poem ought to be a painting that speaks; a painting ought to be a silent poem." The phrase Turnbull attributes to Horace, "A painting is a silent poem," does not appear in Horace's writings. Rather, Horace writes in *Ars poetica,* line 361, that "A poem is like a picture."]
38. "Painting is silent poetry, poetry is talking painting."

ished, in Proportion as the Reader, in Consequence of being accustomed to study Nature, and compare good Pictures with it, is abler to paint in his Imagination; so, on the other side, fine Prospects of Nature's Beauties will be more highly delightful, when they recall to the Mind a beautiful lively Description of it, or of any like Prospect in some good Poet.

BUT the Conclusion I have now chiefly in View is, that good moral Paintings, whether by Words, or by the Pencil, are proper Samples in moral Philosophy, and ought therefore to be employed in teaching it, for the same Reason that Experiments are made use of in teaching natural Philosophy. And this is as certain, as that Experiments or Samples of Manners, Affections, Actions, and Characters, must belong to moral Philosophy, and be proper Samples for evincing and enforcing its Doctrines; for such are moral Paintings. _{Moral Imitations ought therefore to be made use of in teaching moral Philosophy.}

WHEN one considers moral Philosophy in its true Light, as designed to recommend Fortitude, Temperance, Self-denial, Generosity, Publick Spirit, the Contempt of Death for the sake of Liberty and general Happiness, and all the Virtues which render Men happy and great; when moral Philosophy is considered in this View, how many Pictures must immediately occur to those who are acquainted with the best Works of the great Masters, that naturally, and as it were necessarily, call up in the Mind the most virtuous Sentiments, and noblest Resolutions, or that are qualified to operate upon our Minds in the most wholsome, as well as agreeable Manner? And how many more Subjects might easily be named, that if well executed by a good Pencil, would have the like excellent Effects!

IT is indeed just Matter of Regret, that at all times moral Subjects have been too much neglected, and Superstition hath had too great a Share of the Pencil's marvellous Art. But hath not her Sister Poetry had the same Fate? And, while I cannot forbear making this Complaint, yet, to do Justice to Painters antient and modern, I must own, that at this very Moment, my Imagination being carried with Transport thro' the Pictures I have seen, or read Descriptions of; one calls upon me, in the strongest manner, to submit to the cruellest Torments, rather than forego my Honour, Integrity, Country, Religion and Conscience: Another, methinks, enables me to prefer Continence and Self-command to the highest Delights of Sense. One fills my Soul with the noblest Opinion of Publick Spirit and Fortitude, and the _{Several Pictures mentioned, that are proper Samples in teaching Morals.}

sincerest Contempt of a selfish mercenary Temper: Another raises my Abhorrence of base, ungenerous, cruel Lust. One warns me to guard against Anger and Revenge, shewing the Destruction that is quickly brought upon the Mind by every unbridled Passion: Another makes me feel, how divine it is to conquer ourselves, forgive Injuries, and load even the Unthankful with Benefits. In one, I see the Beauty of <149> Meekness and Goodness; in another, the Firmness and Steadiness that becomes a Patriot in the Cause of Liberty and Virtue, and it inspires me with the most heroick Sentiments. On one hand, I am loudly called upon to examine every Fancy and Appetite, maintain the Mastership of my Mind, and not rashly to trust to the most specious Appearances of Pleasure: On the other, I see and tremble at the direful Consequences of the least immoral Indulgence.

Pictures described. WITH what a Variety of human Nature doth one admirable Piece present me;[bb] where almost all the different Tempers of Mankind are represented in a polite elegant Audience to a truly divine Teacher! I see one incredulous of all that is said; another wrapt up in deep Suspense: One says, there is some Reason in what he teaches; another is unwilling to give up a favourite Opinion, and is angry with the Preacher for attacking it: One cares for none of these Things; another scoffs; another is wholly convinced, and holding out his Hands in Rapture, welcomes Light and Truth; while the Generality attend and wait for the Opinion of those who are of leading Characters in the Assembly. Who can behold, unmoved, the Horror and Reverence which appears in that whole Assembly, where the mercenary Man falls down dead? With what Amazement doth that blind Man recover his Sight! How do those Lame, just beginning to feel Life in their Limbs, stand doubtful of their new Strength! How inexpressible is the graceless Indignation of that Sorcerer who is struck blind! But how shall I signify by Words, the deep Feeling which these excellent Men have of the Infirmities which they relieve, by Power and Skill which they do not attribute to themselves! Or the generous Distress they are in, when divine Honours are offered to 'em! Are not these a Representation in the most exquisite Degree of the Beauty of Holiness! As for that inimitable Piece, in which is drawn

bb. This Description of the Cartoons is taken from one of the *Spectators,* No. 226, T. 3. [*The Spectator,* No. 226, 19 November 1711.]

the Appearance of our Saviour, after his Resurrection, who will undertake to describe its Force and Excellency? Present Authority, late Suffering, Humility, and Majesty, despotick Command, and divine Love, are at once settled in his celestial Aspect. The Figures of the Eleven Apostles are all in the Passion of Admiration, but discovered differently, according to their Characters; *Peter* receives his Master's Orders on his Knees, with an Admiration mixed with a more particular Attention; the two next, with a more open Ecstasy, tho' still constrained by their Awe of the divine Presence: The beloved Disciple, who is the Right of the two first Figures, has in his Countenance Wonder drowned in Love; and the last Personage, whose Back is toward the Spectator, and his Side toward the Presence, one would fancy to be St. *Thomas,* as abashed at the Conscience of his former Diffidence; which perplexed Concern, 'tis possible, the great Painter thought too hard a Task to draw, but by this Acknowledgment of the Difficulty to describe it. The whole Work is indeed an Exercise of the highest Piety in the Painter; and all the Touches of a religious Mind are expressed in a manner much more forcible than can possibly be performed by the most moving Eloquence.

BUT when I reflect upon the Power of the Pencil to express Subjects of all Sorts, my Mind is immediately carried into another more distant Gallery, and presents me with a most beautiful Picture of the fine Arts, and of *Apollo* the God of Wisdom, their Father and Lawgiver. See *Apollo* sitting on Mount *Parnassus,* under a Laurel, with a delightful Fountain at his Feet; he is playing upon a musical Instrument, attended by the Muses, and the most famous Poets, with their immortal Crowns on their Heads, all in Postures of Admiration, which is differently expressed according to their Characters. How lovely is the God, and how charming doth his Musick appear to be, by its wonderful Effects on all about him! Upon his right Hand sits *Clio* with her Trumpet, ready to sound with highest Transport the Praises of Gods and godlike Men: Upon the Left is *Urania,* who, turned towards *Apollo,* listens with Rapture to his divine Harmony; she holds a Lyre in her Hand, and her celestial Robe shews her divine Birth, and high Employment. The other Muses stand behind, in two Choirs, with Books and Masks; and tho' each hath a distinguishing Countenance and Mien, they are evidently Virgins and Sisters, the Daughters of *Jove.* Not far from *Clio,*

Pictures described.

on her right hand, stands *Homer,* in a long Robe, full of Inspiration, and accompanying a Heroic Song with correspondent Action. There he is, the old, venerable, blind Bard, the Father of Poets, just as the Ancients have represented him, with the same sweet, yet grave, majestick, prophetical Air! How agreeable is it to see *Virgil* leading *Dante* to *Apollo;* and how charming, how inexpressibly delightful is the whole Representation! How pleasantly doth it point out the Consent and Harmony of all the Arts; and how powerfully doth the Place given to the Ancients, recommend the Study of 'em to all who would arrive at any Perfection in good Taste, and useful Science! See again, in another Piece, the ancient Philosophers, and their Scholars; with what profound Meditation do some study! With what divine Joy do others teach and impart sound Philosophy, and profitable Science; whilst several Students of different Ages and Characters, quite in Love with true Learning, drink in Instruction, or take Notes with the keenest Attention, the most <150> agreeable Docility, and highest Satisfaction! How pleasantly is the true Philosophy of *Pythagoras* represented, who taught that all Nature is Musick, perfect Harmony; and that Virtue is the Harmony of Life; or its Conformity to the Harmony of the all-governing Mind, and his immense melodious Creation!cc

WHAT cannot Painting teach or express in the most forcible Manner! For see there in another Piece the Constancy, the Serenity, the Fortitude of Heroes in the Fury and Danger of Action: How hot and terrible is the Battle! and with what intrepid Bravery does the Chief rush into the thickest of the Enemy! His Countenance bespeaks Victory, ere yet the Tyrant's Defeat is declared: One of the Captains, fraught with glad Tidings, is but beginning to declare his Overthrow, and to point at him, just falling with his Horse thro' the Bridge into the River. How eager do many appear to tell the whole Conquest, and to shew the Emperor the dread Trophies of

cc. See *Diogenes Laertius, lib.* 8. Pythagorei affirmare non dubitabant virtutem harmoniam esse, sanitatem, necnon omne bonum, ipsumque adeo Deum: Proptereaque universa haec harmoniae potissimum beneficio consistere. ["The Pythagoreans did not hesitate to assert that virtue is harmony and health and every good thing, and thus God himself; and therefore that all of these things consist above all in the good which is harmony." Compare Diogenes Laertius, *Lives of Eminent Philosophers,* 8.33: "Virtue is harmony, and so are health and all good and God himself; this is why they say that all things are constructed according to the laws of harmony."]

their Victory; while other Commanders, flushed with Success, eagerly pursue the flying Enemy! But how vain is it to attempt to equal by Words the ineffable Force of such a Pencil!

FROM what hath been said 'tis manifest, that all the liberal Arts and Sciences have the most close and intimate Relation, Dependence and Connection, and that they cannot be severed from one another in Education, without rendering it very incomplete, and indeed incapable of accomplishing its noble End, which is to form betimes the Taste and Love of Beauty, Truth and Harmony in Nature, in Life, and in all the Arts which imitate Nature and moral Life.

Hence we see that the liberal Arts ought not to be severed from Philosophy, or from one another, in Education.

IN whatever View Education is considered, whether as it is designed to improve the Senses and Imagination, or as it is designed to improve our reasoning Powers, and our inward Sense of Beauty natural and moral; or, lastly, as it is designed to form a benevolent, generous, and great Temper of Mind; in which ever of these Lights it is considered, all the Arts and Sciences amicably conspire towards it; and it is by mixing and combining them together, that all or any of these Ends may be most effectually and agreeably accomplished. How can the Temper be better improved, than by Reflections on the Greatness and Benevolence of Nature, and upon the beautiful Effects of like Benevolence and Greatness of Mind in our own Conduct? And when is it that Poetry and Painting shew their Charms, their divine Power to the greatest Perfection? Is it not when they are employed to display the Beauties of Nature, and the Beauties of those Virtues which emulate Nature, and when their Productions are truly beautiful natural Wholes? Is not the Imagination a powerful Faculty, that well deserves Culture and Improvement? Nay, is it not of the greatest Importance to have it early interested in Behalf of true Beauty, and secured against the Delusions of Vice, Luxury, and false Pleasure? And how can this be done, but by early employing it in the Contemplation of Nature, and of the true Beauties of Life, and consequently by calling in all the Arts to exhibit these in their liveliest Colours? What doth the Improvement of Imagination mean, but, in one Word, teaching it to paint, with Spirit and Life, after Nature, according to Truth? Have we a Sense of natural Beauty and Harmony capable of giving us such a vast Variety of truly pure and noble Pleasures? and ought this Sense to be neglected in Education? Is it worth while to form the Ear,

In whatever View Education is consisidered, the Assistance of the Designing Arts is of the greatest Use.

as most certainly it is? and ought not the Eye likewise to be formed to a just, quick, and perfect Relish, of the Harmonies it may be fitted to perceive, and delight in, by due Culture and Exercise? About what ought our reasoning Powers to be exercised, but the Harmonies and Beauties of Nature, the Harmonies and Beauties of Life? The chief Employment of Man's Understanding, is the Order and Regularity he ought to promote within his own Breast, by the right Management of his Affections, and the Order, Harmony and Good, that wholesome Laws, impartially executed, produce in human Society. But what is it can more powerfully inforce the Sense and Love of moral Order, than the Contemplation of the wise and good Order of Nature, and frequent Reflections upon that which constitutes true Order, Beauty and Greatness, in the Arts which imitate Nature? *Atticus* is introduced by *Cicero*, dd after a long Conference about the Foundation of Virtue in our Natures, making a very beautiful Reflection, which must naturally lead every intelligent Reader to the Conclusion I have been all along

A Saying
of *Atticus.*

---

dd. *De legibus, lib.* 2. ab initio. Equidem, qui nunc potissimum huc venerim, satiari non queo: Magnificasque villas, & pavimenta marmorea, & laqueata tecta contemno. Ductus vero aquarum, quos isti tubos & Euripos vocant, quis non, cum haec viderit, irriserit? Itaque, ut tu paulo ante de lege & jure disserens, ad naturam referebas omnia; sic in his rebus, quae ad requietem animi, delectationemque quaeruntur; natura dominatur. —— Quin ipse vere dicam, sum illi villae amicior modo factus, atque huic omni solo, in quo tu ortus, & procreatus es. Movemur enim nescio quo pacto locis ipsis, in quibus eorum quos diligimus, aut admiramur, adsunt vestigia. Me quidem illae nostrae Athenae non tam operibus magnificis, exquisitisque antiquorum artibus delectant, quam recordatione summorum virorum, ubi quisque habitare, ubi sedere, ubi disputare sit solitus: Studioseque etiam eorum Sepulchra contemplor. Quare istum, ubi tu es natus, plus amabo posthac locum, &c. [Cicero, *De legibus,* II.i.2 and II.ii.4: "I cannot grow tired of this place, especially as I have come here now. I despise magnificent villas and marble pavements and coffered ceilings; as for the artificial streams that they call 'pipes' and 'Euripi,' who would not scorn them after seeing all this? And so just as you referred everything back to nature when you were discussing law and right a little while ago, so too nature is predominant in these things which we seek out for mental relaxation and pleasure. In fact I may truly say I have just become more attached to the villa and this whole area where you were engendered and born. For some reason or other we are more moved by the actual places where we find reminders of those whom we love or admire. For me the delight I take in our beloved Athens is not so much from the magnificent buildings and the exquisite works of the old artists as from the recollection of supremely great men, where each one was accustomed to live, to sit, to hold discussions; I even contemplate their Tombs with passion. So from now on I shall have a greater fondness for this place where you were born, etc."]

aiming at; even that Beauty, Truth and Greatness, are the same in Nature, in Life, and in all the Arts. If we attend, says he, to what it is that chiefly pleases us even <151> in rural Prospects, we shall find that it is the same natural Taste and Disposition, from which you have derived Virtue: And now that I feel a particular Attachment to this Place where we are, to what is this Pleasure owing? is it not to my Delight in the Remembrance of great Men and their Virtues, or to some other social affectionate Tie, and kindly Principle deeply inlaid into our Natures? There is likewise a famous Saying of *Aemilius* recorded by *Plutarch,* very much to the present Purpose.[ee] Having given a very elegant Entertainment after the Conquest of *Macedonia,* he was asked how it came about that a Man always employed in great Affairs, the Discipline of Armies, Battles, and military Arts, understood so well the Management even of a Feast: To this he is said to have replied, that 'tis the same Taste that qualifies for the one and the other, to range an Army in Battle-array, or to order a publick Entertainment. These and several such-like antient Apophthegms are pregnant with Instruction, and well deserve to be unfolded and explained to Youth, because they afford Occasion of discoursing fully upon what I have now been endeavouring to shew to be the chief End of Education, and the properest Method it can take. The Sum of all which amounts to this; "That the readiest, the most effectual and most agreeable Manner of forming an universal good Taste, is by shewing from proper Examples, that good Taste is the same everywhere, always founded on the same Principles, and easily transferred from any Subject whatever to any other."

BUT lest, after all that hath been said, this Scheme of Education should appear to any one too complex, and for that Reason hardly practicable; let us but imagine to ourselves a School consisting of different Apartments for Instruction in the several Parts of useful Learning and Philosophy, suitably adorned with Pictures and Sculptures, or good Prints of them; and all I propose must be immediately perceived to be very simple, and easily reducible to Practice. For in reading the antient Poets and Historians, for Example, what could have a better Effect than having recourse to such Pieces of Painting and Sculpture as exhibit the Customs, Rites and

Another of P. Aemilius.

These lead us to the Conclusion now aimed at.

A View of the easy Practicability of this Method of Education by uniting the Designing Arts with the other Parts of liberal Education.

ee. Plutarch. in vita Aemilii. [Plutarch, *Plutarch's Lives,* "Aemilius Paulus," XXVIII.5.]

Manners described or alluded to by them? How agreeable would it be to see the Images of antient celebrated Heroes, while we read their Lives and Characters, or to compare the Gods as they are described by Authors, with the Representations of them that are given us by the Pencil or Chezil? And how much more delightful still would it be to compare Fables or Actions as they are told by an Historian or Poet, with the Representations of 'em the other Arts have given? I need not tell those who are acquainted with the antient Remains in *Italy,* or with the Works of the great modern Masters,[ff] that almost the whole antient Mythology and History, all the Fables, and almost all the great Actions that are the Subjects of antient Poets, or that make the greatest Figure in History, are to be found represented in a very beautiful expressive Manner upon Antiques of one kind or other; and many of those Subjects have been likewise painted by excellent modern Masters. And I think 'tis too obvious to be insisted upon, that such Works, that is, good Designs or Prints of 'em, would have their proper Place, and be of great Use in the Schools, where antient Poets and Historians are read and explained. To be convinced of this, one need only read Mr. *Addison's* Dialogues on Medals, in which he shews what Use may be made of these in explaining the antient Poets, or giving a more lively Idea of the Beauties of their Epithets and Descriptions.[39] Now, if the Schools of natural and moral Philosophy were in like manner furnished with proper Pictures of the natural and moral Kinds; would it not render Lessons on any Subject in Philosophy exceedingly agreeable, and consequently much more strong and insinuating, if to philosophical Reasonings and Arguments, was added an Explication of the ingenious Devices and Contrivances of the Imitative Arts to illustrate the same Subject, or to inforce the same Lesson? Thus, for Instance, in discoursing upon any Virtue, any Vice, any Affection of the human Mind, and its Operations, Effects and Consequences, would it not necessarily have a very pleasant, and therefore a very powerful Effect upon

ff. Only see what Account *Felibien* gives of the Works of *Giulio Romano,* and of *Polydore* and *Mathurino,* and likewise of *Ligorio.* [See the entries on Giulio Romano, Polydore and Mathurino, and Pyrro Ligorio in André Félibien, *Entretiens sur les vies et sur les ouvrages des plus excellens peintres anciens et modernes,* 2nd ed., 2 vols. (Paris, 1685–88), I:339–63, 388–439, 699–700.]

39. Joseph Addison, *Dialogues upon the Usefulness of Ancient Medals. Especially in Relation to the Latin and Greek Poets* ([London], 1726).

young Minds, if they were shewn, not only the Fables, the Allegories, the dramatic Representations, and the other different Methods Poetry hath invented to explain the same moral Truth, but likewise some Paintings and Sculptures of that same Nature and Tendency?

THIS Plan only requires that our Youth should be early instructed in Design or Drawing. For thus in teaching other Sciences, the Beauties of Painting and Sculpture might be fully explained in any Part of their following Studies occasionally, and in Subserviency to a greater Design. And as for teaching the Art of Designing early, the good Consequences of such a Practice in other respects, or with regard even to mechanical Arts, are too evident to need any Proof: 'Tis indeed surprising that an Art of so extensive Use should be so much neglected. *Aristotle* recommends it strongly as a very necessary Part of Education with respect even to the lower Ranks of Mankind;gg and we learn from him, that it was <152> the Practice in *Greece* to instruct the better Sort early in it. The *Romans* too, so soon as they began to educate their Youth in the liberal Sciences, followed this Method. *Paulus Aemilius,* who is celebrated for having taken particular Care of the Education of his Children, employed not only Rhetoricians and Philosophers, but likewise Painters to instruct them.hh It hath been already observed, that *Pamphilus* not only established Academies in *Greece* for the Formation of Painters, but that by his Means it became an universal Custom over all *Greece* to teach the Principles of Design amongst the other elementary Sciences in liberal Education.

IN Truth, the Care that was antiently taken of Education in general, well deserves, on every account, the most serious Attention of those, who having the Interests of their Country at Heart, look upon it (to use the Words of

[marginal notes:] This Manner of Education only requires that Design be taught early, and the other Advantages of this Practice are evident.

The Education of the antient *Greeks* well

gg. Aristot. Polit. Ed. Wechel. *p.* 218. 13. *p.* 219. 12. *p.* 220. 4. *p.* 225. 2. See *Plutarch's Life of Pericles,* where he gives an Account of his Education. [Turnbull's references correspond to the page and line numbers of the text of the *Politics* in volume ten of *Aristotelis opera quae exstant,* edited by Friedrich Sylburg, 11 vols. (Frankfurt, 1587–96). The specific passages cited are *Politics,* 1337b 24ff, 1338a 17ff, 1338a 40ff, and 1340a 28ff; Plutarch, *Plutarch's Lives,* "Pericles," IV.1–4.]

hh. Plutarch. in vita Aemilii. And in like manner we are told, several of the best Emperors, *Marcus Antoninus Philosophus* in particular, had Painters to instruct them in Drawing, and a Taste of Painting. [Plutarch, *Plutarch's Lives,* "Aemilius Paulus," VI.4–5; Julius Capitolinus, "Marcus Antoninus the Philosopher," in *The Scriptores Historiae Augustae,* IV.9: "In addition he gave some attention to painting under the teacher Diognetus."]

deserves our Attention in every respect, since Education is the very Basis of publick or private Happiness. a very great Man) as that by which the Foundation-Stones are laid of publick or private Happiness.[ii] No Part of it seems to have been overlooked by the *Athenians* in their better Times; and hence chiefly their immortal Glory.

I SHALL only add, that what was called by the Antients Musick,[jj] seems to have been a very comprehensive Part of Education, and very different from what now passes under that Name. The Design of it was to form the Ear, the Voice, and the Behaviour, or to teach a graceful Way of reading, speaking, and carrying the Body, not only on publick Occasions, but at all Times, or even in ordinary Conversation. *Cicero* regrets that this Part of Education was so much neglected amongst the *Romans:* And as for the manly Exercises, which had so great a Share in antient Education among the *Greeks* and *Romans,* not merely to form the Body to Vigour and Agility, but chiefly to fortify the Mind, and to fit for Action, Suffering and Hardship in the publick Service; though the same Exercises may perhaps not be the properest in present Circumstances to gain these Ends, yet the Scope intended and pursued by them must be acknowledged to be of lasting Use, or rather Necessity.

But my present Design was only to give some Notion of the Usefulness of the Designing Arts in Education. BUT I have accomplished my present Aim, if what hath been said of the Arts of Design, and of their Usefulness in Philosophy and Education, shall be found in any Degree conducive to give a juster Idea of those Arts than is commonly entertained, and a larger and better Notion of the Ends Education ought to have in View; for we have seen that a good Taste of Life and of all the fine Arts being the same, it must be improved and perfected by the same Means, even by uniting and conjoining all the liberal Arts in Education agreeably to their natural and inseparable Connection and Dependency.

---

ii. Lord *Molesworth* in his Preface to his Account of *Denmark.* [Molesworth, *An Account of Denmark,* p. 14.]

jj. This is plain from the Definition of it by *Aristides Quintilianus, lib.* i. Ars decens in vocibus & motibus. Necessary to all the Ages of Life. [Aristides Quintilianus, *On Music: In Three Books,* translated by Thomas J. Mathiesen (New Haven and London, 1983), 1.4: "an art of the seemly in sounds and motions."] —— See what *Quintilian* says of it, *Inst. lib.* i. *c.* 3, 6, & 12. [Quintilian, *Institutio oratoria,* I.iii.1–2, vi, and xii.2–4.] But see of this, Reflexions Critiques sur la Poesie & sur la Peinture. Troisieme part. [In Part III of the *Réflexions critiques* Du Bos discusses musical practice in ancient Greece and Rome, as well as the relationship between music, poetry, and theatrical performance.]

BIBLIOGRAPHY

Primary Sources

We list here the works referred or alluded to in Turnbull's writings, including editions used in our introduction and annotations.

MANUSCRIPTS

"A Collection of All the Statutes or Rules, and other Printed Papers, Relating to the Management of the Society for the Encouragement of Learning: From the First Plan of It, 1 January 1735; to Its Dissolution, January 31, 1749." Add. MSS 6191. British Library.

"Dr. Birch's Diary, 1716–64." Add. MSS 4478C. British Library.

"Dunbar and Haddington Presbytery Minutes, 1720–34." MS CH2/99/5. National Records of Scotland.

"First Laureation Album." MS IN1/ADS/STA/1/1. Edinburgh University Archives.

James Arbuckle to the Rev. Thomas Drennan, undated. MS D531/2A/3. Public Record Office of Northern Ireland.

"Memoirs of the Society for the Incouragement of Learning taken from the Register of their Meetings, and Minute Books of the Committee." Add. MSS 6185. British Library.

"Minutes of the Society for the Encouragement of Learning." Add. MSS 6187. British Library.

"A Plan for Managing the Designs of the Intended Society for the Encouragement of Learning and Learned Men & Proposed to be Laid before the First General Meeting." Add. MSS 6184. British Library.

Undated list of salaries at Marischal College. MS M 361/10/8. Special Collections Centre, University of Aberdeen.

Wallace, Robert. "A Little Treatise against Imposing Creeds or Confessions of Faith on Ministers or Private Christians as a Necessary Term of Laick or Ministeriall Communion." MS La II 620/18. Centre for Research Collections, Edinburgh University Library, University of Edinburgh.

NEWSPAPERS AND JOURNALS

Champion or Evening Advertiser
Common Sense: Or, The Englishman's Journal
Daily Advertiser
The Daily Post
The Gentleman's Magazine
London Evening Post
The London Magazine: Or, Gentleman's Monthly Intelligencer

OTHER PRINTED SOURCES

Addison, Joseph. *Dialogues upon the Usefulness of Ancient Medals. Especially in relation to the Latin and Greek Poets.* [London], 1726.
———. *The Evidences of the Christian Religion.* London, 1730.
———. *Remarks on Several Parts of Italy, &c. in the Years 1701, 1702, 1703.* London, 1705.
Addison, Joseph, and Sir Richard Steele. *The Spectator.* Edited by Donald F. Bond. 5 vols. Oxford: Clarendon Press, 1965.
Anon. *La Vie et L'Esprit de Spinosa.* [The Hague], 1719.
———. Review of George Turnbull's *Philosophical Enquiry, Bibliothèque raisonée des ouvrages des savans de l'Europe* 7 (1731): 329–54.
Aristides Quintilianus. *On Music: In Three Books.* Translated by Thomas J. Mathiesen. New Haven and London: Yale University Press, 1983.
Aristotle. *Aristotelis opera quae exstant.* Edited by Friedrich Sylburg. 11 vols. Frankfurt, 1587–96.
———. *Poetics.* Edited and translated by Stephen Halliwell. Loeb Classical Library. Cambridge, Mass., and London: Harvard University Press, 1995.
———. *Politics.* Translated by H. Rackham. Loeb Classical Library. Cambridge, Mass.: Harvard University Press, 1944.
Arnauld, Antoine, and Pierre Nicole. *Logic or the Art of Thinking: Containing, Besides Common Rules, Several New Observations, Appropriate for Forming*

Judgment. Translated and edited by Jill Vance Buroker. Cambridge: Cambridge University Press, 1996.

Arrian (Lucius Flavius Arrianus). *Anabasis of Alexander and Indica.* Translated by P. A. Brunt. 2 vols. Loeb Classical Library. Cambridge, Mass.: Harvard University Press, 1976.

Augustine, Saint (Aurelius Augustinus). *The City of God against the Pagans.* Translated by William H. Green and George E. McCracken. 7 vols. Loeb Classical Library. Cambridge, Mass.: Harvard University Press, 1957–72.

Aurelius, Marcus. *The Emperor Marcus Antoninus His Conversation with Himself.* Translated by Jeremy Collier. London, 1701.

Bacon, Francis. *The Major Works.* Edited by Brian Vickers. Oxford: Oxford University Press, 2002.

Beattie, James. *Evidences of the Christian Religion; Briefly and Plainly Stated.* 2 vols. Edinburgh, 1786.

Bentley, Richard. *The Folly and Unreasonableness of Atheism Demonstrated from the Advantage and Pleasure of a Religious Life, the Faculties of Human Souls, the Structure of Animate Bodies, & the Origin and Frame of the World: In Eight Sermons Preached at the Lecture Founded by the Honourable Robert Boyle, Esquire; in the First Year MDCXCII.* London, 1693.

———. *Publii Terentii Afri: Comoediae; Phaedri Fabula Aesopiae; Publii Syri et aliorum veterum Sententiae.* Cambridge and London, 1726.

Berkeley, George. *The Works of George Berkeley Bishop of Cloyne.* Edited by A. A. Luce and T. E. Jessop. 9 vols. London: Thomas Nelson and Sons, 1948–57.

Birch, Thomas. *The History of the Royal Society of London for Improving of Natural Knowledge, from Its First Rise.* 4 vols. London, 1756–57.

Blainville, Monsieur de. *Travels through Holland, Germany, Switzerland, and Other Parts of Europe; but especially Italy.* Translated by George Turnbull, William Guthrie, John Lockman, and Daniel Soyer. 3 vols. London, 1743–45.

Blount, Charles. *Miracles, No Violations of the Laws of Nature.* London, 1683.

———. *The Two First Books, of Philostratus, concerning the Life of Apollonius Tyaneus.* London, 1680.

Boindin, Niçolas. "Discours sur les masques et les habits de theatre des anciens," *Mémoires de littérature tirez des registres de l'Académie Royales des Inscriptions et Belles Lettres. Depuis l'année M.DCCXI. jusques & compris l'année M.DCC.XVII,* 4 (1723): 132–47.

Boyle, Robert. *The Christian Virtuoso: Shewing, that by being addicted to Experimental Philosophy, a Man is rather Assisted, than Indisposed, to be a Good Christian. To which are Subjoyn'd, I. A Discourse about the Distinction, that represents some Things as Above Reason, but not Contrary to Reason. II. The first Chapters of a Discourse, Entituled, Greatness of Mind promoted by Christianity.* [London], 1690.

―――. *A Discourse of Things above Reason, Inquiring whether a Philosopher should admit there are any such.* London, 1681.

―――. *Some Considerations about the Reconcileableness of Reason and Religion.* London, 1675.

―――. *The Works of the Honourable Robert Boyle.* Edited by Thomas Birch. 5 vols. London, 1744.

Busbequius, A. G. *The Four Epistles of A. G. Busbequius, concerning his Embassy into Turkey. Being Remarks upon the Religion, Customs, Riches, Strength and Government of that People. As also a Description of their Chief Cities, and Places of Trade and Commerce.* London, 1694.

Casaubon, Isaac. *Auli Persii Flacci Satirarum Liber. Isaacus Casaubonis recensit, & commentario libro illustravit. Ad virum amplissimum D. Achillem Harlaeum Senatus Principem.* Paris, 1605.

―――. *ΘΕΟΦΡΑΣΤΟΥ ἠθικοὶ χαρακτῆρες. THEOPHRASTI NOTATIONES MORUM. Isaacus Casaubonis recensit, in Latinum sermonem vertit, & libro commentario illustravit. Editio ultima recognita, ac infinitis in locis ultra praecedentes aucta & locupletata, atque paulò ante auctoris obitum recognita.* Lyon, 1617.

Chambers, Ephraim ed. *The History of the Works of the Learned.* 2 vols. London, 1740.

Cicero (Marcus Tullius Cicero). *Brutus and Orator.* Translated by G. L. Hendrickson and H. M. Hubbell. Loeb Classical Library. Cambridge, Mass.: Harvard University Press, 1942.

―――. *De finibus bonorum et malorum.* Translated by H. Rackham. Loeb Classical Library. New York: G. P. Putnam's Sons, 1931.

―――. *De inventione, De optimo genere oratorum, and Topica.* Translated by H. M. Hubbell. Loeb Classical Library. Cambridge, Mass.: Harvard University Press, 1949.

―――. *De natura deorum and Academica.* Translated by H. Rackham. Loeb Classical Library. Cambridge, Mass.: Harvard University Press, 1951.

―――. *De officiis.* Translated by Walter Mitter. Loeb Classical Library. New York: G. P. Putnam's Sons, 1928.

―――. *De oratore, De fato, Paradoxa Stoicorum, and De partitione oratoria.* Translated by E. W. Sutton and H. Rackham. 2 vols. Loeb Classical Library. Cambridge, Mass.: Harvard University Press, 1948.

————. *De re publica and De legibus.* Translated by Clinton Walker Keynes. Loeb Classical Library. Cambridge, Mass.: Harvard University Press, 1959.

————. *De senectute, de amicitia, and de divinatione.* Translated by William Armistead Falconer. Loeb Classical Library. New York: G. P. Putnam's Sons, 1930.

————. *Pro archia poeta.* Translated by N. H. Watts. Loeb Classical Library. Cambridge, Mass.: Harvard University Press, 1923.

————. *Rhetorica ad Herennium.* Translated by Harry Caplan. Loeb Classical Library. Cambridge, Mass.: Harvard University Press, 1981.

————. *Tusculan Disputations.* Translated by J. E. King. Loeb Classical Library. Cambridge, Mass.: Harvard University Press, 1945.

————. *The Verrine Orations.* Translated by L. H. G. Greenwood. 2 vols. Loeb Classical Library. Cambridge, Mass.: Harvard University Press, 1935.

Clarke, John. *A Dissertation upon the Usefulness of Translations of Classick Authors, both Literal and Free, for the Easy Expeditious Attainment of the Latin Tongue.* [London], 1734.

————. *An Essay upon the Education of Youth in Grammar Schools.* 2nd ed. London, 1730.

————. *Justini Historiae Philippicae. Cum versione Anglica. Ad verbum, quantum fieri potuit, facta. Or, the History of Justin. With an English Translation, as literal as possible.* 2nd ed. London, 1735.

Clarke, Samuel. *A Demonstration of the Being and Attributes of God: More Particularly in Answer to Mr. Hobbs, Spinoza, and their Followers.* London, 1705.

————. *A Discourse concerning the Being and Attributes of God, the Obligations of Natural Religion, and the Truth and Certainty of the Christian Revelation.* 7th ed. London, 1728.

————. *A Paraphrase on the Four Evangelists.* 4th ed. 2 vols. London, 1722.

Collins, Anthony. *A Discourse of Free-Thinking. Occasion'd by the Rise and Growth of a Sect call'd Free-Thinkers.* London, 1713.

————. *A Discourse of the Grounds and Reasons of the Christian Religion.* London, 1724.

————. *A Philosophical Inquiry concerning Human Liberty.* London, 1717.

————. *The Scheme of Literal Prophecy Considered; in a View of the Controversy, Occasioned by a Late Book, Intitled, A Discourse of the Grounds and Reasons of the Christian Religion.* 2 vols. [The Hague], 1726.

Cooper, Anthony Ashley, Earl of Shaftesbury. *Characteristicks of Men, Manners, Opinions, Times.* 3 vols. [London], 1711.

————. *Characteristicks of Men, Manners, Opinions, Times.* Edited by Douglas Den Uyl. 3 vols. Indianapolis: Liberty Fund, 2001.

————. *Letters from the Right Honourable the late Earl of Shaftesbury, to Robert Molesworth, Esq., now the Lord Viscount of that Name. With Two Letters written by the Late Sir John Cropley. To which is Prefix'd a Large Introduction by the Editor.* Edited by John Toland. London, 1721.

————. *A Notion of the Historical Draught or Tablature of the Judgment of Hercules, according to Prodicus, Lib.II. Xen. de Mem. Soc.* London, 1713.

————. *Several Letters Written by a Noble Lord to a Young Man at the University.* London, 1716.

Crousaz, Jean-Pierre de. *Traité de beau: ou l'on montre en quoi consiste ce que l'on nomme ainsi, par des examples tirez de la plupart des arts & des sciences.* Amsterdam, 1715.

Cudworth, Ralph. *The True Intellectual System of the Universe: The First Part; Wherein, All the Reason and Philosophy of Atheism Is Confuted; and Its Impossibility Demonstrated.* London, 1678.

Cunningham, Alexander. *Alexandri Cuningamii animadversiones, in Richardi Bentleii notas et emendationes ad Q. Horatium Flaccium.* The Hague, 1721.

————. *Phaedri Augusti liberti Fabularum Aesopiarum libri quinque.* Edinburgh, 1757.

————. *Q. Horatii Flacci poemata, ex antiquis codd. & certis observationibus emendavit variasque scriptorum & impressorum lectiones adjecit Alexander Cuningamius.* The Hague, 1721.

Descartes, René. *Discourse on Method, Optics, Geometry, and Meteorology.* Translated by Paul J. Olscamp. Indianapolis: Bobbs-Merrill, 1965.

Diogenes Laertius. *Lives of Eminent Philosophers.* Translated by R. D. Hicks. 2 vols. Loeb Classical Library. Cambridge, Mass.: Harvard University Press, 1972.

Du Bos, Jean-Baptiste. *Critical Reflections on Poetry, Painting and Music. With an Inquiry into the Rise and Progress of the Theatrical Entertainments of the Ancients.* Translated by Thomas Nugent. 3 vols. London, 1748.

————. *Réflexions critiques sur la poésie et sur la peinture.* Revised edition. 3 vols. Paris, 1733.

Duck, Stephen. *Hints to a School-Master. Address'd to the Revd. Dr. Turnbull.* London, 1741.

Durand, David. *Histoire de la peinture ancienne, extraite de L'Hist. Naturelle de Pline, LIV.XXV.* London, 1725.

Félibien, André. *Entretiens sur les vies et sur les ouvrages des plus excellens peintres anciens et modernes.* 2nd ed. 2 vols. Paris, 1685–88.

Fleming, Caleb. *Animadversions upon Mr. Tho. Chubb's Discourse on Miracles, Considered as Evidences to Prove the Divine Original of Revelation.* London, 1741.

Forbes, Honourable Mrs. Atholl, ed. *Curiosities of a Scots Charta Chest, 1600–1800. With the Travels and Memoranda of Sir Alexander Dick, Baronet of Prestonfield, Midlothian Written by Himself.* Edinburgh, 1897.

Fraguier, Claude-François. "La Gallerrie de Verrés," *Mémoires de littérature tirez des registres de L'Académie Royal des Inscriptions et Belles Lettres. Depuis l'année M.DCCXXVIII. jusques & compris l'année M.DCCXXV,* 6 (1729): 565–76.

Gerard, Alexander. *Dissertations on Subjects Relating to the Genius and Evidences of Christianity.* Edinburgh, 1766.

Gordon, Thomas. *The Character of an Independent Whig.* London, 1719.

Gordon, Thomas, with Anthony Collins and John Trenchard. *The Independent Whig.* London, 1721.

Gordon, Thomas, with John Trenchard. *Cato's Letters.* 4 vols. London, 1723–24.

Grotius, Hugo. *The Truth of the Christian Religion. With Jean Le Clerc's Notes and Additions.* Translated by John Clarke and edited with an introduction by Maria Rosa Antognazza. Indianapolis: Liberty Fund, 2012.

Harrington, James. *The Political Works of James Harrington.* Edited with an introduction by J. G. A. Pocock. Cambridge: Cambridge University Press, 1977.

Heineccius, Johann Gottlieb. *Elementa iuris naturae et gentium, commoda auditoribus methodo adornata.* Halle, 1738.

———. *A Methodical System of Universal Law, with Supplements and a Discourse by George Turnbull.* Edited with an introduction by Thomas Ahnert and Peter Schröder. Indianapolis: Liberty Fund, 2008.

Historical Manuscripts Commission Reports, Various Collections. Vol. 8. London: H.M.S.O., 1913.

Hoadly, Benjamin. *Several Tracts Formerly Published: Now Collected into One Volume.* London, 1715.

Hobbes, Thomas. *Leviathan, or the Matter, Forme, and Power of a Commonwealth Ecclesiasticall and Civill.* London, 1651.

Homer. *The Iliad.* Translated by Alexander Pope. 6 vols. London, 1715–20.

———. *The Odyssey.* Translated by Alexander Pope. 5 vols. London, 1725–26.

Horace (Quintus Horatius Flaccus). *The Odes and Epodes.* Translated by C. E. Bennett. Loeb Classical Library. Cambridge, Mass.: Harvard University Press, 1988.

———. *Satires, Epistles, and Ars Poetica.* Translated by H. Rushton Fairclough. Loeb Classical Library. Cambridge, Mass.: Harvard University Press, 1978.

Hume, David. *Letters of Eminent Persons Addressed to David Hume.* Edited by John Hill Burton. Edinburgh and London, 1849.

Hutcheson, Francis. *An Essay on the Nature and Conduct of the Passions and Affections, with Illustrations of the Moral Sense.* London, 1728.

———. *An Inquiry into the Original of Our Ideas of Beauty and Virtue.* London, 1725.

Julius Capitolinus. "Marcus Antoninus the Philosopher," in *The Scriptores Historiae Augustae.* Translated by David Magie. 3 vols. Loeb Classical Library. Cambridge, Mass.: Harvard University Press, 1960–61.

Junius, Franciscus. *De pictura veterum libri tres.* Amsterdam, 1637.

———. *De pictura veterum libri tres.* Revised edition. London, 1694.

———. *The Painting of the Ancients, in Three Bookes: Declaring by Historical Observations and Examples, the Beginning, Progresse, and Consummation of that most Noble Art.* London, 1638.

———. *The Painting of the Ancients.* Edited by Keith Aldrich, Philipp Fehl, and Raina Fehl. Berkeley, Los Angeles, and Oxford: University of California Press, 1991.

Justin (Marcus Iunianus Iustinus). *Justin's History of the World translated into English* (London, 1742).

Justinian. *The Digest of Justinian.* Edited by Theodore Mommsen and Paul Kruger, and translated by Alan Watson. 4 vols. Philadelphia: University of Pennsylvania Press, 1985.

———. *The Institutes of Justinian: Text, Translation, and Commentary.* Edited and translated by J. A. C. Thomas. Amsterdam and Oxford: North-Holland Publishing Company, 1975.

Juvenal (Decimus Iunius Iuvenalis). *Juvenal and Persius.* Edited and translated by Susanna Morton Braund. Loeb Classical Library. Cambridge, Mass.: Harvard University Press, 2004.

Leibniz, G. W. *Essais de Theodicée sur la bonté de Dieu, la liberté de l'homme, et l'origine du mal.* Amsterdam, 1710.

———. *Godefridi Guilielmi Leibnitii Tentamina Theodicaeae de bonitate dei, libertate hominis et origine mali.* Frankfurt, 1719.

———. *Theodicy: Essays on the Goodness of God, the Freedom of Man, and the Origin of Evil.* Edited by Austin Farrer and translated by E. M. Huggard. La Salle, Ill.: Open Court, 1988.

Limborch, Philip. *De veritate religionis Christianae amica collatio cum erudito Judaeo.* Gouda, 1687.

Livy (Titus Livius). *From the Founding of the City.* Translated by B. O. Foster et al. 14 vols. Loeb Classical Library. Cambridge, Mass.: Harvard University Press, 1919–59.

Locke, John. *An Essay concerning Human Understanding.* Edited by Peter Nidditch. Oxford: Clarendon Press, 1975.

———. *The Reasonableness of Christianity, as delivered in the Scriptures.* Edited by John C. Higgins-Biddle. Oxford: Clarendon Press, 1999.

———. *Some Thoughts concerning Education.* Edited by John W. and Jean S. Yolton. Oxford: Clarendon Press, 1989.

———. *The Works of John Locke Esq.* 3rd ed. 3 vols. London, 1727.

Longinus. *On the Sublime.* Translated by W. H. Fyfe and revised by Donald Russell. Loeb Classical Library. Cambridge, Mass., and London: Harvard University Press, 1995.

Lucretius (Titus Lucretius Carus). *De rerum natura.* Translated by W. H. D. Rouse and revised by Martin Ferguson Smith. Loeb Classical Library. Cambridge, Mass.: Harvard University Press, 1992.

Machiavelli, Niccolò. *Machiavelli: The Chief Works and Others.* Translated by Allan H. Gilbert. 3 vols. Durham, N.C.: Duke University Press, 1965.

Maclaurin, Colin. *The Collected Letters of Colin Maclaurin.* Edited by Stella Mills. Nantwich, U.K.: Shiva Publishing Limited, 1982.

———. *A Treatise of Fluxions. In Two Books.* 2 vols. Edinburgh, 1742.

Malebranche, Nicolas. *The Search after Truth.* Translated and edited by Thomas M. Lennon and Paul J. Olscamp. Cambridge: Cambridge University Press, 1997.

Markland, Jeremiah. *Epistola critica: ad . . . Franciscum Hare . . . in qua Horatii loca aliquot et aliorum veterum emendatur.* Cambridge, 1723.

———. *P. Papirii Statii Silvarum libri quinque.* London, 1728.

Maximus of Tyre. *The Philosophical Orations.* Translated by M. B. Trapp. Oxford: Clarendon Press, 1997.

Milton, John. *The Works of John Milton.* Edited by Frank Allen Patterson. 18 vols. in 21. New York: Columbia University Press, 1931–38.

Minturno, Antonio Sebastiano. *Antonii Sebastiani Minturni de poeta, ad Hectorem Pignatellum, Vibonensium Ducem, libri sex.* Venice, 1559.

Molesworth, Robert. *An Account of Denmark, as it was in the Year 1692*. London, 1694.

———. *An Account of Denmark. With Francogallica and Some Considerations for the Promoting of Agriculture and Employing the Poor*. Edited with an introduction by Justin Champion. Indianapolis: Liberty Fund, 2011.

Morgan, Thomas. *The Moral Philosopher. In a Dialogue between Philalethes a Christian Deist, and Theophanes a Christian Jew*. London, 1737.

———. *The Moral Philosopher. Vol. II. Being a farther Vindication of Moral Truth and Reason: Occasioned by Two Books lately published: One Intitled, The Divine Authority of the Old and New Testaments asserted . . . by the Reverend Mr Leland. The other Intitled Eusebius: Or, the True Christian's Defence, &c. By the Rev. Mr Chapman*. London, 1739.

Newton, Isaac. *Optice: Sive de reflexionibus, refractionibus, inflexionibus, & coloribus lucis libri tres*. London, 1706.

———. *Opticks: Or, a Treatise of the Reflections, Refractions, Inflections, and Colours of Light*. 3rd ed. London, 1721.

———. *Opticks: Or, a Treatise of the Reflections, Refractions, Inflections, and Colours of Light*. 4th ed. London, 1730.

———. *The Principia: Mathematical Principles of Natural Philosophy*. Translated by I. Bernard Cohen, Anne Whitman, and Julia Budenz. Berkeley, Los Angeles, and London: University of California Press, 1999.

Nye, Stephen. *A Discourse concerning Natural and Revealed Religion*. London, 1696.

[Oswald, James]. *Letters concerning the Present State of the Church of Scotland, and the Consequent Danger to Religion and Learning, from the Arbitrary and Unconstitutional Exercise of the Law of Patronage*. Edinburgh, 1767.

Otto, Everhard. *Thesaurus juris Romani, continens rariora meliorum interpretum opuscula, in quibus jus Romanum emendatur, explicatur, illustratur*. 5 vols. Leiden and Utrecht, 1725–35.

Paul, Rev. Robert (ed.). "The Diary of the Rev. George Turnbull, Minister of Alloa and Tyninghame, 1657–1704," in *Miscellany of the Scottish History Society*. Vol. 1. Edinburgh, 1893.

Persius (A. Persius Flaccus). *Juvenal and Persius*. Edited and translated by Susanna Morton Braund. Loeb Classical Library. Cambridge, Mass.: Harvard University Press, 2004.

Philostratus the Elder. *Imagines*. Translated by Arthur Fairbanks. Loeb Classical Library. Cambridge, Mass.: Harvard University Press, 1960.

Plato. *Charmides, Alcibiades I and II, Hipparchus, The Lovers, Theages, Minos and Epinomis*. Translated by W. R. M. Lamb. Loeb Classical Library. Cambridge, Mass.: Harvard University Press, 1955.

————. *Euthyphro, Apology, Crito, Phaedo, and Phaedrus*. Translated by Harold North Fowler. Loeb Classical Library. Cambridge, Mass.: Harvard University Press, 1947.

————. *Laws*. Translated by R. G. Bury. 2 vols. Loeb Classical Library. Cambridge, Mass.: Harvard University Press, 1926.

————. *The Republic*. Translated by Paul Shorey. 2 vols. Loeb Classical Library. Cambridge, Mass.: Harvard University Press, 1930–35.

Pliny the Elder (Gaius Plinius Secundus). *Natural History*. Translated by D. E. Eichholz, W. H. S. Jones, and H. Rackham. 10 vols. Loeb Classical Library. Cambridge, Mass.: Harvard University Press, 1940–62.

Pliny the Younger (Gaius Plinius Caecilius Secundus). *Letters and Panegyricus*. Translated by Betty Radice. 2 vols. Loeb Classical Library. Cambridge, Mass.: Harvard University Press, 1969.

Plutarch (L. Mestrius Plutarchus). *Moralia*. Translated by Frank Cole Babbitt et al. 17 vols. Loeb Classical Library. Cambridge, Mass.: Harvard University Press, 1927–76.

————. *Plutarch's Lives*. Translated by Bernadotte Perrin. 11 vols. Loeb Classical Library. Cambridge, Mass.: Harvard University Press, 2000–2006.

Polybius. *The Histories*. Translated by W. R. Paton. 6 vols. Loeb Classical Library. Cambridge, Mass.: Harvard University Press, 1960.

Pope, Alexander. *Poetical Works*. Edited by Herbert Davis, with an introduction by Pat Rogers. Oxford and New York: Oxford University Press, 1985.

Pringle, Sir John. *Six Discourses, Delivered by Sir John Pringle, Bart. when President of the Royal Society; On Occasion of Six Annual Assignments of Sir Godfrey Copley's Medal. To which is Prefixed the Life of the Author, By Andrew Kippis, D.D. F.R.S. and S.A.* London, 1783.

Quintilian (Marcus Fabius Quintilianus). *Institutio oratoria*. Translated by H. E. Butler. 4 vols. Loeb Classical Library. Cambridge, Mass.: Harvard University Press, 1958–60.

Ramsay, Andrew Michael. *The Travels of Cyrus . . . To which is Annex'd, A Discourse upon the Theology and Mythology of the Ancients*. 2 vols. London, 1727.

————. *Les voyages de Cyrus, avec un discours sur la mythologie*. 2 vols. Paris, 1727.

Rollin, Charles. *The Ancient History of the Egyptians, Carthaginians, Assyrians, Babylonians, Medes and Persians, Macedonians, and Grecians*. 10 vols. London, 1734–36.

————. *The Method of Teaching and Studying the Belles Lettres, or, an Introduction to Languages, Poetry, Rhetoric, History, Moral Philosophy, Physicks, &c.* 4 vols. London, 1734.

St. John, Henry, Lord Bolingbroke. *Historical Writings.* Edited by Isaac Kramnick. Chicago and London: University of Chicago Press, 1972.

Sallust (Gaius Sallustius Crispus). *Catiline and Jugurthine War.* Translated by J. C. Rolfe. Loeb Classical Library. Cambridge, Mass.: Harvard University Press, 1931.

Seneca (Lucius Annaeus Seneca). *The Epistles of Seneca.* Translated by Richard M. Gummere. 3 vols. Loeb Classical Library. Cambridge, Mass.: Harvard University Press, 1943.

————. *Moral Essays.* Translated by John W. Basore. 3 vols. Loeb Classical Library. Cambridge, Mass.: Harvard University Press, 1958.

Serces, Jacques. *Traité sur les miracles.* Amsterdam, 1729.

Smalbroke, Richard. *A Vindication of the Miracles of our Blessed Saviour; in which Mr. Woolston's Discourses on them are particularly Examin'd, his pretended Authorities of the Fathers against the Truth of their literal Sense are set in a just Light, and his Objections in point of Reason are Answer'd.* 2 vols. London, 1729–31.

Spinoza, Benedict de. *Theological-Political Treatise.* Edited by Jonathan Israel and translated by Michael Silverthorne and Jonathan Israel. Cambridge: Cambridge University Press, 2007.

Statius, Publius Papinius. *Statius.* Translated by J. H. Mozley. 2 vols. Loeb Classical Library. London: Heinemann, 1928.

Stobaeus, Joannes. *Florilegium.* Edited by Thomas Gaisford. 4 vols. Oxford: Clarendon Press, 1822.

Suetonius (Gaius Suetonius Tranquillus). *Suetonius.* Translated by J. C. Rolfe. Revised edition. 2 vols. Loeb Classical Library. Cambridge, Mass.: Harvard University Press, 1951.

Tacitus (Cornelius Tacitus). *Tacitus.* Translated by M. Hutton et al. 5 vols. Loeb Classical Library. Cambridge, Mass.: Harvard University Press, 1925–70.

Temple, Sir William. *Observations upon the United Provinces of the Netherlands.* London, 1673.

Thucydides. *Thucydides De bello peloponnesiaco libri octo.* Amsterdam, 1731.

————. *Thucydidis bellum peloponnesiacum. Ex editione Wassii et Dukeri.* 8 vols. Glasgow, 1759.

Tillotson, John. *The Works of the Most Reverend Dr. John Tillotson, Late Lord Archbishop of Canterbury: Containing Fifty four Sermons and Discourses, on*

Several Occasions. Together with the Rule of Faith. Being all that were Published by his Grace Himself. 2nd ed. London, 1699.

———. *The Works of the Most Reverend Dr. John Tillotson, Late Lord Archbishop of Canterbury: Containing Two Hundred Sermons and Discourses, on Several Occasions.* Edited by Ralph Barker. 2nd ed. 2 vols. London, 1717.

Tindal, Matthew. *Christianity as Old as the Creation: Or, the Gospel a Republication of the Religion of Nature.* 2nd ed. London, 1732.

Toland, John. *Letters to Serena.* London, 1704.

———. *Nazarenus: Or, Jewish, Gentile, and Mahometan Christianity.* London, 1718.

Turnbull, George. *A Curious Collection of Ancient Paintings, Accurately Engraved from Excellent Drawings, Lately done after the Originals, by one of the Best Hands at Rome. With an Account Where and When They Were Found, and Where They now are; and Several Critical, Historical, and Mythological Observations upon them.* London, 1741.

———. *A Curious Collection of Ancient Paintings, Accurately Engraved from Excellent Drawings, Lately Done after the Originals, by One of the Best Hands in Rome. With an Account Where and When They were Found, and Where They Now are; and Several Critical, Historical, and Mythological Observations upon Them.* London, 1744.

———. *The History of the World Translated from the Latin of Justin: With Some Necessary Remarks by way of Notes; and a Prefatory Discourse, concerning the Advantages that ought chiefly to be had in view, in reading this or any ancient Historian.* 2nd ed. London, 1746.

———. *Observations upon Liberal Education, in All its Branches.* Edited with an introduction by Terrence O. Moore, Jr. Indianapolis: Liberty Fund, 2003.

———. *A Philosophical Enquiry concerning the Connexion betwixt the Doctrines and Miracles of Jesus Christ. In a Letter to a Friend.* London, 1731.

———. *A Philosophical Enquiry concerning the Connexion between the Doctrines and Miracles of Jesus Christ. In a Letter to a Friend.* 2nd ed. London, 1732.

———. *The Principles of Moral and Christian Philosophy.* Edited with an introduction by Alexander Broadie. 2 vols. Indianapolis: Liberty Fund, 2005.

———. *Three Dissertations; One on the Characters of Augustus, Horace and Agrippa . . . another on the Gallery of Verres . . . a Third on the Nature, Origin, and Use of Masks, in Theatrical Representations among the Ancients.* London, 1740.

———. *A Treatise on Ancient Painting, containing Observations on the Rise, Progress, and Decline of that Art amongst the Greeks and Romans. . . .* London, 1740.

————. *A Treatise on Ancient Painting, 1740.* With an introduction by Vincent M. Bevilacqua. München: Wilhelm Fink, 1971.

Valerius Maximus. *Memorable Doings and Sayings.* Edited and translated by D. R. Shackleton Bailey. 2 vols. Loeb Classical Library. Cambridge, Mass.: Harvard University Press, 2000.

Velleius Paterculus. *Compendium of Roman History.* Translated by Frederick W. Shipley. Loeb Classical Library. Cambridge, Mass.: Harvard University Press, 1961.

Vertot, René Aubert de. "Caractére d'Auguste, avec la comparison entre Agrippa & Mécénas, ministres de ce prince," *Histoire de l'Académie Royale des Inscriptions et Belles Lettres. Avec les mémoires de littérature tirez des registres de cette Académie, depuis L'année M.DCCXXV,* 5 (1729): 235–41.

Vitruvius. *On Architecture.* Translated by Frank Granger. 2 vols. Loeb Classical Library. Cambridge, Mass.: Harvard University Press, 1962.

Wallace, Robert. *The Regard due to Divine Revelation, and to Pretences to it, considered. A Sermon . . . With a Preface, Containing Some Remarks on a Book lately publish'd, Entitled, Christianity as Old as the Creation.* London, 1731.

Walpole, Horace. *The Yale Edition of Horace Walpole's Correspondence.* Edited by W. S. Lewis. 48 vols. New Haven: Yale University Press, 1937–83.

Werenfels, Samuel. *Opuscula theologica, philosophia, et philologica.* Basil, 1718.

Wishart, William. *The Principles of Liberty of Conscience Stated and Defended: In a Letter to a Friend.* Edinburgh, 1739.

Wodrow, Robert. *Analecta: Or, Materials for a History of Remarkable Providences; Mostly Relating to Scotch Ministers and Christians.* 4 vols. Glasgow: The Maitland Club, 1842–43.

Xenophon. *Memorabilia and Oeconomicus.* Translated by E. C. Marchant. Loeb Classical Library. Cambridge, Mass.: Harvard University Press, 1923.

Secondary Literature

We list here all secondary literature used in the preparation of the editors' introduction and the editors' notes to Turnbull's texts.

Ahnert, Thomas. "The 'Science of Man' in the Moral and Political Philosophy of George Turnbull (1698–1748)." In *Human Nature as the Basis of Morality and Society in Early Modern Philosophy,* 89–104. Edited by Juhana Lemetti

and Eva Piirimäe. Acta Philosophica Fennica 83. Helsinki: Philosophical Society of Finland, 2007.

Anderson, P. J., ed. *Fasti Academiae Mariscallanae Aberdoniensis: Selections from
the Records of the Marischal College and University, MDXCIII–MDCCCLX.*
3 vols. Aberdeen: The New Spalding Club, 1889–98.

Atto, Clayton. "The Society for the Encouragement of Learning." *The Library,*
fourth series, 19 (1938): 263–88.

Bevilacqua, Vincent. Introduction to *A Treatise of Ancient Painting, 1740,* by
George Turnbull. München: Wilhelm Fink, 1971.

Brown, Iain Gordon. "Allan Ramsay's Rise and Reputation." *Walpole Society,* 50
(1984): 209–47.

Carter, Jennifer J., and Joan H. Pittock, eds. *Aberdeen and the Enlightenment.*
Aberdeen: Aberdeen University Press, 1987.

Cokayne, George E. *The Complete Peerage of England, Scotland, Ireland, Great
Britain, and the United Kingdom.* Revised edition. Edited by Vicary Gibbs.
12 vols. London: St Catherine Press, 1910–59.

Darnton, Robert. "The High Enlightenment and the Low-Life of Literature."
In Robert Darnton, *The Literary Underground of the Old Regime,* 1–40. Cambridge, Mass.: Harvard University Press, 1982.

Dobai, Johannes. *Die Kunstliteratur des Klassiizmus und der Romantik in England.* 3 vols. München: Benteli, 1974.

Emerson, Roger L. *Academic Patronage in the Scottish Enlightenment: Glasgow,
Edinburgh, and St Andrews Universities.* Edinburgh: Edinburgh University
Press, 2008.

———. "Natural Philosophy and the Problem of the Scottish Enlightenment."
Studies on Voltaire and the Eighteenth Century 242 (1986): 243–91.

———. *Professors, Patronage, and Politics: The Aberdeen Universities in the Eighteenth Century.* Aberdeen: Aberdeen University Press, 1992.

———. "Science and the Origins and Concerns of the Scottish Enlightenment." *History of Science* 26 (1988): 333–66.

———. "Sir Robert Sibbald, Kt, the Royal Society of Scotland, and the Origins
of the Scottish Enlightenment." *Annals of Science* 45 (1988): 41–72.

Foster, Joseph. *Alumni Oxonienses: The Members of the University of Oxford,
1715–1886: Their Parentage, Birthplace, and Year of Birth, with a Record of their
Degrees.* 4 vols. Oxford and London, 1888.

Frasca-Spada, M., and P. J. E. Kail, eds. *Impressions of Hume.* Oxford: Clarendon
Press, 2005.

Gay, Peter. *The Enlightenment: An Interpretation.* 2 vols. New York: Alfred A. Knopf, 1966–69.

Gibson-Wood, Carol. "Painting as Philosophy: George Turnbull's *Treatise on Ancient Painting.*" In *Aberdeen and the Enlightenment,* edited by Jennifer J. Carter and Joan H. Pittock, 189–98. Aberdeen: Aberdeen University Press, 1987.

Gunther, A. E. *An Introduction to the Life of the Rev. Thomas Birch D.D., F.R.S., 1705–1766.* Halesworth, U.K.: Halesworth Press, 1984.

Haakonssen, Knud. *Natural Law and Moral Philosophy: From Grotius to the Scottish Enlightenment.* Cambridge: Cambridge University Press, 1996.

Haakonssen, Knud, ed. *Enlightenment and Religion: Rational Dissent in Eighteenth-Century Britain.* Cambridge: Cambridge University Press, 1996.

Hanson, Craig Ashley. *The English Virtuoso: Art, Medicine, and Antiquarianism in the Age of Empiricism.* Chicago and London: University of Chicago Press, 2009.

Ingamells, John. *A Dictionary of British and Irish Travellers in Italy, 1701–1800.* New Haven and London: Yale University Press, 1997.

Innes Smith, R. W. *English-Speaking Students of Medicine at the University of Leyden.* Edinburgh and London: Oliver and Boyd, 1932.

Jacob, W. M. *The Clerical Profession in the Long Eighteenth Century, 1680–1840.* Oxford: Oxford University Press, 2007.

Jones, Peter, ed. *Philosophy and Science in the Scottish Enlightenment.* Edinburgh: John Donald Publishers Ltd., 1988.

Kendrick, T. F. J. "Sir Robert Walpole, the Old Whigs, and the Bishops, 1733–1736: A Study in Eighteenth-Century Parliamentary Politics." *The Historical Journal* 11 (1968): 421–45.

Kidd, Colin. "Scotland's Invisible Enlightenment: Subscription and Heterodoxy in the Eighteenth Century Kirk." *Records of the Scottish Church History Society* 30 (2000): 28–59.

Kramnick, Isaac. *Bolingbroke and His Circle: The Politics of Nostalgia in the Age of Walpole.* Cambridge, Mass.: Harvard University Press, 1968.

Laing, David. *A Catalogue of the Graduates in the Faculties of Arts, Divinity, and Law, of the University of Edinburgh, since its Foundation.* Edinburgh, 1858.

Laird, John. "George Turnbull." *Aberdeen University Review* 14 (1926–27): 123–35.

Lemetti, Juhana, and Eva Piirimäe, eds. *Human Nature as the Basis of Morality and Society in Early Modern Philosophy.* Acta Philosophica Fennica 83. Helsinki: Philosophical Society of Finland, 2007.

Levine, Joseph M. *Dr. Woodward's Shield: History, Science, and Satire in Augustan England*. Berkeley, Los Angeles, and London: University of California Press, 1977.

Lillywhite, Bryant. *London Coffee Houses. A Reference Book of Coffee Houses of the Seventeenth, Eighteenth, and Nineteenth Centuries*. London: George Allen and Unwin, 1963.

Mackinnon, K. A. B. "George Turnbull's Common Sense Jurisprudence." In *Aberdeen and the Enlightenment*, 104–10. Edited by Jennifer J. Carter and Joan H. Pittock. Aberdeen: Aberdeen University Press, 1987.

McCosh, James. *The Scottish Philosophy, Biographical, Expository, Critical, from Hutcheson to Hamilton*. London: Macmillan and Co., 1875.

Mijers, Esther. *"News from the Republick of Letters": Scottish Students, Charles Mackie, and the United Provinces, 1650–1750*. Leiden and Boston: Brill, 2012.

Moore, James. "Natural Law and the Pyrrhonian Controversy." In *Philosophy and Science in the Scottish Enlightenment*, 20–38. Edited by Peter Jones. Edinburgh: John Donald Publishers Ltd., 1988.

———. "Presbyterianism and the Right of Private Judgement: Church Government in Ireland and Scotland in the Age of Francis Hutcheson." In *Philosophy and Religion in Enlightenment Britain: New Case Studies*, 141–68. Edited by Ruth Savage. Oxford: Oxford University Press, 2012.

Nadel, George H. "Philosophy of History before Historicism." *History and Theory* 3 (1964): 291–315.

Nenadic, Stana, ed. *Scots in London in the Eighteenth Century*. Lewisburg: Bucknell University Press, 2010.

Norton, David Fate. *David Hume: Common-Sense Moralist, Sceptical Metaphysician*. Princeton: Princeton University Press, 1982.

———. "George Turnbull and the Furniture of the Mind." *Journal of the History of Ideas* 35 (1975): 701–16.

Piggott, Stuart. *Ruins in a Landscape: Essays in Antiquarianism*. Edinburgh: Edinburgh University Press, 1976.

Plomer, Henry R. *A Dictionary of the Printers and Booksellers Who Were at Work in England, Scotland, and Ireland from 1668 to 1725*. Edited by Arundell Esdaile. [Oxford]: The Bibliographical Society, 1922.

Plomer, Henry R., with G. H. Bushnell and E. R. McC. Dix. *A Dictionary of the Printers and Booksellers Who Were at Work in England, Scotland, and Ireland from 1726 to 1775*. [Oxford]: The Bibliographical Society, 1932.

Sambrook, James. *James Thomson, 1700–1748: A Life*. Oxford: Clarendon Press, 1991.

Savage, Ruth, ed. *Philosophy and Religion in Enlightenment Britain: New Case Studies*. Oxford: Oxford University Press, 2012.

Sharp, L. W. "Charles Mackie, the First Professor of History at Edinburgh University." *Scottish Historical Review* 41 (1962): 23–45.

Smart, Alastair. *Allan Ramsay: Painter, Essayist, and Man of the Enlightenment*. New Haven and London: Yale University Press, 1992.

Stewart, Dugald. *The Collected Works of Dugald Stewart*. Edited by Sir William Hamilton. 11 vols. Edinburgh: Thomas Constable and Co., 1854–60.

Stewart, M. A. "Berkeley and the Rankenian Club." *Hermathena* 139 (1985): 25–45.

———. "George Turnbull and Educational Reform." In *Aberdeen and the Enlightenment*, 95–103. Edited by Jennifer J. Carter and Joan H. Pittock. Aberdeen: Aberdeen University Press, 1987.

———. "Hume's Intellectual Development, 1711–1752." In *Impressions of Hume*, 11–58. Edited by M. Frasca-Spada and P. J. E. Kail. Oxford: Clarendon Press, 2005.

———. "John Smith and the Molesworth Circle." *Eighteenth-Century Ireland* 2 (1987): 89–102.

———. "Principal Wishart (1692–1753) and the Controversies of His Day." *Records of the Scottish Church History Society* 30 (2000): 61–102.

———. "Rational Dissent in Early Eighteenth-Century Ireland." In *Enlightenment and Religion: Rational Dissent in Eighteenth-Century Britain*, 42–63. Edited by Knud Haakonssen. Cambridge: Cambridge University Press, 1996.

Stewart, M. A., ed. *Studies in the Philosophy of the Scottish Enlightenment*. Oxford: Clarendon Press, 1990.

Stewart-Robertson, J. C. "The Well-Principled Savage, or the Child of the Scottish Enlightenment." *Journal of the History of Ideas* 42 (1981): 503–25.

Voitle, Robert. *The Third Earl of Shaftesbury, 1671–1713*. Baton Rouge and London: Louisiana State University Press, 1984.

Watts, M. R. *The Dissenters*. 2 vols. Oxford: Clarendon Press, 1978–95.

Wood, Paul. *The Aberdeen Enlightenment: The Arts Curriculum in the Eighteenth Century*. Aberdeen: Aberdeen University Press, 1993.

———. "Science and the Pursuit of Virtue in the Aberdeen Enlightenment." In *Studies in the Philosophy of the Scottish Enlightenment*, 127–49. Edited by M. A. Stewart. Oxford: Clarendon Press, 1990.

———. "Thomas Reid and the Tree of the Sciences." *Journal of Scottish Philosophy* 2 (2004): 119–36.

Yeo, Richard. *Encyclopaedic Visions: Scientific Dictionaries and Enlightenment Culture*. Cambridge: Cambridge University Press, 2001.

INDEX

Page numbers followed by an italic *n* indicate a note; thus 311*n*14 guides the reader to note 14 on page 311. Page numbers in *italics* indicate illustrations.

449

This book is set in Adobe Garamond, a modern adaptation by
Robert Slimbach of the typeface originally cut around 1540 by the
French typographer and printer Claude Garamond. The Garamond
face, with its small lowercase height and restrained contrast between
thick and thin strokes, is a classic "old-style" face and has long been
one of the most influential and widely used typefaces.

Printed on paper that is acid-free and meets the requirements of the
American National Standard for Permanence of Paper for Printed
Library Materials, z39.48-1992. ∞

Book design by Louise OFarrell, Gainesville, Florida
Typography by Grapevine Publishing Services, Madison, Wisconsin
Printed and bound by Worzalla Publishing Company, Stevens Point, Wisconsin